THE MUSIC HUNTER

THE MUSIC HUNTER

The Autobiography of a Career

by Laura Boulton

Doubleday & Company, Inc.
Garden City, New York
1969

Library of Congress Catalog Card Number 67–11154

Copyright © 1969 by Laura C. Boulton

Printed in the United States of America

To

My Mother and My Father

ACKNOWLEDGMENTS

I am greatly indebted to an unbelievable number of individuals and governments around the world for their help and cooperation. Although it is not possible to list them, I want to express here my heartfelt thanks to all of them.

For substantial grants and fellowships and for inspiring sponsorship I want to express my deep appreciation to the following:

Foundations: American Council of Learned Societies; American Philosophical Society; Carnegie Corporation of New York (2 grants); East and West Foundation; Phelps Stokes Fund; Wenner-gren Foundation.

Universities, Museums, and Organizations: American Museum of Natural History; Carnegie Museum; Field Museum; Columbia University; Harvard University; Tulane University; University of California; University of Chicago; University of Washington; UNESCO.

I am also deeply grateful to many individuals who have sponsored expeditions or have generously assisted my research, especially the following:

Mrs. Anne Archbold; Mr. and Mrs. Robert Woods Bliss; Mrs. W. Murray Crane; Mrs. Lydia Foote; Mr. Chauncey Hamlin; Mrs. H. H. Jonas; Mrs. John H. Leh; Mr. Leon Mandel; Mr. and Mrs. Ralph Pulitzer; Dr. and Mrs. George Shattuck; Mrs. Oscar Straus; Mrs. Margaret Pope Walker.

I also want to express my appreciation for the privilege of writing portions of this book surrounded by the peace and beauty of the MacDowell Colony, N. H. and on the estates of kind and interested friends: Mrs. Anne Archbold, Nassau; Mrs. Louis Anspacher, Purchase, N.Y.; Mr. and Mrs. Zlatko Balocovic, Camden, Maine; Frances and Alexander McLanahan, Chateau de Missery, Côte d'Or, France.

I also want to express my thanks to the experts from various countries who have taken time to read these chapters and have given valuable comments.

For the constant aid of assistants and secretaries, I am particularly grateful, especially for the invaluable help and suggestions of Elizabeth Webb who encouraged me in my occasional moments of despair while choosing and eliminating material.

My deep gratitude goes to Dean Andrew Cordier for the stimulating cooperation he has given me and for the sympathetic Introduction he has written for this book.

I would like to express warmest thanks to Ken McCormick, editor-in-chief of Doubleday, for his valued help and infinite patience.

For his expert editorial assistance my eternal gratitude goes to John Ardoin.

To Mrs. Oscar Straus I am most indebted for starting me in this career.

To Mr. Julian Clarence Levi through whose wisdom and generosity our research center for World Music at Columbia University was established and continues to grow my gratitude is boundless.

CONTENTS

SECTION III: THE AMERICAS

SECTION IV: EUROPE

SECTION V: AFRICA

LIST OF ILLUSTRATIONS

INTRODUCTION

This extraordinary book, by Dr. Laura Boulton, *The Music Hunter,*
is the fascinating story of the on-the-spot search by its author for
folk and liturgical music in all parts of the world. It records thirty-
five years of determined and dedicated effort to secure the tapes
and records of the music of peoples on all five continents and on
the islands of the seas. She penetrated almost inaccessible places.
Her journeys carried her deep into Eskimo territory, into sub-
Sahara Africa, into Nepal, Thailand, Borneo and elsewhere. She
never chose the easy places, concerned as she was to seek the most
authentic music directly from the people who were its creators
and users. Much of her travel took place before recent improve-
ments in transportation and one is filled with awe that she should
have survived some of her experiences in travel and in local living
conditions. In her travels she felt equally at home as a guest of
great personalities like Dr. Albert Schweitzer, Prime Minister
Nehru, Emperor Haile Selassie or with natives hidden away in the
jungles, the mountains or frozen tundra.

She had a capacity to develop a quick and easy rapport with her
hosts, whoever they might be, and thus elicited from them not
only warm cooperation in the rendition and recording of music,
but, as well, a flood of folk habits which gives music a meaningful
setting. While the book is an exciting diary, it is more than that. It
is alive with acute observations of the folkways of peoples, their
traditions, their customs, their ways of life, their hopes and concerns, their struggle for sheer physical existence. These are the

materials out of which music is born, the crowning jewel of a culture. Music is both the language and the reflection of the lives of peoples.

As Dr. Boulton points out, music is the universal language. It is a form of communication universally understood. Whether as the universal language or as a language of identifiable folk whose lives are carved by custom and tradition, it throws a penetrating light upon values of importance to the human race and to its separate parts.

Under conditions which were often unbelievably difficult Dr. Boulton succeeded in securing recordings and tapes of folk and liturgical music previously unavailable to the outside world. While recording the music she also collected a rich treasure of musical instruments, many primitive in character and unusual in design.

It is fortunate for the world of music that Dr. Boulton engaged in her numerous adventurous expeditions even before improved transportation would have eased her task, for today the spread of popular music through the radio and the disc is blotting out much of the native music which she had the satisfaction to record and from which the world will benefit.

Her collection of thirty thousand recordings and scores of musical instruments form the heart of the Laura Boulton Collection at Columbia University. Surrounded by these rich resources collected on at least twenty-eight expeditions, she is directing today a research program in world music in the School of International Affairs at the University. It is her concern to share this music as widely as possible with students, faculty and the general public, and an increasing number of her recordings are being made into albums for wider distribution.

Andrew W. Cordier,
Acting President
Columbia University
New York City

Section I

AFRICA

Chapter 1

THE BEGINNING

It hardly seems possible that so many years have passed since I made my first recordings in an African rain forest. Little did I know that the ensuing years would take me to every corner of the world, from the frozen wastes of the Arctic to voodoo ceremonies in Haiti, from the snow-capped mountains of Nepal to the Penguin Islands at the tip of Africa, from Tibetan lamasaries to Buddhist temples in Japan, and from the courts of kings to the huts of peasants.

In every instance my object was the same: to capture, absorb, and bring back the world's music; not the music of the concert hall or the opera house, but the music of the people, their expression in songs of sadness and joy, their outpourings in times of tragedy and times of exaltation.

In remote areas of the world, where the tribes were at first very shy with me and distrustful of my recording machine, I devised a game: first I recorded a gay French folk song, singing it with gestures, and then played it back for them. Their faces would inevitably burst into smiles when they recognized my voice and saw they did not need to fear my machine. After that everyone wanted to sing for me at once. Having a quick musical ear, I could soon sing with them some of their own songs. Nothing I could have done would have established me more firmly, more rapidly, as a friend. Bestowal of gifts establishes contact; a sharing of music inspires trust. This bears out what I have always believed:

that music is the one perfect form of communication that knows no barriers.

My wise parents brought me up without prejudices. I have been able to collect rare music and attend sacred ceremonies never previously witnessed by white people, and sometimes in regions where a white woman had never been seen, only because these people knew that my interest in them was not just idle curiosity. I was willing to spend many hazardous months seeking them out because I was genuinely interested in their music and in what that had to teach me.

After twenty-eight expeditions all over the world, where shall I begin? The Chinese say that the longest journey starts with the first step. My first step was a firm background in music, both in theory and in performance. A small fortune had been spent on the training of my voice and the nature of my career seemed never to have been in doubt. As a small child, I am told, I concluded every bedtime prayer with "Dear God, make me a high soprano." This gift and an extensive training were not to be wasted, but none of us could have forseen the direction in which they would take me.

I sang my first solo in an operetta at the age of three and was planning a concert career, but it had barely begun when the invitation came to join the Straus African Expedition for the American Museum of Natural History in New York. In spite of vigorous protest from my musical mentors, I accepted this marvelous opportunity to hear indigenous music in Africa. As serious as my musical interests were on the expedition at the time, I did not dream that the study of the world's music would occupy the rest of my life and lead to long years of research and field work (including university graduate work in musicology and anthropology) combined with lecturing and teaching at major universities in America, Europe, and Asia. When I brought back my first recordings out of Africa, there was no word for my career. I used to be introduced as a musical anthropologist or an anthropological musicologist. Now we have a word: ethnomusicologist.

I am deeply grateful to Mrs. Oscar Straus, the patron of my first expedition, who because of her interest in music encouraged me to take time from the museum collecting of everything that crawled, flew, moved, and breathed to record the songs and rhythms of Africa. This was the beginning of a career that has become increasingly absorbing.

It was Africa that provided for me the first exciting proof of what I had always believed to be true: that music is the most spontaneous and demonstrative form of expression the human family possesses, that truly it is the one language that needs no translation. It was my good fortune that I was able to work in world music before people had changed so much—for example, throughout Africa while villages were still purely African villages, in Vietnam while it was still Indochina and people had time to sing. A great deal of political history has been made in the last thirty-five years and much that was beautiful in the tribal lore has now been lost.

Musicologists today often have a struggle to locate the genuine article; the end product is so often influenced by "civilization," that only keen research reveals how much is worth collecting at all. When I returned to Bechuanaland fifteen years after my first expedition there, I could find only a few of the songs I had recorded before. During a Red Cross campaign to raise money, the Africans, wishing to make their contribution, thought of an ingenious way of raising funds. They organized a concert. There was a cost of sixpence to have a number performed and a shilling not to have it performed. As a shilling was a lot of money to an African in those days, every number was performed and the concert lasted all night. But of the forty-three songs performed, only six were genuine African melodies. All the others were a very poor imitation of Bing Crosby or one of the latest popular singers heard on the radio or in the movies. The ability to distinguish between genuine material and what is hybrid is the result of intensive study and ear development.

Before the invention of portable recording equipment, musical notation was the only way to preserve the music heard, but it simply was not possible to capture all the little quavers, the elaborations, the variations which, on first hearing, eluded the Western ear, however trained. Even with today's highly scientific recording equipment, one must still listen with earphones over and over before the music can be correctly transcribed. Ethnic music has become such a scientific study that we are now developing machines to examine and analyze the melodies and rhythms. There are even computers in which melodies go in one end and come out the other, classified and "transcribed."

While struggling one day with the acoustics involved in recording the ancient Benin ceremony of sacrifice in Southern Nigeria, I could not have known that religious music was to become the major interest of my musical studies, and that I would record not only the primitive rituals of Africans, but also those of Eskimos and American Indians, sacred voodoo ceremonies in Haiti, New World African rites in Brazil, and unique music of the Todas, a disappearing hill tribe of India whose funeral ritual, being secret and profoundly sacred, had never before been heard by an outsider, I was told.

Eventually I was to go on to record, study, and collect representative musical material in all twelve great religions of the world, including Buddhist chants in Tibetan lamaseries, Zoroastrian hymns in Iran, Hindu chanting in Himalayan ashramas during the great Purna Kumbha Mela (Urn Festival), ceremonial music in the golden temple of Amritsar, seat of the Sikh religion, and ancient music of the Far Eastern religions. More recently the early music of Christianity—Byzantine and orthodox music—have been my major interest.

I have retraced my steps to the countries formerly visited and have found everywhere incredible change. Even in the earlier days while working with remote groups, it was difficult if not impossible to find informants who would agree completely in their interpretation of tribal lore, or to witness a ceremony performed in exactly the same way on different occasions. And certainly the so-called authorities in their learned volumes often differ widely in their facts, their spelling of local words—spelled phonetically, of course—and particularly in their interpretations. I have for the most part written of my own observations; world travelers unfortunately can no longer experience the same fascination which these lands formerly held. But this is the way it was.

Chapter 2

UP THE NILE TO THE MOUNTAINS
OF THE MOON AND KENYA

I had to be satisfied with only rubbing shoulders with Alexandria's rich history: with walking where, three hundred years before Christ, Euclid had paced back and forth while expounding the theorems which have formed the basis of our present geometry; where the scholar Eratosthenes accurately mapped the Nile in 250 B.C.; and where Nelson, in more modern context, defeated the French in 1798 and Napoleon the Turks in 1799. The passage of time seems to have left only a superficial imprint on this ancient city. In this century intrigues may be on a wider scale and better organized, but one sensed that the Arabian Nights atmosphere, the intermingling of beauty and ugliness, and the scents and sounds of the city are, and have always been, as fixed as the poles.

In Cairo one felt even more strongly the startling contrast of being catapulted from the New World into the Old. Everywhere there was ceaseless activity: the hubbub and bustle of the bazaar, the raucous cries of the vendors, the hounding of dragomans who insisted on showing us the rare sights and dark secrets of their city, and the pitiful beggars and ragged urchins with hands forever outstretched for baksheesh (to them, anything from money to cigarettes). When the swarming crowds and the heat became too oppressive, one had only to sit on the veranda of the old Shepheard's Hotel to witness the kaleidoscope of the East, for sooner or later everything in Cairo passed by Shepheard's, including one day a party of celebrants singing in procession as

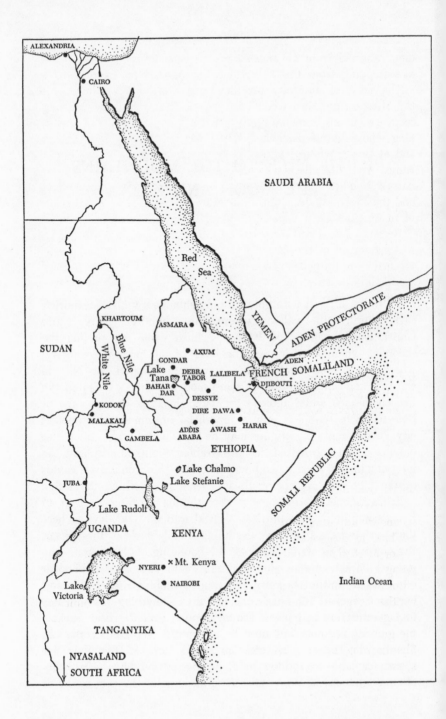

they returned from an ancient circumcision ritual. It was rather like stepping from the Hilton into a page of the Koran.

The sense of antiquity was heightened still further for me in the Museum of Cairo when I saw many of the priceless treasures recovered intact from the tomb of King Tutankhamen, the ancient king whose burial place had been abandoned by grave robbers, and at Luxor, where I visited the excavations in the Valley of the Kings. And then there were Heliopolis, the original site of Cleopatra's Needles (now in London and New York), the Sphinx, and the Pyramids. (Visiting these marvels brought for me the first of many rides on a camel.)

Recently I was in Cairo for the sixth time, and for sentimental reasons stayed at the new Shepheard's Hotel. The original building had been burned down during the anti-British riots. The whole world still paraded in front but this time there were more intensified modern noises: big, smart American and European cars and troupes of grim, revolution-minded Egyptians instead of gay celebrants returning homeward from age-old rituals.

Though a new Egypt has evolved and an independent Sudan has emerged, the Nile still dominates the whole of life, just as it has for past millenniums. Near Cairo the waterway still teems with activity and commerce of every kind; dahabeahs and feluccas and other frail craft sail busily to and fro on the slow-moving brown water, and the boats swarm with Arabs in long Mother Hubbard gowns and turbans which lend them the rakish air of the brigands remembered from childhood picture books. Here, too, the Khamsin (a hot sand storm) attacks without warning, with violent winds overturning small boats and dumping voyagers and cargoes into the river. Saving lives appeared to me to have been of secondary importance to salvaging fruit, carrots, or anything edible bobbing in the water.

For more than 5,500 years the height of the annual Nile flood, rising in April, overflowing in September, on which cultivation of crops was entirely dependent, had been ceremoniously measured by the Egyptians. Then in 1902 the British government built the first Aswan Dam to harness the floodwaters, which made possible the growing of four crops annually in the rich Nile Delta. But with this blessing came misfortune. Some of the oldest monuments known to man were hidden under the waters of the dam. Probably the most famous of these was the Temple of Isis on the island of

Philae. When I was first in Egypt, it still emerged for a few months each year—when the dam gates were opened for irrigation. When the island submerged again I was told that villagers in their small craft could see through the green waters into the narrow streets and walled courtyards which once sheltered the women from men's eyes, and that the boatmen could pick fruit from trees that stood up to their foliage in water.

The backflow from the first damned lake sometimes reached 200 miles upstream submerging innumerable small homes. As in the case of the recent building of the Kariba Dam on the Zambezi River, which provides the biggest hydroelectric plant in Africa, the British compensated landowners deluged by the dam's waters. However, in Kariba many Africans refused to vacate the Zambezi River area until the waters of the new lake were creeping into their villages. Like the animals, they clung uncomprehendingly to the flooded islands until the last possible moment.

The Straus Expedition left the lush lower Nile where gardens and palms grow right to the river's edge and continued from Wadi Halfa to Khartoum, traveling 232 miles through the Nubian Desert. In the comfort of a tropical train, riding from dawn to dusk without seeing a living thing, I tried to picture Kitchener plodding through this sea of molten sand under a blazing sky in order to lay, at the rate of one mile a day, a railroad that would open up the Sudan.

The only water in this bleak and fiery world was at the ten stations set up as storage tanks at intervals along the way to provide for the little train. At one of these desolate outposts we said good-by to a young Englishman with whom we had been visiting on the journey. As the train pulled away, he seemed the very embodiment of the British Empire, standing alone against the terrible backdrop of endless burning sand and shimmering heat. Formerly so much of the grim, resolute courage, tenacity, and fortitude of the British had been to me only words in a history book. As I approached Khartoum this history sprang vividly to life. I remembered and now understood accounts of the agonies of thirst, of parched lips and swollen tongues, of eyes blinded by pelting sand, and of the merciless hardships suffered by the British relief expedition in its heroic but hopeless attempt to reach General Gordon in time to save him from the Mad Mahdi of Omdurman. I marveled that any of the men endured and survived this terrible tract of country. A Bedouin camel caravan may occasionally reach its destination, but the numerous bones scattered along the way, protruding from the sand, testified to the numbers that did not. I imagine that the songs of these lonely travelers must have been very sad indeed, much more tragic than the music I recorded later of the meharists, the camel patrol of the Sahara.

My first intimate contact with African wildlife was in a small zoo in Khartoum where exotic birds (spoonbill and shoebill storks, and secretary birds, the latter so named because of crest feathers resembling quill pens behind their ears), and beautiful golden gazelles balancing on slender legs wandered about freely. It was there that I made my first African animal friend, a baby hippo. He looked forward to our late afternoon visits and, at our approach, would rush to the wire of his enclosure, opening his enormous cavern of pink mouth. When a lump of sugar was dropped into it, he would stand there sucking and looking ridiculous, with tears of pure pleasure pouring down his lumpy cheeks. He had come to expect this daily ration of sugar, for a British officer stationed at Khartoum had spoiled him for many months before our arrival by cultivating his sweet tooth. It was there also that we met our first African lion, a not very kingly, rather shamefaced old fellow with only a stub of a tail. If you have never seen a bobtailed lion, you cannot imagine what a pitiful and incongruous sight he presents. This one had carelessly gone to sleep with part of his formerly proud tail lazily protruding into the next cage, where a hyena had bitten it off. Khartoum rocked with his roars for two weeks.

After the desolation of the Nubian Desert, we looked forward to relief when we boarded a small stern-wheeler, the government mail boat, for our journey southward "up the Nile" to the headwaters at Rejaf. Our boat pulled two barges, one for sleeping and one for eating. The heat in the Sudan was so intense that the cabins on the boat were bearable only long enough to dress. The sudd, floating islands of papyrus grass, made night navigation impossible, so at sunset we anchored offshore and after dinner fell asleep under our nets to the ceaseless clamor of crickets and frogs, and the drone of mosquitoes. These pests surrounded us in ferocious swarms ready to devour anything and everybody the moment the north wind dropped, as it did each evening. In the velvety blackness before daylight we would be awakened by the grunting of hippos plunging and splashing in the water around the boat, and then, waking again to a cup of tea delivered by a smiling attendant, everyone would tumble out in pajamas and dressing gowns to line the rails and watch the dawn. The African dawn is so dramatic, so rapid, that even a minute's dawdling in bed and one can miss the entire spectacle. First the eastern sky fills suddenly with flaming red; then the sun shoots up over the edge, immediately dominating the scene, draining all color from the sky, and drowning our world in an all-pervasive heat. Then out came our dark glasses as we rushed for breakfast to the shade of the canvas awnings on the eating barge.

As we churned up the great waterway we saw hippos in hundreds wallowing and diving around our stern-wheeler, and herds of elephant threading their way in majestic procession through a forest of tall papyrus grass to drink and bathe. They trumpeted and flapped their huge ears in annoyance as we passed within yards of them. The first impact of Africa's glorious wildlife upon the traveler thirty-five years ago was far greater than it is today. Increased traffic on the Nile and the growth of trading posts and villages along the riverbanks have not only diminished herds but also have driven many animals inland.

At times our boat would stick on a sandbank, and the whole crew would jump overboard; delighted with this diversion, they would heave and shove to the beat of a rhythmic song without which the boys seemed quite unable to work. It was the time of Ramadan, and, being Mohammedan, the crew fasted all day and feasted and sang all night. This was unfortunate for those who wished to sleep, but lucky for me. I collected many spontaneous performances of festive and religious singing which I might never have otherwise obtained.

At Khartoum we had been joined for the fourteen-day journey up the Nile by a district commissioner going to the Bari country, the wife of a missionary returning from sick leave, and a charming English bey. All contributed to many wonderful evenings spent singing national songs, arguing amiably on international issues, and telling tales of Africa. The commissioner entertained us with a whole repertoire of delightful African folk tales and songs. The bey informed us that he was on his way "to look for a war." Theoretically, under European rule all tribal warfare had ceased, but news had reached the authorities of a skirmish between two tribes somewhere in the upper reaches of the Nile, and the bey's task was to remove one of the tribes to the opposite side of the river to end the hostilities. The missionary's wife helped greatly as an interpreter. She spoke the language of the picturesque Shilluk and Dinka, those seven-foot willowy people we nicknamed the "Cranes" because of their habit of standing on one leg with the other foot wedged against the knee. Through her I was able to write down the translations of many of their songs.

At Juba, near the end of the Nile voyage, we filmed night dancers in a spectacular ceremony to their wood deities (they worshiped the spirits of fire, wood, and water). Each dancer carried a sizable piece of wood throughout the gyrations. The magnesium flares we used for filming gave off great bursts of smoke which fascinated the natives and which, mingled with the dust churned up by their stamping feet, lent a magical and eerie effect to the whole scene. The songs of the tribal dancing at Juba had never been recorded before, and when an American piece called the "Juba Dance" appeared, I wondered if it might have had any connection with the one I transcribed on that expedition.

Our river journey ended at the headwaters of the upper Nile. When navigation became impossible cars hired by Mrs. Straus were waiting to take us across the Anglo-Egyptian Sudan into the Mountains of the Moon, across Lake Victoria and into Kenya Colony. One of the cars developed a bad radiator leak, and while the engine boiled and bubbled, the driver coaxed it along from one tiny stream to another.

One never loses those first impressions of traveling overland in Africa. Driving through the Sudan I saw remarkably beautiful African women. There was one I remember vividly with a half-calabash—a dried gourd used throughout Africa as a water bottle and a drinking and eating vessel—entirely covering her albino baby to protect it from the sun. I have often wondered if that poor child on the woman's back survived with such feeble protection for its pink eyes and pale, unpigmented skin.

The days were filled with other new and wondrous sights, such as my first giraffe dining on a thorn tree, its elegant spotted head rising above the flat treetop, its long tongue curling around the spiky twigs and its enormous brown eyes with lashes as long and thick as the fringe on an old shawl. The animal's eyes were fixed on our "fire-chariot," as the natives called the automobile. In Latuka, as in many villages of this region, the people were naked. The chief's councilors, however, wore metal helmets like those of Crusaders. It is thought that at least one of the nine military expeditions undertaken in the name of Christianity between 1095 and 1272 passed through this area, leaving behind these relics.

At Fort Portal in Uganda we slept for the first time under thatched roofs in small rest huts, provided by the British officials along the route. The eerie, unidentifiable noises of the African night, the rustlings and scurryings of unseen things, the whir and bump of insects beating against the mosquito netting, and the constant barrage of flying, crawling, squeaking creatures were at first terrors I had previously encountered only in nightmares. Hippos, too, thumping and grunting outside the hut, frequently used the mud wall of the huts as rubbing posts. The large herds of hippos in this area made it necessary to post a notice on the little golf course at Fort Portal to the effect that a player could, without penalty, lift his golf ball out of a hippo track.

In Uganda we followed close on the heels of the Duke of Windsor, then Prince of Wales, who was on safari with Uganda's top white hunter, Captain Salmon—known as Samaki, the local African word for fish. Samaki, a charming English ex-army officer, later told us fascinating tales of his life in Africa, including the royal safaris.

It was not Samaki, however, but another white hunter who took us on our first collecting trek into the snow-capped Mountains of the Moon on the border between Uganda and the Belgian Congo. We camped near a mountain stream where the elephants came to drink and bathe. One night a large herd of these giants plowed through the area, and I have to admit that I slept through the rumpus, for there is no deeper fatigue than that induced by a long, exacting day in the bush. In the morning I saw the spoor everywhere. Trees were uprooted all about us, as if to show the resentment the elephants felt at our intrusion into their private lives.

We had been out only a short time when our hunter did a foolish thing. He shot a hippo to provide meat for our safari boys, and ate some of it. Hippo meat is eaten by the indigenous people of Africa but it apparently was too rich for him. Within a few hours he was desperately ill, in great pain, and convinced that he was going to die. "This is the end," he wailed. "This will do me in."

Though the nearest settlement was about fifteen miles away, I set off with an African guide hoping to find a doctor, leaving the men of our party to break camp and to make the difficult trek down the mountain with a two-hundred-pound invalid in an improvised hammock. Ned, Mrs. Straus's grandson, appalled at the thought of my going off through the mountains with only an African for protection, came crashing after me (he was heavy and unused to strenuous exercise). "Laura, Laura," he panted, "wait for me, wait for me." A doctor was located, the sick hunter was left in his charge, and we were on our way to Entebbe. We crossed Lake Victoria—Africa's largest lake, forming part of the border of East Africa's three territories—to Kampala, now a large city but then only a small village, and went on into Kenya, bumping over rutted dusty roads, crossing the equator at 9,000 feet (it was a weird feeling to be freezing right on the equator), to Nairobi.

Two things I saw for the first time on this journey remain imprinted forever in my mind: the majesty of the Rift Valley, the volcanic cleft which ages ago split open the green heart of east Africa; and the splendor of the flamingos, rising in pink shimmering clouds as we approached the blue waters of Lake Navaisha. Thousands of these graceful birds, much more brilliant than the flamingos of Nassau or our South, come every year to feed on the fish in the lake. Seen at sunset, their bright plumage mingling with the blues, purples, and golds of the hazy light filtering through the valley, they are a breath-taking sight.

In the Kenya Highlands, outside Nyeri, we stayed with Major Walker and his wife in their recently built Outspan Hotel. They had installed a *boma*, an observation platform, high in a tree in the midst of dense forest some miles from the town overlooking a salt pan. Here we saw animals of every kind coming, as they had for centuries, to lick the natural salt from the earth. This first rough boma was later enlarged into a small treetop hotel which eventually became famous throughout the world. While Princess Elizabeth was the guest of the Walkers, her father died. The young woman had climbed into the tree house a princess, and came down a queen.

The original Treetops was burned during the Mau Mau terrors,

but later a compact, modern hotel was built in the heart of another
giant tree with verandas where guests can sit in strictest silence
and look down on herds of rhino, elephant, gazelle, and families
of ridiculous wart hogs, with their wireless-aerial tails, licking
the salt below. The only talking permitted is at a little bar or during meals, and even then it must be carefully modulated so as not
to frighten the animals at the salt pan. To augment the natural
supply, salt is sprinkled over the pan area during the day; when
there is no moon or it is covered by a cloud, there are now concealed floodlights which cleverly filter through the trees to simu-
late moonlight. This apparently hoodwinks the animals completely.

It is not possible to drive through the dense forest to Treetops,
and visitors have an exciting twenty-minute trek going through
the bush in complete silence, guarded by an armed white hunter
and several African guards. Now long slat ladders are fixed to
trees at intervals along the track as uneasy reminders of imminent
attack from rhino and elephant which abound throughout this wild
Aberdare country. There were no such comfortable safeguards
on my first visit.

The Walkers lived in the heart of the Kikuyu territory, where
the murderous, oath-taking Mau Mau movement began, though
the Kikuyu appeared to be a peaceful and contented people
when we were there. Yet only a little more than twenty years
later they had instituted their secret anti-European terrorist movement in which Jomo Kenyatta, the present prime minister of Kenya,
figured so largely. While in Kikuyu territory, we filmed many of
their dances, the most exciting being the vigorous dance of the
circumcision ceremony, in which the initiates made themselves
grotesque by liberal use of paint and other embellishments. Over
their short toga-like garment, which is knotted over one shoulder,
they wore black and white colobus-monkey shawls and handsome
leopard skins that swung out in back as they danced. Symbolic
red and white paint was applied to their heads, faces, arms, and
legs in geometric designs, and bands of cowrie shells hung down
their outside upper legs supporting metal rattles shaped like pea
pods. Each boy carried a short stick topped with plumes made
from cow tails, and a few had small wooden shields brightly
painted in triangles of deep blue and white edged with red. One
wore a mask made from animal skin, and the leader carried a long
staff. It was not possible to record all the sounds of such violent

group activity on my wax-cylinder recorder. To have preserved anything at all with that early equipment was something of a miracle.

Before leaving New York we had booked a safari with Kenya's most sought-after white hunter, Denys Finch-Hatton. The youngest son of the Earl of Winchelsea, he had gone to Kenya on a hunting trip and loved the country so much that he had decided to spend the rest of his life there. Finch-Hatton, too, had recently taken the Prince of Wales on a shooting safari, and we feared that he might be bored with our party because in Kenya we shot only with cameras. But our fears were ungrounded, for he was not only interested in our photographic work but equally interested in studiously observing the game.

He was a tall, striking man, with large blue eyes which revealed his sense of humor more than did his quiet personality. His charm made fireside chats and safari dinners unforgettably happy. His witty conversation and stories full of wisdom and knowledge of Africa made us reluctant to retire at night. On the plains and in the bush we saw demonstrated time and again his rapport with wild animals. He could detect every spoor, anticipate every movement, and by testing the wind tell exactly how close we could approach game. He and his head hunter found the wind's direction by constantly stooping as we cautiously advanced, gathering handfuls of dirt, letting it sift through their fingers, and judging the wind by the direction in which the dust was blown.

Life in camp was made easier by expertly trained and highly efficient camp boys. When we arrived at a campsite hot, dusty, and tired, almost before we were out of the cars there would be a fire going, a cup of tea ready, and soon our tents were up, with beds made. After a hot bath in a folding canvas tub, everyone would gather for drinks and dinner, clean and fresh in bush jacket, slacks, and mosquito boots. Because we were so near the equator, there was no twilight and darkness descended suddenly. I looked forward to these evenings about the campfire. They were the best part of each day.

Our first night in the bush we were thrilled to see a whole family of magnificent lions—a male, two lionesses, and four cubs —prowling about in front of our camp. They appeared to be as fascinated by our movements around the campfire as we were by theirs in the moonlight.

At dawn and dusk we would go into the bush to watch and photograph animals of every kind coming to drink at the water holes: elephant, buffalo, zebra, and great herds of antelope from the awkward wildebeest to the exquisite gazelle. All would lift their heads nervously from time to time, muzzles held high to scent the wind, then scatter wildly at some slight sound or from an instinctive sense that warned of a lioness nearby. Many tragedies occur beside water holes, where animals, absorbed in slaking their thirst, are taken unaware. However, the majority of the animals are saved by their strange form of "radar" which can broadcast throughout a herd in seconds the presence of a killer. On late afternoon drives we often spotted two or three lions crouched in the tufty scrub, cleverly stationed near the water hole, and were delighted to see the herds of zebra and antelope gallop away before the cats had an opportunity to strike.

The cameraman and I had a sharp lesson in emergency behavior while we were camping for a week in the midst of a herd of feeding elephant. One day while we were filming a huge bull elephant, the wind changed and he caught our scent. Trunk raised, ears flapping, he rushed at us trumpeting wildly. On an impulse we raced for an eight-foot anthill and scrambled up it; Finch-Hatton drew the bull's attention away from us, and we crawled down from our perch, but with little dignity. Finch-Hatton then explained that climbing the anthill was the worst thing we could have done. Although these African termite nests are calculated to be twenty-seven times the height of the Empire State Building judged in terms of the size of the insects, even an African anthill would have afforded little protection from a giant elephant weighing six tons, had he really meant business. All we had accomplished was to draw further attention to ourselves.

It was on this safari that we filmed the Masai, a tall, proud, and dignified people, one of the more reticent of African tribes. Before the days of organized protection of wildlife, a Masai lion hunt might continue over many days. When a lion was surrounded, the warriors would close in inch by inch or stand immobile for what seemed hours, ebony statues in the long golden grass, awaiting the signal to advance on their quarry. Their only weapon against the infuriated beast was the traditional long spear, but it was very seldom that they failed to make a kill. For a young

Masai to wound and not kill his lion outright during the blooding ceremony was a dishonor, for the Masai believe that it is better that a young warrior be killed by a wounded lion than survive as a coward. We learned that many chose death in this manner.

All in all, this was one of the happiest episodes in my life. It was in great part due to Denys Finch-Hatton that every day of the safari is still a glorious landmark in my memory. We were very sad when we said good-by to him at Voi on the Tsavo River, and we were deeply shocked to learn of his death about a year after our parting. He had crashed in a small plane which he had bought to survey the herds of game he loved so much. He had been burned to death at Voi, where when we had last seen him he was smiling and waving good-by.

There is a touching tribute to this delightful and cultured man by Isak Dinesen in *Out of Africa.* Having shared much of the same kind of background in their native countries, Baroness Karen Blixen (Dinesen's true name) and Finch-Hatton were very close friends and spent much time together reading the classics, listening to symphonic records, and conversing in Latin for the fun of it.

When I first met the Baroness, she was still living on her African farm, and although I knew her later in her native Copenhagen, it is against the background of the Africa she loved that I see her most vividly. A story she once told me and later published gives an insight into this wonderful woman's character, and illustrates the kindness and affection shown by many European settlers to their African workmen, something rarely remembered in these days of rapid changes. The Baroness had just received a letter from the King of Denmark thanking her for the gift of a magnificent lion skin which she had sent to him, a skin worthy of a king, for which she and Finch-Hatton had searched for a long time. While she was reading the letter, a frightened boy burst into her home to tell her that one of the farm boys had been badly hurt in a wood-chopping accident. Thrusting the letter into the pocket of her bush jacket, she rushed to him.

A king means something special to Africans, and the workers had always loved her stories about her king. On the way to the hospital in the ambulance, she sat beside the boy, pacifying him. To keep his mind off his pain, she showed him the letter she had just received from her king. He begged to touch it, and she gave it to him to hold. Throughout his stay in the hospital, and even in death, the letter (now bloodstained) was clutched to his breast as though it were the last thread holding him to life. She did not have the heart to take it from the boy.

Finch-Hatton had always expressed the wish to be buried in his beloved Ngong hills outside of Nairobi overlooking the Athi plains where the game roamed free in hundreds of thousands. The last thing the Baroness did before leaving Africa forever was to visit her friend's grave. In *Out of Africa* she describes having seen two proud lions, their tawny manes ruffled by the wind, lying quietly on his grave. She wrote: "The lions on Lord Nelson's monument are only made of bronze."

Chapter 3

TANGANYIKA'S MYSTERY MOUNTAIN

After the departure for New York of Mrs. Straus, her grandson, and her companion, we continued the expedition for the American Museum of Natural History through Tanganyika into Nyasaland, where we would begin the Carnegie South African Expedition, ending at Capetown and the Penguin Islands off the southwest coast of South Africa. We said farewell to Mrs. Straus at Nairobi and began our journey to the coastal city of Mombasa. But in spite of our preparedness we were stranded on the banks of the Tsavo River. Heavy rains had caused a flood that had carried away part of the bridge, and we had no choice but to pitch camp and wait for it to be repaired so that our trucks could cross.

Of all the sounds and songs and cries and calls of an African night, there is none so chilling as the roar of the lion. This is a sound to which I could never become accustomed. You can feel your skin prickling as other lions answer the first deep-throated roar. We had not known that there were so many lions in the world until that night.

The only book I had at hand that night was Lieutenant Colonel J. H. Patterson's famous thriller *Man Eaters of Tsavo*, a blood-curdling account of the building of the railway from Nairobi to Mombasa. Progress on the line was seriously delayed when many of the workmen were devoured by man-eating lions. The men were not safe even in the boxcars where they slept; the lions, bold beyond belief, eventually jumped in and hauled them out

into the night. Finally all the workers fled, holding up the laying
of the railroad for almost a year. Later when I recounted my
shattering experience on the Tsavo River to the son of the author,
Dr. Bryan Patterson, an eminent scientist at Harvard, he agreed
that his father's book was not, under the circumstances, the best
inducement to sleep.

At Mombasa we boarded a small steamer en route from India
to England for our voyage to Beira in Mozambique (Portuguese
East Africa). In the harbor of Dar es Salaam, where we anchored
one night, I awoke in the morning insisting that I had heard the
roaring of lions. I was told that I was still dreaming the nightmare
of Tsavo, but when the captain came to breakfast he asked:
"Anyone hear the lions roaring last night?" I was vindicated.
Lions had come into the town during the night and had dragged
an Indian cabinetmaker out of his hut and hauled him off into
the bush. Such things could not happen in modern Dar es Salaam,
but on my first visit, the edge of the town was still bordered by
bush country.

I contracted my first bout of dysentery on that ship and arrived
in Mozambique feeling more dead than alive. But in Beira there
was a wonderful old man named Lawley who had been brought
from England by Cecil Rhodes as an engineer to help build the
mighty bridge over the Zambezi. Lawley had retired to Beira
and had built a small hotel called the Savoy where we all stayed.
He took me under his wing, and I was allowed to eat nothing
but boiled rice and drink nothing but the water in which the rice
was boiled. Everyone else was having penguin eggs shipped in
from Capetown, avocado salad, pawpaws, and other luscious tropical foods which I longed to taste. However, the rice treatment
quickly restored me to life, and to this day it has never failed
to work its magic.

During our stay at the Savoy we were regaled with wondrous
tales by our host, fascinating reminiscences of those early bridge-
building days. He told us that when the bridge was finally completed, some dignitaries from England came for the official opening, and one, not content with Lawley's word as to the exact
height of the structure, was determined to prove it for himself
by the old method of holding a watch in one hand and dropping
a stone from the other, timing the fall. Mr. Lawley loved to

recount how this foppish gentleman opened the wrong hand and "there he stood on the bridge, staring at a stone."

From Beira we went by a tiny boat and a chugging biweekly train to the Shire Highlands of Nyasaland where we stayed with the director of railways at Limbe near Blantyre while arranging our trip through Nyasaland to Mount Rungwe in southern Tanganyika. With the help of our host and the government, we assembled an excellent staff of five personal boys. From Limbe we moved on to Zomba, then little more than a village nestling under the shadow of Mount Zomba. Many parties were given for us by the small European community there, and it was in Zomba that I found the first piano I had come across in Africa. I was kept playing and singing until the early morning hours. The latest song hit was "My Blue Heaven," and whenever I have heard it since, I have been taken back to that evening and have remembered our host firing the cook at three o'clock in the morning because the dinner was cold. (The cook was rehired the next day.)

From Zomba to Mwaya in Tanganyika Territory we eventually sailed on a small government mail steamer, the only water traffic for the entire length of Lake Nyasa. The other passengers in addition to our party were a judge and his three assistants on their way to try a native murder case. Their folk tales and the singing of our boys kept me busy recording throughout the journey. The most anxious moment of the trip came when, at the head of the lake, we were put off on a sandy beach with our mountain of gear, expecting to find porters awaiting us there. All arrangements had been made through government headquarters in Zomba, and porters were to have been sent to us by Karosa, the paramount chief of this area. We had traveled some five thousand miles to reach this isolated spot, the jumping-off point for the real work of the expedition. No land has ever looked so formidable or less welcoming to me. It was an unnerving moment when the boat steamed away leaving the members of our expedition alone on that spit of sand without another human in sight, knowing that it would be a month before the ship returned.

I was not so philosophical then as I am now, nor had I yet heard the story later told me by Ronald V. C. Bodley, a descendant, I was informed, of the founder of Oxford's Bodleian

Library, who lived for a considerable time in the desert while preparing his two-volume work on the life of Mohammed. New to desert life and still Western in moods and attitudes, he had arranged to meet a famous sheik at a certain time in the desert. He waited all day and all night, all the next day and night, and finally after three days the sheik appeared. Bodley, by now raging with impatience and frustration, could not completely hide his feelings. The sheik said to him: "What would you have been doing if you hadn't been here?" "Nothing much, I suppose, but . . ." The sheik interrupted: "Well, couldn't you do nothing much just as well here as there?"

This was our plight on the sandspit except that had we been where we were going we would have been very busy indeed. At last, toward sunset, our porters came straggling out of the rim of bush beyond the beach. When our gear was finally loaded —after much argument among the men as to who would carry the lightest boxes in our mass of equipment—we set off to pay our respects to Karosa. The chief's representative and several tribal headsmen came in slow procession to meet us. Behind them trailed troops of men, women, and children keeping a respectful distance, but excited and curious. A white safari in this remote part of central Africa, especially one with so many porters, was quite an event. A white woman was cause for great excitement.

Karosa had sent to me by his representative a gift of a beautiful white goat, my first present from an African chief. Long afterward I learned that according to the native etiquette of this tribe I should have killed the animal on the spot and sent half of the meat back to the chief. Instead I was so touched by this gesture that I led the little goat many miles into the mountains of Tanganyika, fording rivers and crossing slippery log bridges above rushing mountain streams, but finally in one camp hunger overrode sentiment, and goat chops were added to our menu. My breach of etiquette over the goat was apparently overlooked by Chief Karosa—a fortunate thing, for we were dependent upon him for our porters and their food supply.

On arrival in the village, we were astonished that the ancient Karosa himself appeared to greet us, carried to his throne chair on the back of a strong young girl; we were told later that this was the special privilege of the youngest wife. He was the oldest living creature I have ever seen. His body was shrunken and wrinkled, but from his wizened face shone a pair of vigorous and cunning eyes. The success of our trip up Mount Rungwe depended on winning the friendship of this important chief. After exchanging formal greetings through interpreters, we said that we would like to present some small gifts. I had brought with me the most gorgeous colored baubles I could find, the best Mr. Woolworth had to offer, and I asked the chief to select one for his favorite wife.

His eyes glinted. With one swift movement he took the box from my hands saying: "I have many wives." With that my entire treasure, with which I had hoped to make friends and influence people throughout the length and breadth of Africa, was gone. I find this amusing now. Then it seemed a major tragedy. After polite conversation and the exchange of other gifts, Karosa gave us a guide to a temporary camping place in one of his banana groves nearby. While we were pitching camp, the chief sent a dozen men carrying bunches of plantains (large green bananas) which, roasted in their skins deep in the coals of the campfires, provided a delicious meal.

I had never before fully appreciated the beauty and usefulness of the banana plant. Here in the northern Nyasa region the banana was a most essential commodity, and these graceful plants with their broad, drooping leaves, wine-colored flowers, and bunches of green and yellow fruit were everywhere. Apart from the fruit providing the Africans with their basic diet, the leaves of the tree supplied thatching for their huts, umbrellas against the rain (the African cannot stand being wet and cold), material for "skirts," and they served as wrapping paper and as covers for bamboo milk containers. The leaves were also used as seats, beds, and pads of many sorts. Wilted over the fire, they made handy drinking cups.

The trunk of the banana tree provided the resonator for the natives' favorite instrument, a primitive xylophone. I brought back to the Carnegie Museum one such instrument—which was humorously described by a music critic as "a good old woodpile xylophone made of young railroad ties." The "railroad ties" are keys made from a light wood and cut into pieces about two inches wide, varying in length from one and a half to three feet. These keys, or staves, usually five to nine in number, are placed on "trunks" of banana trees, freshly cut for each occasion, as resonance is lost when the trunk dries. Each key is accurately tuned by chipping away tiny flakes of wood, and held in place by small pegs driven into the trunk. Two boys seat themselves on either side of the huge unwieldy instrument and play it by striking the keys with small wooden beating sticks. They play in syncopated rhythms, and the liquid tones of the keys produce strangely sweet music.

I still have vivid memories of our first night camped in Karosa's banana grove. Our boys were singing at their tasks, the bivouac fires of the porters glowed among the trees, the special guard provided in our honor by Karosa paced up and down proudly with a brightly polished gun on his shoulder, his shadow, thrown by the campfires, stalked silently beside him. During the night our camp was invaded by a battalion of soldier ants on the march, an invasion no gun could stop. There was no sleep for anyone until these tenacious insects had been driven away by the old native method of slowly scorching with bundles of lighted grass every inch of ground around the camp.

It was a hard trek from the banana grove to Tukuyu, and it took us several days to cover the fifty-mile distance, camping en route. This southernmost government post at the foot of Mount Rungwe was our first objective in Tanganyika, and the trip to reach it was lightened by the porters' rhythmic singing. In Tukuyu I made some of the favorite records in my collection, songs sung by a splendid old man, totally unspoiled and an excellent singer. While singing exuberant songs he accompanied himself on a small African zither held under his left arm and plucked with his left fingers. At the same time, he danced brandishing a spear in his right hand. When I played the recording back to him he was beside himself with joy. Through my interpreter he said: "Now I have heard myself sing, I would like to see myself dance," for we had also filmed his performance. I was in a quandary. How could we make this child of nature understand that the motion pictures had to travel thousands of miles back to America to be treated with white man's medicine before they could be seen? Although disappointed and not at all convinced, he did not stop singing and his songs are among my treasures. They created great interest when the wax cylinders were copied recently by the Thomas Edison Rerecording Laboratories.

I seem to have lived through the history of recording for I think I have tried every method and material known. I did not dream that the melodies I captured on that early, glorified Edison recorder would be of interest to the world in general. For African flutes or a single voice, this machine was surprisingly good, but it could not take the volume produced by a chorus or an orchestra of drums. When I returned to Africa on the Straus West African Expedition I had much more adequate equipment, especially designed for me by engineers of Columbia Broadcasting System, thanks to a generous grant from Carnegie Corporation of New York. The recording was done on big aluminum discs thickly coated with heavy grease, really an embossing process. Then came the first commercial portable machine, the Presto, cutting acetate-covered aluminum discs. The wire recorder I did not trust for use in the field; the wire tangled and was easily stretched producing a "wow." Then came tape, a real godsend! The first good field recorder for tape was the Magnacorder; the president of the company presented one to me for my first trip around the world. The results were excellent but it was cumbersome with two cases weighing nearly fifty pounds each, requiring heavy duty batteries. Finally came a tape recorder which is an answer to prayer—it is the Nagra, invented by Kudelski in Lausanne.

The isolated government post at Tukuyu had only three British officials, one with a wife and child. Their day began in the early morning dealing with native affairs (everything from theft to suspected witchcraft), and the late afternoons were devoted to tea and tennis followed by hot baths and "sundowners" (usually scotch and soda). The day ended with dinner in formal dress (black tie and long gowns); the farther from civilization an outpost might be, the more rigid was this rule. Day after day the routine was the same. Perhaps when there were no guests they might have spent an evening alone, but when we were at the post there was little rest, for visitors were rare and new faces meant new conversation and word from the outside. These British officials were doing a wonderful job in the area, and they were kind beyond words in helping me find musicians to record, such as the old man and his excellent songs, and in helping to start our entire party on its way to Mount Rungwe.

In Tukuyu we also met a wonderful old German Lutheran missionary whose hospital had served the local population for many years. He had great scientific knowledge and a splendid library about the area, which he made available to us. We discovered that he was very disturbed about a new mission which had recently been built in the shadow of his own by a highly emotional American religious sect. This form of religion had immediate appeal to the exuberant Africans, and the congregations were flocking from the old church to the new. To make matters worse, an American woman with more dollars than knowledge of the African interior had "felt the call," packed hundreds of Greek Testaments, scores of writing pads, pencils, pens, and storybooks, and had set sail to establish a school for the new sect. When we arrived in Tukuyu the matter had practically become an international issue. We heard after we had left that there had been a fire in which the new mission was destroyed. Whether this was accidental or by divine interference, the crisis was passed and orthodoxy restored. This could not happen today because missionaries are thoroughly screened by very strict boards and the standards required are high.

From Tukuyu we began the climb up Mount Rungwe, an extinct volcanic mountain so isolated that it had never before been explored by a scientific expedition, and I was, I was told, the first white woman to climb to its summit. At the beginning of our ascent we followed small paths made by the local woodcutters who penetrated the forest of the lower mountain, but after three thousand feet we had nothing but animal trails to follow. The only means of crossing rushing mountain streams was by fallen trees slippery with moss, or by native bridges of bamboo bound together with lianas, often so fragile that I marveled that they held together while our stream of a hundred carriers jogged across with their heavy loads. The ordinary load for each was sixty pounds, but many begged to be given a double load in order to have double pay and food. Twenty men were needed just to carry food for themselves and the other eighty.

In the course of my twenty-eight expeditions I have lived the history of transportation—traveling by native dugout canoes and little rafts poled by bamboo poles; by Greek donkeys, Tibetan ponies, and Nepalese dhandi (primitive sedan chair); by African camel, Indian elephant, and Eskimo dog sledge; ultimately by truck, jeep, helicopter, and jet. And still my favorite method of travel, especially in Africa, is on foot. I have trekked hundreds of miles into the mountains, through the bush, and across the plains. Only in this way does one feel close to the people, see every flower, know every scent, hear every bird; a marvelous way of making friends with a strange country . . . and best of all, the porters always sang to make the load lighter, improvising new songs or singing ancient songs that belonged to the former days of trade caravans crossing the continent.

On this march the porters sang constantly as we climbed into beautiful rain forest where mahogany trees, nine and ten feet in diameter reached a height of one hundred eighty feet. They were covered with thick trailing creepers that made the forest so dense that even at midday we were walking through tunnels of deep green gloom, forcing our way through lianas, thick entangling vines which draped themselves from tree to tree making a solid wall of growth. Curious monkeys, black and white colobus and blue Sykes, swung and bounded overhead, and their chatter protesting our presence reverberated eerily through the trees.

At the beginning of the steep climb the porters began a wonderfully vigorous song with each verse imitating a different animal, starting with the fleet gazelle, and going through every species they knew until finally, at the end of the day when they were near exhaustion, they sang: "I am the slow-creeping snail. Shall I ever reach my goal?"

We were interested in making observations and collections in every zone of life at various altitudes on Mount Rungwe. Above the lifezone of the savanna (bush), there was a zone of forest in the foothills up to about three thousand feet, another up to six thousand feet where giant trees towered to nearly two hundred feet and moss-bearded tree ferns grew to a height of over twenty feet, and finally a zone of bamboo, rearing straight and slender fifty feet into the sky, marking the tree line at approximately nine thousand feet, with the scrubby alpine zone reaching to the summit. The bird and animal life changed as dramatically with each zone as did the vegetation; the various belts were almost as clean-cut and distinguishable as though there were actual walls between them.

We made our base camp on Mount Rungwe at six thousand feet on the only level space available, right in the heart of the rain forest. I felt very small and insignificant hemmed in on all sides by enormous wonders of nature. The trees seemed to scratch the sky and the undergrowth was so dense that it took hours to make a clearing big enough for our tents, worktables, campfire, and space for the "kitchen" area and the boys' canvas shelter. The smell of the deep wet foliage, the humid air, heavy and dank, and the pungent scent of moldy decaying leaves and plants pressed in on us from everywhere.

On the way up we had collected two beautiful black colobus monkeys with big white neck ruffs. While the boys were making a clearing and pitching our tents, the monkeys were skinned and the pelts were hung for safekeeping in a tent. The carcasses were then tossed well out into the impenetrable tangle surrounding the camp. In the night we heard loud munchings, crunchings, and deep-throated growls in the forest beyond the circle of firelight. When morning came the boys were clearly uneasy. Although not mountain-forest boys, they knew only too well the sounds of the *chui* (leopard). We hoped to reassure them by promising to find and shoot the big cat. On the second night we staked another monkey carcass well inside the small clearing, darkened the camp early, and stationed ourselves with gun and flashlight in the entrance of a tent. Every few seconds I would flash my light on the carcass. Then suddenly it was gone. Not a sound had been heard, but presently there was once again the crunching and munching from inside the dark rim of forest.

By morning the boys had worked themselves into a panic, and Awami, our "head boy" and cook, was sent to explain that they all wanted to leave. Awami was a treasure. He was our highest-paid boy, earning one pound a month, riches to an African in those days. Without any apparent effort Awami had so far easily controlled not only our personal boys but the porters as well. Now, as he spoke to us, he was calm but firm. "These are no ordinary leopards, *bwana*. They are bewitched. We cannot stay in this place." Only by magic, they said, could anything disappear so silently: meat and stake both gone without a sound while my light flashed and every eye and ear in the camp concentrated on that one spot. It took all our persuasive powers to give the boys enough confidence to keep them in camp one more night. Again a carcass was firmly staked in front of the tent, and the boy with the best reputation as a hunter was stationed beside us to signal us. This time there was no magic, only a swift sleek flash of gold and black in the torch beam and the shattering sound of a shot which sent the leopard leaping and snarling high into the air. It was a terrifying moment for us, knowing that the wounded leopard might spring directly at us. It bounded instead into the dark protection of the forest, and there was little sleep for anyone that night wondering if it might return.

The buffalo hunter will tell you that there is nothing more cunning and dangerous than a wounded buffalo; and the lion hunter considers a wounded lion even worse. We were just as sure that nothing could be more dangerous than a wounded leopard near camp. We knew that it must be found and destroyed, for not only was it a menace in its wounded condition, but the Africans told us that where there is one *chui*, there are always two. With the first rays of daylight we started out with the hunters, guns ready, following a trail of blood through the deep tangle of vines and bushes, expecting any moment to have a pain-maddened beast drop on us from a tree or spring from the undergrowth. After what seemed hours, but was probably no more than half an hour, we found the leopard, dead, a fine female.

News travels fast in Africa. Although we heard no drums, in some magic way word had reached the foot of the mountain that the great man-eater of Mount Rungwe had been killed. Within an hour of sunrise a procession (which continued all day) of woodcutters and their families began the long climb to our camp above the altitude level to which they normally traveled, bowing low before us, pouring out their gratitude. Many people on the mountain had been eaten by a "demon" leopard of exceptional size and the hunters were convinced the one we killed was that very leopard. One old man with intense gestures enacted a dramatic description of the leopard's attack on his brother in the forest while they were cutting wood. So perfect was his miming that one could see the twitching of the leopard's tail above the tangle of brush, the soundless spring, and the flash of gold and black. The old man's brother was dead by the time he and the other woodcutters had managed to drive off the beast. They were firmly convinced that we had been sent by their gods to save them from the leopards.

The leopard's "cough"—like a startled, guttural explosion of breath—is an unmistakable and exciting sound, especially in the dead of night. From the frequent "coughing" we heard we soon learned that the leopard we had shot was but one of many. In fact, it became uncomfortably obvious that we had pitched camp in a leopard-infested area. This was borne out by the fresh claw marks on trees nearby. The bark was raw and ragged from regular use by the leopards in sharpening their claws. For the safety of the camp, as well as for the specimens we wanted, we set traps around the clearing and the next night caught two young leopards, perfect specimens, evidently hunting for the mother we had shot. Altogether we bagged five in our camp.

Throughout the excitement Awami was composed and able to restore calm once again among the boys, while not neglecting his duties as cook. He could perform culinary miracles under appalling conditions. Here in the heart of the rain forest with mountain mists dripping all about us, he would dig a hole in the ground and bake bread, cake, or a pudding fit for royalty. All of our camp boys, for that matter, were resourceful, clean, neat, and meticulous. Being from the Mohammedan Yao tribe in Nyasaland, they wore the fez, one of fine white cotton more practical in the tropics than the usual heavy red felt one. The flat tops of their fezzes were beautifully embroidered in geometrical designs, and in Awami's spare hours he would embroider these in brightly colored floss. They were so pretty that I asked him to embroider a set of twelve for me. They are still admired as table mats in my home.

On every expedition, knowing we would be hundreds of miles from a pharmacy for long periods, we carried a fully stocked medicine chest, and although I had no nursing training, I fell heir to the job. I soon became adept at bandaging wounds (the wood-choppers were always cutting themselves), diagnosing aches and pains, administering medicines, and applying ointments. In the cold dampness of Mount Rungwe the boys were especially susceptible to rheumatic chills and colds, and every morning when I emerged from my tent I would find them, plus dozens of villagers, in line for some white man's magic to cure their ills. The stronger the medicine, the worse it tasted, or the more it stung, the more they loved it and believed in its power to cure. My large bottle of Sloane's Liniment was soon exhausted. I sometimes suspected that they exaggerated their coughs in order to come with cupped hands to receive a little liniment to rub on their chests. This "firewater" warmed them if it did nothing else.

In the line-up one morning was my devoted gunbearer and hunter Wamjabaregi. After I had poured liniment into his hands, instead of rubbing it on his chest as I had carefully demonstrated, he lifted it to his lips and drank it, afterward licking his pink palms greedily. I waited with apprehension all day for signs of some drastic aftereffects, but he was back in line the next morning.

Wamjabaregi was Africa's counterpart of our legendary Ichabod Crane, a gangling youth, ebony black, and all but naked. With long thin arms, spindly legs and a smile like an open piano, he stood well over six feet tall, straight as a sapling. I never saw Wamjabaregi when he did not appear to be on the point of bursting with energy and infectious good fun. He had the contagious exuberance of a big porpoise.

The day I chose him as my personal gun boy in the mountain forest of Tanganyika, I gave Wamjabaregi an old pair of hunting trousers which a scientist in our party had discarded. With the help of the other camp boys he put them on then and there and bounded about, almost hysterical with joy. Thereafter they were removed only in moments of extreme activity when they threatened to hamper his movements. Knowing the boy's devotion to these pants and his unwillingness to be parted from them for an instant, I was truly alarmed one day deep in the forest to see Wamjabaregi suddenly stop on the narrow path, lay down his gun, whip off his pants, and fold them quickly into a pile on the ground. He then shinnied up a tree with the agility of a monkey and vanished into the entanglement of growth overhead.

Had the boy gone berserk? I felt the hair begin to rise on my head; perhaps it was another leopard. With my heart beating like a drum in my ears, I picked up the gun and, pressing my back against a tree trunk, waited for heaven knows what. But no leopard sprang at me from the green wall of the forest, only Wamjabaregi, swinging down from the trees, their thick branches rustling and swaying as he leaped from one to another like a monkey. With a great bound he landed in front of me, and with a beatific grin and that almost reverent courtesy inherent in the unspoiled African, held out to me like a royal gift a large roll of freshly stripped tree bark. Limp with relief I knelt down and unfolded it. Inside was a mound of dark honeycomb, filled with a sweet-scented wild bees' honey such as I have never tasted before or since.

Perhaps Wamjabaregi had smelled the wild honey above us, for all of the senses of the African are much more highly developed than ours. The hunters especially can see and hear and smell things with uncanny perception. On these morning hunts Wamjabaregi frequently identified some animal that had recently crossed in our path by the faint, musky scent it had left behind. On one occasion he pointed out to me on the still warm, flattened grass beside our path the tawny hairs of a leopard that had just bounded away at our approach.

Of all the primitive people I have recorded, Wamjabaregi showed the most spontaneously joyous reaction to hearing his voice for the first time. He whipped off his trousers, grabbed his long spear, and with arms and legs weaving in simultaneous motion, head wagging furiously, eyes rolling, he brandished his weapon aloft with wild whoops of delight. Anyone suddenly coming upon this performance might have justifiably believed that we were all about to be massacred. But that was the kind of person Wamjabaregi was: a lovable extrovert.

When our expedition moved south from Tanganyika, we wrote a glowing note of recommendation in his "work book," which was essential to getting a job even in those early days in East Africa. Many years later we heard from a famous scientist who had gone to Mount Rungwe to collect specimens for his museum that my faithful Wamjabaregi had turned up in search of work, proudly carrying his little book in a split branch. It was grubby and tattered but our comments were still legible. I have often wondered if, with the rapid development of his wild country, he had learned to read and knew that we had written that he was one of the best boys we had ever had.

It was Wamjabaregi who gave me my first understanding of a simple phrase that has remained part of my daily life ever since. If I shot a bird in the forest that was particularly rare or beautiful, I would hear a soft voice near me murmuring, "*Ndaga, bwana*," and see a quick gesture of thanksgiving. If I tripped over a hidden root, but did not fall, again the soft "Ndaga, bwana" as my gun boy gave thanks that I had not fallen. Giving thanks to what? I wondered. To whom? I also heard Wamjabaregi use the phrase when he met another African on the forest path.

There would be a brief brushing of hands in passing and the exchange of greeting: "Ndaga." Thanks for your safekeeping, go safely, there is a friend among and above the tall trees. Like so many commonly used phrases in Africa "Ndaga, bwana" defies literal translation, but it appeared to embrace a gratitude as big as the human heart can hold or bestow. I first heard but did not fully comprehend the phrase from the grateful villagers after we had killed the man-eating leopard. I had been told that the African has no word for "thank you" and apparently this is true among many tribes. But "Ndaga, bwana" suited the villagers' need to thank us. The expression seemed to have a mystical connotation, since they regarded us as being sent by their deities to aid them, in thanking us they were in turn thanking their gods.

One wonders if this humble thanksgiving, this gentle courtesy in Africa, is extended as generously and spontaneously today as thirty-five years ago in the Africa of Wamjabaregi with his good-hearted consideration and enormous capacity for enjoyment. Is it not significant that it should have been from one of these simple, lovable people of the remote forests, as yet unspoiled by white intrusion, that I learned to understand and cherish so eloquent an expression of gratitude, two words in a strange dialect that still, after all these years, come to my mind many times daily and turn my thoughts upward with thanks to Bwana.

In the Mount Rungwe camp I became an expert at bird skinning practically overnight when our ornithologist was stricken with a terrible bout of malaria. There were none of today's cures available then, only quinine taken in large doses at sundown when the mosquitoes became the most vicious. We had trained three boys to help measure, skin, and stuff bird specimens immediately after they were collected, as we had no refrigerators to preserve the birds. For several days and nights I got little sleep, for as well as ministering to the ill man, who became delirious at times when his temperature rose to 105, I was collecting birds and working with the skinners to keep them busy. Time was so very precious; everything we collected on this mountain was immensely valuable, being either a new species or new subspecies. I had sent a runner to the foot of the mountain for medical help but when he returned after several days with word that the doctor was away on an emergency call, the patient's fever had subsided and he soon fully recovered.

During this period I made the mistake of becoming so skilled in preparing some of the most difficult birds that they were thereafter allotted to me. Such a bird was the trogon, whose skin is like wet tissue paper and whose feathers are so lightly attached that if one hit a branch on its fall to earth, we found only a puff of brilliant feathers and a denuded bird. No one who has not skinned and stuffed one of these beautiful birds can imagine with what care and delicate skill it must be handled. Another mistake I made was in becoming too adept at preparing the thumb-sized sunbirds, the African equivalent of our hummingbirds. Although they were brought down with the smallest possible shot, even a pinprick in such tiny creatures added to the difficulty of preparing them as museum specimens.

When it became known in any region that we would pay for all kinds of creatures, large or small, dead or alive, we had a menagerie in no time. The variety of creatures in our zoo was amazing, and it was here that "Puzi," a baby vervet monkey, made a dramatic entrance into my life. He arrived one day more dead than alive, dragged at the end of a rope that had cut deep into his tender middle. I paid a shilling for him, hoping to make his last hours comfortable. With the help of my boy Cholie, who had proved himself an excellent bird skinner and who seemed more gentle in his handling of animals than most Africans, we got the rope cut from Puzi's waist without being too severely bitten by the terrified little creature. We made a tiny belt of gauze which kept him from licking the thick application of zinc ointment on his wound and which enabled us to attach a small harness by which to tether him. A pen of sharpened stakes was built in the boys' quarters and every sundown I took a little time off from work to play with Puzi. When I approached, he would dive into my arms, curl up, and coo like a baby, gazing lovingly into my eyes while I fed him his favorite food, bananas. Fortunately we always had plenty of them around.

I know nothing about the color sense of monkeys or whether they choose their food or perhaps even friends and enemies by color. But Puzi certainly was antiblack. He had been so mistreated by the fellow who had brought him to me that he always repulsed with angry chattering any African who came near him except my camp boys, who usually fed him when I was occupied. Puzi so endeared himself to us that he became a part of the expedition family and traveled with us thousands of miles through Africa to Capetown and eventually to America. He was wickedly mischievous and usually managed to leave a trail of havoc in his wake, but in spite of this everyone loved him.

Another specimen brought in alive was a beautiful crowned crane. This graceful bird stands over three feet high. It has a golden crest, a white and red face patch, a soft gray body, and mahogany-colored wings and is the most beautiful and elegant of all the cranes. In Kenya we had witnessed the rarely seen courtship dance of these cranes, a ballet of great beauty. The males walk on tiptoe with spread wings, bowing and strutting to win favor with their would-be mates. At that time it did not occur to me that I would have one for a pet. We could not bear the thought of killing this new arrival for the museum collection and so built a pen to house him in our camp. He soon became quite tame and would eat out of our hands.

At night we moved him from his pen and tied him for safety to the frame of my bed, not more than a foot from my head. On our last night in this exotic mountain camp I was awakened by a great whirring of wings beside me—no other sound. Snatching the flashlight from under my pillow, I leaped out of bed. A small length of rope still dangled from the bedframe. Even my tent had proved unsafe. Strewn into the clearing were all the skins that had been drying in the safety of the tent, and my bird was gone. While I stood there shivering in the cold, I heard that dreadful sound of munching and crunching in the blackness of the forest about me. In the morning we found leopard tracks inside the tent and, in the undergrowth near the clearing, a little pile of blue-gray feathers, all that was left of my favorite bird. Fortunately the crane was more to the leopard's taste than I, under my fragile protection of a mosquito net.

This incident disproved two theories that I have always been told. First, that a member of the cat family in the wilds would never come near a light. In spite of the campfire which we kept blazing throughout every night, and the lighted lantern hanging in the entrance to my tent, this leopard came inside to snatch his prey. And second, that cats will never pass through or under entangling devices. Yet this one deliberately walked under the low guy ropes of the tent from the forest behind us. But despite leopards, the cold and dripping damp of the forest, there were marvelous compensations in this high-altitude camp. Each day the boys covered the floor of the tents and the small camp clearing with fresh, vivid green fronds of tree fern, and all around us the earth was decorated with delicate lavender ground orchids; climbing lilies made brilliant splashes of red and gold amid the green, and rare birds flashed their colors in the tangle around us and filled the air from dawn to dark with singing. For me the exquisite tones of species of thrushes I heard here even challenged the much-extolled song of the nightingale.

Every evening a crowd of boisterous trumpeter hornbills with their ridiculous white helmets came to roost in the trees about the camp and bombarded our eardrums with their raucous cries. As in the bush, the forest, in the depth of night, was filled with rustlings and eerie nocturnal activity.

On our ascent to the summit of Mount Rungwe, which reached almost ten thousand feet into the clouds, we climbed through the forest and the lush bamboo zone and came suddenly into a rocky belt; it looked as though the heavy vegetation had been shorn off with a knife. This expanse of lava, rocks, and chasms made the last fifteen hundred feet of our climb very difficult. The alpine growth here was beautiful, however. A kind of heather grew among the rocks, and many-colored gladioli tossed on slender stalks in the gusty mist that shrouded the crest most of the time. As on our later expedition to African mountains, we built a cairn of stones on the peak of Mount Rungwe, burying there a bottle containing our names, the date, and scientific data. In the brief moments when the mists cleared from the peak, the highest for many thousands of square miles, we were confronted with a breath-taking panorama. Away to the north other blue peaks cut into the sky, and far to the south Lake Nyasa lay glistening in the sunlight within its deep protective shawl of mountains. We could have gazed about us forever but a blanket of cold clouds came and blotted out the rest of the world, and with a steep descent of five thousand feet to make before nightfall, we could not risk waiting for it to clear.

It was dark when we reached camp again, and in the night the realization came to me: how fortunate I was to have had this experience. I had attained my first mountain peak while still young and yet mature enough to be deeply moved and indelibly impressed by what I had felt, a glorious inner peace, a sense of universal perspective I had not known before. I felt then that human trivialities could never disturb me deeply again. Perhaps some do not need to climb a mountain peak to achieve this kind of strength and insulation. But I firmly believe that when, some years later, my life was badly disrupted, one of the reasons that I was able to pick up the threads again quickly was largely because of the insight I had gained from this view that was so much more than merely a view; it had put me in proper perspective with my world.

Chapter 4

NYASALAND TO CAPETOWN

Leaving the "miracle" mountain behind us, we began the long trek back to Lake Nyasa, collecting as we went. We paid our porters and chartered a tiny barge about thirty feet long for our journey southward to Florence Bay. The trip took several days along the western shore of the lake and provided me with one of the most perfect illustrations of the rhythmic impulse that governs the whole life of the African.

It is impossible to say whether or not the African sages of long ago recognized the beneficial influence of rhythm, as did the Greeks, and consciously introduced it into work by singing and into play by drums and other musical instruments. Rather, one supposes that primitive rhythm is an unconscious means of correlating emotions and muscular effort. Rhythm arouses the individual to activity and makes possible an interested and continued effort which would otherwise be difficult. The amount of work accomplished is greatly increased as labor becomes, through music, almost play. Small wonder that the Europeans in Africa soon learned to employ singing workers; the louder and longer they sang, the sooner the task at hand was completed. Boats are paddled, corn is hoed, and spears are sharpened to the rhythm of song. I am convinced that rhythm alone made possible certain long, monotonous tasks required of our boys in central Africa.

Into our fragile craft for the journey down Lake Nyasa we loaded our huge mound of equipment, our specimens, a crew of ten boatmen, our own staff of five, and ourselves. The crew, five in a shift, one as pilot, propelled us along the shores of the lake with twenty-foot-long bamboo poles. Their songs and chants eased the strenuous labor of guiding the heavily loaded barge against almost gale winds. The Bantu boatmen's songs were of great interest to me; they were extremely different from the Arabic boat songs with their oriental flavor which I had recorded going up the Nile.

Our personal boys from Blantyre were unused to any great body of water, and in this tiny barge they were much too close to it for comfort. They begged to be allowed to walk, complaining that "the road on the lake" was very bad. Puzi heartily agreed with them. He was desperately seasick for the entire voyage and for three days after reaching land. How he must have longed for his rain forest on Mount Rungwe. The wind at this season was very strong against us, and there was such a high sea that travel during the day was impossible. At three in the afternoon when the gales died down, our journey would begin, and we had the joy of spending the glorious sunset hour on the water.

The sun, after beating down on us mercilessly through the day, slowly sank behind the jagged peaks which pierce the Vipya Plateau, and then, in quick succession, delicate shades of rose, orange, yellow, green, and purple suffused the clouds resting on the mountaintops. The water of the lake reflected like a mirror the whole inverted bowl of flaming sky so that we had the unforgettable experience of being bathed in a maze of celestial color. Large flocks of cormorants flew overhead during sunset to their roosting places in the reeds which thickly fringed the shore. Approaching our barge the flocks divided, half passing to the right, half to the left, then once again reuniting behind us and continuing their flight.

Beyond doubt the most thrilling bird of Lake Nyasa was the fishing eagle. We frequently saw him plunge into the waters of the lake, then soar in spiral flight so high that we could barely follow him in the sky. No matter what task we were involved in, we could never resist turning our eyes upward when we heard his triumphant cry which came down to us from the zenith of his spectacular flight. I often thought that it would not be at all bad to be reincarnated as one of these huge, noble birds.

Each evening about eight o'clock we would draw in to shore, build a campfire, and have dinner before resuming our trip. Back on board again, I found it difficult to sleep, because the boys continued their singing and shouting throughout the night as they poled. I have rarely seen such poetic motion as the swing of their bodies while they wielded the light bamboo poles. With each thrust the barge rolled to one side and a great splash of sea came pouring into our faces. In the morning the wind arose forcefully, and sunrise on the water was almost as beautiful as sunset, but much more swift and never so blazingly flamboyant.

We would go ashore after breakfast to collect and prepare our specimens under the shelter of palms or thorny acacia trees. It was exceedingly hot on those marshy shores, but a constant breeze made life endurable. Within minutes of landing we would be surrounded by scores of natives curious about us, our errand, our equipment, our pet monkey—everything. All day they would work for us with cheerful enthusiasm, bringing us specimens of all sorts: fish, flesh, and fowl. They were wonderfully kind and generous, coming in long processions bearing gifts for the strangers: milk, eggs, chicken, fruit, and mealy flour. In return we gave them handfuls of salt which from their point of view was infinitely preferable to what they had brought to us. In the little villages by the lake we were again able to observe African life closely. We watched while babies were bathed, children fed, and cows milked. The latter was a strange and marvelous operation. When an African wished milk he approached a likely looking animal, threw it to the ground, tied its feet firmly, and proceeded to milk it while in this undignified position. It is small wonder then that the cows gave barely a cupful of milk. They are inferior beasts compared with our specialized breeds, although their appearance is impressive with horns similar to those of the Texas longhorn. They receive little care and wander about at will, herded by small boys who amuse themselves from time to time by riding and prodding the cows with a stick. At night the cows are driven to the cattle kraal, a small unroofed enclosure near the huts intended to protect the animals from wild beasts—a precaution that frequently proves inadequate.

Each day we found new surprises awaiting us at our camping spot wherever it might be along the lake. One morning as we were disembarking and preparing a "sitting tree" for the center of our day's activities, a European clad in gaily striped pajamas suddenly appeared. He was confused and apologetic for his unconventional attire when he found a woman in camp. His boys had rushed to tell him that some *bwanas* (in my bush clothes with pants I was constantly regarded as bwana) had arrived, and since visitors were rare and very welcome in his hermit life, he had come at once from his house, only a few hundred yards from our camp, to invite us for breakfast. After our long isolation in the mountain camps, he was an equally welcome sight.

At the house he excused himself, reappearing shortly (simultaneously with the arrival of tea) clean-shaven and clad in immaculate slacks and bush shirt. He had snow-white hair, merry blue eyes, and was very lively in spite of his advanced years. The typical Englishman, Commander Rhodes was neat and precise. We drank tea from the biggest cups I have ever seen. They were of the blue willow pattern and the size of bowls. When I exclaimed at their size he said he loved his tea and had written to Fortnum & Mason in London asking them to send him half a dozen of the biggest teacups they had, and these "bowls" had arrived. For the first time I had met someone who loved tea as much as I did. They were his proudest possession, along with twenty-three cats of every color and size, which overran the house.

Many years before he had been captain of the H.M.S. *Gwendolyn*, the British mail boat which plied Lake Nyasa and which had brought us up the lake months before. He told an amusing tale of his one-man victory over the Germans in World War I. Tanganyika was under German rule before the war and a German mail boat also made a monthly trip between Nyasaland and Tanganyika. It was touch and go when hostilities began as to whether the English boat would capture the German first or vice versa. It depended, of course, on which of them first got word of the declaration of war. Our host was the lucky one, and one morning he pulled alongside the German boat and said to his good friend, the captain, "You are my prisoner!" Probably this was the first German boat captured in the war.

After retirement Commander Rhodes had no desire to return to life in an English village. Instead he selected a perfect spot on his beloved lake, and with the help of a few Africans built a low, cool bungalow on a wooded hill from which he could look across the dark blue waters to the deep purple mountains beyond. He had also built a small yacht, and when he could not resist the nautical urge, he would cruise leisurely up and down his old route. While others collected specimens that day, I stayed with the captain and recorded many songs, folk tales, and local tribal lore which he and his boys knew so well.

Of all the equipment on our barge, perhaps the most used was a great piece of blue and white calico bought from some trader years before. It was the crew's most precious treasure. In the hot afternoon sun, stretched across upright poles, it served as a sunshade. During the chilly nights, as the crew took turns sleeping, it served as a blanket. When it was necessary to sail from one point to another, due to the rocky shore or the great depth of water, the calico was rigged up as a precarious sail. The world about us at this time was very beautiful. The rains had ceased in April, and everything was a brilliant green. The trees—red, yellow, and lavender—were all in bloom and pouring forth their fragrance. Their blossom-laden branches were surrounded with clouds of butterflies, bees, jewel-like sunbirds, and hundreds of weaverbirds in velvety coats of gold and black. Their gorgeous colors flashed in and out of their small grass basket-like nests that dangled in colonies from slender branches overhanging the water.

Reaching the mission station, Livingstonia, named after David Livingstone, I met his granddaughter and her children, still doing exceptional work among the lake tribes. The head of the mission was a tall and hospitable Scot, Dr. MacKenzie. His wife, blonde and gracious, was one of the people encountered on my early African expeditions of whom I think most often. She was a fine musician and with her help I collected many valuable songs and folk tales. Mrs. MacKenzie was the first missionary, I feel sure, who collected African tunes and set to them hymn words, translated into Chinyanja, the official language of Nyasaland. The hymnbook she created and which she gave to me is now a collector's item.

In the many missions I have visited, I have noted with sorrow that missionaries, instead of encouraging natives in their own music, have taught them Gospel hymns, in many cases the rambunctious revival tunes of the Moody and Sankey type. Had they taught them instead only beautiful music from our early church hymnals it might not have been so bad. Even so I have always felt strongly that it was wrong to make Africans, or any ethnic group, feel that their own forms of musical expression must be discarded once they become mission converts. It is surely insular and very foolish of us to imply that only Western music is valid for worship. Mrs. MacKenzie had taught the Africans that they could reach God through their own music. I have preached this belief throughout the world when visiting other mission stations and have always cited Mrs. MacKenzie as the shining example to follow. On recent trips I have been pleased to see more and more evidence of indigenous music being encouraged for use in worship by missionaries not only in Africa but in India, Asia, and even the Caribbean and South America.

We continued southward in Nyasaland, and on one occasion collecting game on the Bua River we walked about two hundred miles in nine days, sometimes covering as much as thirty-five miles in one day so as to have time to stop to shoot and prepare specimens. As it was just before the rainy season, the earth was parched and the heat intense. But the hours passed cheerfully as our feet kept time to the rhythmic singing of the porters. It was impossible to walk out of step, for caravan or traveling songs have a marvelous swing, and they even manage to sound joyful when they deal with so sad a topic as homesickness. Most of the tunes of the caravan songs were old, and often extemporaneous words were set to them. The soloist created the lines, usually about the journey and his companions (including us) or about the animals and birds around us. The chorus responded, repeating his words.

Responsorial singing such as this is common throughout Africa. It is found so often that it must be considered basic. With no notation, songs are passed on by oral tradition from generation to generation, and partly for that reason there is great variation of detail in performance. It is only in secular music, however, that a performer becomes a creator, adding his own inspired changes. Ritual music, on the other hand, is preserved with exactitude within a tribe. Though secular songs at times are sung in unison, part singing is the general rule, and according to early navigators, the Africans had evolved a striking form of polyphony long before the Western world began its first crude attempts at harmony.

The essential element of all African music is its rhythm, and I am certain that these so-called primitive musicians have forgotten more about it than most of us have ever known. An extremely popular means of expressing rhythm in Africa is through dance. By singing, beating drums, clapping hands, stamping feet, and swaying the entire body, or even, as in certain dances, contracting and expanding individual muscles, chiefly of the abdomen, the natives find an outlet for the tremendous surge of rhythm within them.

It was thrilling to me to hear for the first time syncopation uninfluenced by European music. In both vocal and instrumental music the foundation of this syncopation was in the drums. They were often placed in groups of three, five, or more, but each retained its individual rhythmic patterns and tones and was quite distinct from the others. I have frequently seen a small boy playing two drums simultaneously with separate and varying rhythms on each instrument.

One of the most interesting of all instruments that I recorded in central Africa was the *gubu,* or musical bow. A gourd is attached by a fiber loop to the center of a long, strong hunter's bow. The player taps on this divided bowstring, producing distinct tones and overtones which are amplified by the gourd resonator pressed with varying force against his exposed chest or bare abdomen. In this way his whole body becomes a resonating chamber.

The gubu was originally a Zulu instrument, and I found it here played only by the old men of the Angoni tribe in northern Nyasaland. The instrument reached Nyasaland more than a hundred years ago when, during the reign of Tchaka, king of the Zulus in Natal, a general of one of his *impis,* or regiments, was defeated in battle. Rather than return to his king and the certain death that awaited him, the general fled to the north and established a new nation, taking the Zulu customs with him. This group became the renowned Angoni nation, especially powerful under King Mombera. When I first visited the tribe, the old men still remembered the ancient Zulu customs and continued to play the early instruments and sing the old Zulu songs. The young men, however, had taken on the customs, songs, and tales of their neighbors. As these old Angoni warriors sang the ancient songs and told their tales for me to record, their voices were weak and distant. But with the singing and telling, new life seemed to come into their eyes and new strength flowed through their veins. At the end of the recording session they seemed to have been rejuvenated.

Throughout Bantu Africa there are numerous types of musical bows. Nearly twenty years later in Swaziland and Zululand I found the same type that was played in Nyasaland. On one occasion I stopped my truck on a lonely road to talk with a Swazi youth playing a bow. As in Nyasaland, this boy's bow had a gourd resonator dividing the bowstring and he played it in the same way as did the Angoni; by pressing the gourd against his bare abdomen. He had a splendid voice and an interesting repertoire of songs. I have often wished that I could have remained there long enough to make a comparative study of his songs and those of the old Angoni men.

I also recorded some two hundred fascinating folk tales in central Africa, all interesting in themselves but doubly so because many of them are ancestors of our Uncle Remus stories of Br'er Rabbit, brought to America by Negro slaves and collected by Joel Chandler Harris. In central Africa the rabbit's name is Kalulu. He is a cunning fellow who invariably outwits the other animals. These tales solved the riddles of the universe: how the leopard got his spots, why the tortoise pulls in his head when it rains, even how to get rid of a superfluous mother-in-law. Often music is introduced that adds appeal to the folk tales, which are usually told by the old men of a tribe. My favorite storyteller was Zeeayah. After everyone had gathered about the fire in the evening, he would begin his tale only when there was absolute quiet and all were ready to listen. He would then proceed with great dignity, squatting on the ground before the fire, pulling his blanket of skins around his shoulders as his shins, glazed and cracked from years of proximity to the flames, gleamed in the firelight. Reaching out, he would slowly draw from the embers a glowing coal which he carefully placed on the bowl of his long carved pipe. By then all eyes were riveted on him, and when his pipe was drawing well he began his tale, punctuating it with great puffs of smoke. The listeners hung on every word and rolled with laughter at the jokes.

On one such evening he told us this tale, a popular one that illustrates the role music plays in many folk stories. A big, fat toad was sitting one day on the bank of a river playing his *sanza*, little "thumb piano," and singing a song to the trees and sky.

A bright green frog jumped out of the water, sat beside him, and asked to play the beautiful sanza. The kind old toad let him take it, but instead of returning the instrument, the wily frog jumped back into the water with it and swam to the other side of the river. He called back to the unhappy toad, calling his admiring wives:

> *Mbira dza ene dzi no tamboga.*
> [The instrument is too beautiful to play on.]
> *Ndidzo dza rure.*
> [It is very good.]
> *Dzi no riedzwa nga va ne papundu.*
> [It was played on by one with warts.]
> *Ndidzo dza rure.*
> [It is very good.]
> *Ku siye su saru sakadya.*
> [But we are given smooth bodies.]
> *Ndidzo dza rure.*
> [It is very good.]
> *Heha he heha, Dzauya, woye!*
> [It is ours, Dzauya, come!]
> *Heha he heha, Muneta, woye!*
> [It is ours, Muneta, come!]
> *Heha he heha, Dzakatsa, woye!*
> [It is ours, Dzakatsa, come!]
> *Heha he heha, Maibase, woye!*
> [It is ours, Maibase, come!]
> *Heha he heha, Hwaguma, woye!*
> [It is ours, Hwaguma, come!]

One of our final camps in Nyasaland was on Lake Chilwa. It was a most unhealthy place in which to linger, but it was the habitat of many water birds which the museum wanted. It is the only place in the world where I have been forced to work all day inside a mosquito net. Whenever we emerged from under this protection, it was imperative to wear a net over our sun helmets like those used by beekeepers. In addition to many valuable examples of bird life, we assembled a remarkable collection of insects. They came to our lanterns in such swarms that we were bottling rare creatures never before preserved simply by holding a cyanide bottle close to the hurricane lamp and corking the bottle as they toppled in. No butterfly-net technique was needed here.

In the stifling heat when I could not sleep, I lay listening to the persistent buzzing of the mosquitoes as they dive-bombed my tent. Having never before heard such swarms of these insects in full cry, I was fascinated by the wide range of tones in their buzzing, and I thought of a day when I might be able to record them. Now we have recordings of the mating calls and songs of anger and love of crickets and mosquitoes. We even have the madrigal of the bees. In the British Museum I found a book dated 1609 called *The Feminine Monarchie* which refers to the madrigal of the bees and insists that the origins of music can be traced to the songs of the queen bee and her court. This absorbing volume also notes: "If any man dislike the harshness of the seconds and sevenths [of the bees] . . . he showeth himself no experienced artist . . . there must sometimes be discords . . . to make sweet concords the sweeter." The author concludes that if music was ever lost, it might be found again with the birds and bees.

Leaving Lake Chilwa and its mosquitoes, we turned our sights to Mount Mlanje on the border of Mozambique, Portuguese East Africa. While planning this difficult ascent, we stayed at a tea plantation about two thousand feet above sea level. Climbing Mount Mlanje was such a dangerous undertaking that we had to deposit with the local government officials a sum of money for each porter, to be turned over to his family should he not return. This was the only time in Africa that we were required to provide such "insurance" for our boys. It had been necessary to establish this regulation because many parties had perished in the unpredictable and violent storms which rage on Mount Mlanje. The storms were called *Chipironi*, after the huge mountain of the same name across the border in Mozambique.

There was something strange about Mount Mlanje. The natives were frightened of it, and even the white man spoke of it respectfully. It was the unique habitat of a tree popularly called the Mlanje cedar, actually an age-old conifer, one of the few woods in Africa which termites will not attack. In the hope of preventing its extinction, government officials had begun a forestry-replanting project. Obtaining our porters for the climb was extremely difficult because of their fear of the evil spirits who rode in the ghostly black mist that descended on the mountain when the sudden storms broke. I am certain that the unpredictable temperament of the mountain was behind much of the fear and superstition of both officials and porters.

It would be suicide, we were told, to set out if we saw threatening black clouds forming on Mount Chipironi. If the mountain was clear, however, it was safe to start, but even then we could not be sure that a storm would not suddenly overtake us before we could reach the forester's hut on the mountain's plateau where we planned to camp and collect for several weeks. Twenty porters were finally persuaded to go, and soon everything was in readiness and the loads equally divided. All we needed was a favorable nod from Mount Chipironi. A fair day came, and we started out full of optimism. But before evening a heavy, freezing mist began to enshroud us, and we became worried about our porters, who had gone on ahead. We had provided them with clothing warmer than their usual tropical attire, but still they were unaccustomed to cold and might not survive a night of exposure in one of these savage storms. There was nothing to do but plod on and hope that we could reach the hut before being lost, and pray that our porters had arrived safely and would be awaiting us. We finally struggled to the hut, but found no one. The men in our group decided they must go out at once as a search party in spite of the wild weather.

One of the most tortured experiences of my life was being alone in the hut with only my personal boy, realizing that I was powerless to aid those confronting the violence of the storm. I also knew that the mountain was infested with leopards, not a consoling thought. We managed to keep busy by building and feeding a fire, brewing tea for the drenched and shivering party upon their return, lighting lanterns to guide them to us, and relighting them as fast as the gale snuffed them out. It required every bit of faith we could muster to bolster our spirits. Eventually we heard the sound of voices, and one by one they straggled in more exhausted from the cold than from the climb. Everyone was accounted for, and the room, so recently gloomy with foreboding, was suddenly glowing and joyous as they all warmed themselves in front of the explosive flames of the resinous cedar logs and drank tin mugs of steaming sweet tea. Looking about the room I quietly breathed, "Ndaga, bwana."

The collections made there were invaluable, and I often wondered if the museum fully appreciated what we went through to acquire them. But beyond the intrinsic worth of the specimens we brought back, the whole experience had a special meaning to me. Magic moments on another majestic peak brought the realization once more that when problems seem insurmountable, I can transport myself mentally to a mountaintop and recapture the sense of being "in tune with the universe," as Emerson put it.

We returned to the foot of the mountain with all our boys well and eager to see their families again. Our "deposits" for the boys were refunded, and after farewells we headed toward Rhodesia, where a tremendous variety of experiences awaited. Aided by the missionaries at Mount Selinda in Rhodesia, I found wonderful songs to record. The birds we collected were equally valuable. Some of the most interesting species were found on the farm of a retired British army officer and his wife and in the beautiful Mount Selinda forest, the only place in the world where the rare little Swinnerton's robin can be seen.

The four hundred families of birds in Rhodesia include all sorts from bright small birds to the huge ostrich (on one farm I had my first ostrich ride, which was both bumpy and precarious). The widow birds were mating at this time, the best season in which to see them, for the males develop brilliant plumage and long swishing tails that obviously appeal to the females whose feathers are drab (no merry widows here). The male widow bird has a harem of from ten to fifteen wives. Throughout Rhodesia we also found the small oxpeckers sitting on the backs of cattle and game searching for the main item in their diet, ticks. Here, too, we again found the stately secretary bird strutting about the veld.

The grandeur of Victoria Falls, more than twice as high as Niagara with double the volume of water, was overwhelming. The rainbows in the dancing spray by day and by night in the moonlight can never be forgotten. It is impossible to see from one position the mile-wide cataract dropping abruptly a full four hundred and twenty feet into a crevice in the basalt rock, the peaceful Zambezi River whipped into a whirlpool by countercurrents, and the gorge so filled that the water is piled up three to four feet higher in the center of the channel than at the shore: the river is too hurried to correct itself. This enormous phenomenon of nature must be seen from many angles if one is to grasp the full magnitude of its splendor.

We also visited the shrine to Cecil Rhodes, the great British empire builder whose life and influence continue even today through the remarkable Rhodes Scholarships he established for study at Oxford University. My greatest surprise in Rhodesia was Zimbabwe, which, we were told, was the ruined temple, fortress, and city built by the workers of King Solomon's mines or by a lost race. When these ruins near Victoria in Mashonaland were discovered in 1868, they were thought possibly to have been constructed more than a thousand years ago by an oriental people from the Near East who, with Bantu slaves, mined the gold, transported it to the coast by slave caravans and shipped it to Persia and Arabia. But since the explorations in 1905 it is believed that Zimbabwe was built not earlier than the fourteenth century, and it has been attributed to the Bantu people, who also built the stone-fenced kraals still found between the Limpopo and Zambezi rivers.

The most famous of the three groups of ruins is the Elliptical Temple, an irregular enclosure surrounded by a massive wall, in places thirty feet high by fourteen feet wide, which dwarfed me as I stood near it. Granite monoliths decorate the wall on the south and southeast, though gold seekers and amateur digging parties have destroyed much of the interior. The great kraal has two impressive conical towers, thought by some scientists to be phallic shrines. The Acropolis with its fortress is even more remarkable, rising from two hundred to three hundred feet above the valley and built with extraordinary ingenuity from stone and some form of cement. The Valley Ruins are smaller buildings, probably the dwelling of traders who bartered the gold bought from mines farther in the interior.

Zimbabwe was thought to have been the center for distributing the gold between the coast Mohammedans and the mythical Monomotapa, whose name means "Lord of the Water Elephants." Even today the hippopotamus is sacred to the people of this region of Rhodesia. This powerful Bantu group was discovered by the early Portuguese navigators, who named the Monomotapa capital Zimbabwe, or "King's residence." Some say that their territory covered an extensive region from the Zambezi "nearly to the Cape of Good Hope," doubtless an exaggeration.

My initial interest in the Bushmen began with my first study of their cave paintings and petroglyphs, rock engravings, in Southern Rodesia and the Transvaal. At this time I had no idea that eighteen years later the Bushmen would be the focal point of one of my expeditions, and that I would visit them in the Kalahari Desert of South West Africa, where they eke out a precarious living. I was disappointed that there was no time to visit the renowned Zulu tribe because my interest in them had been stimulated by the work I did with their offspring, the Angoni in Nyasaland. As with the Bushmen, my first visit to the Zulus would have to wait until 1947 and the University of California expedition.

At the South African government house in Pretoria we met friends from England staying with the Earl of Athlone, Queen Mary's brother, who was then Governor General of South Africa. His wife, Princess Alice, was very musical and much interested in the African music I had been recording. Years later, when Lord Athlone was Governor General of Canada, Princess Alice was extremely helpful to me in a project I undertook for the Canadian government, recording the music of Canada's peoples.

How our little pet Puzi survived all the ordeals he had faced from Mount Rungwe to Capetown, our final stop, I will never know. But thrive he did through heat and cold, high and low country, sometimes parched and longing for a drop of rain, at other times drenched in the misty rain forest or a sudden cloudburst. Everywhere we went he proved an entertaining though sometimes destructive guest. His reach even when on leash was unbelievable, and on more than one occasion he pulled a tablecloth covered with dishes crashing to the floor. But he was always forgiven, even by us who paid his bills. All through Rhodesia, the Transvaal, and Cape Province people begged to adopt Puzi, but we could not bear to part with him even though he was a luxury.

In Capetown, Puzi was left temporarily with a page boy in our hotel while we went to the Penguin Islands off the coast of South Africa. The jackass penguins swim from their usual habitat in the Antarctic to nest on these islands, and during this period there is scarcely room enough to walk among the thousands of nests. The territory of each female penguin sitting on her eggs is as far as she can reach with her razor-sharp bill, and other penguins have learned to respect this rule. They were quite undisturbed by our presence, viewing us probably as extra-large penguins. They seemed to know instinctively that their only enemies are in the sea. The penguins were carefully guarded by an old whaler, appointed by the South African government to protect the birds from intruders.

We were able to secure government permission to collect a few for the museum.

The whaler, eager to please us, cooked a dozen and a half penguin eggs for our dinner. He ate his share with gusto; in fact, I believe that he devoured six. I ate only one and found it somewhat fishy and as filling as a Thanksgiving dinner. From time to time the whaler had found washed up on Jutten Island treasures that had been hoarded by the sea since the days of the early Portuguese navigators sailing around the Cape of Good Hope bound for the East. He gave me my most prized coin, a huge silver-alloy piece about the size of our silver dollar. It is dated 1602 and is embossed with a portrait of "Philip, the Fourth, King of India and Spain." It was undoubtedly from a ship wrecked off this island on its way to India for silks and spices in the early seventeenth century. The wreck of such a ship was recorded in that decade.

On returning to Capetown we learned that Puzi had had a wonderful time with his new friend seeing the sights of the city. When I appeared he rushed into my arms and clung to me as though he would never let me go. The next day when I went to buy a ticket for his ship passage to England, I left him tied in a cool, protected spot in the lovely hotel garden. When I returned with his ticket (it cost $150) there was no sign of Puzi in the garden. I found only an empty, dangling chain. Soon I saw the treetops above me bouncing and swaying, and there he was, free for the first time since he had come to me as a baby. Most of the guests in the hotel joined in the efforts to entice him from his lofty playground. Eventually, near sundown, he was hungry enough to respond to a tempting banana I held aloft and offered with pleading tones. Perhaps what finally brought him down was not only the banana but a realization that it was the hour of day that I always set aside to play with him.

On the ship, during the three-week voyage home, he was the most popular passenger. He and a French count dressed as an organ grinder won first prize at the ship's masquerade party. An English lady was so enchanted by him that she insisted that Puzi stay with her in the country while we were spending two weeks in London. I shall never forget his supercilious expression as he rode away with her from Southampton in the back seat of his hostess's Rolls-Royce. When we returned to Southampton for the voyage to America, Puzi arrived to meet us, riding alone with the chauffeur and looking quite pleased with himself.

In America, Puzi was the center of attention when reporters met us. There were stories about him with his photograph in the daily papers, so that when I later walked him in the park, troops of small boys followed, begging to take him to a baseball game or home to show their parents. I felt like the Pied Piper of Hamelin on such occasions. After I had been in the United States only two months, an invitation came to return to Africa, and with about a week's notice I was off to Angola on the Pulitzer expedition. It was impossible to take Puzi along, so one of his many friends, a zoology professor at the University of Pittsburgh, begged to have him. Puzi was terribly spoiled by his doting keeper, who fed him hothouse grapes, bananas, and rare fruits and vegetables even out of season, and frequently got up in the middle of the night to see if he was properly tucked into his little bed. The last I heard of Puzi, our friend wrote that he was working on his doctor's degree. His thesis subject no doubt was on tropical fruits.

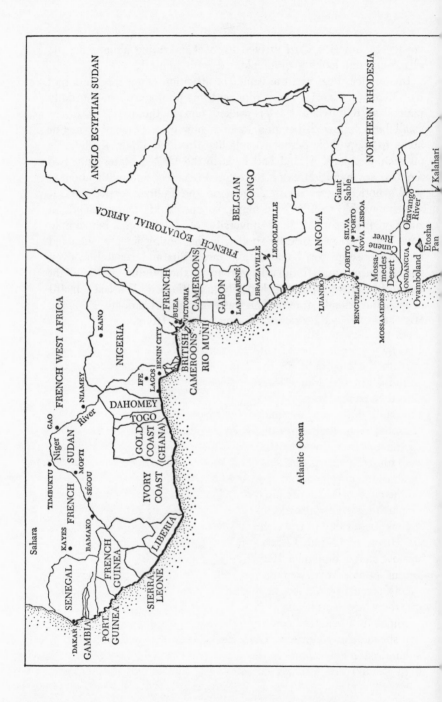

Chapter 5

ANGOLA: GATEWAY TO PORTUGUESE WEST AFRICA

Seven years before Columbus discovered America, Angola was annexed to Portugal to become the first European colony in Africa. The early Portuguese navigators who explored the African coast from the Senegal River to the Cape of Good Hope between 1446 and 1503 were fascinated with the possibilities of Angola as a gateway to the continent. In the sixteenth century it became an outpost for the Catholic Church, and since 1571 Portugal has maintained a strong colony there. With a coastline extending over a thousand miles, farther than from New York to Florida, Angola stretches from the mouth of the Congo in the north to the mouth of the Cunene River in the south. It is twice the size of Texas and fourteen times the size of Portugal. From Benguela on the west coast it is possible to cross the African continent to Beira on the coast of Mozambique three thousand miles away by a system of narrow-gauge railroads, provided you are not pressed for time: it took me all day to travel the two hundred fifty miles from Lobito to Huambo (Nova Lisboa) in the Angola Highlands by the narrow-gauge Benguela Railroad. It is difficult to make a correct census of the area's population, but there are about (1965 estimate) some five million people in Angola, approximately 250,000 of whom are Europeans.

Angola is a beautiful country with mountains, plains, lakes, rivers, and spectacular waterfalls. The coast is rather forbidding, but about a hundred miles inland is the great plateau, and leading to this high ground are terraces covered with vegetation and cut with

deep-forested gullies. A dense tropical forest lines the coast as far
south as Benguela with plentiful mangoes and oil palms flourishing
in its hot, damp climate. Coffee and cotton grow abundantly in the
rolling plains and on the low hills of the rich plateau in a healthy
and invigorating climate. The plateau, where pastureland is plentiful, is excellent too for cattle, pigs, horses, donkeys, sheep, and goats.
Even silkworms thrive here.

Luando, founded in 1576, is Angola's capital; the country's second most important city is Huambo or Nova Lisboa with an altitude
of 6000 feet on the plateau of central Angola. The seaports, Luando,
Lobito, Pôrto Amboim and Mossamedes, are all heads of railroads
to the interior. If the country's natural resources could be fully
developed, Angola's highlands would be as healthy and prosperous
as Kenya and Tanganyika have been for many years. Angola's tropical region yields many valuable woods and other products such
as wild rubber, asphalt, some petroleum, diamonds, manganese,
copper, iron, uranium, tin, sulfur, and marble. There is a cold
current flowing along the coast so the fishing is excellent and
trawling is an important industry. Beeswax is exported in large
quantities, and collectors are aided in their search for hives by the
famous bird, the honey guide. In the interior especially in the south
there is good hunting: lion, elephant, giraffe, cheetah, zebra, buffalo, rhinoceros, hippopotamus, monkeys, and many kinds of antelope. The antelope most prized by hunters is the giant sable
antelope, found only in a small region of central Angola.

It was for this rare and carefully protected animal that Ralph
Pulitzer organized the expedition to Angola in the early thirties and
though this was his primary objective, I was invited to join the
expedition to continue my work on African music. Accompanying
Ralph (who with his brother owned the *New York World*) in
addition to the scientists and white hunters were his wife, the well-
known writer Margaret Leech; his son Seward, who celebrated his
eighteenth birthday in Angola; Saunders, the English butler and
former member of the Coldstream Guards; and Saunders' French
wife, Georgette, Mrs. Pulitzer's maid.

We sailed from New York to London, where we stocked up—
with staples unavailable in Africa—at Fortnum & Mason, famous
for supplying all expedition needs from biscuits to the latest terai
(double felt sun hat). From England we began a three-week voyage on the German-African Line down the west coast of Africa

dressing for dinner every night and dancing to the music of a provincial German orchestra. On all expeditions evening clothes were an essential equipment, not only for shipboard but also for the frequent functions given by government officers and other officials and dignitaries. In remote back country, where settlers rarely saw a new face, our visits were great occasions and called for formal dress.

Alan Black, who had been Ralph's white hunter on an earlier safari in Kenya, was invited to Angola to join Seward, who had gone on ahead of us. As it turned out, this was not a good idea, for Black did not know Angola and its game, did not speak the language, and consequently got into trouble with the Portuguese, who thought that Black and Seward had enough guns and ammunition to start a small revolution. The officials confiscated the firearms, emptied the boxes of ammunition and counted it shell by shell, which took ages. Black and Seward had become practically house prisoners by the time we arrived, and it required a hasty trip to Luando and a vast amount of diplomacy to straighten things out with the governor.

Black, a crusty old character, was a man's man and took a violent dislike to some members of our group, refused to speak to them. I remember long conferences in which he poured out his complaints about the country, the people, everything—which I was then supposed to pass on. I breathed a sigh of relief when he and Ralph finally started for the antelope country, a tiny triangle between the Luando and Cuanza rivers in the heart of Angola. The giant sable antelope, for which they were searching, has scimitar-shaped horns so long that he can tip his head back and scratch his flanks. These antelope are stunning in herds—the bull is black; the cow, red-brown; and the calf, yellow.

While Ralph pursued his antelope for a group in the African Hall of the Carnegie Museum, Pittsburgh, we were collecting, at various campsites, all kinds of other specimens: animals, birds, butterflies; in fact, every kind of creature we came across. Georgette became expert at skinning birds and preparing butterflies, and Saunders, a very good shot, did his share of collecting with us each morning. For many reasons this couple was delightful to have along, and from my point of view they were indispensable. Georgette took care of all of Peggy's camping needs; and Saunders took over the commissary, to my great relief. An expedition, like an army, travels on its stomach, and it would have taxed my imagination to provide a sufficiently varied menu for this discriminating group.

One of the niceties of life provided by the Pulitzers was excellent Portuguese wine for dinner. It was especially welcome when we camped in the Mossamedes Desert. Quantities of wine were kept in the kitchen tent in a locked box, as we did not want to tempt the staff. However, returning to camp one day after a long hunt, we found that our cook had broken into the wine supply and, with murder in his eye, was pursuing our Portuguese driver around the camp with a gun. We arrived just in time to prevent a tragedy, and hustling both of them into a truck, drove them that night underguard to the nearest government officer. The fact that they were being taken to the police quickly sobered them, and they calmed down. It was a long, tedious trip, and for me especially difficult as it came in the middle of one of my bouts with dysentery.

We reached the coast the next morning and delivered our charges to the officials, who put them on a ship leaving for the capital. Our last glimpse of them was the unbelievable sight of the two, now thoroughly sober, going up the gangplank arm in arm, laughing together.

We returned to our desert camp, and once again the expedition was on the move. According to our typical travel arrangement, Ralph, Peggy, and I traveled in their sedan, and the men rode on the trucks, with the camp boys sitting on top. En route one of the men shot a hawk, a rare and much desired one that was perched in a treetop. As it plummeted down into the deep grass below, one of our bird skinners jumped from the truck to retrieve it. Just as he leaned over to pick it up a cobra lifted its head and shot venom directly into his eyes. He fell to the ground writhing in pain, his eyes rolling until we could see only the whites. It was a terrible moment; we had an adequate medicine box and a book dealing with snakebites, but they were of no help in this emergency.

The Africans, trying to be helpful, were pulling out their pipe-stems about to blow tobacco juice into their friend's eyes. We pushed them aside and prevented what might have blinded him. We quickly made a solution of boric acid, and kept it on his eyes all night. By morning they had cleared and were not even bloodshot. We had washed them out just in time. As for the cobra, it was shot immediately for the museum collection. It measured more than nine feet in length.

Ralph had received two intriguing gifts for his trip; both were new at that time, not yet perfected for the market. One was a raincoat which folded into a small envelope of the same thin synthetic material. The other was a fancy cocktail shaker which made its own ice through a chemical in a separate compartment of the mechanism. Both were thoughtful items, very imaginative and useful. The first day that Ralph wore the coat he was lighting his pipe when a spark fell, and in seconds it was in flames. The fire was smothered immediately and what was left of the coat removed, but not before his left arm was badly burned. Fortunately, Ralph was in camp at the time with a good medicine chest at hand, rather than on the hunting trip which was about to start. His fine sense of humor and his perseverance did not fail him, and he continued to hunt throughout the entire expedition. In spite of a heavily bandaged arm, he bagged his prized antelope.

The cocktail-shaker incident took place near the end of the Pulitzers' stay in Africa and during our Thanksgiving Day celebration. We had located an honest-to-goodness turkey on a farm and persuaded the Portuguese settler to sell it to us. Saunders planned a wonderful dinner aided by the former assistant cook who had been promoted after the escapade of our head cook. (When our food continued to be as delicious as ever, we discovered that the assistant cook had been doing most of the cooking from the beginning of the trip.)

As the cocktail shaker had not yet been tried, we felt that this festive occasion was the opportune moment. Ralph and Seward whipped up a tempting mixture in the gadget, shook it vigorously according to the instructions, tasted it, and were highly pleased with the results. All of us enjoyed the concoction tremendously, and that dinner was the gayest, most exuberant feast imaginable. But soon after dinner we, one by one, began having severe stomach pains. Apparently some of the freezing chemical had seeped into the drinks, and I had visions of the whole expedition being snuffed out then and there. I had drunk very little, as cocktails never agree with me at best, but some of the others had been less abstemious and were violently ill. Happily everyone recovered quickly, and the consequences did not delay the Pulitzers' sailing for America, which was planned for shortly after Thanksgiving in order to be home in time for Christmas. I saw them off at Lobito sadly, knowing that their warmth and cheerfulness on the balance of the trip would be greatly missed.

Returning to the interior, our party went to the antelope country, which I had not yet seen, since our base camp had been some three hundred miles southward. We found that in the ten-foot-tall grass (following the rainy season) the herds were moving so fast that it was impossible to work from a permanent camp. It was necessary to travel light in order to keep up with the antelope, resting each night in a temporary shelter, and by day gathering the grass, flowers, tree leaves and bark, and even soil needed to make the exhibit authentic. Because the men could not stop to pitch camp, I took fifty porters, camp boys, my gun boy and most of the gear; traveled back across the river; and made camp there.

To my dismay I discovered that the area was infested with puff adders and I was many miles from any white settlement. Poisonous snakes abound in Africa, but in this camp I was surrounded by the most poisonous of them all. The local tribesmen, as always, soon learned that I would pay them for anything that lived, moved, or breathed, so why not puff adders? They evidently knew the rocks where these short fat reptiles liked to sun themselves and were bringing them into camp dangling on little grass nooses. The currency here was salt and, as no one had been insane enough to pay for adders before, the collectors and I agreed on a price of two handfuls of salt per snake. The specimens came in faster than I could inject them with formalin, and one day when I tripped over something near my tent, there was a puff adder on the ground at my feet with only a fragile string around his neck. The boy who had brought it in had not bothered to mention it to anyone. Fortunately the creature was as surprised as I, and he was plunged into the formalin jar before he had a chance to bite me. Altogether I collected fifteen in this camp.

On another day a native brought me a beautiful game bird about the size of a pheasant. The bird looked new and different to me, but I am not an ornithologist and did not want to collect and skin it only to find that it was a local domestic species that had escaped from a farm. So I made a small pen for it, and fed it native corn until the experts arrived. It turned out to be extremely rare. Another bird we collected was the ground hornbill, a huge bird about the size of a turkey. The hornbill's name comes from its immense beak which gives it a grotesque, top-heavy appearance, especially the smaller species. Actually these ridiculous bills are not so heavy as they appear, for they are of a hard spongy tissue, quite light in weight. While these bills look extremely clumsy, the birds use them with great delicacy and dexterity in catching insects and small rodents.

The hornbills have unique habits during their nesting period. The female finds a hollow tree, enters a comfortable hole, and prepares the nest. The male then seals up the hole with mud and saliva, leaving only a small opening through which he brings his wife food which he has partially digested. She is sealed in the tree not just to keep her at home but also to protect her from marauding enemies. She sits there happily until her offspring, usually only one, is hatched and ready to emerge into the world. The hornbill is called in Umbundu *epumumu*, or rain bird, because the natives believe that when he calls, it will surely rain. They insist that the male's loud booming voice says to his wife, "Come and cook my dinner," and that the female answers, "No, I can't come. It's going to rain; I have to stay and hoe that corn." This is typical of the many stories and songs about birds and animals so common among the Africans. They endow all creatures with their attributes, personalities, and expressions.

The honey guide found in many parts of Africa, is also well-known in Angola. If you follow him, he will take you to the wild bees' hive, but if you do not share this delicious feast with him it is said that he will lead you to some dangerous animal or other misfortune. (The natives love the flower-flavored honey, and the wax is also of great value to them, being one of the few products that can be sold to the whites.) One day I had enough time to follow a honey guide, knowing that a trip with this enterprising bird might take a few minutes or possibly several hours. He darted back and forth a few yards ahead of me, and then rested in a tree until I caught up with him. He scolded me if I hesitated, but answered my occasional whistling with cheerful chattering. Our journey ended in finding a cache of honey that gave enormous pleasure for both of us.

Various tribes have different lore about this strange small bird, and some include him in their creation myths. Their belief in him is so strong that they would never dream of deceiving him or harming him in any way. James Chapin, an authority on birds of the Congo, notes that the Azande tribe in the Congo was so superstitious about the honey guide that, before the arrival of the white man, the chief would cut off the ears of anyone so stupid as to kill one.

The honey guide is plain and brownish-gray, about the size of an American bluebird. He is extremely clever—"too much clever," as my cook, Awami, used to say. His ability to locate beehives is uncanny, and the mystery is how this bird adopted for his diet a food that he is powerless to obtain alone. He must persuade a conspirator, either man or animal, to come to his aid. Such an animal might often be the honey badger, which is black and white, about three and a half feet long, with short legs and strong claws. If a honey badger is hungry, the bird can easily "badger" him into joining in the search for honey. When a hive is found, the badger claws it open and both share in a feast of honey and juicy bee larvae. What the badger cannot eat he often stores in a hole near a tree or a stump, where it will be at hand when he is hungry. The honey remains intact in such a hiding place during the dry season, but if rain gets into the badger's cache, when the hot sun returns, a fermenting process begins in the honey. The Africans told me of seeing a badger cavort about gleefully after a meal of fermented honey, clawing and scratching the earth about him. When they found such a torn-up spot, they used to say: "The old man has been drinking again." If the honey guide cannot find a badger to join him, he then pursues a man. Many times a honey guide hovered above me noisily insisting that I stop my work and come to his aid. All birds are vocal, but the honey guide's call could hardly be termed song. It is a loud, excited, insistent chatter designed to gain attention and help.

A new species of bird which we collected at sixty-six hundred feet on Mount Moco was apparently confined to the mountain rain forest of the Benguela highlands. It belonged to the family of old world warblers. At the Carnegie Museum this new bird was formally named after me: *Seicercus laurae,* or Laura's flycatcher. This trim, attractive yellowish-green bird has an eye ring of bright yellow; throat, upper breast, and cheek of lemon yellow; belly of white; and the edge of wing tips bright yellow. It was the first of its genus found in southwestern Africa, I was told.

Another new species found at 2200 feet in the district of Benguela was an old world warbler, a brownish-olive bird somewhat smaller, than my namesake. It was named *Macrosphenus pulitzeri* in honor of the sponsors of the expedition. The many fine species of birds, insects, amphibians, mollusks, plants, and even some fossil animals proved the prodigious richness of this country for scientific research. And though the mounted group of the giant sable antelope was the most spectacular result of our trip, for me it was the people and their music which proved the most memorable and held the greatest excitement.

I have frequently been asked what is my favorite place in Africa. I have always been torn between the Angola highlands and Nyasaland. Angola, though the oldest colony in Africa, is still un-spoiled from my musical point of view. The game has been con-siderably depleted, but animal life is relatively plentiful, especially in the highlands. Nyasaland, the last area to be annexed by a European country, was completely unspoiled when I was first there. A few Englishmen administered the country, and protected the game, but animals were not found in great herds that would attract hunters, as in Kenya. Also, since Nyasaland is inland, it had not yet been discovered by tourists. Now both Angola and Nyasaland are so subject to various political pressures that they have lost some of their attraction for visitors.

We reached the Benguela highlands by the narrow-gauge Ben-guela Railroad. At Huambo, we stayed in a comfortable house belonging to the railroad company and, while collecting in the area, developed and printed photographs, caught up on our notes, and did all the chores needed to service an expedition. It was here that we had as pets two young chimpanzees which lived in our garden. They were so devoted and affectionate that it was dif-ficult for me to get any work done. One day I was terrified to discover that our quart bottle of ink had been consumed by one of my little friends. The cook told me that the chimp had downed the ink in one long swig. I watched him anxiously for the balance of the day, fearing the worst, but fortunately nothing happened. They were continually in mischief of this sort, and I particularly remember how they loved to take our bath towels, throw them around their shoulders like shawls, and rush for the nearest mud-hole to roll over and over in it. That year we had the chimps for Christmas dinner—not on the menu, but as honored guests.

We also had parrots as pets: beautiful gray ones with rose-red tails, the best talkers of all. One of them had been trained by a Scot.

From time to time he called out with a broad Scottish accent, "MacPherson swore a feud against the Clan MacTavish," or, "Let's all go down to the Strand and have a banana," and, "I kissed her in the morning before the break of day." The bird would then get all three phrases mixed up with hilarious results. He wandered about the house freely and developed the habit of eating whatever soap he could find. It became his favorite diet. We brought three young parrots home to America with us. They lived quite happily in one cage, but occasionally one would take a bite out of another, which would bring forth a furious squawk— answered by, "Ha, ha, ha, what a joke!" At times like this they seemed almost to think.

Later it became necessary for us to part with them, so I let it be known that the parrots were for sale. One day a charming voice called and inquired about the birds. I explained that they were rather expensive, but this did not discourage the person from making an appointment to see our pets. At the appointed hour an attractive Negro couple arrived, found the birds to their liking, and paid our price without a quibble. They told us that they had a vaudeville bird act and were highly pleased with these young parrots who could be so easily trained. We then had no further worries about the future of our parrots because we knew that show birds are extremely valuable after the period of training involved and are treated with the utmost care: special foods, constant temperature, and the best of everything.

In addition to our parrots we returned with twenty-eight rare birds, three small monkeys, one of our chimps, and a very unfriendly mandrill, a type of baboon, for the Brookfield Zoo near Chicago, which was trying to build up its exotic population. We had a problem in getting our little menagerie to Chicago; it meant a three-week trip up the African coast to England, where the small "zoo" would be transferred to the ship for our Atlantic crossing. For the ship home from England we had booked our return passage in tourist class in order to have more expedition money while in Africa. The animals, however, were required to ride in swank kennels with the first-class poodles and other pets. I found it amusing that a steward was necessary to escort me through first-class each day to visit my elegant family.

On board also was the socialite, Woolworth Donahue, who was bringing home a pet cheetah. During the visiting hours he would walk his large cat while I walked my chimp, and he apparently was chagrined that my cheerful, amusing chimp constantly drew attention away from his magnificent cheetah. The drafty train trip from New York to Chicago was the most precarious lap of the entire trip, but our tender care of the birds and animals was rewarded by getting our charges all safe and sound to the zoo. The mandrill, whom we had named Charley, was found to be a female, so her name was promptly changed to Rosie. I heard later that Rosie had grown so increasingly bad-tempered that she was traded to a zoo in Germany for a kangaroo.

Chapter 6

THE OVIMBUNDU OF ANGOLA

There is no such thing as a pure African race because of the many migrations through Africa. It is believed that Angola, for example, was settled by waves of people from the lake region of central Africa, from north of the equator, and possibly from the south; the invaders assimilated, conquered, or killed the aboriginal people who lived there. Many believe that this accounts for the great diversity of physical types and many shades of color—tea, coffee, chocolate, and licorice—found among the Bantu of Angola, though the two predominating types are those light-colored and slim and those shorter, darker, and sturdier.

The tribes I worked with were primarily the Ovimbundu of central Angola, the most numerous and powerful; the Vachokue, formerly a fierce and warlike group, now considerably mixed with the Ovimbundu; and the Kuanyama-Ambo in the south, one of the subtribes of the Ovambo. Early in Angola's history the Ovimbundu became a dominating power. Their trade routes, crossing the continent transporting ivory and slaves, made them extremely wealthy. Their strongly regulated tribal society, through more than four centuries of European contact, has not been destroyed, and the basic elements of their mode of living have been preserved.

The Ovimbundu are primarily an agricultural people, though they also raise a few head of cattle. Their society is patrilocal in that a bride always goes to live in her husband's village (a young man may never seek a wife in his own community). The immediate or limited family consists of the husband, his wives—often two, but as many as he can afford—and their children. Adopted children may include former domestic slaves who have served to repay their maternal uncles' debts. The extended family includes the grandparents, their sons with their wives and children, and any unmarried daughters. A village is a unit of several families, immediate and extended, under a chief or *sekulu,* and a large group of villages is a kingdom ruled by a king or *osoma,* who, with his tribal council, is responsible for law enforcement and government.

The Ovimbundu are fairly successful and prosperous as compared with other tribes. Division of labor is firmly fixed for men and women, and tasks are so regulated that a boy who works for a white family will not do certain jobs, for to him they are woman's work and thus degrading. The women, first of all, are occupied with having and caring for children; for a woman to be childless is the worst possible fate; in fact, it is grounds for divorce. In this agricultural society, where gardens are of paramount importance, the women not only tend the crops but do the harvesting. The men do the heavy work of cutting and burning the trees and preparing the ground for cultivation. Not only cooking but gathering food is reserved for the women—except for collecting honey since this involves climbing trees to reach the beehives. This is a man's job, as are the harvesting of products of the palm tree—oil and palm hearts—and making weapons and domestic equipment.

Transition ceremonies (birth, initiation, marriage, and death) are all conducted by men, supervised by the medicine man. Many songs in Angola are for men only, though there are specific dances and games for women only; I have never seen a musical instrument made or played by a woman there. Music in connection with ceremonials has a very important function in strengthening the bonds of unity within any primitive group. The collective action of rituals brings about a feeling of solidarity in the community, and the importance of music and dance in restoring the euphoria of the group after the balance or equilibrium of the tribe has been disturbed cannot be overemphasized.

For example, death in a village produces dysphoria and demands a community response to combat this "attack" by an outside force. Certain rituals must be carried out by the group as a whole to restore social cohesion. At such a time wailing songs are sung which seem related to the sad call of the mourning dove, which

the natives interpret as "My father has gone; I am abandoned."
This collective singing relieves the uneasiness and restores the original strength of the group. The significant thing is that everyone
takes part in the ceremony, singing the same songs with the same
emotions to achieve the same purpose. The group participating
approves, by its presence the carrying out of certain obligations
inherent to the society. A widow, for instance, is allowed and
expected to sing songs at her husband's funeral which would
normally be obscene but which at this time provide her with an
emotional release with the full approval of her people.

Again in the wedding rites, the group as a whole joins in the
ceremony, and such ancient practices as bride-stealing are enacted
symbolically through dance, the men in one group, the women in
another nearby. Suddenly the bridegroom rushes into the group
of dancing women, catches his bride, and races as fast as possible
with her to their newly decorated hut which he has prepared. The
other women run to block the doorway and make a show of
preventing his entrance into the hut. If he fails to break through
their barricade, he must pay them a pig or an ox. This payment
for the bride represents an indemnity. The tribe suffers a loss
when the girl goes to her husband's village to live, and the payment is given in exchange for the injury done the community.

When a young man decides to marry, he goes to a distant
village where the girls are reported to be beautiful and industrious.
When he arrives, he is housed in the village guest quarters, and
at sunset food is brought to him. After eating, he calls at the
special meeting house of the community and talks to the eligible
girls in the proverbs and the puns used by all young men when
courting. For example he might say, "The path is worn down
because they walked on it," meaning that every phenomenon has
a cause and reason, or, "I have come here for a special purpose."
He might continue by saying, "A fine bottle of birdseed is food
for birds," meaning marriageable girls exist for the purpose of
marrying, which in Africa is completely true. When he says, "The
wild fig and the mudongu tree are ornaments of a home," he
means a bride adorns a home—a pun, since the word for fig tree
is nearly identical with the word for making love, and the word
for mudongu tree is similar to the word for bride.

After considerable conversation with all the girls, he says to his chosen one, "I came because of you." If she accepts him and her parents are willing, he returns to the guest house for the night; and in the morning asks her father's permission to marry her. They settle on the bride-price or amount he must pay for his wife (perhaps two pigs or a cow), and the boy then returns to his own village. The payment given the bride's parents is not a price paid for goods but rather a pledge and symbol of the contract. Later, if a husband refuses his wife new cloth or palm oil, beats her too often, or is impotent, she may return to her parents, and he loses his price or pledge. If, on the other hand, she is too quarrelsome, not a good gardener or cook, or unfaithful, the parents must return what the husband has paid them.

All wedding dances are vigorous and riotous. The singing and shouting are boisterous and prolonged, and the bridegroom is required to furnish an ample feast for the tribe, as well as great quantities of beer and palm wine. The function of the wedding dance is to assemble the whole social group to witness and, by doing so, give their approval of the union. The newly married couple are thus made to feel that their marriage concerns the entire community and not merely themselves, and they are further made to understand that their positions within the tribe have changed. They now have new duties, new responsibilities, and new social status. The attitude of the community toward them has also changed, for they command greater respect as man and wife than they did when single.

There are numerous bride songs. Here is a great favorite among the Umbundu women; it is sung to the bride by the girls and women of her new village.

Ka limi KaciKenge.
[*KaciKenge* (the bridegroom) doesn't work in his fields.]
Ka limi KaciKenge, we!
[*KaciKenge* does not work in his fields, alas!]
Ondombo e yo talula!
[Though it is the rainy season, he is fascinated (by his bride) The little bride takes all of his attention!]
Ka limi we!
[He does not work in his field, alas!]
KaciKenge la limi we!
[*KaciKenge* does not work in his fields, alas!]

This song has a simple descending melody with many small variations. In the forty-nine repetitions of it I recorded, there were twelve distinct changes or variations depending in some cases, but not always, on the text. The melody consisted of two parts, the first corresponding to a lifting motion, the second to a dropping motion. The rhythm was free; in fact, no time signature can be indicated. The melody consisted of six tones with G as the fundamental. Second in importance was B; the other tones were of minor importance; and the final two notes, F and E, were doubtless accidental.

The most important ceremony in the life of any Umbundu man or woman is the coming-of-age ceremony, particularly where they have been influenced by their southern and eastern neighbors. At this time they put away the things of childhood and become members of the adult society, maintaining unity and conformity within the tribe. For the girls, endurance is the test; for the boys, bravery. Both go through long periods of exposure to extreme cold, followed by extreme heat and by hunger, followed by feasting. During initiation they also learn the ceremonies, beliefs, and traditions of the tribe. The coming-of-age rites often last as long as six months for the boys, but are generally shorter for the girls and less rigorous; often boys do not live through their testing period. The age of initiation varies from tribe to tribe, but usually the ages range from ten to fifteen since the ceremony has to be performed when a sufficient number of children have reached puberty. The ritual, which may occur only every three or four years, involves circumcision for the boys, and, in certain tribes, mutilation for the girls.

In southern Angola among the Ovambo and other neighboring tribes, the young women prior to the coming-of-age ceremony proudly build their hair into spectacular headdresses resembling birds, cartwheels over their ears, or other strange forms. Beads and shells are also important decorations, and the most prized is the snow-white *omba* shell with a diameter about that of a teacup. These shells are valuable heirlooms handed down from mother to daughter, like precious family jewels and one of them, I was told, has the value of six months of work. After a girl marries and her first baby is born, the headdress is shaved off to denote that she has become a mature woman and outgrown such frivolity.

Iloy-Iloy, one of these beautiful girls, became my tribal sister.

Her headdress was exceptionally fine, consisting of two big wing-like forms on either side of her head, with a black ostrich plume decorating one of them. Our camp was near her village, and she followed me about daily as I worked. Finally she expressed the wish that her tribe adopt me, and, instead of the usual blood ritual, we agreed upon a simple exchange of bracelets. I still wear the wide copper one she gave me with its geometrical designs, and she seemed thrilled with the one I gave her.

I was unable to witness Iloy-Iloy's initiation, for when I was among the Ovimbundu on the Pulitzer expedition, it was the time for the initiation of the boys. They were kept in a camp some distance from the village under the supervision of the elders, one instructor for each boy. Food was brought to the camp daily in gourd containers by the mothers. If a boy failed to survive an ordeal, his gourd was broken and tossed out of the encampment. When a mother saw this, she knew that the spirits had taken her son, and she asked no questions. A mother who lost her son during the testing period was allowed to come to the final cere-mony, but could not participate.

As a woman, I was not permitted to approach the remote initiation camp. In fact, I think very few men outside of the tribe could do so. The whole initiation period is so secret that no one is allowed to see the boys, and they are taught under penalty of death, never to reveal any part of their rites. The only time during the en-tire period that they are seen is when as part of their training they race through the countryside to hunt, kill, and bring back to camp some wild animal. When I saw them during this phase they were covered with white ash and wore only a loincloth. The men accompanying them wore costumes and masks representing the spirits. Above their cries came the wild sound of the bull-roarer, a thin, oval piece of wood attached to the end of a string and whirled to produce a whistling sound, thought to be the voices of the spirits.

The ritual ends in a great feast and a dance which stresses the phallic nature of the ceremony. The survivors come for this dance garbed in fantastic costumes of strong dyed fiber woven with sym-bolic geometric designs. On each leg they wear a rattle of five or six tiny gourds fastened together forming a square or oblong. While the boys dance, these gourds provide a rattling accompani-ment to the drums. A double-headed drum and a cone-shaped drum with one head are used in the ceremony, together with the unique drum of the medicine man. His drum has only one head, but attached to the center of the membrane extending through the drum is a long, strong reed. The medicine man's apprentice, with his hand wet, reaches through the bottom of the drum and rubs the reed, thus vibrating the drumhead. The sound produced is a wailing, fluctuating tone which represents the voices of the spirits present at the feast.

The men conducting the ceremony wear headdresses of tightly woven fiber which are truly spectacular. These are attached to beautifully carved masks dyed brown and deep henna. Elaborate beads around their necks link the headdress to the rest of their regalia. In the costumes I collected then, only the natural color of the fiber, henna and brownish-black dye made from rocks and soil, were used. I have recently seen some with blue, white, bright red, and orange (all commercial colors); the tendency is toward even more brilliant costumes. The Portuguese government has now forbidden all but the great feast of the initiation rites, for over the years too many of the young boys did not survive. But in addition to the feasting, one other phase of the old ceremony persists, that of the initiate changing his name upon reaching adulthood as a symbol that he has been reborn into adult society.

Nontransition rituals take many forms, such as the coronation and other ceremonies pertaining to a king, the initiation of the medicine man and the blacksmith (molten metal is sacred, and thus the one who handles it is of enormous importance), and the cleansing ceremonies. While among the Ovimbundu I witnessed a cleansing ceremony which was held to drive evil spirits from the village. It was conducted by a medicine man and a medicine woman who wore leopard or wildcat skins because of the ferocious nature of the animals. The ceremony took place during a full moon (the usual time for such a ritual), and each wore a skin in front and one in back. An antelope horn held by the man in his left hand was filled with pulverized charcoal made into a charmed paste with herbs, castor oil, and honey. This horn, containing a smaller one filled with medicine, was wrapped in a skin and tied with a special cloth. In his right hand the man held a small ax used exclusively for this ceremony. As he waved it in the air while dancing a special step, he rubbed his finger inside the horn and applied the sacred paste to his tongue and to the bottoms of his feet. After dancing for some time he put the horn on the ground and the ax beside it.

He then climbed a twenty-foot pole—one used to be found in the center of every Umbundu village—and sat at the top cursing the evil spirits to drive them away. At first he cursed alone, but later, as drum music began, the whole village appeared and danced and chanted around the base of the pole. He stayed aloft for an hour ("as long as to walk four miles," as the Africans say), continually cursing the spirits with apparently no set text. While the man was sitting and cursing, the woman put on a headband of bark rope from the *olumanu* tree decorated with cowrie shells. She began twirling a small gourd filled with salt and meal. While the villagers were chanting with the man, she put some of the salt and meal in her mouth, threw a bit to the spirits, and began speaking. She was then supposedly in contact with them and able to remove the curse from the village. The medicine man also possessed this power while on the pole. During the entire ritual, the people continued to dance and sing while musicians accompanied the singing with rattles and drums. The implements for the ceremony (ax, headband, and gourds), were kept on a handsomely carved chair in the spirit house and were removed only for this ceremony.

Among the nontransitional ceremonies pertaining to the king is the *osaka*, a dance which takes place when a monarch is sick. A strong man is required to dance for many hours holding in his outstretched hand a dried round fruit containing seeds which rattle. It is covered with cloth to which a lizard skin is attached. The men dancing with him hit the muscles of the main dancer's outstretched arm with their fists, attempting to make him drop the ball. If he does so, another man will promptly take it up. This endurance test goes on for hours in an effort to bring strength to the sick king.

In addition to ritual dances, secular dances play an important role in the life of a tribe. They are especially popular in May and June, when maize is plentiful for making beer. There is always dancing when the new moon appears: "So that there will be no sickness during this moon," the people say. There are secular dances to commemorate important events of the past in which only the men dance, and for these an ox is killed; there is much beer drinking while an old man of the tribe chants a war story accompanied by the shuffling feet of the dancing men. If there is no special occasion, the Africans dance for pure pleasure. The dancers may form lines, the men and women advancing toward and retreating from each other, or they may dance in a circle around the drums, taking small steps and swaying rhythmically. The dance *onyaca* perhaps had a significant part in an ancient agricultural ritual, for the song sung with this dance goes: "There is grain in the house; may it never be out." Today, however, the onyaca is danced only for pleasure.

As the Ovimbundu are a typical Bantu tribe, their music has the general characteristics of Bantu music throughout Africa. There is a marked tendency for the melodies to progress downward from tension to rest. Usually the musical phrases are short and repetitive, and fractional intervals (tones outside the Western scale) are regularly employed. The scales are many and varied, but none is fixed or typical. Thus every melody is a law unto itself. Rhythmic structure is more often than not quite complex, and most drum music contains many conflicting patterns. Even the rhythms of songs are so involved that they can be notated only with great difficulty.

The music of most primitive people of the world consists only of melody and rhythm, but the African, through part singing, has evolved a distinctive style of harmony as well. In his singing there is a definite technique characteristic of all Africans: a frequent vagueness of pitch, a short glissando preceding the actual attack, a raucous vocal quality cultivated by the women, various *Sprechstimme* devices, and occasional humming in place of singing. These characteristics are so typical that they came with the Negro to the New World and gave his singing here an African flavor.

In Angola I found the indigenous music still quite pure in spite of the long contact with the Portuguese. It plays a vital part among the Ovimbundu not only in ceremonial usage, but in everyday work and play. Games and secular singing and dancing are not merely for amusement, but also have educational value as well as coordinating the forces of tribal life. Each tribe has certain songs which can be sung only by certain singers, such as the medicine man, the old man who sings the genealogy songs, and the men who make and play the drums. There are also

members of each tribe who are recognized as professional singers
and instrumentalists and who perform for ceremonials and secular
dances. They do not wander from village to village as the itinerant
musicians of the French Sudan do, and are happy to be paid
with food or a gourd of beer for their services. These professionals
also have specific songs that are exclusively theirs. But there are
many songs, including game songs, which may be sung by any
member of the tribe.

The melodies for game songs are rather simple, moving within a
restricted range with uninvolved rhythms. The same short melodic
fragment is repeated as long as the game requires it, or may be
changed slightly to suit the words. The children's game songs are
even simpler, often with very amusing texts. The songs of the
elders are much more elaborate. The Umbundu word for game is
omapalo. The games are not seasonal; every game may be played
at any time. The children imitate the occupations of their elders.
For example, the boys play at making war (taking prisoners, tying
them with bark rope) or imitating the hunt (some represent game
animals, some the dogs that aid the hunters). The Ovimbundu
have long been famous for their caravans, and the porters are
often imitated by young boys in their singing games. The boys
also have a form of hide-and-seek. A knife is hidden, and the
boy who has to find it is guided by music. His proximity to the
knife is indicated on a musical bow. When the boy approaches
the hidden knife, the bow player strikes a distinctive note, *yelula*,
which means, "Pick it up, pick it up."

Dancing and singing with the Umbundu women I learned
charming play dances, some of them reminiscent of folk dances
and games of the Western world. In these games they may imitate
animals, such as the monkey or the leopard; they may enact
scenes, such as the bridegroom searching for a bride; or they may
demonstrate certain types of work, like pounding. I had particular
pleasure in filming them and recording this pounding song which
they accompanied with work movements:

> Oh, my mother!
> My mother pounds like that.
> Her little neck is like the little crane,
> Her mouth is like a little cup.
> Oh, my mother!

My mother cultivates her fields like that.
Her little neck is like the little crane,
Her mouth is like a little cup.
Oh, my mother! . . .

The song continues through the sowing, reaping, harvesting, and preparing of the grain for food. Near each village there are special pounding rocks which have been consecrated with ceremonial rites, for, as the main diet of these people is a porridge made from cornmeal, its preparation is of great importance. Every morning the women and girls assemble at the rocks to grind the day's supply of flour. Little girls begin pounding with their mothers at an early age. Youngsters six or eight years old soon become quite efficient and can pound for long periods, shifting their mallet from one hand to the other without losing a beat and always to the rhythm of a pounding song. In the evenings, when the work is done, this same song is often used as a game song, and as the women and girls sing it they enact the various phases of planting and harvesting. If this or other game songs ever had a ritual significance, it has been lost. At present they are performed merely for amusement.

Another interesting game song I recorded had these words:

My mother has made me a cornmeal cake,
She has put it on the rocks
To roast for me.
It is roasting, roasting, roasting.

This song has a unique accompaniment which I tried to learn but with limited success. The women, as they sang, placed their right hand in their left armpit and brought the left upper arm down sharply against the hand, producing a smacking sound. At the same time, their cupped left hand beat a fast rhythm against their lips, making a bubbling sound. Since the women had no musical instruments to accompany their dancing, this provided a fine substitute.

Many songs have to do with food. One which I recorded has a proverbial twist and also makes a point of etiquette. These are the words:

Do not put the brother of your friend
In the kitchen.
There the food is bitter.

The motions accompanying this song are rather like our children's game called "Pease porridge hot." The girls and women in two lines facing each other strike the palms of the dancers opposite them with very fast and complicated rhythms.

Through song, one can learn about many obscure tribal customs. The question-and-answer method of obtaining information is tedious to the research worker and often objectionable to the informant. However, since all people love to sing, the musical approach to the study of a culture is both pleasant and profitable. For example, through recording one song I learned the marriage and divorce customs of the Vachokue tribe and discovered that lack of children was the most frequent grounds for divorce among them. This is the wail of a childless woman who, indicating her empty cradled arms, sang this song:

> I want a child here.
> You have denied me.
> I have fed you;
> I have no child.
> I am going home.

Another significant discovery was Angola's genealogy songs. While staying at a mission at Galangue, I recorded an old man singing what proved to be a song of genealogy. Although my hosts knew Umbundu songs well, they had never heard this type before. Some Angola tribes, like the Djabu tribe of eastern Liberia, hand down family lineages by song. With no written records, song was the only way to keep a family tree straight. In Angola it was the men who sang the genealogy songs rather than the old women as among the Djabu. When someone was sick and certain to die, the singer would brush up on all the family names of the ill person, going back for many generations, for the deceased's genealogy must be chanted during the funeral ceremonies.

Among the most interesting play dances I recorded was the ball game, in which the girls and women sat in two rows facing each other with their legs straight out and interlocked. They bounced a small cloth ball, loosely rolled for the occasion, from one end of the line to the other by rhythmic motions of their legs (they could not touch the ball with their hands). The rhythms of this game song were complicated and strenuous, but everyone seemed to love it. Even the babies on their mothers' backs enjoyed this game at an

early age, and sometimes the ball would be snatched up by a baby
and thrown down the line to the amusement of everyone. The
words for this song were:

> O the little ball, let it come.
> My father has given me a little ball.
> O father, let it come.

Then each member of the family was called upon to send the
ball: "O mother," "O sister," "O brother." This song continued verse
after verse until all were exhausted.

Another game song dealt with the monkey:

> My father has a little monkey,
> It has not one tail but two.
> Look at me, I have a tail.
> I have not two tails, only one.

For this dance each participant attached a small piece of cloth to
the back of her garment—usually a piece of calico knotted under
the arm—which served as her "tail." Then each performed animated steps designed to show off her "tail" to best advantage. To
my great amazement, I discovered that this dance was almost
identical with the Charleston.

Most of the game songs have no accompaniment except the
clapping of hands and the stamping of feet. However, I recorded
one in which the grain-pounding sticks were used to form an instrument. Two pestles were placed on the ground parallel to each
other; a third resting on them formed a right angle. Two women
sat at opposite ends of the third pestle, striking the parallel sticks
with the third stick in elaborate rhythms. The dancer performed
her steps with the third stick rising and falling in rapid rhythm
between her legs and feet. I learned by experience how difficult
this was. If one's feet are not in time with the stick, the results are
disastrous. While learning the rhythms, I had black-and-blue ankles
for two weeks.

I also witnessed a very pretty game played only when the moon
is full: the leopard game. A common tree of Angola has leaves
which are silvery on one side, almost white in the moonlight.
While a girl crouched on the ground like a leopard, her friends
danced around her, covering her black body with these bright
leaves. The effect was startling. The accompanying song included

raucous, throaty sounds in imitation of the leopard's cough. The dancers spanked their buttocks with a brisk rhythm, creating an amusing smacking accompaniment and provoking hilarious gaiety for everyone.

In Angola I also found a tremendous number of unusual caravan songs (originally sung on the old trade routes, across Africa); they persist today as secular dance songs, game songs, sung by porters on journeys. In addition to imitating animals and birds, these songs are frequently philosophical. One such thoughtful song sung on trading journeys and sometimes around the campfire of the home village has these words:

> I choose which?
> Shall we choose laughter or wealth?

This song shows that the African is faced with the same basic problem that confronts Western man: should life be a pursuit of happiness or of wealth? This was a choice I faced and resolved early in my life when I refused a very lucrative executive position in order to devote my energies to music, a notoriously unlucrative business.

One of my favorite caravan songs was a "homesick" song the porters sang when our journeys took them far from their villages and families. It began, "Kapalandanda, He is weeping for his country." It was a response song, with the chorus repeating the solo line. The melody was more developed than most game and dance songs, and there was a definite correlation between the two parts as well as among the four phrases which comprised the whole. The rhythm was very free; in fact, it was impossible to bar exactly. In general it suggested alternate divisions of % and % time signatures.

It is rarely possible to fix the date of an African song, just as it is impossible to date African sculpture precisely. However, the song "We Ko Vava" was an exception, for according to tradition, it was composed when the first white men came in ships to the coast of Angola in the fifteenth century. This song was also special in that it had no accompaniment of any kind, neither instrumental nor hand-clapping. Further, it had no connection with any particular activity, but was often sung by the boys while marching.

Nearly every African tribe has songs in its repertoire dealing with the white man, his queer customs, his mode of living, his unaccountable bursts of anger, or his kindness and generosity. These often take the form of either praise or satire. "We Ko Vava" is probably the oldest of these songs dealing with the white man. The text is:

> The white man came up
> Out of the waters.
> His grave is in the waters.

The reference here is to the white man arriving out of the sea in ships and then returning into the sea, disappearing over the horizon.

The principal melodic line was sung first by the soloist. The last half was repeated by the chorus. Then a new melodic line entered, followed by the second; then both the third and the second were sung again by the chorus. The rhythm was very free, rather in the nature of a recitative or free declamation. The solo was lively, but the choruses were so sluggish that the notes almost doubled in time value. This was quite rare: a chorus holding back and weighing down the melodic phrase. So in addition to its historical significance, this unforgettable melody has important musical interest.

In Angola, musical instruments usually accompany songs and dances other than game songs, and many of them are also played solo—for example, the stringed bow. The first of these is the notched bow made of a thin bent stick with a twisted fiber string or split reed. The player holds the string or reed near his open lips and plucks it with his right hand. With the left hand he rubs a small stick back and forth against the notched bow, producing a humming accompaniment. The *mbulambumba* is another form of musical bow which corresponds to the gubu of the Zulus. A gourd, attached to the center of a long strong bow, is pressed with varying force against the exposed chest or abdomen of the player. The musical bow (the ancestor of the Egyptian harp according to Curt Sachs), has been found in some form in Africa, North and South America, Asia, India, the Malay Archipelago, Melanesia, and Polynesia. A third type of stringed instrument is a sort of primitive fiddle played with a bow and always solo. The strings are made of fiber.

Among the interesting percussion instruments I found were the scraping stick, various forms of rattles, and iron gongs. The scraping stick is considered a magic instrument, as it is in the province of the chief and of the medicine man when healing the sick. It is made from a bamboo stick cut open along one side and hollowed out, then notched on the other side. The player rubs a tiny piece of wood over the notches to produce a humming sound. In this way it is not unlike the notched bow. Sticks of wood are also used by the initiates during the circumcision dance. They are struck together to regulate the tempo of the dancing and singing. Rattles are used in innumerable forms: woven-basket rattles, large and small gourd rattles, and the dumbbell (a stick with a basket rattle at each end). Small iron gongs, used only ritually today, once were sounded to announce a declaration of war by the king and also to warn him of approaching enemies in the night.

An instrument found frequently with the Ovimbundu, and one of my favorites, is the *ochisanji*. It is not found any place in the world but in the Bantu belt across Africa from the west coast to the east. In my collection of material instruments I have about twenty different members of the *sansa* (sanza) family, or the ochisanji, as it is called in Angola. Its long and narrow keys are made of highly tempered steel by the village blacksmith. He alone may see the molten metal used in the making of the ochisanji; he formerly made the metal only in the dead of night so that he would be assured that no outsider—especially a female—would see the metal in its sacred molten form. I heard that if by chance any woman, or even a female cow or pig, saw it, she would have been killed instantly in the old days, for it was felt that any female gazing on the molten metal would bring bad luck.

The keys are attached to a foundation board made from hard, resonant African mahogany, sometimes beautifully decorated. The ochisanji is played by holding it between the palms, the thumbs plucking the keys in a downward motion. In some cases there are two sets of keys. The tones may be changed by sticking small balls of wax on to the underside of the keys. In areas where there is no iron, keys are made from bamboo, making the instrument more fragile and the tone more delicate. Modern ones have been seen with keys made from nails or even umbrella stays.

There is always some device for vibration, either bits of metal or shells attached to the sounding board or a string of beads placed over the keys. A gourd or box resonator or even a tortoise' shell may be attached to amplify the sound. The ochisanji is not a ritual instrument, but is played for aesthetic pleasure. It was brought to the New World by the Negroes and later developed into a much larger bass rhythm instrument popular in Cuba and certain areas of the Caribbean.

Much of the instrumental music and even many of the forms and uses of the instruments themselves are unique to Angola—for instance, the *malimba* or xylophone (called marimba in some tribes). It is found in many forms in Africa, but that of the Ovimbundu is unique. The keys or staves of hard resonant African mahogany are assembled in a curve with a gourd resonator attached under each key. The resonators are in graduated order from tiny ones for high tones to huge ones for bass tones, and are especially chosen over a long period of time so that the vibrations of each gourd will match the vibrations of the key whose tones it will amplify. As Africans like vibration effects, they cut little openings in the gourd resonators and cover the holes with a particular kind of spider's nest which is like strong parchment. These coverings are heated before the instrument is played, in the same way that drumheads are heated before playing, thus producing a very special and delicate buzzing effect. The sound of the keys is made more liquid by playing with sticks tipped with rubber balls which are chewed before playing to make them resilient.

I knew that this particular curved xylophone had existed in Angola and I repeatedly traveled miles to some remote village in search of it only to find a few broken gourds and some abandoned staves. The villagers would tell me, "Oh, the old man who played it is now dead and nobody else knows how to build another or play it." Finally I sent out a messenger, saying, "Don't come back until you find one for me. You'll be well rewarded." My messenger was gone for about ten days, and when he returned it was with an old man, his xylophone, and two young singers.

The curved keyboard was about eight feet in length, and the musician played it beautifully while his two assistants tapped the gourd resonators in a wonderful rhythmic accompaniment. They sang as they played, but the xylophone was always more prominent than the song. I would have paid them a fortune for the instrument had they demanded it, but all they wanted were our brightly striped shirts, which I gladly gave them, together with two large bags of salt, the currency of the area. The old man was very happy with the bargain and said that he would begin construction of a new xylophone as soon as he returned to his village. When I got this enormous instrument back to America (it was a cubic ton when packed for shipping) there was no room in my apartment to house it. I gave it to the Field Museum of Natural History where it has been on display ever since in the African Hall.

Also unique to Angola were the three-sectioned royal flutes, always played by a trio of musicians who accompanied their king wherever he went. The first time I encountered the royal flutes remains an unforgettable moment in my life. Accompanied by John Tucker, a missionary who spoke Umbundu perfectly and a good friend of the Umbundu king, I visited the king's capital, or *ombala*, near the Dondi mission. The capital held particular interest for me, not only because this was the scene of the ceremonies which honored the ancient kings who became deities at death, but also because of the special music I knew was to be heard there.

Word had been sent to the king that I would like to call on him and hoped to record his musicians. A cordial invitation was sent to me by runners. We set off from Dondi early one morning, and left our car on the small road a short distance from the ombala, continuing on foot by a native path to the capital. The welcoming ceremony was overwhelming. Long before we reached the village, songs of greeting were heard as all the women rushed to meet us, trilling, shouting, and waving huge green ceremonial branches. We entered through a ring of tall ancestral trees which encircled the entire area. A special tree was planted for each king at his installation, and after his death, and here offerings were made to his spirit, which was thought to inhabit the tree.

Proceeding to the carved "throne," the king, in ceremonial robes, rose to greet us. He was not a large man, but his quiet dignity made him seem taller than he was. His wisdom and philosophical comments made us feel he was a just ruler rather than a tyrant such as we had heard of among certain other tribes. He acted as our host for a tour of the village, explaining the life and customs of his people, including the background of the sacred trees which were flourishing, a good sign from the spirit world.

Accompanying the king during the entire visit were three royal flutists, playing, as we later learned, melodies reserved for times when the king received distinguished visitors. Though the homes of the flutists were in other villages, during the months when they attended the king they lived in the capital. When they returned to their own villages to see their wives and children, three others came to take their place, but the instruments never left the capital. As they told me, the flutes had to "sleep" in the royal enclosure and accompany every activity of the king. The playing of the flutes was a hereditary profession; fathers taught their sons the royal melodies, one for every occasion or activity.

I recorded a large body of these tunes, such as those played when the king went on a journey to another village or was sitting on his throne, or was in his private quarters. For whatever was happening in his life there were special songs on the flutes. Each flute consisted of three parts: a wooden mouthpiece, an endpiece, and a tube of bamboo in the center with seven finger holes. The tones produced were delightfully melodious. The music was two-part. The first flute carried the melody (ostinato) while the second and third played a lower accompaniment—like the bourdon principle of the bagpipe but more elaborate.

As the king showed us his capital, our group proceeded in a fixed order with the flutes playing extremely spirited and melodious walking songs. The order was, first, the *kesongo* or "captain of the army hosts"; second, the king; third, the three flutists; fourth, the *kalei*, the carrier of the king's chair; fifth, a wife of the king carrying on her head food and beer for the king's use (not the head wife, but a concubine); and finally the elders of the village, the headmen, and the important wives in no particular order. The people brought up the rear, walking slowly like *chanja* or branch; they say that "when one is dragging a large, heavy branch, one goes slowly."

As our visit was as important an occasion for the village as a feast day (such as weddings, funerals, or social dance), the three musicians were required to play almost unceasingly. Toward evening they played what was described to me as a homesick song; it was the melody they played to the king when they were tired and wanted to be relieved so they could visit their families. It was an elaborate and appealing tune with much variation within phrases and great freedom of rhythm. No wonder they were weary and longed to be relieved. After their continuous playing to accompany our visit and for my recordings, they must have felt the need of a long vacation.

All in all, the Pulitzer expedition, for many reasons, was one of the happiest trips of my life. Although I had done my share of collecting for the museum, I had more time for music than on previous expeditions. I was able to make extremely valuable recordings—the first, I was told, ever to come out of Angola, and as far as I know, the only sizable collection available even now.

Chapter 7

FROM TIMBUKTU TO THE CAMEROONS

After returning from Angola I was given a generous grant by the Carnegie Corporation of New York to continue my research in African music. This made possible my first excellent recording equipment especially built by Columbia Broadcasting engineers. When Mrs. Oscar Straus, the patron of my first African expedition, heard of the grant her immediate reaction was: "Well, Laura, you'll have to go back. Couldn't I come along?" Under Mrs. Straus's patronage, our expedition, my fourth in Africa, had a threefold purpose: to collect specimens for the new hall of exotic birds in the Field Museum of Natural History, to film the customs and ceremonies of tribal life, and to record the music of French and British West Africa.

During the course of the trip we traveled eight thousand miles, enduring such opposing climates as the hot, dry Sahara and the dank Cameroon rain forest, with one of the highest rainfalls on earth, more than thirty feet annually. I studied the highly developed kingdoms of the Sundanese peoples and the simpler life of the small Cameroon Bantu tribes. I worked among the huts of the cliff dwellers of Sangha and in the spacious palace of the King of Benin. This journey of contrasts began at Dakar, the port of Senegal, French West Africa. On the edge of the continent's westward bulge, its good harbor attracted much sea traffic, and now, with its fine airport, Dakar has become a jumping-off place for planes crossing from Europe and Africa to South America.

When we were in Dakar, it was called "a bit of Paris trans-

planted to the tropics." But though there were statues honoring
famous French citizens and a sizable garden in the heart of the
city, there were no artists sketching in the tropical sun, nor lovers
wandering hand in hand. The night life, however, was very gay
and centered around the Highlife Café (locally pronounced "Hig-
lif"), where soldiers, settlers, and traders amused themselves. By
daylight the city was colorful with its clean streets and shining
white, pink, and blue houses, many with flower-decked balconies
and pleasant gardens surrounded by bougainvillaea-covered walls.
The native quarter, some distance from the center of town, was
noisy and pungent, especially in the markets when morning bargaining was at its height.

The French first came to this part of Africa in 1364, but it was
not until much later that a permanent settlement was formed.
Undoubtedly Cardinal Richelieu never dreamed, when he formed
the Compagnie Normande in the early seventeenth century, that
this small trading colony would be the forerunner of a spacious
French empire in the heart of Africa, larger than the United
States. Nor did I dream that ten years after my visit this obscure
port would be the scene of an important naval battle during World
War II, and, as a result, that its name would suddenly be known
to every American school child.

As we entered the harbor, we saw huge yellow mounds about
forty feet high lined in regular formation along the shore. We soon
discovered that these piles were neither sand nor rock, but peanuts—or "ground nuts," as they are called almost everywhere outside America. Peanuts formed the principal export of French
West Africa in those days, and the half million tons shipped
annually to European and even American ports before the last
war were made into oil for the manufacture of soap and numerous
other articles. What cotton is to our South, the peanut was to
Senegal. Each native harvested his own crop and carried it in
sacks on his head or on a donkey—if he was prosperous enough
to own one—to the nearest trader. Eventually these reached the
coast by rail, truck, or boat from the interior.

As soon as it was known in Dakar that we were American and
had enough guns and ammunition to start a war, we were viewed
with curiosity and not a little distrust. Suspicions were dispelled
when the word was spread by grapevine that we had come to the
Governor General of French West Africa armed not only with

bullets but with letters from the American Secretary of State, from the French Colonial Office, and from the late Jesse Straus, then American ambassador to France and a nephew of Mrs. Straus. Through the efficient aid of government officials we were able to prepare for the inland journey in a short time.

Organizing a safari for penetrating the interior of Africa is like getting together a small army. The comfort and health of the party would depend on our staff. It seemed as if half the ninety-three thousand people who inhabited Dakar at this time wanted jobs as our personal attendants. But within a few days our retinue had begun to take shape and we had assembled nine personal servants, including a head boy, camp boys, the cook, and his assistant. An important task on an expedition, just as at home, is hiring a good cook. Then comes the marketing with the cook's assistance. In Dakar we bought our groceries in little French shops, such staples as flour, oatmeal, rice, beans, tea, and coffee. But even in camp, where the open air sharpens the appetite, one craves a few delicacies, and those we had brought from New York: jam, wafers, and such canned goods as spinach, tomato juice, and pork and beans.

In the bush we shot game birds and antelope for fresh meat—the skins and skeletons went to the museum—and native chicken was always a possible last resort. One has to live in Africa to realize how tedious a chicken diet can become, especially when the chicken tastes like cooked string. The unfortunate African chicken has no kindly farmer's wife to scatter corn for him. He must go out and scratch for his own living, and it is usually a poor living indeed. In certain regions we feasted on fresh tropical fruits such as mango and melon-like papaya which could be had for a few cents. Near towns we occasionally managed to get fresh vegetables such as native yams and beans.

In our caravan of one sedan and two trucks brought from America, we left the damp coast bound for the interior, driving two or three hundred miles each day, making camp at night as near a river as possible in this arid country. Four tents and a shelter for the boys had to be pitched every evening except for a few memorable nights when we drove until sundown and chose to sleep under the stars, despite the dangers involved. But even when we dispensed with tents, our six folding beds had to be set up and prepared, complete with blankets, sheets, pillows, and mosquito

nets. The mosquitoes in this dry country were never too serious
a problem, but one night we were routed out by driver ants which
invaded our camp and had to be fought off by burning a circle in
the growth surrounding us.

On arrival at a chosen campsite, everyone was put to work by
the head boy. While some boys set up the tents and others made
beds, the cook and his assistant built fires, boiled drinking water,
made tea, prepared baths, and began preparing the evening meal.
One dreadful day our biggest truck broke down en route and the
men of our party were detained for some days and nights repairing it. The task of supervising the camp to make sure that our
expedition family was supplied with water, firewood, and food
(not an easy job in this barren land) fell on me. To add to my
problems I found that the region in which we were camped was
thickly populated by hyenas, the stealthiest thieves in the world.
Their eerie "laughter" made the nights hideous. My conscience
required that I stand guard over the camp through the dark hours,
gun in hand. A sleeping villager nearby had his shoes eaten from
his feet by a hyena one night, we were told, but fortunately, these
marauders bypassed us.

Our route inland took us across the Falémé and Bafing rivers.
As there were no bridges in this region, we were ferried across
precariously on small rafts which carried one car at a time, and
we barely managed to get our biggest truck on board. These rafts
were propelled by human power, the natives pulling us across by
cables, chanting the while in rhythm with their work. Once across
we drove on, passing thousands of acacia trees, from which is
produced much of the gum arabic which goes into medicines and
confectionary; it is also used in calico printing. These trees grow
wild and require no care, and in certain months become covered
with masses of blooms which fill the land with color and fragrance.

As we approached the Sahara, the trees became fewer and
more dwarfed until finally the vegetation ceased, except for occasional low scrubby thorn bushes. The rainfall gradually became
less, and, at Timbuktu, where the Niger River makes its most
northerly bend and encroaches on the desert, it almost never
rains. We had only one rain during our entire sojourn in the arid
regions of French West Africa, and our expedition had the novel
experience of being stuck in the mud in the Sahara. But even
without rain or mud, as we traveled over rough roads of rock and

sand, the boys often had to jump out and extricate us from deep ruts and sand beds. Over some stretches of desert, a good day's run was only fifty miles.

One hot, breathless night while we were camped on the edge of the desert, one of our boys vanished into the darkness with our tin money box and other valuables. He had come to us the night before we left the coast with excellent recommendations from a former expedition. They must have been forged! As the other boys we had hired were new on safari, this one seemed a real find with his previous experience. But our pleasure at finding him was short-lived. When the theft was discovered the entire expedition turned out in the night and began a frantic search, for we knew the boy could not go very far, as we were surrounded by desert. Finally we apprehended him some distance from camp with our belongings intact. The local police discovered the reason for his action. The boy was ill and we had arranged for him to be examined by the local doctor the next day. As he feared dismissal because of his sickness, he decided to flee with whatever of value he could find. Though I felt sorry for the lad, the experience bore out what I had always been told, that bush boys were usually more dependable and loyal than town boys.

One day, about one hundred fifty miles south of Timbuktu, after a long climb through rocky, eroded badlands, we seemed suddenly to be at the end of the world—the jumping-off place, literally. We arrived at the edge of a precipice and to go farther meant descending by ropes. The scene was like a fantastic stage set with cliffs, caves, gorges, tunnels, and palisades. A cluster of small villages, seemingly perpendicular, were clinging precariously to the cliffs resembling a stronghold of the Middle Ages. They reminded us vaguely of the homes of the ancient cliff dwellers of our American Southwest, and were in striking contrast to the thatched huts of so many African tribes. On the roofs of the houses near the entrance to the central village were big rocks, which, we discovered, served as doorbells. Travelers approaching the town at night had to throw stones against these rocks to attract attention and satisfy the inhabitants of their intentions before they were allowed to enter.

These villages were collectively known as Sangha. The chief's house, in the center of town, was a mud structure two stories high. There were stables for his fine horses, granaries, and gardens, all tended by slaves who did his bidding. The chief and the nobles were impressive in long, flowing cotton robes with huge hats of woven grasses bound with gaily colored leather. The slaves wore short smocks of hand-woven fabric. On the rocks about the village were altars where the young boys of the tribe offered sacrifices when they reached puberty and were initiated into the mysteries of adult society. At the end of the initiation period, the boys, without the assistance of their elders, pounded millet into flour and mixed it with warm water, making a paste which they poured as an offering on phallic shrines sculptured in clay. Then each boy killed some wild thing and sprinkled its blood on the altars.

Though the ruler lived in modest affluence, surrounded by loyal subjects, life was not easy in this barren place. A few beans and onions were grown in tiny patches where a bit of soil could be found. The beans were taken to the pounding rocks where they were ground by the women into a fine flour to be used in making a sort of porridge. The onions, too, were beaten into a soft pulp. This pulp was then formed into huge white masses resembling popcorn balls to be sold in the marketplace or exchanged for tooled-leather bracelets, cowrie shells, a bit of cloth, or a medicine man's charm.

Nobody missed the weekly market day, for it was a time not only for trading but for all the latest gossip to be heard. At the Sangha market cowrie shells, which have been used as money since the time of the Phoenicians, were still being used as currency. All over West Africa this little shell, which had traveled some three thousand miles from its native Indian Ocean, was used in magic rituals and, in addition to its value as a charm, had real monetary worth. In the Sangha market a large handful of cowrie shells was the equivalent of one cent in our money, or enough to buy a peck of meal. For two handfuls I bought an attractive leather bracelet. Cowrie shells were more valuable before the harvest than after. Even among primitive people money fluctuates.

The Habbe (Tombo) people living here believed that they had wandered from their original home to their present rocky stronghold, directed by their fetishes or gods and pursued by their ancient enemies, the Peul (Fulani) tribe. In their wanderings they came to the Niger River and were carried across on the backs of friendly crocodiles. Miracles performed by their witch doctors and fetishes saved them from their pursuers and from the hunger and thirst they had to endure before finally reaching their mountain home. They found the caves occupied by a quiet, friendly people whose religion the Habbe combined with their own fetish worship. The migrating tribe intermarried with the cave dwellers and they became one people. I learned all of this while we were in Sangha through an important ritual in progress which depicted the tribe's history. Surprisingly, and unlike the practice in most African tribes, in this ceremony honoring a dead chief the dancing took place in the daytime accompanied by singing and drumming and the violent explosion of native gunpowder made from natural sulphur or phosphate deposits in their caves.

The dances, highly dignified and formal, told the story of the tribe and were different from the frenzied performances typical of many peoples in central Africa. Some of the dancers wore huge wooden headdresses with tall, swastika-like crosses representing the crocodiles that befriended the Habbe and were revered as ancestors. Others wore fantastic masks with cowrie shells woven into fiber headdresses or hoods, with shirts, anklets, and armlets of grass. These weird-looking performers represented the Peul tribe. Included in the performances was a dance concerning theft, for in Sangha, where life is very precarious, theft was formerly punished by death. When a theft was discovered, the old medicine man assembled the people to smell out the thief. This was done by a dance in which each dancer carried a dancing stick representing the head of an antelope. At a given moment the dancers threw themselves to the ground and listened intently. The spirits were supposed to whisper to them the name of the thief, whereupon he was properly dealt with.

From Sangha we turned toward Timbuktu, and on my first visit there it still seemed as poetically remote as when Thackeray wrote:

> In Africa (a portion of the world)
> Men's skins are black, their hair is crisped and curled;
> And somewhere there, unknown to public view,
> A mighty city stands, called Timbuctoo.

The poet then goes on to describe the "stalking tigers" (there are no tigers in Africa; he doubtless meant leopards) and the roaring lions, and adds in a footnote: "The site of Timbuctoo is doubtful." To some the site of Timbuktu is still doubtful, and both Thackeray's

spelling of its name and the official French spelling—Tombouctou—
add to the confusion. Even recently, a young woman, a graduate of
a large university, asked me, "On what continent is Timbuktu?"
This city in the heart of the Sahara, about eight hundred miles
inland from the nearest coast, thrives as a busy, colorful crossroads
of vast native commerce.

When I first gazed on Timbuktu I had the same sensation of
unreality that I experienced on my first African expedition when
I saw the "great, grey-green, greasy Limpopo River, all set about
with fever-trees," as described by Kipling in his "Elephant's Child."
From afar Timbuktu looked colorless and unprepossessing, but,
as in the case of the Limpopo, there was the thrill of seeing something that I had known before only in exotic storybooks. The
reality was a busy city where about sixty-six hundred people
were living at the time. This number greatly increased when a
caravan arrived.

As we drew near, Timbuktu rose out of the desert, a straggling
gray, mud-brick city set in the midst of the hot, simmering plain,
with a skyline of flat mud roofs and a few mosque minarets beyond.
Entering the town, we found a maze of narrow, winding alleys
lined with neat, square mud houses. The alleys and connecting
passageways made such a confusing labyrinth that we did not
dream of venturing out after dark for fear of getting lost (there
were, of course, no street lights). The narrow thoroughfares led to
an open marketplace in the heart of the city which was crowded
on market days with camels, donkeys, horses, veiled Tuaregs,
proud Moors, black Sudanese, and crafty-eyed Syrian traders.

Shopping here was even more exciting than Christmas in an
American department store. One could buy anything from mangy
camels to articles of gaily colored leather. But the bracelets of
hammered silver caught my eye. They were made on the spot by
a native silversmith, and I bought two which I still wear. We could
not resist the piles of tempting green desert melons and bought
huge quantities only to find them juicy but completely tasteless—
each one seemed worse than the last. The Africans, however, devoured them with gusto.

In Timbuktu many African cultures met—Moors and Tuaregs
of Arabic and Berber stock from the north; Sudanese, among the
most highly developed of all Africans; and the more primitive
blacks, the Bela tribe from the south, who had been enslaved

and treated cruelly for centuries by the Tuaregs. Slaves, however, were not badly treated in most other African communities. They were simply members of the family group who were expected to perform menial tasks. In many tribes they may purchase their freedom, but rarely become prosperous enough to do so.

Timbuktu, so far from what we consider civilization, was once a university town. From the fifteenth to the seventeenth century the city's fame as a center of learning was so great that it was said, "We shall one day correct our Greek and Latin classics by the manuscripts preserved there." Here was a highly important cultural center of the black Islamic Empire which covered a large part of northern Africa. Learned men came to the University of Sankoré and brought their manuscripts (one, a dozen, or as many as they possessed) to study and compare. In those days one of the foremost collections of Arabic classic manuscripts in existence was assembled at Timbuktu. After the decline of the city many of these manuscripts were carried by their owners across the desert to widely scattered regions, but those that remained formed a valuable part of the city's treasure.

The city's wealth in gold and ostrich plumes was pictured to the outside world by Moslem scholars as being so great that Louis XIV of France planned an expedition to it, but this never materialized. It was probably just as well, for in those days Europeans were not welcome in Timbuktu. History tells of a French sailor who was taken captive there in 1591 and died a slave within the city. At the beginning of the eighteenth century a Frenchman, René Caille, spent two months in Timbuktu disguised as a Moor. He was the first European to get out alive. In 1825 the English sent Major Alexander Gordon Lang there, but in less than a year he was killed and his volumes of notes destroyed because, according to local tradition, this mecca for Mohammedans could not be desecrated by the presence of a Christian.

Finally in 1894 a French expedition conquered the city and the Sudanese inhabitants welcomed the invaders as saviors freeing them from the oppression of the Tuaregs. The White Fathers (Augustinian monks) then entered the Sudan, and Père Yakouba came to establish the first Catholic mission. The "White Monk of Timbuktu" was the first permanent white resident, and after forty years, was still the town's most famous citizen.

In 1934 when I met Père Yakouba, he was about seventy

years old, a sturdy man of medium height, with red cheeks, snow-white hair, a walrus mustache, and a flowing beard. His alert blue eyes twinkled through metal-rimmed spectacles, and his general expression reflected wisdom, kindness, and a great sense of humor. Seeing him in the marketplace in an old beret, khaki jacket, baggy Arab trousers, and rawhide sandals, one would not have guessed that he was Timbuktu's leading white citizen, still holding three government jobs long after the ordinary retirement age. Later, as we sat on his roof top under the stars, he looked more like what I had expected. He had on a white tropical suit and wore his French medals in our honor. As he shook the ashes from his ever-present pipe, he sipped Pernod, joked, instructed us, and showed us his meticulous notes and careful drawings made during his lifetime in French West Africa.

He was probably never meant for the priesthood, but at the age of ten, having shown little interest in his family's farm, he was sent by his widowed mother to the Petit Seminaire at Soissons, in the north of France. After eight years he emerged, in 1889, a typical rural priest, with beard, black robes, shovel hat, and hobnailed shoes. He was much too lively a priest, however, and went astray so often that in 1890 he was sent to become a novice in the mother house of the White Fathers in Algiers, an order which was founded in 1868 by the first archbishop of Algiers and which wore the white desert costume of the Arabs. Here, with a foundation of Latin, Greek, and Hebrew obtained in his seminary years, Père Yakouba perfected his knowledge of the Arabic, Bambara, and Kabyle languages.

In 1894, with a superior, he was sent by his archbishop to Timbuktu. He arrived in May of 1895, just before the rain and tornado season began. It was twilight when the two priests were shown through the labyrinth of sandy streets between flat-roofed houses to an empty one that had been made ready for them. They set up their camp gear by candlelight and went to bed promptly after dinner: the same procedure we followed forty years later when we arrived in Timbuktu. The next morning, when Yakouba saw the city, it was love at first sight. Eventually he would lose all interest in Europe as well as any urge to see other parts of Africa. There was a mystic, inexplicable something that bound him to Timbuktu.

Yakouba and his fellow priest walked through the market, and the robed black people of this Islam metropolis were amazed to hear this white Marabou (holy man) greet them in the local languages. Later they returned home and, according to native etiquette, waited for callers. The black chief of the city came, followed by his retinue with drums, and in a few minutes he was sitting on the floor with Père Yakouba treating a sore on the chieftain's leg with zinc ointment. Then followed other prominent citizens, scholars, and finally the head of the most powerful Mohammedan secret society in the city.

Yakouba discussed with them in Arabic their holy books, comparing the doctrines and texts, and immediately a friendship began between them and the white monk that became warm and permanent. Later, when he had gained their admiration as a classic Arabic scholar, the wise men brought to him in secret priceless manuscripts that had survived the disintegration of the University of Sankoré. Local descendants of professors and theologians had guarded within their families these manuscripts and scraps of manuscripts, and among them was one particularly famous document: the history of the Black Empire, of which Timbuktu had been the center at the height of its glory.

Within a short while the priests were able to hire a contractor to build their mission buildings with walls of sun-dried clay bricks, plastered over with soft clay, and flat roofs of the same material, reinforced with reeds, straw matting, and hewn beams. Shortly thereafter they opened a school, a shelter for escaped slaves, and a clinic. The free clinic became so popular that it stretched out and took over the street. All Timbuktu, high and low, sick and curious, crowded the walls of the clinic from dawn till dusk. All were received with the same welcome. If the Sultan himself had come, he would have had to sit in the sun and wait his turn.

Later a chapel was built, a small rectangular room with an alcove for an altar with a canopy of white cotton draped over it. There were candles, flowers, and a little plaster figure of the Virgin, our Lady of Timbuktu, enthroned as Queen of the Sahara. The bishop had hoped to build a cathedral in Timbuktu, but this was not to be. When we were there, the mission was dead and the chapel had long ago disappeared, but the school and clinic still flourished. Doubtless the cathedral would have become a reality and the mission would have flourished had Père Yakouba not discarded his robes, abandoned the church, and married Salama, the daughter of a wealthy Timbuktu family. Yet he loved the Catholic church until his death.

In time a university was founded which brought him prestige, honor, and a secure income. The French military also realized the special qualities of Yakouba's linguistic accomplishments, and he became their chief interpreter. He was without question the greatest linguist in the modern colonial history of Africa. He frequently served as interpreter for military excursions, archaeological explorations, and even a botanical expedition. He became the Commandant of Goundam (a kind of local king) for two years and wore a uniform with gold braid, epaulets, tassels, and a sword. He laughed boisterously when he told us about this episode in his life.

He lived a free, rich, and useful life, and distinguished visitors to the city were more eager to find this grand old man than the gold-braided government functionaries. Not only white rulers but black notables admired his wisdom and honesty and came to him with their secrets and troubles. I think of him often, as we left him—surrounded by his friends and cronies, his devoted but domineering wife, and his many children and grandchildren. It was obvious that he had found a good life—one of peace, security, and satisfaction.

Behind the walls of Timbuktu and the bleak, forbidding, metal-studded doors, the city was vitally alive. The image of the great and wealthy Timbuktu of the legends came to mind: "Timbuktu, Queen of the Sudan"; "The Holy Mecca"; "The Great Center of Learning"; "The Light of the Niger River Valley." The activity in the city during our visit was unusual because of the arrival of a large caravan of four thousand camels and their leaders. Traveling in single file, the procession extended as far as the eye could see. They had come 425 miles from the Taoudenni salt mines in the center of the Sahara, a journey of about ten days from Timbuktu. Each camel was carrying, carefully balanced and strapped to its sides, two or more blocks of salt resembling slabs of marble. Each slab was roughly four feet long, two feet wide, and perhaps six inches thick.

Twice a year, in fall, the arrival of the salt caravans was the occasion for combined business and carnival. Traders from far and near assembled to spend their days in bargaining and their nights in reveling like sailors on shore leave. A few days or weeks of gaiety provided a welcome release after months spent in some tiny village downriver where life flowed as quietly as the water itself. Timbuktu was the center of commerce in this area of the world, the meeting place of the camel and the canoe. Salt, coming by caravans across the desert, and dried fish, grain, rice, and other produce coming by canoe up the Niger River met here to be sold and traded. From the city itself caravans were sent to villages on the fringe of the desert and canoes were loaded with goods for villages downstream. A good percentage of the salt supply for the rest of West Africa was distributed from this point, and was more highly prized than the commercial variety imported from Europe. It was the favorite salt for ritual use throughout Africa.

This ancient city furnished rich material for my research in native music. Many singers were eager to perform for a few francs, or even better, for a feast for everybody. Here, just as always when I recorded, the Africans were at first fearful of and amazed by my recording apparatus but finally considered it a grand game. Then they all wanted to perform at the same time, and I had to have a guard to keep the crowd back. It was like amateur night on the radio with all the performers trying to get before the microphone at once. I first recorded my own voice and played it back to them. This did not seem so remarkable to them, however, for they felt white people had their own magic and could "even fly in the air like birds." But when they heard their own voices in their own language, they were astonished.

The voice is the instrument which plays the largest part in the music of any primitive group, and people are often distinguishable more by the manner in which they sing than by what they sing. Certain groups develop definite techniques, and one can often recognize the songs of particular tribes more easily by the manner of delivery than by the melodic or rhythmic structure. This fact is well illustrated by the voices of the Tuaregs I recorded in Timbuktu—those fierce, aristocratic people believed to be descended from the same original stock as the Berbers of North Africa. The voice production of the Tuaregs, like that of some of our American Indian tribes, requires great tension of the throat muscles. In the woman's songs the raucous quality of the voice is no accident but is deliberately cultivated and is a definite trait of the tribe.

Three very typical Tuareg songs I recorded were a herding song, sung by two boys without accompaniment, telling their goats and camels that they are going to war; a marriage dance-song, sung by a solo male voice with a chorus of sixteen females; and a lullaby, in which the mother sang:

> My son, why do you cry?
> Your father has money,
> Goats, camels, sheep, and many slaves.
> Do not cry.
> You will be a rich man soon.

I was intrigued by the words of this lullaby when I recorded it. All the lullabies I had ever known told the child to sleep, for its mother was nearby, or God in heaven was watching over him. But here the Tuareg mother was quieting her child by telling him that his father was wealthy and so he could sleep without fear. Later, when I first heard Gershwin's *Porgy and Bess*, I was amazed at the similarity of the idea in the famous lullaby "Summertime" sung in the first act by a Negro mother. At the time I wondered if possibly Ira Gershwin had based his lyrics on an actual Afro-American lullaby which had been brought to our South by the slaves, though, of course, no slaves were taken from the Timbuktu area. But songs do travel widely throughout Africa, and it is not impossible that this Tuareg lullaby had reached the Bantu tribes farther south, possibly through Bela slaves escaped from their Tuareg masters.

The marriage dance-song was accompanied by a water drum, a wooden pot with a central diameter of eighteen inches, and a sheepskin stretched across the opening twelve inches in diameter. The pot was partly filled with water and was tuned not by the usual method of heating but by tipping it from time to time to moisten the membrane, thus changing the tautness of the drumhead and its pitch. This was the first instance that I remember of having seen a drum in Africa played by women rather than by men. As they played they sang:

> Play well, dance well,
> For a fine man is marrying.
> He is good, rich, generous.
> He will give us splendid gifts.

The Tuaregs are very proud of their ancestral heroes and many of their songs I recorded were about them. One war song sung for me by a very old man extolled the bravery of a great chief and his marvelous horse named Yali. By singing of the warlike qualities of their ancestors, the young warriors were stirred to fighting pitch. The old man accompanied this song on the *tehardent*, a three-stringed instrument closely resembling the Egyptian harp.

The famous camel patrol, the Sahara's own mounted police, called the *meharists*, from *mehara*, the Arabic word for "racing camel," was also in Timbuktu at this time. One French officer with a small group of handsome Berbers made up the patrol and these units pursued bandits and maintained order throughout the desert (all Tuaregs are trained as fearless fighters).

We were amazed to see the officer, a cultured gentleman, sitting on his camel with bare feet and a monocle. Never was the monocle dislodged, not even when his spirited camel was dashing full speed. He was barefoot not for comfort's sake in the hot climate but in order to direct the camel, since one drives a camel, like an automobile, partly by pressure from the feet. In prewar days this intrepid camel cavalry was often away from its base of supply for as long as six months at a time. During this period the white officer might never see another European. These hardy troopers could go for days in the saddle with nothing to sustain them but a meager supply of dates and nuts and a limited amount of water.

We had a terrifying display of their horsemanship. From some distance away they rode straight at us, spears pointing directly at our hearts. Since we had been invited as their guests to witness their prowess on horseback, we had to check our instinct to run. Several yards from us, but what seemed like inches to me, they pivoted sharply and unexpectedly, and raced off as we caught our breath. The captain and his riders later took me for an exciting camel trip into the desert. I was unaccustomed to the necessary foot motion, and it was rather like riding in a large animated rocking chair, without the faintest idea of what the chair would do next. When they escorted me back to camp, the men and even the camels recorded songs and sounds of many types, among them numerous songs recounting the great deeds of their ancestors. Incidentally, the records of camel noises resemble nothing so much as the roaring of lions.

One morning while we were in this region, it was discovered that two hundred camels had disappeared in the night from a camp forty miles away. Government airplanes were sent to find them, but there was no trace of the missing beasts, this in a land where there was not one tree or bush large enough to hide a jackal. Tuareg bandits had stolen them and had traveled all night by forced march under cover of darkness. When daylight came the camels were weary, and while they were resting the bandits had thrown sand over them, making each one look like just another sand dune. In this way the caravan reached the border of Rio de Oro, the Spanish colony on the coast, about 750 miles across the desert. Once across the line, like car thieves, they rebranded the camels and sold them for fancy prices.

The Tuareg nomads of the desert are called "People of the Veil" because the men wrap their heads in a deep blue veil. Apparently its original purpose was protection against the sand, sun, and flies, for anyone who does not wear it is called "mouth for flies." The veil is never removed, and it is said that the Tuaregs could not recognize their nearest friends and relatives without it. We were assured it was not even taken off for eating, and consequently a special spoon with a curved handle had been developed by the Tuaregs. These aloof people, who always kept to themselves, were despised by other Sudanese groups who called them "thieves, hyenas, and the abandoned of God." Such critics said that theft with the Tuaregs not only was a natural industry but might be considered a part of their education.

Their religion was chiefly a belief in talismans; wealthy Tuaregs wore around their necks from twenty to forty charms in tooled-leather cases of great beauty containing the "blessings of Allah." They had a definite caste system, but it was less elaborate than that of India. Their Sudanese enemies said of them: "Nobles, serfs, and slaves they have, but nobility, none." For emphasis they added: "The word of a Tuareg, like water fallen on the sand, is never to be found again."

The time which Mrs. Straus was able to spend with us was at an end. Intrepid and cheerful traveler that she was, she decided that the five-hundred mile trek across the Sahara to the Mediterranean, however hazardous and exhausting, was the most feasible way to proceed to Europe. Her Swiss companion, who had almost died from amoebic dysentery, was eager to get home by the shortest route. I regretfully said good-by to the party as they started across the formidable desert. My worry for the safety of Mrs. Straus and her party was groundless, for they reached home without incident.

Some two hundred miles down the Niger River from Timbuktu was Gao (pronounced to rhyme with "cow"). It was important at the time as a French military air base and a station on the military air route across the Sahara. Once it had been the capital of the powerful Songhai nation. The ancient kings of Songhai were great potentates ruling over thousands of Sudanese subjects occupying a huge territory in the region later known as the French Sudan. These powerful kings were buried in Gao and their resting place had become a shrine. It was so important to the Mohammedans of French West Africa that three visits there were the equivalent of one pilgrimage to Mecca. The Songhai were still considered an important tribe in the region, but the days of their glory had passed.

The road to Gao was filled with rocky ruts and heavy sand, and our cars once labored seven hours to cross sixty-five yards—this in a temperature which we were never able to record accurately because our thermometer registered only up to 157 degrees and then burst.

In Gao among the birds I collected was the weaverbird which built its nests in the acacia trees that the French had brought in and planted here along the river. The bird's name connotes its habit of weaving straw and grass to make a firm "basket" nest. For the weaverbirds, Gao was a sort of oasis in the desert because it was the only region for many miles where there were trees. Abdim storks and spoonbills also came here to nest in the acacias. The interesting little tickbird was welcomed by the cattle grazing near the river. These birds had learned that ticks, their primary diet, could be found not only on the hides of such wild creatures as rhino, giraffe, and elephant, but also on ordinary domestic cattle. As do woodpeckers, tickbirds use their tails as props, holding themselves on perpendicular surfaces by this stiff support while they feed.

Most exciting of all the birds to watch were the black egrets. They have one peculiar and quite spectacular habit: they spread their wings while fishing to cast a shadow in front of them on the water. It is not certain whether they do this to make a cool spot where the fish will seek refuge or whether their shadow helps them to see better under water. If we had not brought back

proof in motion pictures, probably no one would have believed
that they fish in this fashion, looking like little umbrellas or native
huts with thatched roofs. The sacred ibises eating with them are
able to find their food without spreading their wings, so I wondered
what advantage the egret's peculiar fishing habits had.

While at Gao I made records of the songs of the Niger boatmen
and fishermen—songs which accompany the dancing and work
such as hoeing the garden, lullabies, and ancient war and ceremonial
songs. There were songs for practically every daily activity from
work to worship. I also recorded the wandering minstrels of the
region who played beautiful melodies on their flutes and accompanied their singing by the marimba. Pursuing the rhythms of
various tribes, we traveled southward to the coast capital of Porto-
Novo through the then military territory of Niger. Then we proceeded through Dahomey, the original home of many of the slaves
who brought to the New World stories, songs, beliefs, and customs
that have persisted with Negroes in little pockets, especially of
South America and the Caribbean. A short boat trip via Lagos,
the port of Nigeria, brought us to Victoria (British Cameroons)
en route to Mount Cameroon, a semiactive volcano rising out of
the Atlantic to a height of 13,353 feet almost on the equator.

After the intense heat of the Sahara, it was a joy to reach
the mountain forest where it was pleasantly cool, and where the
rainfall approximates 360 inches a year. After burning sands and
glaring sun, which we could endure only with the aid of very dark
glasses, the deep, all but impenetrable forest growth brought immense relief. On the slopes of Mount Cameroon live the Bakwiri,
a Bantu tribe whose villages and little plantations are found from
the seashore up the flanks of the mountain.

At the British government resthouse in Buea, at three thousand
feet, we assembled additional camp boys and fifty porters to carry
our equipment to our next mountain camp at six thousand feet.
Here we found Nmanga, one of the finest native hunters we have
ever had. On Mount Cameroon the hunter's profession was especially important, and Nmanga, who became our chief hunter, had
great prestige in the native community. By the time we left, his
stock was high with us, too. Through his aid and amazing knowledge of the forest creatures we were able to obtain a splendid
set of specimens including the rare Cameroon francolin, a species
first discovered in 1909. It is one of the rarest and least-known

game birds of Africa, and there were no specimens in America
of it up to that time. Nmanga knew the francolins and their
habits, roosts, favorite paths, and feeding grounds, and set his
traps accordingly.

From our camp at six thousand feet we climbed through the
dense forest tangle a thousand feet higher where the undergrowth
ended sharply as though cut off by a gigantic knife. Then came a
belt of grassland and growth very much like that found on the
higher Alps. The climb from here to the summit was more difficult
as we had to labor over lava and cinders. On the very top of
the mountain we made weather observations and deposited data
with our names in a bottle in a stone cairn which later expeditions
to Mount Cameroon have undoubtedly found on the summit.
Mount Cameroon was an important goal because of its height, and
a survey of its bird life was necessary for the expedition's study of
the distribution of birds in the rain forests of African mountains.
On three previous expeditions we had already studied birds of
mountains in Kenya, Nyasaland, Southern Rhodesia, and Angola
(including Mount Kilimanjaro, in Tanganyika, over nineteen thousand feet, the highest mountain in Africa), and on the climb
to the top of Mount Cameroon we continued the study of life
zones on African mountains. Rising like an island, this mountain
harbors birds distinct from those of the surrounding sea of hot,
steaming lowland forest. On Mount Cameroon there were twenty-
two kinds of birds not found elsewhere in the world, and we
were fortunate enough to acquire specimens of eighteen of the
twenty-two. These birds are, so to speak, marooned on this mountain as on an island. Although they have relatives in the mountain
forests of Angola and East Africa, two thousand miles away, they
never fly from one mountain forest to another over the sea of
lowland country where they would be entirely out of their element.

Mount Cameroon is like a cross section of the world's climates,
ranging from tropical at the bottom to alpine on the summit. As
we ascended the mountain we passed, as on Mount Rungwe,
through a succession of definite zones of plant, animal, and bird
life corresponding to each climatic belt. When we reached the
summit the temperature at high noon was only forty-five degrees
Fahrenheit, although we were almost on the equator, but we kept

1. The author, Mrs. Straus, her grandson, and Denys Finch-Hatton, at lunch

2. Wamjaberege and boys, Mount Rungwe, Tanganyika

3. Author recording dancer-musician in Tanganyika

4. Author feeding Shoko

5. Puzi nursing Shoko

6. Pulitzer party at lunch, Angola

7. Iloy-Iloy, author's tribal sister, Angola

8. Recording royal flute, Angola

9. Participants in Ovimbundu circumcision ceremony, Angola

10. Yakouba, White Monk of Timbuktu

Courtesy of Field Museum of Natural History

Courtesy of Field Museum of Natural History

11. The author with the famous meharists (camel corps) near Timbuktu

12. Sixty-five yards in seven hours in the Sahara

13. Recording Tuaregs in Timbuktu

Courtesy of Field Museum of Natural History

14. Obba of Benin

Courtesy of Field Museum of Natural History

15. Awni of Ife

16. Obba's musicians

17. Musician playing kora

18. Malinki musicians playing bulon bata in French Sudan

19. Drum orchestra

20. A gubu player with musical bow

21. Curved xylophone and singers, Angola

warm, for we were literally sitting on a volcano. Mount Cameroon erupts every few years, and an eruption was long overdue. Large cracks had appeared on the mountain top, some so wide that we could scarcely jump across them. The steam poured out like a smoke screen, and the surface at these cracks was so hot that it was unbearable to touch the ground with a bare hand.

But our base camp at six thousand feet was a paradise amid a deep tangle of tropical forest growth. Giant mahogany trees towered more than two hundred feet, all festooned with climbing vines and gay with orchids and mosses. While out collecting one morning with my gun boy, I noticed above my head a great cluster of delicate creamy orchids, twenty-two stalks growing on a single host. With it, I began a collection of sixty species of orchids all from that one mountain. Birds of unbelievable beauty and brilliance darted about us constantly, and we were enveloped by the liquid tones of large-eyed birds of the deep forest such as thrushes and babblers which lived in the thick shade of the forest floor. Although they are active and seek their food in the daytime, their eyes are extraordinarily large to enable them to see in the dim twilight which prevails here all day.

Monkeys chattered gaily in the forest and tempted the natives to pursue them. All the native hunts for monkeys and other game were directed by means of a large hunting horn which was often heard resounding through the ravines. Signals blown on the horn told the hunters which way the animal was moving, and the leader of the hunt would thus guide the pursuers for hours until the quarry was cornered and dispatched with spears and arrows. After one such spectacular hunt we had our first taste of roast monkey with caterpillar sauce at a ceremonial feast. This was just one of the many exotic dishes I have been obliged to eat out of courtesy and for art's sake.

The music of the Bakwiri of Mount Cameroon, like their language, is similar to that of the great Duala group of the French Cameroons. Both are of Bantu stock and the music of the Bakwiri is closer to the music of the central African groups than any of the other melodies I recorded in West Africa. Their hunting songs, the songs of their many secret societies, their dance songs, all of their musical outpourings have a spontaneity sometimes lacking among the more highly developed groups of West Africa such as the Sudanese. The Bakwiri also have fewer and less elaborate musical instruments than the tribes of the French Sudan. Among the most interesting of the wind instruments I recorded were the horns made from elephant tusks, antelope horn, or wood. The antelope horn used for directing the hunt was also used during wrestling matches. Wrestling is a common form of amusement in West African communities, and the wrestlers, like the Sudanese professional troupes of dancers and wandering minstrels, were usually found in the marketplace. During a match the wrestlers were encouraged by singing, shouting, and blowing messages on the horn. I found these songs the nearest African approach to organized cheering of the Western world. Sometimes whole phrases were poured out on a single note, as recitative.

The Bakwiri made extraordinary use of the musical bow to accompany their songs. Here a hunter's bow was played quite differently from the *gubu* of central and South Africa. The musician held the lower end of it firmly by the last three fingers of the left hand, leaving the index finger and thumb free to hold a stick, which was pressed from time to time against the string. In his right hand the player held another small stick or reed with which he tapped the bowstring with a staccato action. The bowstring was held close to his mouth so that the string vibrated between his open lips but did not touch them. Using the cavity of the mouth as a resonator, each harmonic of the bow's fundamental tone was isolated and amplified, similar to the technique that is used in playing a jew's-harp. By leaving the string free or by stopping it with the stick in his left hand, the player could produce two different fundamental tones in succession. Since these two tones were constantly accompanied by the amplified harmonics, they produced the effect of two consecutively alternating chords. The fundamental tones are frequently at an interval of a major second.

This instrument is of great musical interest, for it shows that the musician, when he taps the string, hears and makes use of acoustically natural harmonies which he uses to color the music. Aside from this coloristic effect, the particular selection of harmonics is also responsible for the unusual melodic line that results. In my recordings the melodies are executed on the harmonics sounding above the bass of the fundamental tones of the string. In one of the songs accompanied by the musical bow, the singer represents the wail of an orphan, singing:

> My mother is dead,
> My father is dead,
> I am alone, alone, alone.

This soft-voiced instrument produces such a fragile tone that it is sometimes difficult to hear it even when one stands nearby. Without modern recording equipment these quiet melodies would never have been captured and preserved.

Some time ago when the prime ministers of former British African colonies were meeting at the United Nations at a reception, I was talking to a dignitary from the Cameroons about my visit there and my interest in African music. He told me that before he left the Cameroons several people had asked him to try to find in America "a lady who came here some years ago and recorded our songs." When he said he knew that that would be like looking for a needle in a haystack, I answered: "Here I am."

After the reception I was going to a dinner party at a friend's home and had been asked to bring my album of West African music to play for the guests. I showed him the album and in the accompanying booklet pointed out especially the music from the Cameroons and the pictures of the musicians with the musical bow. He exclaimed: "Of course, you are Dr. Laura Boulton. It was my uncle who assembled these musicians for you. I wonder if you know that one of the songs you recorded with the musical bow is now the signature tune of Cameroons Radio." I gave him the album on the spot!

Chapter 8

BRONZE ARTISTS OF BENIN

As we entered Great Benin in 1934, we recalled the tales of her past glories and horrors. Since the early Portuguese navigators discovered Benin in the fifteenth century, the great West African kingdoms, particularly that of Southern Nigeria, have furnished the Western world with many romantic, vivid, and often frightening stories of these strange people and their weird ceremonies.

Benin was an important metropolis in the fifteenth century, the capital of the kingdom of the same name, and the political and religious center of a wide area. Under its powerful rulers Benin expanded through the sixteenth and seventeenth centuries for hundreds of miles east and west from Lagos to Bonny and northward into the savanna country. Regiments of tribesmen went forth from Benin to conquer new territories, and if an important general was vanquished, he dared not return. If, however, he was victorious he established himself as the chief of the newly acquired territory and paid tribute to the *obba* (king) of Benin rather than continue in his service.

The Bini are an offshot of the Yoruba nation, though their language differs somewhat. Still, their customs, traditions, religious practices, and beliefs link the two tribes together ethnologically. According to accounts of the early Europeans who visited the area, the obba, king of Benin, although a mighty ruler of a great kingdom, received his investiture from another powerful monarch who lived "toward the east" and who sent each new king a staff, a cross, and a cap of shining brass. Heads of bronze were also sent as gifts to the new king. It is believed that this mysterious potentate was the *awni* of Ife, the spiritual leader of the Yoruba nation. I was eager to study the art which had made this sacred city famous throughout the world and, if possible, to record the court musicians of the spiritual head of the kingdom. So before paying our official call on the obba at Benin we went to the awni in Ife.

The sacred city of Ife boasts a long and glorious past. The Yoruba have a tradition that their ancestors came from Egypt and settled there and that their nation increased and spread until, when I was there, it numbered millions of people, covering a huge area in Southern Nigeria. Native tradition tells us that through the centuries there have always been a secular ruler and a spiritual one. The first king was Oduduwa, an almost mythical personage, a great leader who brought his people safely through the northern desert to Nigeria. He died at Ife and later was deified and identified with the Earth Goddess. His grandson Awranyan, who succeeded him to the throne, is regarded as the father of today's Yoruba.

Awranyan moved his capital to Oyo, a city near Ife, and left a henchman in charge of the treasures of Ife. This man, as high priest, became very powerful and received the title of awni of Ife. His descendants still held sway over the religious life of the Yoruba and were the rulers of the spiritual affairs of the natives while the temporal head ruled from Oyo. This ancient capital was later transplanted to Great Benin. Near one of Ife's sacred groves, where religious rites are performed, I photographed a granite obelisk about twelve feet high and four feet square at the base. It is known as the Opa Awranyan, or Awranyan's staff; the Yoruba say that the king carried it about with him as a walking stick to prove his might. This obelisk was erected on the spot where Awranyan is supposedly buried. There was evidence that a storm had blown it over and had damaged it considerably. A section four feet in length at the top had been replaced by new stone, and several fragments lying about the base indicated that it was once much taller.

On one of its faces there were three rows of nails with coiled heads. In the center from the bottom, reaching nearly to the top, was a row of sixty-one nails. About four inches on each side of these were two parallel rows of thirty-one nails each. One explanation for the nails was that the sixty-one represented the years Awranyan lived; one row of thirty-one indicated that he was thirty-one when he came to the throne; and the other thirty-one, that he ruled thirty-one years, counting the first year of his reign twice according to Yoruba custom. There were also ancient hieroglyphs which perhaps represented his name. The interesting part of this obelisk was that the art of carving or drilling in stone such as was used here has long since been lost. The Yoruba believed that the staff was once wood and the nails were driven into it then, and that it turned to stone when Awranyan was deified.

In the grove nearby were the sacred trees, Dracaena. It has been suggested that these trees have a symbolic meaning and are planted in the sacred groves because of the similarity of their sap to the blood of human beings. A Dracaena I brought back with me flourished and grew to such heights that I had to give it away or cut a hole in my ceiling. I decided against the latter. Remarkable sculptured heads and figures in terra cotta and bronze have also been found in these groves. The Yoruba explanation of these antiquities is that the ancient rulers were deified and at the same time petrified. They believe the bodies had in most cases disappeared, but the heads remained to receive adoration and offerings. When the German scientist Frobenius discovered some of these in 1910, he believed he had found the descendants of the lost Atlantans. Since then many theories have been advanced regarding these works of art. The natives held them in highest respect as sacred objects, and during my visit many of the heads were being collected and brought from the groves into the awni's palace to be kept in chests carefully protected from the elements and marauders.

Our party made every effort to observe the local native etiquette so that nothing might stand in the way of our plans to visit the awni. I was delighted when word was sent that he would receive our party in the throne room, where great chairs were provided for us beside his. He also sent for his priests, many of them coming from outlying regions to meet with us. Their salutation of their high priest was an immensely impressive ceremony with each prostrating himself before the throne: first the greater priests, then the lesser ones, all chanting a prayer for the long life and prosperity of the awni. He responded briefly to each phrase of the chant.

Although the awni understood English, an official conversation was carried on between us through an interpreter. Through him we explained how many thousands of miles we had come to visit him, and among other pleasantries, what large quantities of his cocoa we bought in America. As cocoa was their chief produce for export, this remark drew wide smiles of appreciation from the assembled chiefs. The awni, in a very quiet and dignified manner, gave a long greeting in Yoruba which the interpreter translated as a glowing speech of welcome. It was then my turn. I assured him that we were tremendously honored and happy to be in his kingdom and were very deeply interested in the customs of his people, especially their music and art, and were eager for our own people in America to hear it.

Ceremoniously, the awni presented us with large gourds of kola nuts to seal our friendship. These nuts, so important in every ceremony or contract in West Africa, could not be refused. We had to eat them then and there. They may have been bonbons to the natives, but they were bitter as gall to me, and it was all that I could do to swallow a few. Then the awni had chests of ancient treasures brought out, and we were permitted to photograph the sacred heads and the sacred carved doors, to measure all of these objects and record data about them, and to go wherever we wished in the palace and the sacred grove.

The awni also assembled his court musicians to perform the tribe's ceremonial music. I was terribly excited by the full-throated choirs with a soloist answered by a large chorus in responsorial singing that would put many of our Western choral groups to shame. It gave me a chill to realize that the deep-toned orchestra of drums and ritualistic rattles had accompanied the age-old sacrifices of former days of which I had read so much. As the ultimate gesture of his high regard for us, the awni, in saying farewell, commanded that the *kakiki*, the royal trumpet, blown only for the king, be sounded. This great instrument, so long that an assistant had to support the far end while a musician blew it, produced a terrific blast which seemed to make the whole earth quake.

Leaving Ife, we traveled the hard-surfaced road to Benin which followed the path that the awni's messengers once traveled on foot as they brought tributes of brass and bronze to their obba. The journey then must have taken many days, but with our fast car and a good highway, the distance between these two historic cities was covered in only a matter of hours. Situated more than fifty

miles from the coast, Benin has long been historically famous as
the "City of Blood." It is said that a Catholic mission was established there in 1485, but its prosperity was short-lived. In return for
"the small consideration of a Portuguese wife," the obba had
promised to drive all of his subjects to the bosom of the church,
and it is said the mission soon had more than a thousand members. However, the extreme heat of the lowlands was unhealthy for
Europeans and the natives were not sufficiently enthusiastic about
Christianity, so missionary efforts were abandoned.

The obba of Benin, however, continued to be friendly toward
Europeans, and trade prospered throughout the sixteenth and seventeenth centuries, although European traders were not encouraged to visit Benin itself. Certainly the human sacrificial rites were
rarely if ever witnessed by outsiders. Early Portuguese navigators
and later Dutch and Swedish travelers brought back to Europe
rumors of a mighty kingdom with a capital city five miles wide
surrounded by a moat and a wall ten feet high. It was said that
the king's palace then was very spacious and filled with magnificent carvings in ivory and wood and castings in brass and bronze.
However, a report which reached the Western world in 1825 stated
that much of the ancient splendor had disappeared. When in 1892
an English officer, Captain Gallway, visited Benin, he noted that
the town was greatly reduced in wealth and size. Civil wars had
ravaged the city, and when remunerative slave raids ended and
all trade relations with Europeans were forbidden by the obba,
much of the city's former greatness had vanished.

In 1896 an English expedition left the coast carrying gifts and
merchandise to Benin. Neighboring chiefs urged them not to approach the city at that particular time, and Overami, then the
obba, warned them not to come, as the Bini tribe was celebrating
the great feast that marked the anniversary of the death of Adolo,
Overami's father. Courageously, but very unwisely, the small group
proceeded unarmed toward Benin and walked directly into an
ambush. All were massacred except two who escaped and after
terrible hardships reached the English settlement at the coast
to tell the tale. Within five weeks at the outset of 1897, a punitive
expedition advanced on Benin and after fierce fighting took the
city. The obba fled to the dense forest nearby, but finally, tired
of bush life, surrendered and was brought back with certain of his
chiefs to be tried for the massacre. Seven chiefs, one for each of

the seven whites who were killed, were sentenced to death. The obba, whose innocence was established by all witnesses, was exiled to Calabar. As he was a great *jujuman* (medicine man), it was necessary to send him far from his province in order to end the influence he held over the Bini. Of all the riches that had formerly been his to command, nothing was left. His lands were taken over by new rulers. His eighty wives and many concubines were sent back to their families with the exception of two favorite wives whom he took with him into exile.

Due to the sacrificial rites which were being observed when the invading English entered the city, Benin was in a terrible state of bloodshed and disorder, which explained its name to Westerners, the "City of Blood." The obba was not regarded by his subjects, perhaps not even by the relatives of the humans sacrificed, as a cruel or bloodthirsty man. He was simply carrying on the tribal traditions which had been handed down through a score of dynasties from the reign of the great Yoruba ruler Awranyan of Ife.

We had been told that the obba of my visit was a well-educated, intelligent young man, but even so, we were a little surprised, when paying our official call, to find him seated in a beautifully carved chair with a volume of Chesterfield's *Letters to His Son* in his hand. The obba ruled over nearly a million people scattered over a large area and presided over his court in all the ancient splendor of his forefathers. Like all native houses in this region, his palace was built of mud or adobe blocks, plastered over with mud, but in this case, ornamented with impressive carved wooden pillars and doors. To have a ready-made topic of conversation I brought a few Bini songs which I had recorded in Ife. The obba was delighted to hear the songs of his people on records, but added: "My court musicians could perform much, much better. Would you like to have them sing for you?" This, of course, was exactly what I had hoped would be his reaction, and a day was scheduled for me to bring my recording apparatus to the palace. When I arrived to record, I was met by an important dignitary and escorted into a hall of the spacious building. Leaving the hall, we plunged into the blackness of a totally unlighted stairway and proceeded by faith and feeling until we finally reached another large hall above. Here I was ushered to an enormous seat and left to await the king.

Presently there were sounds of great excitement outside, and hurrying to a window I was just in time to see the salutation ceremony, the participants quite unaware that they were being observed from above by an outsider. The obba, in ceremonial robes, emerged from his private quarters in the palace, attended by his retinue. His headdress was a magnificent creation of coral (which represents royalty among the Bini), designed so that only his face could be seen. His necklaces and bracelets and even the coverings for his feet were coral. It was undoubtably brought by early traders, for this is a land where there is no coral. The obba's garments were of brilliant brocades that flashed their colors with every movement.

Among the remarkable group following the obba were, first in importance, the chiefs who made up the body of elders and who had great authority. There were about fifty of these, all tall, splendid, and handsome with their hair shaved into the form of a coronet; they wore coral bracelets which stood out against their skin, and "skirts" drawn tightly about the hips and knotted at the waist.

There were two groups of musicians, one playing flutes, the other playing horns of elephant tusks and gigantic gourd rattles. The sign of the obba's office was a huge executioner's knife with a blade of native wrought iron and a carved ivory handle. The knife shadowed the obba constantly. If he advanced a step, the knife held by its bearer advanced. If he retreated, the knife also retreated. Two boys were at the side of their ruler literally acting as his arm bearers, for each supported an arm at the wrist and elbow when the obba walked. When he paused, he rested his whole weight on the head of one boy. Another boy shaded the obba with an enormous multicolored umbrella. Here was the entire court assembled in their ceremonial regalia to record for me. I became so absorbed in the spectacle of the people prostrating themselves at the feet of the obba, chanting their salutations, that I did not hear the attendant return until he stood beside me. With quiet and somewhat stern dignity, he escorted me back to my seat for the arrival of the king. When the obba entered the hall and formal greetings had been exchanged, we moved in slow procession to the sacred court amid a cheering throng of several hundred of his subjects. The flutists led the royal procession and bringing up the rear were the drummers, preceding me and six porters bearing my recording equipment. A ceremonial umbrella was also held above me, and I suddenly felt very self-conscious in the splendor of it all. I had arrived in my working costume, expecting only the musicians, and suddenly found myself in the midst of elaborate tribal ritual. I had dressed correctly when I first called on the king, and had I known that he would attend the recording session, I would have put on my "court" clothes, too.

In the inner ceremonial court, memorial mounds had been erected for the previous obbas and were piled high with ivory tusks beautifully carved to depict events in the life of the king. Here, too, were heads, figures and groups of brass or bronze representing the activities of the obbas. There were also brass bells with exceedingly sweet tones used to call the spirits of the dead obbas to accept proffered sacrifices. As soon as the king was seated on his throne, the musicians, who were also magnificently attired, prepared to perform for my recording machine. This presented me with one of the major challenges of my career, for I was not certain whether my equipment would faithfully capture such a large body of performers. However, the final results are among the most prized records in my collection.

The old men who recorded for me had actually performed this ancient ceremony when it had included human sacrifices. These royal musicians had considerable prestige and commanded great respect in the community. Their songs, however, were so old that although the singers knew the meaning of each and its exact place in the ceremony, they could not give me a direct translation of the text, which had come from the dim past. The songs and dances performed were from the ceremony of worship of kings who had, at death, become deities. It was given only once a year, and in the old days lasted three months, day and night, and was an orgy of human and animal sacrifice: twelve slaves, twelve head of cattle, twelve goats. Now it covered little more than twenty-four hours, for since the advent of the British, the sacrifice consisted only of domestic animals, more expensive than human life once was.

Most of the songs during the ceremony were normally accompanied by dancing but this was impossible because of my microphone. First came the songs for the great chiefs, followed by those for the lesser chiefs, and finally those for the obba's wives, which continued for such a long time that I decided it was because

he had so many wives. I did not manage to discover the exact
number, but I was told that his grandfather had fifty of his
favorite wives buried with him to minister to his needs in the next
world. The songs were sung by a solo voice and a responding
chorus of fifty chiefs chanting above strident rattles, soft-voiced
flutes, and great drums with carved figures of deities, and with a
carrying power of twenty miles. The ceremony concluded with the
songs and prayers for the former kings. This directly preceded the
priest's offering of the sacrifices on a blood-caked altar. It was a
fitting climax to a crowded parade of impressions, contrasts, dangers, and delights sufficient to fill a lifetime. It was probably the
only time in my life when I was happy to have been too late to record a ritual in its original form.

The taking of Benin City by the British had also led to the discovery of art treasures exceeding all expectation, and having recorded the king's musicians, I was anxious to see and learn more
about the famous bronze castings of the Bini tribe. Travelers in
West Africa had for centuries reported seeing in the king's compound and in the *juju* houses remarkable works in bronze, brass,
and ivory, but no traveler or ethnologist dreamed of the vast
quantity and variety of objects hidden there. I was most fortunate
in obtaining the king's permission to see and photograph these
treasures, with the help of special guides.

Every house had its altar, and sometimes beautiful bronze objects were buried in the altar itself or in the surrounding walls. In
such unexpected places bronze jugs, vases, heads, and figures were
found. Plaques with intricate designs decorated the obba's palace,
and the most spectacular works were on the sacred altar. Early
descriptions of these altars indicated to me that the same sort of
objects decorated them as in 1934. Many of the ancient works were
removed to European museums soon after the capture of Benin, but
the bronze artists continued to fashion them, casting in the same
style and using the same methods. The altars we saw were filled
with traditional ceremonial objects, some ancient and some doubtlessly made since the capture of Benin. Large carved ivory tusks
in intricate designs were supported by life-size bronze heads. There
were smaller bronze heads and figures of equal excellence and
beautifully executed brass bells. Also on the altar were metal
swords and staves of wood carved to resemble bamboo, which
served as both musical rattles and clubs.

All of these bronze castings were made by the well-known cire-perdue (lost-wax) process, which we saw in operation. This technique has been passed on as a heritage of certain families of the tribe for countless generations. We were allowed to film the entire process. A core of special clay was formed on which the figure was molded in beeswax. The very fine details, such as the coral beads of the headdress and necklace, were attached to the model by means of a heated wire which served as a soldering iron. The wax model was then carefully coated with fine clay and eventually completely covered with a heavy mass of coarser clay in which an outlet was made for the wax to excape when melted. The mold was then baked in charcoal embers; a mold of exactly the design of the original wax model remained after the wax had melted.

Molten bronze was then poured into this mold and filled every hollow left by the wax. After the metal cooled, the clay was broken away. Obviously only one casting could be made from the wax model, and this accounts for the fact that no two works are identical. Incidentally, this complicated method used with such success and familiarity by the Bini is the same process as that used in Italy during the Renaissance. By no other conceivable method could such elaborate detail and such extravagant relief be obtained as that which I found on the plaques or tablets in the obba's palace, which represented the victories of the Bini over their enemies. A series of about three hundred of these panels is now in the British Museum. The composition and the masterful way in which the detail is treated indicate that these highly developed castings were produced by a people long familiar with the art of working metals. The plaques show only one phase of the bronze casting of Benin, but these artists are equally as successful with objects in full relief such as heads, bells, vases, and smaller objects.

The question invariably arises as to where and from whom these people of Southern Nigeria learned the art of metalworking. Both in Ife and in Benin we found bronze castings that are unique. The method of casting may or may not be indigenous, but the style is definitely African. All the Benin productions represent a form of native art with stylistic features that are fundamentally Negroid. I was tremendously impressed by the grave simplicity, perfect proportions, strength, vigor and boldness of the modeling, and the extraordinary feeling for rhythm and design. As with the music of the region, with its forceful, free melodic outlines and rhythmic complexities, the ancestral art forms provide continuing evidence of the innate, artistic sense of the Negro.

Chapter 9

SONGS AND INSTRUMENTS OF JUNGLE AND BUSH

The animal life, the geographical exploration, and the political intrigue of Africa have been of concern for generations. The two hundred million natives belonging to eight hundred tribes have been studied by anthropologists; explorers, traders, government officials, and missionaries have long ago opened trails into the heart of this great land; and curious investigators have penetrated many of its most deeply hidden secrets. Geographers have navigated its great rivers and climbed its important mountain peaks; scientists have collected and classified its varied species of the bird, animal, and insect kingdoms; and many thousands of Europeans have made Africa their home.

We who are involved in the arts have looked to Africa with special interest. Of all preliterate people, the African Negro has had perhaps the most positive and far-reaching influence on the artistic achievement of our own epoch. Modern artists and composers of the Western world have been profoundly impressed by these ancient art forms, many of which have been a catalyst in producing much that is fine and significant in the artistic expressions of this century. The introduction of the plastic principles of Negro sculpture in the Western world awakened new feeling for abstract forms; for modern artists, weary of old traditions and seeking new means of expression, found in them fresh stimulation. African music, however, is much less well known, and a study of the music of the African Negro gives additional evidence of his

genuine art sense. He has definitely, though unconsciously, contributed to the artistic life of the Western world.

It is impossible to overemphasize the importance of music in
the life of an African. From morning until night, from cradle to
grave, everything is done to the rhythm of a song. Whether
sharpening his knife, paddling his canoe, or making a sacrifice
to his gods, he performs his task to the accompaniment of music.
The songs of so-called primitive people are by their very nature
immortal. They will live forever by virtue of their simplicity and
spontaneity and because they deal with the realities of tribal experience.

The texts of their songs make up the poetry of the people. The
verses show the same feeling for form, balance, and symmetry
which is apparent in all their art forms. The subtle power of the
rhythmic beat of the lines of their song-poems is strongly felt and
is comparable to the stimulating pulse of their music and dance.
There is a directness and forcefulness which is lacking in much
of our sophisticated poetry, a vital quality which never fails to
stir us and to create our sympathetic interest. Poems may be
lyrical, expressing the feelings of the heart, or epical, relating
events or even the whole history of a tribe. Lyric poems are sung,
epics are chanted. The subject matter of the poetry is usually
meager, but the group repertoire covers a wide range of subjects.
Some songs are very old, some are comparatively new. Every experience, occasion, or activity has its song or groups of songs.
There are war songs, love songs, historical songs, fervent religious
chants, frenzied dance tunes, gentle lullabies, and songs of praise
to a king or chief.

The latter are of immense importance in every African tribe.
Among the Chopi of Mozambique, songs of praise were sometimes used as popular dance songs, accompanied by orchestras of
from sixteen to thirty xylophones, playing extremely inventive
music with beautiful melodies and cross-rhythms. One of my recordings has, in addition to a xylophone orchestra, an interesting accompaniment of clapping and ululations (special high, shrill trilling with the tongue, usually produced by women). The dance
was performed by men draped with skins of leopard and civet
cats and wearing fantastic headdresses of ostrich plumes. Their
anklets of dried seed-pod rattles added a soft liquid sound and

an additional rhythmic accompaniment to every movement of the dance.

In Zululand I discovered a unique type of song of praise which I found nowhere else in Africa. In the chief's village every day at dawn, a special solo singer passed by each hut singing, without accompaniment, loud songs of praise to the chief. I have found that usually such songs are sung by a soloist and chorus on a ceremonial occasion honoring a chief, and this solitary singer was unique in my experience. The Zulus' interesting songs of praise and beautiful praise poetry nearly all pertain to their king. They deal with the king's virtues and bravery in war, and the great deeds of the ancestors.

Special songs of praise and songs of satire, which serve as a moral agent in the community, are sung and improvised by wandering minstrels in the French Sudan. For instance, certain songs extol worthy citizens, praising them for their excellence and encouraging others of the village to follow them as an example. On the other hand, songs of satire wield great power, for there is no punishment an African dreads more than being held up to the ridicule of his fellow man. One song of satire I recorded was about a very attractive young woman. I do not know what she had done to annoy the composer, but he was certainly taking his revenge by describing her as a terrible hag with hideous hair and other unlovable features. He emphasized the unattractiveness of her derrière and ended with the worst insult of all, that she had dirty teeth. You can imagine what the belle of a village would do to avoid a song like that. The minstrels could also make terrible trouble for their enemies by singing songs that aroused hatred or suspicions of witchcraft throughout the community.

The professional minstrels had a social status curiously like that of their European counterpart of a few centuries ago, but in West Africa they were more powerful, and their tendency to use songs for blackmail purposes made them greatly feared. They collected tribute both for the satire they withheld and for the praise they bestowed. Many of them grew wealthier than the chiefs themselves. In certain tribes these blackmailers were not regarded as reputable and were even denied the rites of burial.

In Nigeria I also recorded songs of the secret societies, which were common throughout West Africa and which had religious, medical, economic, and social purposes. Some of them even had the power of life and death over the people. One of their ancient songs I captured was from the *ashiko* society, a song used to call their group together. There were seven singers and part of the repetitive theme was: "We are ready brothers, *adingo, adingo . . .*" This song was accompanied by five rectangular tambourine-like drums called *bebe, samba, briz, jiagban,* and *dadu.* A drumhead of vellum was attached by pegs to a square frame of heavy, resonant African mahogany. An inner frame, which could be pushed against the drumhead by means of wedges at the ends of a crossbar, provided a means for holding the drum and controlling the pitch. The manufacture and playing of these drums were special professions.

Often the African improvised his songs about news events and people who made the news. The same goes on today. Not long ago a news item from Stanleyville listed the lastest songs in the Congo as "Independence, Cha-Cha-Cha," "Vive, Patrice Lumumba," "The Round Table" (inspired by the first conference on independence with Belgian Prime Minister Spaak), "The Spaak Cha-Cha-Cha," and "Reconciliation Song" (referring to the reconciliation and reunion effort). The main difference between these popular numbers of 1964 and the xylophone-playing minstrels of the Sudan of 1934 appear to be that the Congolese now use steel guitars, and with the change in politics some of the composers have landed in jail.

Songs survive in the group repertoire when the events or persons that inspired them are important. Often, however, inconsequential songs have survived, just as in the West, for no reason other than that the melody and particularly the rhythm appealed to popular taste. Often new words have been set to favorite old tunes, also a common practice in the most modern countries.

Studying the music of the African is like living the history of music and instruments, and nowhere is his inventiveness and ingenuity more marked. There are simple melodies of three or four notes and elaborate melodies played by complete orchestras; instruments of the string family which range from the *dingidu,* a one-stringed fiddle, to the *kora,* a twenty-one-stringed harp; wind instruments from a tiny one-toned whistle to sophisticated flutes; drums so simple that they are no more than a skin stretched tautly between two men and beaten by a third to complex drum orchestras that create whole symphonies of rhythm.

In West Africa there are unusual combinations of instruments, producing amazing tonal effects; for example, drums with bells and trumpets and even flutes and whistles; stringed instruments with gongs and rattles, sometimes assisted by empty bottles; or flutes with sanza, horns, and drums.

Of all the wind instruments in Africa it is the flutes that perform the most elaborate melodies. Throughout West Africa they are played widely and usually two or three together, sometimes accompanied by drums and even bells. Flute players are often attached to the court of a king, or paramount chief, and frequently become famous for their virtuosity. In a dance song I recorded among the Sudanese Bambara, two flutes called *fle*, made of bamboo with five holes each, were played in unison and accompanied by a small iron bell (*chiningini mongo*) struck with a wart hog's tusk, two small drums (*perinkaba*), and three arm-pressure drums (*dunka*).

In the French Sudan I found the curious *bulon bata*, a combination string and percussion instrument. One piece played on this instrument that I recorded was a dramatic war song of the Malinke, a well-known tribe of Sudanese Negroes. A melody was played on the three strings of the instrument while a rhythmic accompaniment was beaten out on its gourd resonator. The resonator's open end was covered with a goatskin membrane, laced onto it by leather thongs. An oblong opening in the resonator was considered essential for the desired tonal effect. Three strings of sinew were stretched from the resonator to a curved neck, on the end of which was an oblong piece of tin with a border of small metal rings loosely attached. This provided a device which constantly vibrated as the strings were plucked and gave a much-admired humming background to the melody. The instrument was called a war drum because in the former days of tribal warfare the musicians who played it led the king and warriors into battle, beating rhythmic accompaniments on the gourd resonators as though they were drums. A war song I recorded was formerly used to incite warriors to fight, and although the bulon bata in this case was accompanied by three drums, its three strings (approximately E flat, B flat, and G) were definitely distinguishable, even through the intricate rhythms of accompanying drums.

One of the most melodious instruments, the Malinke's form of the xylophone, called in their tribe the *balafon*, was described by a

Portuguese explorer as early as 1586. Each key or stave has a gourd resonator, the gourds carefully graduated from tiny ones for high tones to huge ones for low tones like those on the curved xylophones in Angola. Another type I recorded in the Sudan consisted of a strong light frame, low and flat, supporting sixteen staves of wood of different lengths. This version had two small round gourds of uniform size per key suspended below the staves on the wooden frame. It was carried hanging from the neck, and these skilled musicians were able to sing, dance, and play the instrument simultaneously. Africans are especially skilled in playing the xylophone. They play it with or without other instruments, alone or in groups of four or five, and in Southeast Africa I found them in orchestras of as many as thirty. In each hand, performers usually held one or two small beaters like drumsticks, tipped with little balls of native rubber. The Malinke musicians even wore bells on their hands to provide a percussive background for the melody.

The kora was the most elaborate instrument that I recorded anywhere in Africa. Like the more primitive war harp, it belongs to the harp family, as its strings are perpendicular to the resonator rather than parallel as in the zither. It has twenty-one strings of unequal length, stretched on both sides of a high bridge, ten strings on one side, eleven on the other. A sturdy straight neck passes through a huge skin-covered gourd resonator, extending beyond the gourd several inches so that it can be firmly wedged into the ground while the instrument is played. The strings are attached to the upper part of the neck with cloth or leather rings which serve in place of pegs. At the lower end they are fastened to a prop where the neck emerges from the gourd. The instrument is tuned by twisting the cloth rings, making the strings more or less taut. The strings are plucked as one plucks those of a modern harp. While recording a song of praise to the chief and other fascinating melodies played on the kora, I found that the musician was humming an accompaniment to the instrument rather than using the instrument to accompany his song.

A splendid orchestra of five xylophones played the accompaniment for the dance of the Concuba festival I recorded. The spirit in whose honor the dance was being given was impersonated by a dancer in a loose flowing robe of scarlet with an impressive ostrich-plume headdress and attended by dancing women and small boys in scarlet robes and masks. The dance performed by these fetish dancers was highly stylized and most impressive.

The Bambara of the French Sudan also have highly developed music and musical instruments; their own forms of the xylophone and kora were played by professional musicians who, like the Malinke, wandered from village to village.

As the oldest music is ritual music, so the oldest instruments are those used in sacred rites, particularly rattles and special drums. Among the Bambara of the French Sudan I was told that interesting symbolism is associated with certain instruments. For example, the *tabale*, a drum reserved for kings and great chiefs, was related to the spirits of light, sound, and water, and to the speech of the people. Their eight-string harp is surely not so ancient as drums and rattles, yet I was told that each of its strings represents a prayer and that certain tones are thought to have meanings like "plenty" or "lack of plenty," "completeness" or "incompleteness."

The use of musical instruments as a means of communication throughout Africa is well known. Travelers have observed it and scientists have described the practice. But the technique is of particular interest to students of linguistics because the messages played on the instruments are closely related to the language of the people. Since most West African languages are "tone" languages (usually four tones), definite pitches or registers convey definite meanings. The drum language is not a system like our Morse code of dots and dashes; it is based on the musical elements of speech, rhythm, and melody. The signals of horns as of drums are based on the tones and rhythm of language and frequently follow patterns of speech closely. Communication instruments common among West Africans vary from tiny whistles of baked clay to elaborately carved ivory horns. Horn communication may use as few as ten signals, depending on the instrument, or an almost unlimited conversation may take place between two players remote from each other. At other times horns may be used purely for display of virtuosity by those adept in the art of trumpeting.

War horns, vitally important in the days of tribal warfare, praised the fighters, abused the enemy, directed the fighters, and announced each development of the battle. Messages which I recorded from a Liberian Kru ivory war horn (calling warriors to battle, directing their action, announcing the victorious outcome)

were translated into native Kru and then by my African interpreter into West African pidgin English, at times almost as difficult
for me to understand as his own language:

Everyone be prepared! The war's coming!
If anybody run away, he's going to get the whip [the draft]!
The warriors tell him to run quickly to the military.
Gather in all the women from the farm!
They [the enemy] are coming off the right hand of the farm
    on the right side.
They are now cross the river on the other side.
Gather troops on the left!
They are not retreating! They are coming!
Come here quick! Run, run, run, quick!
The guns! The guns fire! The guns fire now!
That's right. They get them, they get them, they are get them now!

This was followed by a tremendous shout of victory, but the victorious cries were, as always, mingled with the wailing of women
whose men did not return from battle.

In some tribes there is communication through whistling, though
women are forbidden to learn that language; in fact, they are not
allowed to whistle at all. We even have a tradition in the Western
world, a warning for women: "A whistling girl and a cackling hen
always come to some bad end."

Musical instruments have a vital role from the point of view of
cultural research—they can be seen, handled, and measured—but
even more important is their function in the spiritual and mental
life of the people through secular and ritual use. From the crude,
sacred whirring instruments, which come from early times when
magic became an important part of the African philosophy, to the
most elaborate and highly developed instruments, all demonstrate
the musical achievement of the people and the cultural significance
of their music. However, no instrument compares in this respect
with the drum.

The Africans with their prodigious sense of rhythm have developed the drum more fully than any other people in the
world, and nowhere has the drum such varied forms and so many
uses. There are whole orchestras of drums which produce symphonies of rhythm and melody. The arm-pressure or hourglass
drum, for instance, is one of the most interesting; it can actually

play melodies. The resonating chamber of wood is carved in the form of an hourglass; and its two drumheads, usually of calfskin, are attached to each other by thongs of untanned hide. The drummer beats the drumhead with a small curved stick while holding the instrument under his left arm in such a way as to tighten or relax the thongs, which may vary the pitch as much as two octaves. When played in orchestras of from five to twelve, hourglass drums produce melodies and rhythms of remarkable subtlety.

In West Africa I also found a counterpart of the modern timpani. These drums were played in pairs, one at each end of a trumpet orchestra. The drummers wore rattles on their wrists to give the effect of snares. Another unusual drum is a small square tambourine form used by some of the secret societies of the Bini tribe of Southern Nigeria. The rhythms of this drum, too complicated to be described here, combine with deep resonant tones to produce performances long to be remembered. The incision drum, a highly specialized instrument, is remarkably developed for long distance signaling. It is made from a log hollowed out through a narrow slit and is played by striking the lips near the slit. It is sometimes cylindrical and sometimes triangular. When this drum is played near a river, the sound is carried over the water and can be heard for great distances.

The triangular slit drum or incision drum of West Africa was also reported among the Swahili in East Africa, where it was used not for signaling, but for exorcising evil spirits. When someone was possessed by spirits, the medicine man treated the patient with several days of constant drumming and with intricate machinations of tones destined to destroy the nervous system, if not the devils.

In Africa some drums are beaten with a stick plus the hand, others with the hands alone, and still others are not beaten at all. Probably the most curious is the friction drum. I have in my collection an example that an old Umbundu witch doctor in Angola gave to me. It is approximately a foot and a half long, and the log was so tapered in the course of its manufacture that the drumhead is eight inches in diameter; and the base or open end, seven inches. Sound is produced by pulling on a reed twelve inches long which is inside the drum, securely attached through the center of the drumhead to a small knob of leather and cloth on the outside of the membrane. The player holds the drum between his legs, and keeping his fingers constantly moist from a gourd of water by his side, pulls the reed inside the drum hand over hand, letting it slip through his fingers and at the same time exerting pressure. The Umbundu word for playing this drum is the same as the word for milking a cow I was told; the motion is, as you might imagine, identical. The rapid vibration of the drumhead set up by this technique produces a sound fearsome in itself, and doubly so to the native of Angola or of the southwest Congo, for it is used by the witch doctor to smell out guilt; it speaks of murder, death, and poison.

Quite another use of the friction drum is made by the Nandi in East Africa, where it is essential to the initiation ceremony, the drum itself being called "female," and the reed inside, "male." For the circumcision rites a "lion" friction drum is used, a small wooden instrument shaped like a barrel, one end covered by goatskin. This drum, like the bull-roarer, is used for the boys' initiation, and may not be seen by any woman or uncircumcised man. The drum used for the girls' ceremony is made by stretching skin over the end of a water jug; it is played by the old women, and no man or uninitiated woman may see it. The sound is supposed to resemble a leopard's growl. This is one of the very rare instances in Africa when a woman is allowed to play an instrument.

Still another use of the friction drum is found with the Ashanti in West Africa. There it is known as the "leopard" drum, partly for its sound, but also because of its association with royalty. It is played not by means of a reed drawn down its center, but by rubbing a curved drumstick back and forth across the membrane. These Ashanti drums are used in pairs, "male" and "female," to announce the coming forth of the king from his palace. Other tribes, among them the Bambala and Bushongo of the Congo, refer to their friction drum as the "village leopard" because of its sound. For the girls' initiation ceremony among the Balilla of Northern Rhodesia a friction drum is improvised from an ordinary grain mortar by covering the open end with dressed skin and placing a reed upright upon it.

A still more exceptional drum, its use apparently confined to the villages of Badjok and Batetele in the equatorial forest, is the humming drum. In appearance it is an ordinary double membrane drum, two feet high, one foot in diameter, and ornamented with curved designs. On one side, however, is a hole into which a funnel-shaped calabash has been cemented with native rubber. A second hole near the narrow end of the calabash is partly covered with the web of a certain spider, like the gourd resonators on the xylophones of the Ovimbundu. When the drum is beaten, air is alternately sucked in and expelled, and the sound is not unlike the hum of a low-flying airplane.

While speaking of these highly developed drums, I must not forget the simple free-membrane drum, possibly the first type of drum ever conceived. I found such a drum still in use among the Bechuana of southern Africa. An oxhide was stretched taut by several men, and then beaten with sticks to furnish rhythmic accompaniment for a ceremonial dance. The method of playing was similar to the process used in preparing a skin for leather-work; but the players beat it as a drum, thus making it a musical instrument.

If a proper drum is not at hand at a moment when drum music is needed for work or play, the African is never at a loss. The Bushmen, for instance, improvise a dance drum by stretching a piece of skin over the mouth of a clay pot, calabash, or tortoise shell. On safari, when our boys felt the need of drumming, any-thing served: a packing box, a stretched-out skin, two sticks struck together, or a gasoline can. When we traveled by canoe, our paddlers turned the dugout itself into a drum; the paddles, hitting the rim of the boat with each stroke, served as drumsticks.

An added fascination about African drums is the fact that there is no standardization even within types. I found an infinite variety of uses, sizes, and shapes as I traveled from tribe to tribe, from region to region. The clove-scented island of Zanzibar has small, fat, barrel-shaped drums; the lower Congo, long, thin cylinders; Somaliland, small round ones; and Sangha, near Timbuktu, pot-shaped drums, with a dark spot near the center where a magic substance has been applied. It was not surprising to find the beautiful classic vase-shaped drum of the Ovimbundu of Angola among the Waru in the Congo, as their cultures appear to be related. The Beyansi have drums with four legs; the Wachewa of Nyasaland in Central Africa, drums with three legs. Even within the same tribe, however, many different shapes and sizes are found.

The manufacture of drums is a very special profession, usually hereditary. But among the Ashanti, at least, it was not a profession handed down from father to son, for it was their belief that when a drum maker taught his art to his son, he would die as soon as the son had mastered it. In most tribes the ordinary cylindrical drum was made according to definite specifications but without ceremony. A tree was chosen for species and size, felled, and a suitable portion removed and hollowed out with a long-handled gouge. When the walls of the cylinder had been reduced to the desired thinness, the exterior was smoothed (for this the Baganda used a special leaf whose rough spiky surface made excellent sandpaper) and carved near the top and bottom with geometrical designs.

The membrane might be of oxhide, goatskin, or lizard according to the tribe and type of drum, but calfskin was the most common material used. For the ordinary dance drum the skin was scraped, stretched, moistened, and pegged to the top of the hollowed-out log. When it had dried to the desired tautness, the pegs were cut level with the drumhead, and the membrane was treated with vegetable oil to keep it pliable. Among the Baganda, butter was used for this purpose. By another process, twisted thongs or sinews were used instead of pegs, or the skin was attached to a second skin by laces.

When the manufacture of a sacred drum was in question, however, elaborate ritual was an important element of manufacture. For example, Ashanti drum makers, commissioned to make a talking drum, first chose as fine an example as possible of the *tweneboa* or cedar, believed "to contain wood from all the other forest trees." But the tree was not cut until an egg had been broken on the trunk to appease the vindictive spirit of the tree and a prayer had been said to avert evil from the drum makers and their people. Then, to the accompaniment of further offerings and prayers, the tree came down. From this moment the drum became a potential home of the tree spirit and also of the elephant spirit whose ears formed the membrane of the drumhead. Each step in hollowing out the tree, the preparation of the membrane, and the attaching of the sinews was accompanied by propitiatory acts. At last the drum was consecrated and was said to have been "given eyes."

Certain sacred drums, designed to be inhabited by particular spirits, were carved with the masks of the spirits. The drum of the *awni,* the spiritual leader of the Yoruba nation, which I recorded in Ife, was carved with the mask of a former ruler, now worshiped as a deity. On the royal drums I recorded in Benin, not the mask but the whole figure of the god (a king deified at death) appeared. Often a fetish was placed inside a sacred drum. To feel in close touch with the supernatural, I have only to pick up my Baganda royal drum and shake it. The mysterious rattle of the fetish inside speaks to me of African ritual, of hidden shrines deep in the forest, and of secret ceremonies rarely witnessed by white men.

Around the drums have developed the most ancient traditions and the greatest ritualistic significance of all African instruments. Therefore there are many taboos connected with them. Because of their great importance in life, the drums are man's province. For example, an Umbundu woman would not dream of touching a drum—particularly if she was pregnant, for it was believed that she would then bear a drum instead of a child.

To become an expert performer, a drummer must learn hundreds of rhythmic patterns, must perfect an amazing technique, and must play with an inner fervor that works magic on the listeners. Since pitch is an important element in African drum music, tuning always precedes playing. This is usually accomplished not by any mechanical means, but by heating the drumhead either over a communal fire or by throwing a handful of dry grass inside and lighting it.

Drums serve a variety of social purposes ranging from work rhythms to religious rituals, from kingly ceremonies to the celebration of such semiprivate events as the birth of twins. Among the Baganda when twins were born, one drum was beaten to tell of the mother's activities—whenever she bathed the children or nursed them or ate her own meals—and another announced to those outside the family enclosure what the father was doing. Later when the husband made his round of visits to invite members of the clan and others to the naming ceremony, the drums and two spears tied together went with him. These told the whole story without a spoken word.

In Uganda there were royal drums for the king and drums for each chieftainship. But as their proverb said: "The drum beats for the office, and not for the person who holds it." In addition to the drum of his office, each chief had a private drum of his clan, beaten from time to time to ensure permanence of tenure. Each office was known by the rhythm of its drums. The royal drums, *majaguzo*, numbered ninety-three in all, two very large, forty of diminishing sizes, and fifty-one small ones. They were the joint responsibility of all the professional drummers who in relays played for the king a month at a time. They were beaten to announce the coronation of a new king, or the death of one of the king's children, to declare war, or to celebrate the full moon or the entrance of the king into a new house. Each drum had its own name. In former days when the drum *kaule* needed a new covering an ox was killed for its skin, and its blood was run into the drum, then a man was decapitated, and his blood run into it. This was believed to give new life to the king.

A new king went into mourning for six months while the late king's body was being embalmed. When it was put into the tomb, the drum named *mansigo* announced the end of the period of mourning and the beginning of the coronation of the new king. For the coronation itself the drum *kibonsbone* was beaten. At the close of the feast that followed, the keepers of the drums would purposefully remove all the instruments except the drum named *busemba*. There would always be some obliging person in the crowd who noticed the supposed oversight and returned busemba to its keeper. This person would then be killed, and the bones of his upper arms made into drumsticks to be used the next time a king was crowned, for this was the only occasion on which busemba was used. Princes in direct line of succession were called "princes of the drums."

The daily audience of the king with his chiefs was announced by drums; and if the meeting brought a decision to declare war, a drummer sounded the war drums in the royal enclosure; the chiefs took up the rhythm in their own enclosures, and the sound was then carried in ever-widening circles until the war drums of the whole country had called everyone to arms. In the war party itself, each chief had his own drum and could theoretically call his own men to his side; but in practice his drum usually took its cue from that of the commander in chief.

Among the Batusi in Uganda when a new king received from his people a drum named *kalinge,* he beat it and clapped his hands. The people never saw the drum again while it was in his possession, but each month the blood of a bull was smeared over it. As is usual for the coronation of a ruler, drums were an essential part of the regalia used at the installation of the emir of Fike. A small "drum of succession" carried hidden under an officer's gown was struck three times. A big ceremonial drum was sounded three times at the close of the ceremony. After seven days of feasting and dancing, the officer gave the king the small drum that he had kept hidden, and the king secreted it in an earthenware pot in his house with a horse's bit, a length of chain, an arrowhead, and a sickle. This drum (eight and a half inches long, eight inches wide, three inches deep) was pear-shaped, of metal, covered with tightly stretched skin, and had two small brass rings set in its side.

Even more important than the part drums played in the king's life was their connection with the religious practices of the people. Royal and religious functions were, in fact, closely related, since dead kings played the principal role in African religion. Since these tribes were ancestor worshipers, their kings became at death deities and their most revered gods. The ghosts of dead kings were thought to be present in the decorated Baganda sacred drums; each drum contained a fetish, and had a time of playing and a rhythm of its own. Two of these sacred drums were named *betabango* and *nemikono*. The former, the larger of the two, used human bones for drumsticks and announced the appearance of the new moon and signaled the people's monthly cessation from work. It was also beaten at fixed intervals, day and night, during the annual twenty-one-day festival.

In two principle ceremonies of the Ashanti—the *odwira*, an annual celebration when dead kings were propitiated in the interest of crops and the first fruits, and the *adae*, a ceremony held every forty-two days—the drum had an important function. In the old days twelve human sacrifices were made at the tombs of the ancestral kings during the odwira. As the king stopped before each skeleton of previous victims, a particular rhythm from the *utumpane* drums was the signal for a new victim to be killed and his blood to be smeared on specific drums. If the victim was a captive of note, his skull was later attached to one of the *fontomfrom*, or "proverb drums," which were dressed in silk and treated as dignitaries. When the king returned to his palace he was entertained by his *kete* orchestra, which consisted of reed pipes and small drums and singers who named the dead and recounted in rhythm their martial achievements.

At the *adae* ceremonies, eleven types of drums accompanied the paramount chief as he went from one blackened sacred stool to another making offerings to the spirit occupant of each. When the chief retired to change into his robes of state, the hour was filled by a drummer telling clan history on his two utumpane, the performance ending with the signal, "The king has sat down," played when the chief reappeared.

The psychological effect of the drum is frequently spectacular, almost as powerful on a Westerner as on an African. Many a night it would draw us, no matter how weary, from our beds to dress and walk miles to some village dance to sit for hours on rare old carved stools offered by some courteous participant while dancers whirled and shouted and the drums led us through mazes of rhythm from which we lost all desire to extricate ourselves. Even later when playing my records during lectures with nothing to hold the eye, I have known rhythms to start strange impulses in a sophisticated audience. The effect is both hypnotic and stimulating. The succession of beats goes on and on, building overtones one upon another until the ear is in a state of complete confusion. To rhythms so intricate that it is often a morning's task for me to notate a single line of one is often added an element of melody just as complicated. The deep and sonorous notes of the drums are indeed stirring, but the rhythms are inescapable.

The drum is the pulse beat of Africa. To the African it gives life its continuity. He is born to it, dies to it, works to it, worships to it, and dances to it for days and nights on end. It brings dignity to the coronation of kings and terror to the witch-smelling ceremony. Whether the rhythms are gay or somber, pompous or sinister, they are always insistent and never to be forgotten.

Chapter 10

THROUGH SOUTH WEST AFRICA:
WASTELAND, WONDERLAND

South West Africa has been largely by-passed by history. As early as 1484 a Portuguese explorer named Diogo Cão, seeking a way to the Indies, stepped ashore near the present port of Swakopmund and planted a stone cross. A little later Portugal laid claim to Angola as the first European colony in Africa. But the barren, unfriendly coast of South West Africa repelled the white explorers who came by sea. For centuries only a trickle of Boer (Dutch) and English settlers seeped up into the land from the Cape colony. In 1885, since no one else wanted the territory, Germany annexed South West Africa, but lost it after World War I through a League of Nations mandate. Only in recent years, when India questioned this mandate in the United Nations, did most of the world hear of this territory for the first time.

The land itself explains its isolation. On a map it looks like an exaggerated saucepan, nine hundred miles deep and an average of four hundred miles wide, with a narrow "handle" running three hundred miles eastward into the heart of the continent. This strip is called Caprivi Strip after a German, Count Caprivi, who planned it as a contact with the mighty Zambezi River. He hoped to give South West Africa a navigable outlet to the Indian Ocean. As it turned out, he hit the Zambezi sixty miles north of Victoria Falls, which effectively cut short any such dream.

South West Africa is a land of space and emptiness, deserts and mountains, strange animals and fascinating native life, modern cities and isolated mines. Much of the country is bare, blazing desert, yet it has lush lowlands whose regular flooding forces people to move about by boat. We saw dusty villages with tiny hospitals as up-to-date as the Mayo Clinic and hunting grounds of aborigines almost as primitive as the ancient cave Bushmen. Diamonds lay loose on the beaches, and ranchers waxed wealthy, growing luxury pelts for Western markets.

Along the Atlantic, South West Africa runs from river to river—from the Cunene, at the border of Angola, to the Orange, the traditional limit of the Republic of South Africa. Between the rivers there is almost no surface water, only intermittent streams, springs, and water holes. Not in almost a thousand miles of coast is there a good natural harbor, a lack which has brought more than one vessel to grief in the pounding surf of the coastline, which is edged by the Namib Desert, a sandy ribbon up to fifty miles wide where rain almost never falls.

Beyond the coast the land rises gradually to a central ridge whose highest peaks approach eight thousand feet. Here there is more rain and most of the towns are in this region. Eastward stretches the high plateau called the Kalahari, a barren waste of more than one-half million square miles which takes in all of Bechuanaland and reaches into Angola, the Rhodesias, and the Republic of South Africa. With all of this, South West Africa is also a small paradise for game.

The area had a nonwhite population of about 315,000 when I was there. Included are two tribes which sprang from Central Africa's great Bantu stock, the Ovambo and Herero; two imported unrelated groups, the Nama (Hottentots) and the Berg Damara; and the charming, timid little people of the Kalahari, the Bushmen. Under the League of Nations mandate, more than one third of the South West's area has been set aside as native reserves. The natives may live elsewhere if they wish, but no white man may own land in a reserve or enter one without special permission.

I had such permission because of my connection with the expedition sent to Africa in 1947 by the University of California, where I was then on the music faculty. It was comprised of thirty-five people in four units. One was working in South Africa on paleontology, botany, and zoology; another in the north and east on anthropology and archaeology; and another in Ovamboland on a detailed study of a single tribe, the Ovambo; and my unit working on music in South West Africa and Angola.

A world war had caused a break in my studies of African music, and I was eager to pick up where I had left off. My unit of the 1947 expedition entered the continent by air, landing in Johannesburg, South Africa, and then proceeded to Pretoria, where we obtained permission to travel into the native reserves of South West Africa.

One-sixth the size of the United States, South Africa then had about as many people as New York City. The natives are both pure-blooded and mixed, and the Europeans are a blend of Dutch, British, French, and other nationalities. There are two official languages: Afrikaans, or Taal (which is basically seventeenth-century Dutch, much modified), and English.

For many decades South Africa was a farming country, and it still raises tremendous numbers of sheep and cattle. The discovery of gold, diamonds, and other valuable minerals in the late 1800s brought a flood of new settlers and set up a trend toward industrialization which is still continuing. As a result, the nation's main metropolis, Johannesburg, was then a center of nearly six hundred thousand people, bristling with American-style skyscrapers, overcrowded, bustling, and proud of its smoking factories, fine hotels, and modern homes. But just a few hours by air is the primeval bush, lonely and silent, haunt of wild men and wilder beasts. Such contrasts are a national characteristic.

In a single day's drive one can range from the great port of Durban, whose foam-flecked beaches are washed by the warm Indian Ocean, to sleepy villages where only Afrikaans is understood; along soaring mountain highways from Zululand, protected realm of the once-warlike Zulus, to the sunny grape country of the Cape Province, settled long ago by French wine makers; or from the bush country to the cosmopolitan city of Capetown, ending the day at an exclusive country club where one's golfing partner speaks pure, clipped Oxford. South Africa offers the majestic sweep of Victoria Falls, the pulsing mines of the Witwatersrand ("White Water's Ridge"), the fabulous hundred-mile gold reef which underlies Johannesburg; Swazi, Basuto, Bechuana, and many other tribes; and the world's biggest park, the Kruger National Park, larger than the state of Massachusetts.

After what seemed endless weeks dealing with government officials, at last with all necessary permits and the blessings of Jan Christiaan Smuts, then South Africa's Prime Minister, we left the capital of Pretoria on a fine morning in September (spring below the equator) and headed southwest. My assistant and I alternated at the wheel of our half-ton Chevrolet van, one of ten vehicles provided for the various expedition groups by General Motors. We carried gas and oil in drums plus maps all donated by Shell Oil Company; the Union government had loaned us camp gear: tents, cots, folding chairs, cooking utensils, and even DDT and spray guns. We had cameras and film through the courtesy of the U. S. Navy, and the all-important recording equipment had been provided by the Presto Corporation of New York. It was a heavy load but an essential one.

Our first destination was Taungs, a village in the northern Cape Province where the expedition's paleontologists headed by Dr. Charles Camp, were hard at work. My interest was in recording the songs of the Bechuana and other tribes who labored in the local limestone quarries. I knew that their tribal cultures were breaking down under the impact of white civilization, and I wanted to preserve what I could while time remained.

From Taungs we went on to Kimberley, the city of diamonds. The famous "Big Hole" was no longer being worked, but I was allowed to don miner's clothes and go deep into a newer mine where the same "blue ground" was being profitably exploited. Later in the DeBeers syndicate's office, I held a small "rock" in each hand and was told that each was worth some $13,500.

Beyond Kimberley, the road began to deteriorate. Though South Africa had made great progress with her highways, very little hard surface was to be found in this region. After one interminably long, narrow, rutted stretch, we came to a settlement with a single store. Were these roads, we asked the storekeeper, likely to continue? He nodded with some amusement. And what about South West Africa itself? "Madame," he said with an almost courtly air, "South West Africa prides itself on having the worst roads in the world!"

With this pleasant reassurance we jounced on, sometimes going for hours without seeing another car. At the isolated village of Upington we crossed the Orange River much as had the earlier trekkers fleeing the trammels of Cape civilization. They had had to ford, of course; we at least had a steel bridge. Then with the thermometer mounting steadily, we put another ninety miles behind us and arrived in South West Africa.

The border was marked by a simple signpost. On either side

the land looked the same: hot, dry, rugged, treeless. Yet somehow we felt a difference. We lurched on, and gradually the spell of the land settled with finality over us. It was a compound of many things: barren hills, marching off toward the horizon, at once terrifying and challenging; stretches of naked sand, blown into serrated ridges by the hot wind; strange plants that store water underground and so survive, such plants as the leafless *nara* and the aloe called *kokerboom;* and the sudden, unexpected animal life, such as brilliant flashing lizards, scurrying brown hares, and distant figures at dusk that might have been kudu, eland, or gemsbok.

As we chugged northward, we could almost trace the history of South West Africa by the names we encountered. Some of them were of Boer origin: Karasburg, Stampriet, and all the "fonteins": Kalkfontein, Grootfontein, and Rietfontein, each a witness that some early wanderer had stumbled onto a welcome spring. Many more were native; Karibib, Usakos, Gobabis, and Maltahöhe, each with a meaning to the tribesman who first enunciated it (Omaruru, for example, means "The Place of Scorpions," which I understood all too well when I found one in my shoe the morning we broke camp there).

After the first long, desolate stretch we began to climb. With altitude came evidence of greater rainfall, and finally an honest-to-goodness town. It was called Keetmanshoop, after a Rhenish missionary who established a settlement there in 1866. The wide, dusty streets and simple frame houses reflected the days of German occupation. This tranquil community, incidentally, had a population of thirteen thousand (three thousand whites) which made it the second largest metropolis of the whole territory.

Keetmanshoop was on the north-south railway line, and from here a single line also ran straight west to another memento of German days: the port of Lüderitz, shipped minerals, beef, hides, and other commodities including guano from offshore islands which boasted such names as Possession, Plum Pudding, and Roast Beef. The town, however, was curiously isolated. Past its placid bay flows a chill current right from the Antarctic. Inland lies the Namib Desert whose complete aridity is perhaps best shown by the rare broad-leaved *Welwitschia mirabilis* which grows only in southern Angola and parched wastelands of South West Africa. This dwarf member of the pine family hugs the ground and nurses tiny cones in its center. It resembles an octopus with its writhing twenty-foot-long leaves waving in the desert winds. Although it gets its moisture solely from sea fogs drifting in from the Atlantic, it can live for a hundred years.

Occasionally along our route we had seen Hottentots, but in Windhoek we observed this interesting tribe at close range. The Hottentots have yellowish skin, peppercorn hair growing in tufts, little triangular faces, small delicate hands and feet, and very protuberant buttocks which in the women are considered a sign of beauty. The tribe came from the south sometime after the Herero had arrived from the north (about A.D. 1550), and for years they fought each other but later united in guerrilla warfare against the Germans. Today the Herero and Hottentots seem quite compatible and even intermarry.

The reed-flute orchestras of the Hottentots provided some of the most interesting music I recorded in South West Africa. Their flutes were the first instruments described by travelers to South Africa. As early as 1497, Vasco da Gama told of being entertained by a huge band of Hottentots playing flutes, and in 1661 a Dutch explorer described bands of one and two hundred musicians each with a hollow reed flute dancing in a great circle, playing "in harmony" their one-toned instruments.

The huge orchestras of those days have dwindled to small groups of five to nine. The ones I recorded had seven players, and every flute had a different tone. Each musician played the single tone for which he was responsible with enormous pride. The band made up what you might call a living pipe organ, each pipe of which was played by a different person. The sounds produced resembled those of a circus calliope, but the performance was perfect.

The dances were always circle dances such as the Dutch writer described in the seventeenth century. In the center of the circle there was a leader, and around him danced a circle of women singing and clapping. The flute players danced in the outer circle. Each song had its own action as well as text, and the dancing was highly dramatic. The reed-flute dances were royal performances held by the commander in chief.

Apparently these reed-flute ensembles antedate the panpipes. Though they were performed always in harmony, the Hottentots never reached the stage of joining several flutes together to be played by one performer as is the case with panpipes.

The making of the flutes was complicated. When the country

was extremely dry and no reeds could be found, the roots of an acacia tree were used as substitutes. The root was cut open along its length, and the inner core removed. The root was then squeezed together again and its edges joined and sealed. The pipe was rubbed with cow dung, fat, and red ocher. Some of the inner bark was chewed and the fibers formed in a wad which was pushed up into the pipe, tuning it to the desired pitch. The tubes were made airtight by binding them with strips of thin bark. When the instrument was not in use a stopper of wood was placed in one end, and the pipe was filled with milk or water to keep it supple. Each flute had a name like "weeping" or "weeping later" or "cow" and so on. I have a set of Hottentot flutes in my collection, made from bark stripped from saplings, but unfortunately they become too dry and brittle ever to be played more than once. They have to be prepared anew for each performance.

Another interesting group in this area was the Berg Damara, a small-statured, very black-skinned people who seem to have lagged behind their neighbors in some respects. Migrating to the southwest about the time the Hottentots did, they were promptly enslaved by them. In their wild state the Berg Damara wear almost nothing and never wash. Surprisingly, however, they take exceptional care of their lustrous white teeth. In Windhoek we found them serving chiefly in domestic and other unskilled work. They are thought by a few scholars to have brought to this region the stone tool culture and the rock and cave painting. These, however, are usually attributed to the Bushmen.

From Windhoek we proceeded north to Ovamboland. It was here that Sam Coles, a missionary whom I had first met during the Pulitzer Angola Expedition, made a dramatic re-entry into my story. I was working on my notes and cataloguing recordings one day when the quiet of the camp was shattered by the noise of an approaching truck. I was amazed and delighted to discover that the visitor was Sam. By bush telegraph, that mysterious communication system unique to Africa, Sam at his mission station over two hundred miles to the north had learned that I had returned to Africa and had set off to find me.

Sam was a huge man, broad, strong, and straight as a tree trunk. His name suited him well because he was as black as coal with the broadest smile I have ever seen on a human face. His infectious laugh was as huge and hearty as the man himself. Gentleness was written in every deep-drawn line of his face, and there was something compelling about his animated eyes. His spontaneous personality was as powerful as his body and both seemed always on the point of bursting.

Looking at the old truck in which Sam had roared into camp, I was reminded of something a missionary had said to me on an earlier expedition: "You'll find God in the most unexpected places in Africa. He might be looking down at you from a tree through the eyes of a leopard, or he might come bouncing down the road one day in an old jalopy." To a lot of people in his part of Africa Sam was very nearly God. To me he remained one of the most remarkable characters I have encountered throughout many journeys back and forth across the globe.

The son of Alabama slaves born before the Civil War, Sam Coles had been a menial Negro laborer in the South, working in lumber camps until he was twenty years old. He had never had a chance to make any use of his quick, bright mind, only of his hands. Like most Negroes in Alabama, he had gone to work very young. But later Sam decided to find a school that would take him as a student. In two and a half years he covered the work of eight grades. His teachers were so thrilled by his keenness and tireless ability that they made extra time for him. Starting at twenty-four, Sam skipped quickly through school, served in World War I, got an A.B. degree at Talladega, a Negro college in Alabama, and then persuaded a teacher at the school to marry him and go with him to Africa, where he longed to be an agricultural missionary. He eventually became one of the few Negroes in charge of a mission station in Angola.

His wife, Bertha, charming and sedate, complemented him perfectly. She was tolerant, but like others, felt that Sam had far too many ideas and tackled too much. But Sam worked on the principle that if you plan to do twenty things in a day, you may get nineteen of them done; plan only one thing and you may not even get that done. This has always been my theory of work, too.

It was like old home week in our camp as Sam and I talked of our Angola friends, and he exacted a promise from me that I would visit his mission at Galangue. The journey was an indescribably difficult one in our half-ton truck through desert and rough bush country, and it took several strenuous days before we sighted the lights of the little mission, a joyful sight.

Every day that I spent at Galangue revealed some new, unexpected side of Sam which demonstrated his wit, wisdom, and love of humanity. While there, Sam and Bertha were running the whole mission: a hospital, a farm, a school, a blacksmith shop, a tile factory, and, of course, a church.

The day began at dawn, even when Sam had been working all night to solve a personal or technical problem. He was a pioneer, a one-man Point Four program, an entire Peace Corps. In the many years that I knew him I never heard him utter a discouraging word about his work or the future. He had tremendous courage to tackle any job or to stand up to any obstacle. His energy was boundless, his ideas soaring. His dreams did not end with his youth but increased with age. He was practical, inventive, and persistent in mastering any task that he undertook. In the affectionate words of one of his colleagues, "His words were pearls, his voice was a song. He was a hopeless optimist."

In the school Bertha and her African teachers taught not only the usual studies but also household arts and practical crafts. Several of her students later became teachers themselves and others found work with the government. Mrs. Coles also headed the hospital while the doctor was away on home leave; most of her medical knowledge was learned through practical experience. Sam had had no medical training, but he did have what he called his "Big Book," a vast medical dictionary of such antiquity that a modern doctor would have donated it to a museum. Sam had used it for so long and with such frequency that the pages barely hung together. But from those pages Sam had acquired so much knowledge that many times patients who had been given up as hopeless came to him and were helped.

Sam never turned anyone away. While I was in Galangue there was a man whose symptoms were so strange that Sam sat up all one night searching through those tattered pages until he found what the "Big Book" advised him to do about the man's trouble. The patient got well and he left the hospital. How much of his recovery was due to faith and how much to the "Big Book" one will never know. Another night an African with his son dragged himself through miles of bush, his body a mass of horrifying burns. Lightning had struck his thatched hut, and it had gone up like tinder. Being near the door the man had managed to escape, but his wife had been trapped inside, and the man said she was dying.

While Mrs. Coles took the poor creature into the hospital, Sam asked if I would take him to the hut in our truck to bring the wife to the mission hospital.

It was a black night and the road little more than a winding native path, but the young boy who had helped his father to the mission guided us. Nothing was left of the hut but cracked and blackened mud walls. The woman lay on a straw mat spread on the ground, her flesh so burned that it looked as if at the slightest touch it would fall off her bones. I had never before smelled burnt human flesh. I still consider it the most terrible odor I have ever encountered.

Sam filled the back of the truck with leaves and grass to make a sort of mattress and picked the woman up, straw mat and all, in his strong arms and gently laid her on the improvised bed, careful not to touch her flesh. Nobody believed that she could survive; I did not even expect her husband to be alive when we returned. But under the tender ministrations of Sam, his wife, and the mission nurse, both recovered completely.

Another healing impressed me tremendously. A young mother in the hospital badly needed surgery after her baby was born, and it was imperative that she be taken to the big mission hospital at Dondi. With Sam I took her and her children in our truck together with a twelve-year-old girl to care for the children. Sam sat in front with me, and the ill woman stretched out in the back with the girl and the children. As we were bumping along the rutted roads I heard a weird noise coming from behind. Sam heard it, too, and exclaimed: "We'd better stop. Have you any salt in your kit?" Surprised, I told him I had (one never moves in Africa without a box of food, a can of water, and other basic essentials).

We quickly lifted the box down and got the salt and went around to the back of the truck. The noises were now terrifying. The young girl was writhing and twisting in a violent epileptic fit. Grasping her firmly in his arms, Sam placed a teaspoon of salt under her lolling tongue and held her mouth closed for a moment. Almost immediately the seizure became less frantic, and then ceased altogether. The girl relaxed, and her eyes once again focused normally. As we drove on I asked: "How in the world did you know to do that, Sam?" "I read it in the 'Big Book,'" he answered.

I was happy to learn that even the local witch doctor marveled at Sam's ritual with the "Big Book" and the irrefutable "cures" that always seemed to follow. Indeed, while I was in Galangue, I observed that everybody in trouble—often the Portuguese, too—came straight to *Nala Kao* (Mr. Coles, in Umbundu) as the one person most likely to help them. No matter what the problem, they by-passed the Portuguese settlers, the British businessmen, and the German farmers and went directly to Sam, even though it often meant walking many miles in the bush perhaps even in the middle of the night.

Sam was quiet and efficient, always unhurried and unruffled, and seemed to know instinctively how to do things in the right way. To Sam every problem had a spiritual approach. The natives treated him as they did all missionaries, with respect and devotion. Perhaps his being black, too, brought them closer to him than to the white missionary, but they also believed, as Sam did, that a power even greater was at work. When Sam preached a simple sermon on Sunday mornings, this was deeply evident. Although he spoke to his congregation in Umbundu, which I did not understand, I felt the power underlying his words. The natives, even the children, listened to him wide-eyed, still, and with little of the fidgeting that rustles within a congregation whose interest is only partly held.

Sam told me that he began his preaching when he was only five years old by practicing for hours on his older brother, for, before his parents died, they had instilled in him a simple, deep-rooted love of God. Sam's untiring helpfulness, already extended in many directions, spread even further to include my work. The natives, encouraged by his enthusiasm, flocked eagerly to the mission to sing for me. Sam was as excited as I when we discovered a type of song which neither of us had known existed there. When Sam was translating for me a song of his tilemaker, we found that the old man was the singer of the tribal genealogies. His songs were exactly like the Book of Genesis: "Melandi begat Ndolo . . . Ndolo begat . . ."

Sam took me to villages hidden deep in the bush, so remote that the music I recorded there will probably never be found again. His friendly approach to everyone, including the powerful witch doctor, helped me in collecting ceremonial songs and musical instruments which were forbidden to outsiders.

Sam and his wife reached Angola in 1923 with what he called his "Ph.D. in ox-driving" acquired in the Alabama lumber camps.

He began by teaching the natives how to make simple plows to use in their fields instead of having to dig the hard earth with sticks. He taught them to make wheelbarrows and ditching plows to lighten their heavy work which included road work for the Portuguese government. The Portuguese, also, soon had complete confidence in Sam's ability and desire to help the people. They called the chiefs and elders together and urged them to plant and cultivate new crops (wheat, buckwheat, rice, soybeans, etc.) as Sam had shown them to do. They sent young men to Sam to be trained in growing crops, in animal care, and in making agricultural tools and equipment. They even sent him oxen to be trained to pull plows and oxcarts being made at the mission. Most important of all, the Portuguese government gave Sam financial support which, added to help from American friends, churches, and foundations, made it possible for Sam's many projects to prosper.

If Sam was ambitious, it was for the natives rather than for himself. Over the years his energy was devoted to improving their lot, not his own. Sam spent every one of his home leaves learning some new technique which would help the natives to help themselves toward economic independence and self-respect. For example, one leave was spent studying blacksmithing and another was spent at Pratt Institute learning ceramics so that he could teach the Africans to make tiles for their floors and roofs. Later the natives produced tiles of such excellent quality that the Portuguese came long distances to buy them. Eventually the little tile "factory" at Galangue could not keep pace with the demand.

Some of Sam's experiments in educating the Africans in agriculture demanded great imagination. In the meager gardens of the Ovimbundu, native corn, struggling for survival in the hard, dry soil, rarely grew more than a foot high. Sam asked the natives why corn was not planted in the lush land along the river which was flooded in the rainy season, making the land always fertile. They were horrified at the suggestion. It would "disturb the spirits." Their children were buried there because the babies could not walk and must be near the river so that their spirits could drink.

Sam understood their fears, for he remembered a similar superstition from his childhood. He never tried to force or badger the natives, believing that example is the best teacher. So he quietly went to the river and planted a field of corn which grew to six or seven feet with great fat ears. When he brought the natives to see it, they marveled but were afraid that some fearful fate would overtake Sam for offending the spirits. When no apparent harm came, they were persuaded to move their crops to the river valley where they flourished.

When Sam and Bertha eventually retired to America, the love and gratitude of the Africans followed him. I saw a letter from one of Bertha's students written from Angola in which he said that, thanks to Sam, he had just returned from town after selling his crop of corn, loaded in an oxcart instead of on his back, for nearly five hundred dollars which would be saved for his children's schooling and for improving the house that he and his sons had built for the family.

The sun-soaked Africans with their leisurely culture are not, by nature, hard-working. What Sam had done was to teach them to make practical use of what nature had given them. He always stressed that the church at Galangue was built with spades, hoes, and plows, as well as with prayers and faith. He once told me of the great dream he had for the years after his retirement from his Angola mission. He had found support to establish a children's shelter in Angola under the auspices of the Pestalozzi Foundation, named for the noted Swiss educator. In this agricultural and industrial school, he planned to gather from all over Portuguese West Africa orphans and destitute children and teach them to be self-supporting citizens.

This, however, was not to be. A fatal heart attack in 1957 ended Sam's dream of yet another step for the betterment of the natives. But the work he accomplished will always stand, an indestructible monument to a dedicated man, the "Preacher with a Plow."

Chapter 11

COMING OF AGE IN OVAMBOLAND

I had two primary objectives on the 1947 University of California expedition. The first was to attend and, if humanly possible, to record an *efundula,* the coming-of-age ceremony for Ovambo girls, and the second was to find the Kalahari Bushmen and to record their music.

This would prove to be an interesting bracketing of native life, since the Bushmen were among the most primitive of tribes, and the Ovambo culture was one of the most highly developed African cultures. Although I had received little encouragement when I asked for permission to record this sacred ceremony, I was, as always, optmisitic.

The Ovambo are of Bantu stock and are the largest tribal group in South West Africa; they numbered some 155,000 when we were there. They live under the authority of native chiefs and tribal councils whose regimes have been so effective and enlightened that tribal wars have been completely eliminated. At the time of our visit, there was not a single white policeman to be found on their reservation. This was most rare, for in the rest of Africa tribes functioned under European police protection.

Our road lay north from Windhoek, capital of South West Africa, through villages with musical Bantu names like Okahandja and Otjiwarongo, and over roads so corrugated that we thought our teeth would be shaken from our heads; on through Groot-fontein, center of a thriving rich ranch area, to the Tsumeb Copper Mine, the only mine of any size in the whole territory, although for many centuries the Ovambo have been fashioning copper into massive ornaments. Eventually, after jolting over endless miles of hot, dry, dusty country, we reached Namutoni, which is the gateway to Ovamboland. Set in an absolutely arid terrain, Namutoni was to us an oasis. A spring of clear, cool water gushing from a mound of reeds had led the Germans many years before to build a fort here, white-walled with crenelated towers in the best Foreign Legion tradition. As we arrived, the sunset was turning the white walls to gleaming gold, and one would not have been surprised to see the great iron-studded gates swing open and Beau Geste himself gallop out on a black Arab steed.

Ovamboland was under the trusteeship of the South African government, and at this point we had to present our credentials before we could travel into the reservation. Many weeks later, when returning to the fort, I was to find it less enchanting, for we were required to be disinfected for any possible hoof-and-mouth-disease germs picked up in the game preserve. Not only did we have to drive our truck through a huge vat of foul-smelling liquid, but, despite protestations, we had orders to march through it on foot. I feel sure that the liquid dispensed with any germs on our shoes, for it was so effective that it completely dissolved all of the stitching in my expensive custom-made desert boots, and I later walked out of the soles!

However, on arrival everything was delightful, and we made our first camp in Ovamboland just inside the fort. We were ecstatic to find a welcoming pool with cold, gushing spring water which provided us with our evening bath. We set off at dawn the next morning to cross the Etosha Pan, a huge expanse of sand in which we were frequently bogged down to the axles. Fortunately we were joined by a truck convoy of Ovambo boys returning home after completing their work contract with territory ranchers, and without their help, we could never have coaxed our truck through the treacherous sand. During the day temperatures soared so high that our thermometer burst, and we frequently had to let the air out of the truck tires to prevent them from exploding. After my Sahara experiences I fully realized that sand could grip wheels just as relentlessly as the heaviest mud. Only the combined shunting and shoving of the Ovambo boys could get us free when we became entrapped.

As it was, I walked the last couple of miles to the commissioner's house at Ondangua where we stayed the night and made plans for our work with the Ovambo. The truck, however, became so hopelessly embedded back up the road that it took most of the next day with all of our Ovambo friends grunting and pushing to rescue it. Commissioner Eades sent help and proved himself to be a very good friend after he overcame his initial suspicion of me. At first I could not imagine what was troubling him. Perhaps he disliked Americans, or perhaps he disliked women. But finally he came out with his reason: "It's easy enough for the officials at Pretoria to give outsiders permission to go into the reservation; they don't have to face the problems that might result. I'm the one who must try to keep things tranquil up here."

I quickly assured him that I was not afraid. He grinned and said, "I wasn't thinking of protecting you, Madam, but the natives. You're the one who is invading." I shall always think that it was his discovery over dinner that we shared a love of symphonic music that decided him to give me the help and permission I so badly needed. We became immersed in a discussion of Beethoven and Brahms, and at one point he jumped up from the table and exclaimed, "You must hear this, you simply must hear this."

In the next room there was a very decrepit windup phonograph, and on this, with infinite reverence, he placed a record so warped by desert heat and scratched from innumerable playings that one could scarcely recognize above the surface noise the beauty of the Brahms Requiem. At the end of the disc, he lifted the needle and turned to me with a rapt expression that said as clearly as if he had spoken, "Have you ever heard anything more beautiful than that?" Here was a man who loved Africa, loved the natives under his charge, but still hungered after those aspects of civilization from which he had so long been separated. Briskly he arose, with the air of a man who has already remembered too much, and said, "Well, now, so you want to record *efundula* music. . . . We must see what we can do to help you."

The next day we left the commissioner's cool house built in the native style with thatched roof and walls of hand-woven reed mats, and moved into tents in our permanent camp several miles away. Here we joined the well-known anthropologist of our expedition Dr. Edwin Loeb, and his wife, who had gone on before and were also interested in studying the efundula. Our camp boys and cook provided by the assistant commissioner were excellent, but our greatest treasure was Elandi, the old man who served as interpreter. He was a tribal headman and therefore had tremendous influence throughout the whole region.

The Ovambo are an intensely interesting people, tall, dark, but not black-skinned, proud, and self-reliant. They include seven main tribes of Ovamboland, and their land is basically a sandy plain laced, for the greater part of the year, by dry watercourses. But when the rains come the soil turns into a sea of mud; the Cunene River overflows its banks and makeshift roads disappear. During the rains cattle and goats are driven to high ground, farmers turn fishermen, and boats are the standard means of locomotion. But normally the Ovambo live by agriculture, raising kaffir corn, millet, and other hardy crops and storing the excess of good years in huge conical baskets as a reserve against lean ones, a wise practice, unique with this tribe.

The Ovambo live in elaborate kraals: villages of grass-roofed huts surrounded by high wooden stockades. Several families usually occupy a kraal; the headman's hut stands in the center of the maze and around it are the huts of his wives (like all Bantu, the Ovambo are polygamous) and other relatives. Cooking spaces, council areas, granaries, and cattle enclosures round out the complete kraal. An intruder entering such a stockaded village would find himself in a bewildering maze.

The witch doctors formerly held great power over the Ovambo. Nowadays a medicine man is more inclined to confine his practice to conducting rituals and to the making of queer concoctions of herbs and native remedies. The Ovambo are deeply superstitious, however; a comet in the sky, for example, is, for them, a certain sign that an important personage will die. Late one night I saw a brilliant orb in the sky, which I thought was a comet, and I learned later that I was right; scientists from far and wide had come to South Africa especially to study it. Strangely enough, that same night, the head wife of the neighboring kraal headman died.

The next morning we were awaked before dawn by the sound of wailing for the dead woman; it went on, increasing in volume, until almost midday, when the mourners stopped to eat. It continued like that for days, since everyone who had known the deceased was expected to come and pay his vocal respects. Since the Ovambo do not believe in death from natural causes, anyone who failed to show up and wail might be held a contributor by witchcraft to the woman's death, by thought if not by deed. I was fortunate enough to record the lamentations, undoubtably the first time these chants had ever been recorded.

The chanting sounded at times wild and undisciplined. Each new arrival began to chant, mentioning his relationship to the deceased ("O my sister" or "O my friend") and the previous mourners poured out their passionate grief in louder and more heart-rending wails than before ("O my wife," "O my daughter," or "O my mother"). Yet there was an order to it as the short descending phrases were repeated over and over again on different pitch levels, in brief melodies of no more than five notes. After each outburst of unrestrained mourning, the slow, sad chanting grew quieter and more monotonous, even subsiding completely from time to time before bursting out anew with the arrival of another mourner. I have found dirges or funeral songs among most peoples of the world, often sung by professional mourners, but I have never heard elsewhere this form of lamentation with its melancholy cadences. It sounded not at all like artificial wailing but rather an expression of grief from deep within the heart.

One day the Commissioner sent word that he had learned the efundula was to take place in a kraal not too far from our camp and that the ceremony was about to begin. At once we climbed into the truck and set off again through that terrible sand to another part of the reservation. The commissioner was still not at all sure that I would be allowed to attend or even record the ritual, but he assured me that if anyone could manage this permission, Elandi could. When we arrived near the efundula kraal, Elandi indicated that we must on no account appear until he had called on the headman and had talked with him. I tried to forget my anxiety, for I had set my heart on recording this unique and secret coming-of-age ceremony, the most important ceremony in the life of every Ovambo woman.

All about me was an unearthly silence, the sun had set, the darkness was deepening. It had been a wearying day. I dozed off for a few moments, but was shortly awakened by the throbbing of a drum. For a moment I thought it was a pulse beat in my head and throat. I jumped up, startled. The sound came persistently from the distance, drumbeats such as I had never heard before. They had the quality of a hoarse spirit voice, an eerie compulsive sound that sent an involuntary shudder through me.

Suddenly Elandi appeared out of the darkness. *"Efundula!"* he said urgently. We climbed into the truck, and the roar of the motor drowned out the beating drums temporarily. We navigated toward the ceremony by following Elandi's pointing arm, and, in the moonless night, roaring over a ribbon of sand that seemed to unwind from nowhere in the glare of our headlights, I had the strange sensation that the earth was spinning away from under me. A faint light appeared on the horizon as from a star hanging low in the blackness, and after driving for what seemed hours, we saw that the "star" was a huge fire in the center of a kraal, its light flickering through the tall, sharpened thorn-tree poles of the stockade and reaching upward into the sky.

When we stopped the truck some distance away and switched off the engine, there was a sudden silence which fell on us like a mantle as we walked toward the kraal. Where was the throbbing drum now? Where was everybody? I had been told that the whole tribe assembled in one spot from great distances for this prolonged ritual, some even coming from across the border in Angola. Elandi's face was inscrutable . . . nothing to be learned here. I followed him toward the kraal and through the entrance. Inside was emptiness and a deathlike silence. No dogs ran barking and growling to greet us, no children played, the doors to the huts hung open; only the fire was alive and cast its golden glow on a row of deserted drums. Twice Elandi walked around the fire, and I followed while he peered into several of the thatched huts. Finally he went to the kraal entrance, and his great ringing shout carried through the maze of corridors and narrow passages.

In the thick darkness beyond the ring of light, something moved in the gloom, took the shape of a man who slowly approached us. As he entered the rim of reflected firelight we knew by his dignified appearance and by the deference with which Elandi greeted him that he must be the headman of this village. His kraal, centrally located and accessible to all members of the tribe, had been chosen for the ceremony, and the permission to witness the efundula must come from him. For some time he and Elandi spoke together in low tones, gesticulating every now and then in our direction. It was not until later that we learned from Elandi that the roar of our truck and its headlights forming two unblinking golden eyes in the black night had convinced the tribe that they must have offended the spirits and that "something" was coming to ruin their sacred ceremony.

His talk with Elandi finished, the headman came to stand directly in front of me and, without speaking, stared into my eyes. I knew the significance of this ritual I wanted so desperately to record. The entire clan was present, not only the living, but, by tribal belief, all those who had gone before and those who were still unborn. I knew the power of the drums to bring the spirit world close to man for the all-important rites of puberty. Did this primitive man believe that one's eyes were the windows of the soul, and did he hope to read in mine whether I was merely there out of curiosity or had come with respect in my heart, even understanding? I returned his stare without blinking and after what seemed an interminable time he appeared satisfied. He turned away and shouted into the darkness.

At once the witch doctor approached within the ring of flickering firelight, wearing a fantastic headdress; at his heels came half a dozen drummers. At the headman's command they took up positions before their drums and beat out rhythms that summoned the rest of the tribe to return to the kraal to resume the ceremony we had interrupted. One by one they appeared: first the elders, then the younger men, then the women, and finally the pubescent girls, the chief participants of the efundula. There were twelve girls in all, ranging in age from twelve to fifteen, all about to put behind them the carefree days of childhood and be initiated into the serious lore of adult society with its responsibilities and duties.

For long years an African family prepares for this ceremony, for their daughter must be presented wearing the most beautiful regalia the family can afford. Watching the girls file past, one sensed that proud mothers had been grooming them for weeks for this supreme moment. Their hair had been built up with rancid butter and cow dung, as though sculptured out of clay, into fantastic shapes. Cowrie shells, which had both monetary value and a deeply religious significance, had been woven into their tall headdresses and the whole of the head ornamentation had been daubed with red clay. The effect was stunning, and from Elandi I learned that these headdresses were of significance as a symbol of the ritual as well as a decoration. Actually there are two: the *olende*, worn for a year before the girl's efundula, and the five-peaked *omatela*, worn after the final dance of the ceremony when she becomes a bride.

The headdresses are tended daily by the girls' mothers during the entire ritual. Eventually, after her first child is born, the whole glorious concoction is shaved off, indicating that the comely young woman has become one of the wise old married women of the tribe. But this was in the future. For the moment they were basking proudly in the full glory of maidenhood. Around their necks the girls wore numerous strings of varicolored beads and necklaces of rare and delicate shells. Like the huge, flat-coiled shells that adorned their belts and hung on strips of leather over their skirts, these were heirlooms handed down from mother to daughter, generation after generation. On arms and ankles they wore massive copper ornaments of great value, so heavy that I wondered how the girls could bear the weight of them during the hours of strenuous dancing that lay ahead. In her right hand each girl carried a switch topped with a massive plume of cowtail hair.

Perhaps the most stunning feature of the efundula costumes were the skirts. Ankle length, almost circular in width, they hung in folds that rippled with every movement, shiny as satin, exquisitely soft to the touch, and the rich brown color of ranch mink. The skins of many unborn calves had been specially treated and sewn together laboriously so that each skirt cascaded from waist to ankles in one shimmering, soft, unbroken sweep. The girls' bodies, bare to the waist, had been annointed with oil from head to toe and rubbed with red ocher mixed with fragrant spices. When they stepped in front of the fire, they seemed to glow with an opalescent light of their own, and every movement caught and reflected the red gold of the firelight on their gleaming bodies.

I gathered that our presence was being explained to the tribe by the headman, for there were curious glances in our direction. But soon we were forgotten, since not even the unprecedented presence of white people could detract from the excitement and drama of an efundula. The drummers took up their positions, stroking the heads of their instruments, tuning them at the fire, listening to the tone with bent heads. For this ceremony they used only the tall, cone-shaped drums that stood on end and had a single membrane.

The girls were being prepared by their mothers, who fussed over them, patted their hair, straightened their skirts, adjusted a bracelet or a shell ornament, and whispered last-minute instructions and encouragement. Though thousands of miles separated this scene from America, and though costumes, setting, and music were centuries removed from those of our own culture, I was nevertheless struck by the similarity between these preparations and those for a coming-out party of young debutantes in any large American city. The mothers exhibited exactly the same attitudes of pride and fussy apprehension, and for all the oil and ocher and herb scent, the jangling copper anklets and long native necklaces, these African debutantes appeared just as composed, fresh, and pretty in their own fashion as do our daughters. This drama of child becoming woman, regardless of the attendant ceremonies, is ageless, and this one in particular I found very moving.

Suddenly the drums burst forth with a surge of sound, an explosive, demanding rhythm to which the twelve initiates began to dance. They performed with the precision of a skilled *corps de ballet*. They moved first in a circle, but as the drums throbbed louder, more persistently, the circle dissolved and they advanced upon the drummers, four abreast, holding the thick cowtail switches to veil their faces and performing small intricate heel-tapping steps with a slight knee-bending motion that pivoted their hips and set their heavy skirts billowing and swirling about their young legs. It was a simple dance but precise to the point where the girls seemed to be pulled forward by the hypnotic effect of the drumming, which was now augmented by strident clanging notes produced by the rhythmic striking together of iron hoe heads. The hoe is the work tool employed almost exclusively by women in Africa, and so in this ceremony, it held a significance that was deeper than that of an ordinary musical instrument. The girls' complete concentration on the drumbeat and the long schooling in performing every part of the ritual absolutely correctly gave the impression that they danced under a spell. Perhaps they did, for there were times when the drums all but hypnotized me.

Elandi told us that throughout the efundula the girls could get only snatches of sleep, for they never knew at what moment the witch doctor's drum might summon them back for the next phase of the ceremony. There would be long periods of strenuous dancing, sometimes under the scorching sun, sometimes under the moon. They had to endure long fasts followed by elaborate feasts, suffer intense cold and heat, and by every means possible be driven to the point of exhaustion. The efundula was one continuous period of testing—an age-old trial which, if survived, proved that the maidens would make strong, healthy wives and mothers.

During these days and nights of feverish dancing and ritual I became nearly as exhausted as the initiates must have been, but I was buoyed up by an underlying excitement; I was recording and preserving this timeless ritual, never before recorded and rarely seen by white men. At one point I crept away from the dancing for a short rest and dropped onto a grass mat in a secluded corner of the kraal, shutting my eyes and wondering if I could ever stand upright again. But when the witch doctor's drum summoned the girls for a new phase of the ceremony, away I went, too. It was not only that I could not bear to lose any moment of this privilege granted me by the Ovambo, but there was something about that commanding drumbeat that could not be ignored.

Elandi's niece, Melodie, was one of the initiates: a tall, beautifully built girl, self-assured, the natural leader of the group both by her own endowments and by the high social position of her family. Melodie and I became friends, and sometimes, when I had slipped away to rest, she would send her attendant younger sister to find me. She did not want me to miss a thing. It was, in fact, Melodie who insisted that I be allowed to join in one aspect of the ceremony which I would just as soon have avoided.

Curled up on my mat in the truck one night, I was awakened by the deep resonant tones of the witch doctor's drum. I glanced at my watch; it was exactly three o'clock. The girls were being called out of their sleeping quarters in the hut of the number-one wife of the village headman, which had been turned over to them for the duration of the initiation period. Drowsy with sleep, I hurried to the hut where the girls, no less sleepy-eyed, were emerging into the cold night. (No matter how hot it may be in the daytime here on the edge of the desert, the nights can be intensely cold.) I stood shivering near the hut while the girls, moving with small shuffling steps to the beat of the drum, gathered in a circle around the squatting witch doctor, as his amazing feather headdress swayed rhythmically in the light of the fire. At his feet was a large earthen jar filled with a thick, whitish liquid. From time to time he gestured at the jar, accompanying the gestures with loud incantations. Finally he filled a gourd with the liquid and passed it to the girls. One by one they took a long drink from the gourd, and when they had all finished, Melodie made an unmistakable gesture in my direction. She was asking that I also be allowed to drink. The witch doctor eyed me sternly for several minutes during which I willed him to refuse, but to my dismay he refilled and offered me the gourd. I could not refuse, of course. With all eyes turned on me, I swallowed a little of the bitter-sour substance. Later I learned what was in it, and the contents were so horrifying that I cannot bring myself to divulge them even now.

The witch doctor performed a few more intricate gestures over the jar, and the girls then went into another dance. This was the first time that I had seen them in the compound of the headman; always before it had been in the big communal space of the kraal. As the cold early dawn dimmed the light of the full moon, the tribe began to reassemble in the kraal compound, and, with the initiates and the witch doctor, I joined them there. The girls began another dancing ritual while the old men sat, gravely intent, and the women watched, perhaps remembering their own youth when they endured this same ordeal. Small girls, younger sisters of the initiates who served as their handmaidens, no doubt dreamed, as they watched the dancers, of the time when they would be the center of attention for the few short weeks during their coming-out ritual. The young men, their minds on love and marriage, watched with lusty enthusiasm this parade of beauty as the girls swayed rhythmically, their skirts rippling in waves and their skin gleaming like burnished bronze in the firelight.

The next day brought the most vital, the most harrowing ordeal of all: the test of virginity. Some tribes do not require the girls to be virgins at the time of marriage, but the Ovambo place great emphasis upon this virtue, and woe betide the girl who cannot pass this all-important test. With his drum beating a slow rhythm, the witch doctor led the girls in single file through the narrow, twisting passages between the walls which separated the various sections of the kraal. In and out they wound with a shuffling step. As always with African dance, I had a sense of interminable time as hours of repetition, hours of swaying and stamping and gyrating preceded the climax. The barriers of time seemed to stretch into eternity.

At last the crucial moment came. The tension throughout the entire gathering was almost tangible. Even the children and the babies at their mothers' breasts were stilled and silent. It was easy to see among the onlookers which were the fathers of the dancers. Their bodies strained forward, their eyes were filled with anxiety. The expressions of the girls were set and gave no sign of emotion, but the faces of their mothers, who stood along the wall of the kraal, were openly apprehensive. The moment of testing approached as the doctor slowed the pace of the dancing line and standing aside pointed dramatically to a spot where a forked stick had been plunged into the dirt at the entrance to a passage. He then pointed to the first girl in line, my friend Melodie, and then to the stick. She had to step over the fork of the stick four times, and in doing so would declare herself a virgin. If she stepped over the stick and was not a virgin, they believed the magic stick would know and the spirits might deal out a punishment as harsh as death as a penalty for her deception.

Melodie lifted her head proudly as she moved forward and confidently executed the ritual. She was followed by the second girl, the third, and on down the line until it came to the tenth. She approached the stick with lagging feet and with a look of blank terror in her eyes. She hesitated, started twice to step over it, and then walked around it. A gasp of sharply indrawn breath rippled around the enclosure. One of the women against the wall, the girl's mother, turned her face away while the others stared with amazed disapproval. From that moment on the girl was shunned. This was the greatest disgrace that she could have brought upon herself and her family. I was told that in former days she would have been killed and her lover driven away.

Now, she had to complete her change to womanhood in a lesser ceremony—the "small-drums" ritual. Her mother was no longer allowed to groom her and her headdress; the girl had to sit apart at feasts and eat only scraps; and, worst of all, her marriage to her betrothed was canceled. If her lover refused to marry her, he would have to pay four cows; eventually a husband would be found for her, probably an old man who already had several wives and needed not love but only another servant to care for him in his late years.

As part of the efundula the girls, when not engaged in rituals or dancing, attended sessions which might be called "classes." Here the elder women of the tribe gave them sex education and made clear their responsibilities as mothers and wives. The practical went hand in hand with the psychological, and they learned the many rituals connected with planting and harvesting, with grinding meal and cooking and other sacred lore of the tribe.

One of the most significant parts of the entire ritual came at the very end and increased my respect for the wisdom of the witch doctor and the tribal customs which he enforced. After a strenuous period of dancing and drumming, starving, feasting, and testing, one afternoon I followed the girls back to the cool shelter of green boughs which served as their "dressing room" throughout the whole period. Inside, their mothers, under the direction of the witch doctor, removed their beautiful skirts and their many ornaments and scrubbed the scented oil and ocher from their bodies, covering them completely from head to toe with white wood ash, rubbing it well into their skin. Around their necks were placed phallic necklaces of small twigs, from their waists were hung skirts of sticks reaching midway between thigh and knee, and into each of their right hands was thrust a heavy hunting club.

After chanting over them for some time, evidently employing some of his most potent spells, the witch doctor dismissed them and they came charging out of the bower shouting as though the devil possessed them, wildly brandishing their clubs. The transformation of these meek and disciplined initiates astonished me. They fell at once upon the nearest group of men, beating them, snatching their weapons from them, shouting what I was told were degrading epithets, and ordering them about in a most imperious manner. Meekly the men submitted.

I sought out Elandi. "What in the world are they doing now?" I asked.

"The girls are men now," he replied, smiling. To resist an "ash girl" is strictly taboo, I learned. The ceremony in the bower had symbolically changed the girls into men, and for a month, "the time of a single moon," they could assume all male prerogatives. They could roam the countryside insulting, beating, and degrading any man in sight, especially their grooms-to-be. The men had no choice but to accept this and do their bidding. In the lead and most imperious in her manner was my gentle friend, Melodie. I could scarcely believe my eyes when I saw her grab a young hunter's spear and with menacing shouts and threats goad her future husband out of the compound.

Roaming in a band, the girl-men sang at the top of their voices: "We are men, we are men, we are men." They also took on the names of ancient tribal heroes and chanted proudly, "I am Nehemiah," etc. During this interlude they released pent-up animosity toward the male, for African women are continually subject to the whims and commands of their fathers and brothers and later their husbands. Now they could vent, for the first and last time in their lives, their resentment toward men, for after marriage, the husbands could push them around as much as they liked and even beat them when they pleased. Short as this unique display of emotional hostility is, it probably helps them in overriding some of the tribulations to follow in married life. This transformation into "men" used to be of a much longer duration prior to our visit, but the elders decided that the crops suffered if the women, the sole caretakers of the gardens, were absent too long from the work.

Following this phase of the ceremony, the girls were again taken to the dressing bower where, again under the witch doctor's supervision, their mothers washed off the white ash, annointed their bodies with oil, covered them once more with scented red ocher, and clothed them in their precious ornaments and glimmering skirts. They were then ready for the last ordeal.

At high noon, under the brassy sun in the hottest part of the day and the hottest time of the year, the girls were led to the pounding area of the kraal where the large mortars and pestles were kept. Here, under the direction of the witch doctor, every girl had to prove her expert ability in a pounding ceremony that went on for hours. This was a test not only of her physical endurance but of her skill in converting grain into meal. The witch doctor moved about inspecting their techniques carefully and critically, ceremonially pounding with each girl for a moment, indicating that they now were once again women and had to know woman's work to which they would be bound for the rest of their lives. To the rhythm of singing and drumming the girls pounded and pounded, changing the pestle from hand to hand without missing a beat. When I thought that they would surely drop from exhaustion in the merciless heat, the ritual ended. There was little doubt in my mind that after surviving the wear and tear of the past weeks these girls would make good strong wives.

The final stage of the efundula was the wedding feast. The young men had been gathering from their various villages accompanied by their best friends, leading the cattle that were the bride-price or *lobolo*. Before the feast the "best man" of each groom ceremoniously chased his friend's future bride and captured her. Tossing her on his back he ran a short distance while she beat him laughingly with a small switch. This was an amusing dramatization of the ancient practice of bride-stealing. The bridegrooms, distinguishable at the feast by their elegant plumed headdresses and cloaks of skins, were for the moment the center of attention. While the girls were being tested, they had been busy in their villages, with the help of friends and relatives, erecting splendid new huts to which they would presently bring their brides to live.

After a night of dancing during which the women were preparing the food, the final celebration took place, the feast itself, in the large outer compound near the cattle kraal. The orchestra of seven drums which accompanied the ritual dancing produced a volume of sound so stirring that there could have been little sleep for any living creature within miles of the kraal. During the feasting I saw Melodie beside her betrothed and was struck by the change that had taken place. Gone was the amazon. Here was a demure maiden proudly submissive to her handsome bridegroom. I could not call it "true love" because Africans do not enter into marriage as Westerners do. Their concern is one of tribe and family rather than emotion. Through Elandi I asked her how she had felt when she was a "man." She smiled. "It was good at first, but . . ." She did not need to finish. She glanced at her young man with such admiration it was clear that she much preferred being a woman.

The feasting over, the girls, utterly weary but wiser than before the long ceremony began, returned to their own villages with their families where they would rest until their grooms came to claim them. After simple nuptials they would be taken to their husbands' villages to live. I, too, was weary but elated at having gone through the efundula and thrilled that I had been the first to capture the ceremonial songs, the drumming that summoned the ancestors to participate in the ritual, the songs of the girls when they took the names of heroes who had become deities, and the chants begging the spirits to witness the ordeal. In this primitive ceremonial I had seen once again the eternal verity: how singing and dancing unite to bind the living members of a tribe together with their ancestors. These religious songs and dances, handed down for centuries as living art forms, establish a continuity, maintain a strong feeling of solidarity, and have a potent influence on the whole social group, binding them together with a sense of mutual spiritual harmony.

By such traditional acts, individuals, young and old, are linked with ancestors and realize their oneness with those who have gone as well as with those who are still to come. When all the excitement had subsided, the kraal seemed strangely empty. After my recording equipment was loaded onto the truck, I made a final call on the headman and the witch doctor to say good-by. It is the witch doctor who has stayed with me most clearly in memory: an old man with a wizened face and bird-bright eyes that flickered over my face with an intensity that gave me something of the same sensation as having a feather passed lightly over my skin. I found myself looking into those eyes after the ceremony with a new appreciation of the wisdom hidden behind them.

Had he not known in common with other doctors and psychologists through the ages the resentment women so often feel because of the submissive role they are expected to play in life, and the hostilities that build up from that repressed resentment? One had to come to Africa to find young girls being given the chance to release fully their aggressions on their male oppressors, no matter for how short a time. More than that, had they not been given a chance "for the time of a single moon" to find out for themselves that they were not really physically or emotionally equipped to play the dominant role in marriage?

And so while we chugged our way back across the reserve toward our own brand of civilization, they were preparing to begin with husbands an adult life, infinitely wiser and more content with their lot. I wonder whether, in our twentieth-century society, our emancipated career women have solved this problem of the sexes any better.

Chapter 12

BUSHMEN OF THE KALAHARI

According to a 1963 census, the Bushmen of South West Africa now number no more than 16,200. Probably the purest of this fast-diminishing race are to be found in Ovamboland, the Okavango, and Caprivi Strip. Those I visited were eking out a precarious living in the barren Kalahari Desert near Ovamboland on the southern border of Angola in Portuguese West Africa.

I have always regarded intelligence as the ability to adjust to one's environment, and surely the Bushman is a perfect example of this. With the coming of the white settler to South Africa, tens of thousands of Bushmen were killed in little more than two hundred years. Robert Bloom noted in his *Natives of South Africa* (1923) that "in the early days they were looked upon by the white farmers who had invaded their hunting grounds as quite untamable savages and were shot at sight."

The Bushmen were a superb race of hunters who could integrate themselves cleverly with their background. It was never known where they might be lurking, ready to discharge their poisoned arrows, and as they gave and asked no quarter, and furthermore refused to distinguish between the sheep and cattle of the farmers and the wild buck of the bushveld, it is no wonder that they were hunted down and nearly exterminated. There was no United Nations Organization in those days to whom the weak could appeal, and, like the Australian aborigines and certain American Indian tribes, the Bushmen were killed or driven to land that was of little use to man or beast. As if this were not enough, a

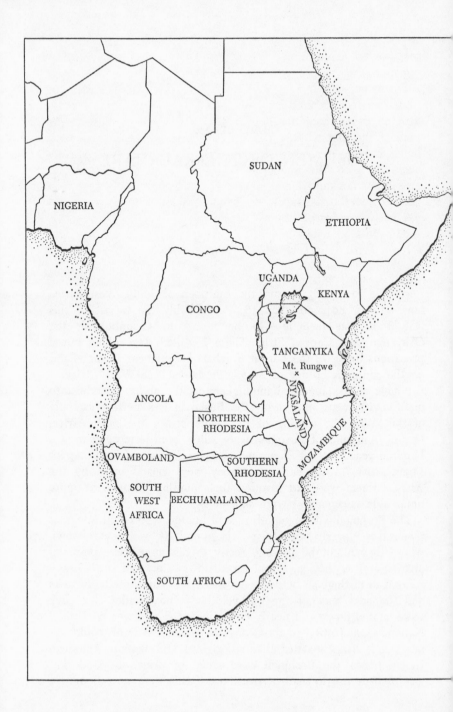

smallpox epidemic in 1951 wiped out a large number of the few remaining.

For many years it was thought that the Bushman's size, varying from four feet six inches to five feet two inches, was due to the extreme desert conditions under which he existed. But, at the time of the first white settlement in 1652, small Bushmen were living in many districts, especially the mountainous areas of the Cape Province, the Orange Free State, Natal, and Basutoland; and it was not until the beginning of this century that they were pushed into the Kalahari Desert, where I found them.

Three centuries of hostility and hybridization as the result of Bantu-speaking tribes advancing down the east coast, European settlers expanding northward and eastward from the Cape of Good Hope, and Hottentots harrying them in the hinterland left the dwindling Bushmen with only the most arid parts of the subcontinent for their home. No other tribe had managed to survive in this sandy wasteland. So, contrary to popular belief, it is only comparatively recently that the Bushman became exclusively a desert dweller. The Bushmen are no better adapted to these climatic conditions than are climatized Europeans. All scientific evidence gathered from published records, exhumed skeletons, and rock paintings indicates that the Bushman who once lived in lush areas was essentially the same anatomical being as the present Kalahari dwellers.

One point to be noted, however, is that when the Bushman adapts himself to the "agrarian revolution" of such neighbors as the Bechuana tribe, his numbers increase dramatically. Where Bushmen have taken to living on farms under more settled conditions with assured food and water and some medical protection, their children tend to develop and grow to greater stature. These are called "tame" Bushmen, and as more and more of the "wild" Bushmen become acculturated to this settled mode of living, the numbers of hunting and food-gathering Bushmen are declining.

On the University of California expedition I wanted to contact the nomadic Kalahari Bushmen who hunt in extended family groups living under the same extreme primitive conditions that have prevailed throughout their struggle for existence in this barren region. Here the Bushman is still an archer. His bow is small, and his light, fragile arrows rarely kill outright or even seriously wound game. He has therefore learned to use poison-smeared arrow tips. Lacking the broad shoulders of other tribes with which to wield strong arrows from big bows or hurl a heavy stabbing spear, the Bushman relies on his extraordinary tracking ability, smallness of build, and fleet-footedness to approach a grazing herd and make his kill. Any open cut is generally sufficient for the poison to penetrate the animal's bloodstream, but it may mean days of strenuous pursuit before the Bushman can close in on the dying animal and deliver the deathblow. I bought a bow and a quiver of arrows from one of the hunters, and I was relieved to see him carefully scrape off every bit of his precious poison into a little skin bag.

Many characteristics tend to set the Bushman apart from his neighbors. He has infantile features and beautifully small hands and feet. His nose is flat, his skin is yellowish and prone to burn easily, and both men and women in a good season develop steatopygia (great storage of fat on hips and buttocks) which sustains them in long periods of famine and child rearing and is much prized as a sign of beauty. This, scientists believe, could be an adaptive trait associated with their meager economy.

The Bushmen have perhaps provided scientists with more intense and interesting study than any other African people. Marston Bates's findings on the cultural acclimatization of the Bushman are interesting in that he believes culture not only modifies the man but also modifies the environment. The culture by which the Bushman has surrounded himself might easily have evolved as a protection against his physical environment. For instance, like his Australian aborigine counterpart, he does not build a fixed hut but erects, wherever he is, a grass-and-bough shelter as a windbreak or shade; he wraps himself in an animal skin, curling up inside, entirely enveloping himself in it as in a tent against the cold winter nights. He sleeps with his body very close to his fire, and some have even earned the nickname "gray bellies" because of the callousing of their stomach skin through overexposure to the blaze.

The Bushman treats his skin with the juices of plants and with animal fats and blood, covering it with a fine layer of sand, as protection from the sun and the scorching desert winds. In some parts an oily substance provided by a desert melon is also smeared over his body and rubbed in well, much in the same way that we use cold cream to prevent our skin from drying out.

The Bushman has a custom of killing one child or both when twins are born, and in some groups if a mother dies in childbirth her baby is buried alive with her. The "wild" Bushmen are completely nomadic and when following game or moving in a forced march to the nearest natural water source, old people who are unable to keep pace are sometimes placed in a bush shelter, given firewood, and, if there is any to spare, a little food and water. They are then abandoned. If the hunting proves good the old ones are rescued in time. If not, they die quickly, and the hyenas quickly remove all traces of the tragedy. A similar custom I was later to see repeated among the Eskimo.

The Bushman owns very little apart from his animal-skin "apron," cloak, and his bow and arrow; a small skin bag can usually hold all of his possessions. Most precious of these is the ostrich eggshell in which he stores water in a good season and which he carefully buries in the ground against cruel drought periods. He prepares the eggshell by making a small hole and sucking out its contents. This provides not only a water bottle but also a meal. I exchanged with a Bushman: his ostrich eggshell for a much desired bag of salt. I have felt guilty ever since wondering how long it took him to replace the fragile water container.

When his water supply is exhausted, the Bushman must rely on plant roots, berries, the little tsama melon, and a species of wild cucumber as well as the juices from the intestines of any game he may kill. In some areas, water, detectable only to these people of the desert, lies not too far below the surface; when such a place is discovered, the Bushman scoops out a hole and sucks the water with a "sip reed," a hollow stem of dry grass, and carefully transfers it to his eggshell bottle.

European and African farmers have moved in on the few natural permanent springs that were once the ancestral watering places of the Bushman, many of whom, driven by drought and desperation, return to these old sources in the hope of finding water, and thus make their first contact with a farming community. Finding a more secure life, they remain. Once the Bushman can be persuaded to overcome his quite understandable mistrust of a stranger, he displays a natural courtesy, charm, and high intelligence.

For far too long he has been maligned as one of the lowest forms of humanity, possessing meager awareness and no morals, gorging beside his kill until he cannot move, and understanding only "the language of the rifle." Actually Bushmen have a moral code and customs, developed and maintained through the solidarity of the family group through centuries. When Laurence and Lorna Marshall (*!Kung Bushmen of South West Africa,* 1956) asked !Kung Bushmen what kind of behavior they considered good or bad, they always mentioned sharing food as a great virtue and the greatest wrong making crooked arrows or fighting and quarreling. The Marshalls found in their myths or legends no Bushman culture hero who is glorified for fighting. "Fighting is very foolish and causes much trouble," they said. (Note: The ! in !Kung represents the sound of a clicked consonant.)

Another characteristic that holds the !Kung Bushmen closely together is the name relationship. A !Kung Bushman applies a kinship term to anyone who has the same name as himself or one of his family. There may be no blood ties, but if a man meets another who has the same name as his brother, for example, he uses the term "brother" in addressing him. No doubt it is a comfort to these people to feel the nearness and sense of belonging that the use of a kinship term gives.

The Bushman tribal organization is a loose one. Nomadic hunters in a land where game is becoming increasingly scarce, they group themselves into small bands of rarely more than twenty. This usually comprises two or three families, and although they may join other family groups in time of great need or celebration, they mostly hunt and live alone. Some anthropologists consider the Bushman to be the original inhabitants of central Africa and distantly related to the Pygmies, but isolated from all close relatives.

On my previous Angola expedition there had been a Bushman among our camp boys, but he was so shy that it was very difficult to learn from him of his people's culture. I knew something of the Bushmen from my anthropological studies, and I had taken rubbings of Bushmen petroglyphs and photographed cave paintings in Rhodesia and the Transvaal on previous expeditions. Wherever the ancient Bushmen wandered they left paintings that show an extraordinary artistic sense. Mostly the pictures are of animals, accurately and delicately portrayed, often quite beautifully tinted with root and berry dyes which have survived for centuries. One remarkable painting has been interpreted as a musical instrument.

It shows overlapping hunting bows with strings turned upward for plucking. I felt that if their art was so striking, their music must be equally significant.

Approaching the Kalahari, where we hoped to make contact with the Bushmen, I realized that no matter how frequently one returns to Africa one is never quite prepared for the assault this country makes on the senses. The sun penetrates your double felt bush hat, perspiration saturates your shirt and slacks, and the weight of the buckskin desert boots makes it difficult to move. The early desert mornings are cool, shining, and scented; the evenings are chill enough to call for a blanket on one's camp bed. But during the day in the Bushman's desert I felt as though we had stumbled into an inferno beyond Dante's imagination. As the sun climbed overhead, the earth became drained of color, the horizon shimmered and waved in the glare; and what plant life there was was stunted and leafless, dried of sap, and twisted by nature to fit this gaunt environment. It seemed almost a surprise to see any form of life here. Over everything there was the hot breath of ever-present drought, a kind of brooding silence that belongs to Africa.

There was more to adjust to than weather and scenery on this part of the expedition. There were many responsibilities as well as thrills and apprehensions to be mastered over again, just as in the past. For instance one of my assistants was a member of the fierce Herero tribe. He was dignified and appeared to be completely trustworthy, but one could not help wondering about his attitude toward us: what was he thinking in those long silences when he seemed to be contemplating us and yet looked through and beyond us? When the Germans conquered South West Africa before World War I, the Herero had resisted the loss of their lands and freedom more defiantly than the other tribes and consequently had suffered the greatest repressions and brutality. For minor infractions of the law they had their ears cut off; for major offenses they were killed. At one stage in history the Germans even placed a bounty on their heads and they were hunted like destructive animals. This happened many years ago, but such things become part of tribal lore and one wondered what inherited tribal resentments were in his heart. Although he was aware that we were American and not German, how much did such a geographic distinction counter the fact that we, too, had white skins?

Each morning of the journey as our gear was packed into the truck, I had made a quick mental check of all the equipment, reassuring myself: I counted our trunks; checked my precious recording apparatus; checked the medicine chest with its treasure trove of antitoxin for snake and scorpion bites, specifics for tetanus, ointments for sunburn, antiseptics for wounds, pills for dysentery, and medicines for almost every known tropical disease. Most of our food was in tins; we had guns and shells, barrels of gasoline and oil, spare tires and extra engine parts, and a radio to communicate with the outside world. In short, we were prepared for almost any eventuality and as safe as it was possible to be in a country hostile only because of its natural elements.

When we finally settled in the camp in Ovamboland we were near the Bushmen we had traveled far to see. We had found signs of them at the water holes in the desert, but where were they? It was obvious we must find some way to persuade them to meet us. After considerable discussion with the commissioner, it was arranged that an Ovambo interpreter from his office would go out to try to contact these desert people to tell them that we would meet them in a desert camp and buy cattle from the Ovambo tribe for a huge feast.

And so the messenger was dispatched to spread the word that in five days we would give a feast at our camp on the edge of the desert and all were invited. We had a little difficulty in persuading the Ovambo to part with the cattle, but at last, for a generous payment, they agreed and we settled down to wait to see who would come to our "party." The first group appeared, wavering like figures in a dream, through the shimmering heat of noon, advancing toward us slowly, hesitating every now and then to consult among themselves. Eventually they settled down some fifty yards away in a little circle, and looking, not at us, but out beyond us as if they knew that soon, out of that dancing wall of heat, more shadowy figures would presently appear. And they did, in groups of three or four, swelling the family circle or sitting a little apart and talking softly among themselves as if we were not there at all.

This gave us a wonderful opportunity to study them without intruding on their shyness and their privacy. All appeared to be of the same short stature with exceedingly wrinkled skin of a light yellowish or reddish-brown hue with very little facial and body hair. The short black hair on their narrow heads was clustered in tight peppercorn spirals above low foreheads. Their faces were flat and rather rectangular with high cheekbones, broad noses, and brown eyes that were little more than slits because of the prominent but un-Mongoloid eye fold. Their lips seemed to protrude slightly but were thin and quite un-Negroid. Their chins were pointed, and except where the women had developed that strange but practical physical trait of storing reserved fat in bulging buttocks and thighs, they were slender.

Most of them were naked except for a narrow skin loincloth, and we knew that they had brought with them all of their worldly belongings. Most of the men were carrying bows or spears, and on their backs were slung long quivers full of arrows. Many of the women carried children in animal skins over their hips or backs; and others unslung a soft animal-skin shawl (probably from the skin of the duiker, the smallest of the antelope family) from their shoulders and took from it such treasures as the ornamented ostrich-shell water carriers and a kind of wooden mortar and pestle which are said to be their ultimate mark of Bushman womanhood. Many of the women and young girls also carried grubbing sticks, essential for digging edible roots.

When night fell, their fires glowed all around us and dawn showed them waiting, trustingly. Eventually more than fifty Bushmen, possibly more than had been gathered in one place for many years, assembled at our camp. With our interpreter we made a formal presentation of the cattle to be slaughtered and prepared in their own way, for we knew that there were certain strict ceremonies for eating meat to be observed by the tribe. At once our camp sprang into buzzing activity. The cattle were killed and skinned by the men, while the women busied themselves collecting brushwood and sticks for the roasting fire. When the bellies of the cattle were opened, all the entrails were removed and cleaned carefully, for nothing was wasted. Bags, made from the stomachs and intestines, were filled with the blood which was used by some of the women as liquid in cooking the meat.

When the animals were cut into pieces, the men and women approached, apparently according to some fixed order, to eat or carry away different parts. The elders were given the delicacy of the livers, and long strips of meat were cut and hung to dry on branches of the low camel-thorn trees. The hide of the beasts was cut into bowstrings and sandals on the spot; bones were cracked open and the marrow eaten; and finally the heads were buried in hot coals and slowly roasted, to be eaten later. At the end of the feast, which went on for hours, only a pile of bones remained, and these would be used for crude knives and arrow tips.

We also supplied them with native beer so essential to every African ceremony (this we had brought from the Ovambo), and now, filled with food and drink, the Bushmen began to dance. They had a very keen sense of rhythm and their agility was remarkable—rhythm flowed through them. They danced exuberantly, portraying aspects of many hunts; then with a slow deliberation, using small shuffling steps, they suddenly seemed, outlined against that bleak background, like traced figures as delicately imaginative as their stone carvings and rock paintings which for so many centuries have decorated the caves of southern Africa. It was abundantly clear that they possessed an instinctive feeling for music. Indeed, the Bushman speech, with its rhythmic clicking sounds, is in itself a form of primitive music and very difficult for the European tongue.

One of their dances was the "Jackal Dance," and the women formed a semicircle and sang, establishing the rhythm by clapping hands. Into the center of the circle jumped a man representing a hyena who with grotesque writhings and gyrations, began to feed from an imaginary carcass. Other dancers, representing hungry jackals, stealthily and cunningly tried to approach the carcass but were driven off by the hyena. In the "Zebra Dance" the women clapped hands in an astonishingly realistic portrayal of pounding hoofs. For this the men wore dance rattles on their ankles made from moth cocoons, with pebbles inside; these made a soft swishing sound, providing a rhythmic accompaniment.

The "Gemsbok Dance" was more complicated musically. A dancer representing a bull gemsbok rushed about, swinging above his head a fly switch made of hair from animal tails. The gemsbok was pursued by hunters who, with rhythmic movements, pretended to shoot arrows into the animal. The wounded bull fought back in very realistic fashion, charging hunters with his horns. Finally the brave bull died and the chief hunter stood above him to announce the fact with a shrill blast on a tiny whistle made from the shinbone of an antelope.

Later in the festivities I recorded a Bushman playing on the hunting bow. A young hunter held the bowstring in front of his open lips and tapped the string with an arrow. The overtones of the vibrating string were amplified in his oral and nasal cavities, as in the case of the bow players in the Cameroons, producing various tones simply by changing the shape of his mouth. The effect was most interesting, and when accompanied by a vocal shushing sound with complicated rhythms from the surrounding Bushmen, was both melodic and stirring.

Sometimes a woman would join the dance briefly. I was able to examine closely the little rattles the women had tied to their ankles. These were made from the ears of the springbok into which had been sewn little pieces of ostrich eggshell which supplied a gentle rhythmic accompaniment to the singing. The dances were so realistic that I soon did not need a translation to follow them. I was delighted that dances so primitive and fundamental should possess such subtleties of movement and melody.

When it all ended, the Bushmen dispersed quickly to their bough shelters and their fires. I tried through my interpreter to thank them for their dancing and music for I knew how very fortunate I had been to record the unspoiled music of these people. They smiled their acceptance of my thanks, but how I hoped that they could sense the joy I had felt in sharing their intimate and ageless dances. What we had seen and recorded was more than an exuberant expression of well-being after a feast: we had been privileged for a while to glimpse a bit of the little-known mystic life of the Bushman.

Two of the young Bushmen were persuaded to accompany us back from the desert camp to our main camp in Ovamboland near the edge of the Kalahari. They were very quiet and dignified and seemed to have a constant hidden chuckle behind their calm far-seeing expression. They were extremely intelligent and alert and took in every detail of our camp. I would love to have heard the tales they took back to their people. Viewing with European eyes their change in fortune, one might imagine the Bushmen would have wished to remain with us forever—untold quantities of food, a tent to sleep in, and other luxuries they had never envisaged before; all this in return just for answering questions through our interpreter about Bushman life and culture.

One unexpected outcome of having them with us was my experiment in giving the two a stack of drawing paper and some colored crayons. I was fascinated to find that the subjects they elected to draw were precisely the same as those in the paintings I had photographed years earlier, especially in the caves of Rhodesia—giraffe, antelope, and ostrich. They also drew a Bushman with his bow and what they probably considered pure inspiration, a thing with wheels for which our truck was clearly the model. The forms of the animals, however, were almost identical with those done so many centuries ago, and although these young men had practically the whole range of color to choose from, their preference was for the browns, reds, ochers, and oranges found in early Bushman paintings.

My most treasured and poignant memory of this all-too-short time with the Bushmen happened on the last evening they were with us in Ovamboland. Most of the camp was asleep. The fire threw its golden circle in the velvet night and the stars were so intensely bright that they seemed to blaze with life just over my head. The thorn trees stood in silhouette against this brilliant canopy and the air was soft and cool, making it hard to picture our friends moving off the next day at first light into the scorching furnace of the midday desert sun. But for the moment there was such utter peace that I lingered, reluctant to break the spell. Toward midnight, as usual, we tuned the short-wave radio to the nightly broadcast of music from Leopoldville, hundreds of miles away in the Belgian Congo. Turning the dial, I heard the stirring strains of a symphony. Resting in my camp chair just outside the fringe of firelight, I leaned back and let the music transport me far away.

I could not at first believe what presently I saw. Forms moved from the darkness into the light of our campfire against the backdrop of dark thorn trees. It was the Bushmen moving softly toward me out of the night, silently, stealthily, with movements usually associated with one animal stalking another. My body grew tense, in anticipation, but I soon realized that what had drawn them from the darkness was the radio several feet distant from me. With a shuffling, soundless dance step they moved circling past me, completely absorbed.

I wondered what they were feeling listening to the music, and as if in answer to my question they began to dance. Perhaps they danced in ancient ritual; perhaps they improvised as they went along. I only know that for me in that stupendous moment they danced to this symphony exactly as it should be danced to, with a profound primeval reverence. It was Beethoven's Ninth, the setting of Schiller's "Ode to Joy," in which he proclaimed the brotherhood of all men everywhere.

The Bushmen danced the Beethoven to the very end. Only when the last notes faded in the air did they turn and like smoke before a gusty wind vanish into the night. Quickly I got up and turned off the radio lest the announcer's voice shatter the beauty of the moment. Alone in the silent night I remembered that Beethoven had once written: "Let this music go from the heart to the heart."

Chapter 13

ALBERT SCHWEITZER:
TWENTIETH-CENTURY SAINT

At last in 1956 I was able to accept Albert Schweitzer's invitation
to visit his hospital at Lambaréné and to record the music of
that area of Africa. Nearly ten years earlier he had urged me
to come, as he put it, "before it is too late." I knew full well
what he meant, for it had become increasingly difficult in modern
Africa to find truly indigenous music, so great was the influence
of the West through radio, records and movies. As I was on my way
to spend a year in Asia recording music of the oriental religions, I
decided to cross Africa on my way to India in order to visit in
Lambaréné.

The African sun beat down on our pith helmets as the large
pirogue in which I rode through the yellow waters of the Ogowe
River carried us closer to Dr. Schweitzer's hospital at Lambaréné.
I was accompanied by Mlle Neff, a tall, strong, cheerful Dutch
nurse who was sent by Dr. Schweitzer to the river landing near
the airport to escort me down the river. Our canoe was manned
by four energetic patients from the hospital's leper village who
chanted as they paddled to keep time, "Yah-nyah, hay-nyeh—
hyneeeeeeen-hay"!

The paddlers kept close to shore, following the channel. As we
slowly progressed, we occasionally met other pirogues on their
way to and from market, and our headman in the bow called
out greetings. White clouds and magnificent *okoume* trees were
reflected in the river, while the tips of waving palms brushed the
waters. A green parrot in a tree squawked at a kingfisher which

dived near us, and bright birds darting above us merged with the beauty of land, water, and sky.

It was about four-thirty in the afternoon when the oarsmen with a final spurt of energy sped the pirogue onto the beach at Lambaréné, ending my trip which had begun on a small plane from Brazzaville at dawn that morning. Walking down to meet me was the doctor in his informal Khaki trousers and white shirt open at the throat. With him were Mrs. Schweitzer and several nurses dressed in white, all wearing pith helmets.

After a brief chat with the Schweitzers, Mlle Neff escorted me to my room to rest until dinner, where I found tea with wafers and hot water for a bath awaiting me. Having visited numerous African hospitals and rest camps, I would not have been surprised to have found an earthen floor, adobe walls, and thatched roof. On the contrary, my room was snowy white and orderly, located in a long building similar to the one in which the Schweitzers lived, built on piles as protection against river floods and torrential rains that swept down the hillside during the long wet season. I entered through a screen door; across the room was a large screened window with a sweeping view overlooking treetops on the hillside, the hospital roofs below, and the river beyond. The room—with its bed, small writing table, chair, improvised cupboard, washstand, small chest of drawers, and oil lamp—was vacant while a nurse was home on leave.

Promptly at seven came the clanging sound of the improvised gong made of two sections of railroad track, hung outside the dining-hall window. The twenty-seven staff members presented a pleasant picture in the glow from the four kerosene lamps set at intervals down the center of the long dining table. The hearty meal was delicious and included vegetable soup, wild-buffalo meat, eggplant, avocados, bread hot from the oven, and a large tray of bananas which I later learned were a part of every meal. Best of all was the raw salad. Here was one of the few places in Africa I would dare touch uncooked vegetables. At that time Dr. Schweitzer ate a meager dinner of fresh tomatoes and eggs.

He prided himself on growing practically every fruit and vegetable which could flourish in this land of heavy humidity and burning sun. His remarkable gardens fed the entire staff. It was his delight to serve newcomers a novel food at each meal, and as he passed breadfruit to me he asked eagerly: "Have you ever

tasted *that* before?" He seemed a little disappointed when I said
yes. My familiarity with the various dishes defied his ingenuity,
and it became a sort of game at each meal for him to challenge
my experience with a gleam of mischief. Finally one day I ad-
mitted I had never tasted the strawberry guava (a special guava),
he offered me. He seized the chance to retort teasingly, "You must
have stayed all your life in cities!"—knowing full well I was on my
nineteenth expedition. It was this mischievous spirit coupled with
his firm authority, his understanding and kindness that endeared
him to his workers, helping them perform their relentless load of
duties.

At dinner the conversation in French and German was sparked
by Dr. Schweitzer's witty banter. All expressed warm interest in my
work and made me feel welcome and at home. The staff was almost like a little United Nations, speaking Swiss, Dutch, German,
Danish, French, and English. The general conversation at table
was carried on in French. I gave Dr. Schweitzer news from Dr.
Emory Ross, treasurer of the Schweitzer Fellowship in New York
City, from Dr. Eugene Exman of Harper, publisher of many
of his books, from Dr. Charles Joy, his translator, and from
other mutual friends whom I had seen just before leaving America.

When we had finished, he stood up, announced in German a
hymn, walked over to an ancient upright piano, and played the
broken ivories with such reverence and tenderness that it could
have been a concert grand. Later I tried to coax a tune from this
well-worn instrument, only to discover that some keys struck while
others made no sound, but these defects were minimized by the
doctor's skilled and knowing fingers. Back at the dinner table he
read in French from the Bible the parable of the seeds sown in
good and barren soil, concluding the daily evening service.

Dr. Schweitzer then retired quietly to a small table in a far
corner of the dining hall, as usual, to provide an opportunity for
any staff member troubled with a hospital or personal problem to
discuss it with him. His massive head with its thick, tousled iron-
gray hair, bushy brows, and walrus mustache was caught in the
light from a kerosene lamp nearby. Mrs. Schweitzer invited me to
a big table in another corner of the room where we had mint
tea with the nurses. Without appearing to watch, I was irresistibly
compelled to observe the scene.

Shortly the other two doctors whom I had met at supper joined
Dr. Schweitzer to discuss a patient. Both doctors were Dutch, one
a dark-haired young man with a handsome, intellectual face and
the other a young woman with her blond hair in a ponytail. Dr.
Schweitzer's elbows were leaning on the red-and-white checked
tablecloth, his head resting on his hands, his eyes lowered as he
listened with an expression of complete concentration, wholly immersed in the problems of the patients and deeply involved in
the suffering of each. Although we were supposedly absorbed in
our own conversation, it was impossible to be unaware of his
presence.

His consultation ended, Dr. Schweitzer joined us briefly, weary
and distraught not only by the pressing cases in the hospital but
by an outside problem as well. He had to go to the local administration the first thing in the morning to attend to a new rule about
cards of identity, a bothersome business. In spite of the late hour
the day's chores were not yet over, and soon the staff disappeared
to jobs including accounts, correspondence, and translations. Certain nurses cared for the sick, others had the duties of housekeeping, gardening, and tending the chickens, sheep, and goats. In
their devotion to *le grand docteur* all were eager to protect him
as much as possible from minor cares involved in maintaining the
hospital community of between three and four hundred patients
and staff members in approximately forty buildings on 220 acres
of land.

Dr. Schweitzer left the dining room for the desk in his office
to begin his evening's work. Mlle Mathilde Kottmann, a tall, au-
thoritative woman with an aristocratic mien, who had been a nurse
at Lambaréné from the early days (1924) of the hospital, told me:
"His light is the last to go out every night. He becomes so absorbed
he would work until morning unless one of us rapped on his door
and reminded him, 'It's midnight, Dr. Schweitzer.'" Mlle Mathilde's
long devotion made her a watchdog intent on quietly guarding Dr.
Schweitzer and preventing him from wasting his strength. "He is
so busy, he is so tired, and he has so much to do."

Life at the hospital started promptly at six-thirty in the morning,
and as I awakened I heard the noise of goats, sheep, and chickens
released to wander over the hills during the daytime. The gong
sounded for breakfast at seven-thirty on the dot. Throughout my
stay I was impressed by Dr. Schweitzer's insistence on promptness

in every activity, which kept the hospital operating with factory precision. Not one minute was wasted by anyone, and the staff accepted this discipline cheerfully because of their devotion to him and their dedication to their work.

Certain strict rules were adhered to by all at the hospital, even guests. First, you had to wear a pith helmet outdoors during daylight hours. I think I would have been sent home if I had arrived without one, but fortunately when I visited Robert McGregor, our American Consul General in Leopoldville in the Belgian Congo, his wife lent me hers. I have always preferred a double felt terai in the jungle to the much heavier pith helmet. Like everything else this rule was for our own good, as Dr. Schweitzer insisted that even a few minutes of that African sun on the head of a white person could result in severe stroke. A second rule was that all lanterns were lighted at six-thirty in the evening, and from then until morning you were not to step out of your door without a lantern in your hand. If you should stumble in the dark and fall because you did not carry a light, it was practically a crime. A third ironclad rule was that you had to move very briskly when you went through a screen door and shut it as fast as possible so that not one mosquito could accompany you, for all the rooms were carefully screened with mosquito wire mesh as a protection against malaria.

Hospital regulations were explained to me by Mlle Emma Haussknecht the famous nurse who had lectured on Dr. Schweitzer's work in the United States and who was still at Lambaréné though very ill. She had come to Africa from Alsace-Lorraine in 1925. The gentleness and understanding of this serious, intelligent, blond woman with her fine sense of humor counteracted any feeling of severity in the strict routine. Somewhere along the way to Lambaréné I had picked up a germ that led to a tropical intestinal disorder which fortunately did not disable me, but caused considerable discomfort. I confided this to Mlle Emma, to whom I took all my problems. She in turn arranged for Mlle Marie, a dark, wiry, and efficient Dutch nurse to give me a thorough examination. Mlle Marie promptly prescribed some very big pills that proved so potent I was better in a couple of days.

After Dr. Schweitzer had left for the government office to attend to the business of the identity cards, Mrs. Schweitzer invited me to sit with her as she did each morning for a chat and a fresh fruit drink on her veranda. The long building where they lived was the first dwelling quarters erected when the hospital was established on this site. The end room nearest the hospital was Dr. Schweitzer's study-office-bedroom, where he wrote many of his great philosophical works that have had such a powerful influence on the lives and thoughts of people all over the world. Next to his office was a small, narrow room jammed with his books and the famous piano presented to him by the Paris Bach Society. The other rooms in the building were occupied by Mrs. Schweitzer and some of the nurses.

The long, narrow veranda where we sat overlooked a clearing. "Many things happen on the clearing," my hostess said. "It is here that the Africans are called to receive their food rations and the ambulatory patients are given their medical doses." We spoke of the beginning of the hospital in 1913, and she discussed her early work here as well as her experience as a teacher in England before her marriage. In spite of the time that had passed, she was still a beautiful woman with merry eyes, a gentle and assured manner, and the clear, waxen complexion of those who live in Africa protected by pith helmets with skin never touched directly by the dangerous sun. Mrs. Schweitzer had returned to Lambaréné only recently and she spoke of her joy at being back after a long period in Europe due to illness.

Dr. Schweitzer came back unexpectedly from his business, annoyed by the fact that three of the six officials were out and he would be forced to make the trip again the next day. He invited me to walk with him. Not far from the hospital an African was trimming the branches of a palm tree with zeal, throwing the fronds to the ground in wild disorder. Dr. Schweitzer stopped to survey the lack of organization, leaned over and arranged the fallen branches in a neat row, then stood up to reproach the man in vigorous tones: "Can't you be more orderly? Do you want people to think you are a savage?" The African smiled warmly and resumed his pruning with greater neatness.

We walked along a path through the forest of tall trees to the top of a high hill, passing the small mission cemetery. "Come, let's sit here," Dr. Schweitzer said and motioned to a wooden bench. We looked out over the river through breadfruit, grapefruit, orange, mandarin, mango, and palm trees all carefully planted under the personal supervision of the doctor. We talked of his work briefly, then directed the discussion to my interests, but he was careful to make the point that to him example was everything. And in retrospect, the most meaningful thing I took with me from my visit was the experience of seeing him, by example, live his principles of love and reverence of life.

He did not take me to the leper village that morning but later assigned Mlle Marie to be my guide there. A forest path led us to the leper colony, which was separated from the hospital by a quarter of a mile of dense tropical growth. The straight and neat buildings were erected by Dr. Schweitzer with his Nobel Prize money. The happiness and hope in the lepers' faces were in marked contrast to my first visit in a leper colony more than twenty years before. Then, little could have been done for these wretched people, and their helpless condition had made me violently ill. I felt no such hopelessness in Lambaréné.

"Dr. Schweitzer personally measured the buildings with a carpenter's square to be certain of correct angles and proportions, and with his own hands, aided by African workers, constructed them," Mlle Marie told me. "If he left it to the Africans," she said, "he would have African houses—charming but a bit lopsided. There are from two hundred to two hundred fifty leprosy victims here most of the time. We now have one hundred twenty men, sixty women, and ten children living in the village." The buildings faced each other, with neat narrow streets between, and included a chapel, a pharmacy, a storeroom, a laundry, a main kitchen, and a temporary construction house.

A cheerful nine-year-old boy, his intelligent face wreathed in smiles though he was permanently crippled by the disease, hobbled up to us on crutches. Mlle Marie stopped to chat with him and learned he was on the way to the woodcarver with whom he would spend the morning working. After he departed, Mlle Marie explained to me that he had been "left" on the shore in the middle of the night by relatives, as many of the leprosy patients were. "He keeps occupied and happy," she said. "Every one in the leper village is busy. Those who are not well or strong enough to go outside find duties here, but those whose leprosy is in a relatively inactive state are permitted to paddle the pirogue, work in the garden, trim the trees, or perform other tasks as they are able. Some of the former patients who are now cured, but bearing marks of the disease, remain at Lambaréné since it is difficult for them to return to the outside world." I became so interested in the life of their village and in certain patients that I walked over the hill every day to visit them with no more hesitation or dread than I would have felt at entering any hospital.

I presented Dr. Schweitzer with checks for this hospital and with a case of drugs sent by a New York doctor, which I had packed in a leather case. Dr. Schweitzer bowed his massive iron-gray head, silently thanking God before speaking aloud, a gesture typical of the man which I observed many times. Then he said, "You are much too kind," deeply pleased and moved that I had brought further help for his work in Africa. He seemed equally grateful for gifts large or small. We discussed his writings, and he explained that he was so occupied at the hospital that he had very few moments to spare for his own manuscripts. He was still struggling to pen brief answers to the thousands of birthday letters he had received the preceding January. Formerly he wrote every letter in its entirety, but more recently he had been persuaded by the nurses to permit them to assist with his voluminous correspondence. However, he always added in his own handwriting a personal note of greeting and gratitude. He said that he was so constantly besieged by requests for articles, prefaces to books, and special messages of many kinds that for two months he had not touched the four major works he was then writing.

I had with me a small New Testament bound with the Psalms, printed on India paper with a pliable leather cover, light to carry. It has gone round and round the world with me for years. I suggested that it would make me most happy if he would be willing to write on the flyleaf his favorite verse from the Bible. When he returned my Testament I was not surprised to see that he had written in his exquisite meticulous handwriting as his favorite text I Corinthians 13:13: "And now abideth faith, hope, charity, these three; but the greatest of these is charity."

He also insisted on returning to me the leather case in which I had brought the medicines, a strong, useful case I had had made on a former trip to India. He accepted the medicines with joy but he would not accept the gift of the bag. "Never give anything you value to an old person who might die tomorrow. Someone strange would then have it and would not appreciate it."

At another time Dr. Schweitzer and I went to Mlle Alida's room, where I read a brief portion of my manuscript to answer his questions about the nature of a book I was writing. He listened with deep concentration; his suggestions were penetrating and extremely helpful. His final comment was: "Don't have a preface or an introduction, just begin! I used to tell my theology students: 'Write an introduction to your sermon but when you get in the pulpit, tear it up! An introduction is like soup before a good dinner; nobody really wants it.'"

From time to time he stroked the tiny pet antelope, popularly called "dik-dik" (a small duiker), which Mlle Alida had adopted. This delicate animal was one of the many pets brought to Lambaréné by Africans who knew of Dr. Schweitzer's fondness for animals and birds. From time to time I could feel the dik-dik's tongue against my hand as it licked the salty perspiration, always plentiful in Africa. Innumerable cats and dogs, several parrots, antelopes, a baby fawn, a baby gorilla, a chimpanzee, and even a porcupine were part of the animal population at the time of my visit.

At breakfast the next morning an amusing conversation took place in connection with the word "sensible," developing from the fact that in French the word of this spelling means "sensitive," while in English the same word means "practical." The French phrase used for illustration was "une femme sensible." His wife gave the English version, "a sensible woman." Dr. Schweitzer with a merry twinkle in his eyes asked in French, "Does such a one exist?"—this proved that although he refused to speak English he understood it fairly well. He left the dining hall, his shoulders shaking with quiet laughter, mischief in his eyes, very pleased with his little joke.

Soon four Frenchmen arrived, loaded with cameras, to see the hospital. There were many sight-seers and all wanted to meet Dr. Schweitzer. He chatted with the Frenchmen graciously for a short while before assigning them to Mlle Rosalie for the "tour," but he told me later he would have liked to discourage the constant stream of unnecessary visitors because of the drain on his time and strength.

Mlle Emma arranged for me to go to the Protestant Evangelique Mission at Andende on the Ogowe River, where I wanted to make recordings of African music and to see where Dr. Schweitzer had lived and worked his first year in French Equatorial Africa while clearing a forest site for the hospital at Lambaréné. Since the mission head was away, a young French teacher met me at the pirogue and escorted me up the hill to the house where the director's wife received me cordially. She served an appetizing luncheon with fresh antelope meat brought by a grateful patient. A tour of the mission included visiting classrooms, gardens, and workshops. We made plans for a recording session a few days later.

On my second visit to the mission I went to the boys' schoolhouse, a simple frame structure consisting of several rooms, one of the buildings scattered over the mission compound. Gathered together waiting impatiently was an excited group of about twenty young students. Most of them were dressed in clothes made by the African tailor at the mission, the boys in cotton shorts and shirts, some white, some checks or prints, and the girls in dresses of vivid colors and exotic designs. A few of the younger children came wearing a strip of brightly printed cotton wrapped around and knotted under one arm. The students ranged in age from nine to twenty years, and a few were accompanied by relatives, curious to see and hear the strange machine that captured their voices.

A young African teacher, very dashing in his long white trousers and white shirt, translated my French for the musicians. His intelligent though serious face frequently broke into a broad smile and he was obviously highly popular with the students. Followed by the group he took me to a sizable classroom for the recording. On two sides of the room were unscreened windows, while a blackboard with a few words written in French ran the length of a third wall faced by rows of benches. As there was no electricity to operate my recording machine, several strong boys brought heavy-duty batteries from the mechanic's shed where they were used to run mission equipment. All of this took some time, as we discovered one battery needed recharging, and there was a scramble to locate a substitute. While this was in progress, the students chatted eagerly in their own tongue and examined with interest my Magnecorder in two black cases which I had placed one above the other, on a table.

At last all was in order. The musicians sat or squatted on the floor with their instruments. The xylophone consisted of staves, or keys, cut from the hard, resonant wood used for all their musical instruments. They were fastened together with native string and attached to a wooden framework. There were about fifteen staves of graduated sizes from short ones for the high notes to long ones for the bass. The xylophone rested on banana stalks, which served as resonators, freshly cut and dripping with sap. It was similar to the type I had recorded in British Central Africa some years earlier which I had taken back with me to America and exhibited at the Carnegie Museum.

Two boys sat on the floor facing each other to play the xylophone. One was clad in his cotton school shorts and shirt while the other, who had been working in the garden, wore the familiar strip of calico. Each used two beaters, short sticks with local rubber balls on the ends, and they handled them with grace and dexterity, producing delicate and charming music. After recording several xylophone solos they added drum accompaniment; later I recorded drum solos with complex rhythms.

The drum was conical and beautifully carved. The lower surfaces where the wood was gouged out left the natural light color exposed, while the higher surfaces were blackened for contrast and to emphasize the geometric patterns of the carving. The small end resting on the ground was about one foot in diameter, while the drumhead measured approximately eighteen inches across. It was tuned by twisting the wooden pegs which attached the drumhead of antelope skin to the wooden body. Some of the finest drummers in the Gabon are found in a village near the school, and I was told that Dr. Schweitzer sometimes had to have "palaver" with the chief about the drumming which kept his patients awake. The young drummer threw himself into the music with abandonment. It was fascinating to watch his fingers fly as he beat out the fast rhythms, playing on different parts of the drumhead to get different tones, using various parts of the hand—the palm, the heel, or the fingertips—as needed. He was a handsome boy with well-shaped ears, a small, straight nose, and not-too-thick lips—features not uncommon in this part of West Africa. Unlike some of the others he did not wear new school clothes but was simply dressed in an old faded khaki shirt and shorts patched on one leg. His excitement grew greater and greater as he drummed, until he became so warm that he threw off his shirt, revealing a strong young body all muscle without an ounce of extra fat. Everyone swayed and kept time to the music. I recorded their songs, also. The boys' voices were deep and resonant; the girls', high and shrill, childish and very appealing. They sang, as usual in Africa, in parts, the melodies moving along in parallel lines.

I was far from ready to leave when the pirogue boys, looking worried, appeared at the door and said, "We must go. A storm comes." This was February, "the little dry season," with frequent thunderstorms usually in the afternoon or early evening. As we paddled away from the mission, the boys' choir started rehearsing in the church for the next Sunday's service, and their clear young voices were wafted to us over the waters. The storm broke with startling suddenness. The high winds whipped the whitecaps on the river and the waves foamed onto the shore. We hugged the shoreline, following the channels, as palm branches broke off all around us, striking our small pirogue. As the wind whipped about us we stopped with a jolt, stuck on a sandbar, and I wondered with horror whether we were stranded here for the night. Two of the boys jumped into the churning Ogowe and waded and pushed, while the other two pulled with the oars until we were free and finally made our way out into the stream again.

When we reached the hospital Mlle Alida with her pet chimpanzee, Fritzle, was standing on the beach watching for us, extremely upset. I had survived so many tempests and strenuous journeys throughout Africa that I had not realized they would worry and I was amazed and distressed to see how concerned Mlle Emma was when I called in her room. They took word at once to Dr. Schweitzer of my safe arrival.

At dinner he was delighted to see me back safe and sound. I told him that the French missionary's wife had sent her salutations. Dr. Schweitzer turned to his wife and asked in French, "Her what?" Mrs. Schweitzer repeated in French, "Salutations." Dr. Schweitzer with a twinkle in his eyes grunted and said, "What can you do with salutations? Why didn't she send eggs?"

I was touched that he should remember, in spite of his heavy burden of duties, to invite me for some music every day. "Because," he said, "you are a musician." He asked me to sit by him on the long wooden bench before his special piano, zinc-lined as a protection against termites and dampness, and equipped with organ pedals. Usually for a full half-hour he played. I was stirred by the purity of his Bach. From time to time the music would stop and he would talk at length of the importance of playing Bach so that each tone is absolutely clear and distinctive: "Always listen to the inner voices in Bach's music," he said. "Each voice lives its life dependently and independently at the same time, each voice must be allowed to sing out its own beauty." The same philosophy he applied to life. Each of us, while independent, is also dependent on others; we must express our own degree of harmony with life, always recognizing responsibility toward all life.

As I had formerly studied organ, we discussed both the resources of the instrument and organ building. When he resumed his playing, I was fascinated that he could turn so quickly from animated conversation to complete concentration. During my entire visit I was impressed by this faculty for deep absorption that he gave to everything he did from planting a tree to choosing a photograph for the *carte d'identité* required by the government. His grasp of the music was so profound that it more than compensated for the toll that age had taken from his technique. His small brown and white dog came into the room and lay close beside us, his ears raised attentively, and through the window I could see the pet antelopes, in their pen nearby, stop feeding and press their noses against the chicken-wire enclosure to listen.

Following dinner on my last evening at Lambaréné, Dr. Schweitzer invited me to his study for a long conversation in German with his wife as interpreter. His study expressed his austere simplicity and dedication to work; there was nothing luxurious or superfluous in the small, crowded room. His desk was a plain, unvarnished table which he had made, and although termites had eaten long tunnels in the wood, he still cherished it. The top was covered with unanswered letters, papers, and books, while behind were shelves holding neat piles of completed chapters of his manuscripts.

The next morning Mlle Emma told me that ten-thirty would be ample time for our departure, but Dr. Schweitzer said we must leave at ten. Mlle Alida came to take me to Mlle Emma to sign in the guest book. Although very ill, Mlle Emma was busy organizing details for those who would carry on when she left for Europe, perhaps realizing she would never return. Back in my room Mlle Marie brought me more of the big pills to take with me as that bug had become active again. Just before the pirogue arrived, Mlle Emma and Mrs. Schweitzer served tea in the dining hall with bread, cheese, and meat, knowing it would have to be lunch for me also as I would find no more food available until I reached Brazzaville that night.

Dr. Schweitzer came to the dining hall for me, and he, Mlle Mathilde, and several nurses walked with me along the path to the pirogue. Until we were well out of sight he stood at the river, simple, sincere, unaware of his greatness, with the hospital and the forest and the Africans at his back, a saint in a helmet waving me good-by.

Section II

THE EAST

Chapter 14

THE PAGEANT OF INDIA

For a long time afterward, although Dr. Schweitzer was far away, his presence was constantly projected across time and space to fill my thoughts and feelings. My mind was so permeated with the spirit that surrounded him like an aura that I approached my year of continued work and travel in the Orient with a sense of regeneration, a new strength, an inner peace, an inspiration for truer dedication.

On the day I had left Lambaréné, Dr. Schweitzer had asked me to carry his warm greetings to Nehru, a task I regarded as a real privilege. I knew Nehru from my first visit to India in 1949, when I had been a guest of the government soon after the country's independence had been declared. I had enjoyed the cordial hospitality of the Prime Minister and the governors throughout India at that time, and I looked forward to renewing my friendship with both Nehru and the country. I was well aware of the terrible problems that Nehru had faced as the leader of a new country and of the amazing progress his people had made under his guidance by 1956.

But when he heard, upon my arrival in New Delhi, that I carried word from Dr. Schweitzer, he would not speak of his problems or successes; he wanted only to discuss Dr. Schweitzer—his health, his hospital, his ideas, his greatness of spirit. Dr. Schweitzer and Nehru had for some time been corresponding, exchanging views on peace, philosophy, and world problems. Dr. Schweitzer's admiration of Gandhi had endeared him to Nehru, and without ever having visited India, the great doctor had a deep understanding of the mind and spirit of Gandhi and of his disciple Nehru.

During this 1956 visit I saw all about me the advances the new India had made guided by the tireless and single-minded Nehru. One of the biggest problems he faced during my first visit had been the rehabilitation of six million Hindu refugees from Pakistan as a result of partition, one million from East Pakistan alone. This multitude, who had left their homes and all possessions behind, had to be settled anew and provided with shelter, food, clothing, and work.

I had learned of their insecurity and fear of Moslem rule first-hand on my initial visit in late 1949 for I had entered India at Calcutta, where Hindus at the rate of thousands a day were pouring into the city from East Pakistan, traveling by whatever means they could: plane, or oxcart, but mostly on foot. I could not have arrived at a worse time and my first impressions of India were not happy ones.

I shall never forget the drive from the airport to my hotel. Bodies were sprawled all over the roadsides—men, women, little children, sleeping wherever there was enough room for a body to spread itself. Staggering aimlessly among them were wretched cows with great limpid brown eyes, the bones all but protruding through their hides. Because they were "sacred" no one could put them out of their misery, even though many of them were too old and ill to move. And I can still see one old woman with her frail body bent nearly double between the shafts of a heavily loaded wagon she was hauling along a deeply rutted road. We even had to pick our way over sprawling bodies to enter the hotel, which was in the center of the city.

I spent a fitful night, tortured by the misery and suffering about me, oppressed by the heat, and worried that at any moment my room might be filled with monkeys. I had been warned not to leave anything out on my dresser, especially anything bright or attractive, for monkeys came in from the trees in the nearby *maidan*, a great open parklike space, and stole anything that amused them. As it was too hot to sleep with the windows shut, I woke every hour or so to assure myself that the room was not full of uninvited creatures.

I was roused before dawn by a loud chanting outside. Rushing to the window, I saw hundreds of people milling about below. I dressed quickly and went down to inquire what ceremony was going on, hoping, of course, to record something of it.

Rather than a ceremony, I learned it was the one day in the Indian year when all the beggars come out. If they cannot grope, hobble, or crawl by themselves unaided, they are brought to the maidan by friends or relatives. The space was packed—the halt, the lame, the blind—a more pitiful array of human misery the mind can scarcely conceive. People came and went, milling around, giving alms, making much of the mendicants, for on this day beggars are encouraged, in order that people more fortunate may give generously to them, thereby "making merit" (as they say) for future incarnations.

My Indian friends agreed that for forming first impressions my arrival in their country could not have occurred at a worse time. But as I began to move around the country, I found India fascinating, and then happy experiences more than offset my original misgivings. Everywhere I went in India, I received not only generous and often lavish hospitality, but also invaluable help in gaining access to remote places to record rare music and religious rituals, some of them never previously seen and recorded by an outsider.

While the guest of the Maharaja of Bhavnagar, then the Governor of Madras, at the summer capital at Ootacamund, I was able to make unique and valuable recordings with the Todas, a fast-disappearing tribe in the Nilgiris, the Blue Hills of southern India. Here was music seldom if ever before heard by an outsider, for the Todas' rituals were secret and profoundly sacred.

When planning to visit the Todas I was aware, that they lived in very inaccessible country, but it proved a longer and more difficult journey than I had expected, even by car; when the road finally ran out, there was still a long and arduous trek on foot. It was a beautiful day, however, and when we finally reached the village of Nars, a priest (the Kiodhr) of the Toda tribe came to greet me. His name was Morgudn, and I can see him now walking through the sunshine with that slow grace and dignity with which so many oriental priests seem to be blessed, his toga-like garment blowing in the wind, his face bright with his smile of welcome. His greeting, too, was memorable: "Our Blue Mountains are smiling today. We are blessed with good weather for your visit."

My Toda guide and interpreter, Mustoe, paid his respects to the ancient patriarch with the characteristic Toda salutation. Kneeling before the holy man, Mustoe lifted the priest's left foot from the ground, reverently touched it to his own forehead, then with the right foot repeated the gesture before rising from his knees.

I worked for about a month among these people and grew to love and admire them. The few remaining Todas live above the scorching heat of the plains, at an altitude of seventy-five hundred feet on a plateau of rolling, golden downs surrounded by misty blue hills. At the beginning of the century there were nearly a thousand of them, but the impact of Western culture and the changes it brought had affected them seriously, and they were gradually becoming extinct. When I was there in 1949, I was told there were thirteen deaths and only five births reported that year: the tribe numbered less than four hundred. Outside influences sweeping across their tribal territory were affecting their spirit; the loss of precious grazing land for their sacred buffalo was tragic; and only about two hundred acres had been left to the tribe for raising food, principally potatoes, one of their staples.

Another disrupting factor was that some sort of home-distilled liquor had always been regarded as essential to every native ceremonial, and although the Indian Congress declared that prohibition laws would not apply to tribal ceremonies, certain reformers tried to enforce these regulations, thus depriving the hillmen of a valuable tonic and stimulant.

The Todas are beautiful people, aristocratic, intelligent, notable for their honesty, frankness, and humor, and possess great dignity and a winning simplicity. As a tribe they are of special interest to the anthropologist for their highly ritualized buffalo cult and for the practice of polyandry, the custom of a woman having more than one husband. In the latter regard, the woman takes as husbands the brothers and close male relatives of the man she marries. This custom is found in tribes in which there are more men than women and the men are absent from home for considerable periods of time. In the case of the Todas, men must go far afield to graze the buffalo herds. The practice with this tribe does not seem to me to be a successful one as the Todas are steadily diminishing in number. In my travels I have found polygamy far more common than polyandry.

Both Toda men and women wear heavy, white, homespun garments with brilliantly colored borders, thrown over the shoulder like Roman togas, which hang in thick folds to the ground. The men, though they are strong and agile, speak with soft, gentle voices and a charming intonation. They have long, thin, well-shaped noses, full lips, and luxuriant beards; they never shave, and their wavy black hair falls in a ring of soft curls following the contour of their heads. The women spend much of their time dressing their hair, setting it with butter, and twisting it into long, shining curls.

I was told by Tilipa of the Kars clan—a simple and courteous ancient, looking, as did all the others, as though he had just stepped out of the Old Testament—that the Todas have always lived in the Blue Mountains. When I asked Pilkodhr, one of the diviners of the tribe who had vast knowledge of Toda ceremonial, about the Todas' gods, he said: "In the beginning God dropped a pearl on a hill in this region and out of the pearl came our Toda God-Creator, Teikirzi. Teikirzi beat the earth with a rod and out of the dust emerged a Toda and a buffalo with a deep-toned bell tied around its neck."

Pilkodhr believed, as all Todas do, that it is this very bell, handed down from generation to generation, that is still preserved in their sacred temple, Bikapati. All the Toda ceremonies connected with buffalo worship, priestly duties, and the "Dairy Temples" (the dairy is the Toda temple) have come from the teachings of Teikirzi, who showed them "the way to live."

The true origin of this dwindling tribe, so different in physique, religious practices, and customs from their Dravidian neighbors, mystifies the ethnologist. However, many accept the theory that the Todas have descended from the ancient Assyrians, and that in the dim past their ancestors crossed the Arabian Sea, landed on the western coast of India, and moved to the isolation of the Nilgiri Hills.

The first thing I observed on arrival in this remote region was that the picturesque Toda villages, called *mands,* are always found in enchanting hollows, or folds, of the downs, usually a mile or so off the beaten paths worn bare by the feet of Toda men who often travel as far as thirty miles a day in the course of their affairs. The *mand* must be near running water and protected from the winds by a *shola* (copse); behind and in front, the glorious sweeping downs slope away to the mountains. A village consists of from three to six huts built close together with a Dairy Temple, where the sacred milk is kept. The buffalo enclosures are nearby.

One of the wives of the Kanars clan, named Malgiji, invited me to her home. Like all the others in the village, the framework of her house was made of bamboo canes laced together as in basket weavings. The shape of the house, really a hut, was like a wagon top, and the neat, elaborate thatching extended from the apex to the ground. The ends of the "wagon top" were filled in with slabs of wood, set back about five feet under the thatch, which formed a sort of porch over a miniature doorway no more than two by two and a half feet. I was much amused to see the tall Toda men wriggling in and out of these tiny entrances.

Inside, everything was scrupulously neat with black pottery and bright brass utensils set in rows on a shelf at the back. While admiring these, I was on the point of picking one up when Malgiji cried out sharply and I withdrew my hand. Mustoe, my interpreter, explained: "Please do not touch! If an earthenware pot is handled by anyone not of our tribe, it must be broken and thrown away."

Apologetically I edged over into the small space at the left where there was a high raised platform. "This," Mustoe said, "is where they sleep." And pointing to the right side he indicated the fire which was burning brightly, where something was cooking in a black pot. Half choked with smoke, I looked for a window, but there was absolutely no means of ventilation, no escape for the spiraling smoke, except through the minute opening of the doorway. Now I understood why all the pottery was black.

One day Morgudn took me to the Dairy Temple, where he performed his priestly duties. The Temple was enclosed by a wall, and I could not enter this enclosure because no one except the priest is allowed inside.

The Dairy Temple is exactly the same shape as the living huts but more carefully and intricately made; at the ends, blocks of stone instead of wood fill the spaces. Directly over the tiny door were a roughly carved buffalo head, a star of five points, a crescent, and a date. A monolith stood beside the temple enclosure, and

Morgudn explained that at every dairy ceremony milk is poured over this.

"Muttanad, or Pearl," he said, "is one of the most important *mands,* because it is on the Hill of the Creation. It is the only one where sacrifices take place near the huts."

When I visited the village of Muttanad later I saw on top of the hill a curious, pagoda-like, conical temple. It was called Poh. This was the most sacred form of Dairy Temple and there were only three of them in existence. Two sizable slabs of stone flanked the narrow entrance into the enclosure which surrounded this tall temple; a group of stones marked the spot where the sacrificial ceremonies took place. When I asked the priest the meaning of these stones he said: "This is where the young men come to try their strength. Each year they try to lift a heavier ball of rock; and when they finally can lift this one"—he pointed to a rock that might well have weighed a hundred pounds—"they are old enough and strong enough to marry." I noticed one huge stone that only a giant could have moved; I was glad some lovelorn youth's chances of matrimony did not depend on hoisting that one. If it had, the tribe would have been extinct long ago.

I looked at Morgudn, his mild brown eyes gazing out over the distant mountains, and I knew his thoughts were focused on long-ago days when the Todas were truly "lords of the soil" and their villages covered the whole of this beautiful tableland. They are still regarded as lords of the soil and levy tributes on the neighboring Badagas, and even collect rent from the Indian government for the considerable territory which has been taken from them for the popular government hill stations—Wellington, Kotagiri, Ootacamund, and Coonoor—where government officials and vacationing Indians find relief from the lowland heat for six months of the year.

Morgudn shook his fine head sadly as he described the villages which had been wiped out of existence, and the grazing grounds which had been given over to tea and coffee plantations and the vigorous Badagas' agriculture. He pointed to the cairns close to the village with a sweeping gesture, proudly drawing attention to these ancient, ruined structures which had been built by his ancestors nearly two thousand years ago, before the coming of the Badagas and other adjacent tribes.

In spite of the sense of loss one knew he must be feeling, his erect bearing was that of the true aristocrat; his keen, far-seeing eyes suggested the wisdom and vision of the priest; yet his gentle manner, his soft voice, and the poetry of his speech revealed an appealing, vibrant human being.

To the Toda, every sunrise symbolizes a recurrent beginning of life. How important this sun worship is! The newborn child cannot be taken out of the house until it has been officially introduced to the sun. When it is about two weeks old the Dawn Ceremony is held. This is "the baptism of light," the child's presentation to the physical world as well as to the gods. Throughout life, every morning as the sun begins to warm the chill air and the Toda emerges from his hut, his first duty is the ceremony of invocation, of greeting to the sun.

After this comes the milking of the sacred buffalo. The Todas are occupied entirely with the keeping of buffalo. They have three distinct and valuable breeds, and the riches of a man are counted by the number of herds he owns. There are three kinds of Dairy Temples, too, and the priests for these temples, chosen with great care, have different training and different rules, according to the type of Dairy.

The milking ceremony is performed only by the priest. For this the priest divests himself of most of his clothing, produces a holy milking vessel of bamboo, and lets the sacred calves out of their enclosure to suckle their mothers. When he thinks they have nursed long enough, the calves are led away very unwillingly and then the ceremonial milking begins as in any ordinary dairy. I was interested to see that even these sacred animals behaved like ordinary cows and given half a chance were not above kicking over the milking pot, and kicking the priest as well.

These sacred buffalo with their long, light gray coats and very long horns curling downward are immensely proud in bearing. While the Todas are nearby, the sacred buffalo are very docile, but when I, a stranger, approached they dashed off into the wooded ravines like wild creatures.

When the priest had finished milking the sacred buffalo he disappeared into the temple to churn the milk and make the *ghee* (the oil of the clarified butter) which he would later sell for the support of the temple and himself; then the village headman milked the other buffalo and the milk was circulated for use among the families of the village. The secular buffalo with their long legs and smooth, shiny coats are not nearly so handsome as their sacred relatives.

I had first been drawn to these remote people having heard of their rare and beautiful songs, which were musically simple but whose texts were full of poetic charm. The funeral prayers were, I was told, especially moving.

When anyone of the Toda tribe dies, it is a cause of intense mourning, but when a child dies the loss is supreme, because of the dwindling community. There are many childless marriages among the Todas, and if not childless, the family often consists of only one offspring; the largest family I met among this tribe consisted of only three children.

It was through Morgudn's good offices that I was permitted to be present at and record the most sacred and secret of all Toda ceremonials, a funeral. It was almost unbelievable to find, in the middle of the twentieth century, a funeral ritual accompanied by wrestling of the bulls reminiscent of the ancient Cretans.

Never before had I found music accompanying a tribal ceremonial provided by a servant tribe. The funeral I was permitted to attend, by special dispensation, was held for a child who died while I was visiting the tribe.

Every Toda funeral is really two funerals, one a "green" funeral and one a "dry" funeral. The "green" funeral takes place immediately following death and requires the ceremonial cutting off of a lock of the dead person's hair and the cremation of the body with many rites. The "dry" funeral occurs much later and the lock of hair is of great importance in this ceremonial, which may be postponed many times to allow all members of the tribe to arrive and participate. The name of the person who has died must never be mentioned; no name can be duplicated in the Toda clans. When a baby is born an entirely new name is composed from a rock, a hill, a river, or some other thing in nature.

The ceremony I attended was a "green" funeral, as the child had just died. I have never seen such grief. In this tribal society the sorrow of one is the sorrow of the whole tribe. Members of all the clans traveled many miles, some of them on very long journeys through the mountains, to share the grief of the bereaved family. Each new arrival was welcomed in the Todas' unique tribal manner. Some of the women went forth to receive older male relatives, and I also saw the greeting delivered between two men or two women. The only time I saw a man kneel before a woman and touch his forehead with her feet was when homage was paid to the bereaved mother.

The women all helped with the funeral preparations; the older ones assisted in preparing the body of the dead child; the others prepared food for the many visitors. For the feast, which preceded the funeral, groups of young men and old men sat apart on the hillside while the female members of the family ate in or near the hut of the stricken mother. Throughout the feast, music was provided by the Kotas, a neighboring tribe whose musicians are always hired by the Todas for their ceremonials. Regarded by the Todas as a servant tribe and mere artisans, the Kotas were paid as hirelings in grain and buffalo meat; the aristocratic Todas have no social intercourse whatsoever with them.

To me this music had a weird fascination; the eerie tones of the wind instruments, the persistent rhythms of the drums, the sad notes of the bells, the dry clatter of the rattles all contributed to the over-all strangeness of the ensemble. Perhaps the same musicians and the same instruments could arouse merriment at a Toda wedding, but here they emphasized remarkably the somberness of the occasion.

After the feast of rice ceremonially prepared and served with sauces and vegetables (the Todas are vegetarians), the melancholy procession began. Had I been told in advance that the mourners were actually hired, as among the Chinese, I would have believed it, and I would have been very wrong. The mourners at this strange ceremony were genuinely grieving over the greatest imaginable loss to their tribe, the death of a child. The effect was heart-rending.

The mourning mother, supported and accompanied by all the other women of the tribe, left the hut and was led to the hillside where the men were grouped. Then she was lifted into a blanket and carried, as if in a hammock; the child was carried in a small casket of bamboo cane. Everyone moved very slowly toward the burial grounds; everyone, that is, except the young men of the village. They had gone to the grazing grounds to round up two carefully chosen buffalo for the ceremonial sacrifice.

The Todas, like many other peoples, recognize that everything in this world comes from another order of beings, and they seek to enter into communion with that other world, especially at the time of crisis, through a sacrificial act. They take something out of common use and dedicate it to God, or the gods—in other words, make the thing sacred, which is really what sacrifice means.

When the two sacrificial beasts had been chosen, a dozen or more of the virile young men from the village approached and closed in on them. Pushing on their sides, pulling them by their tails, riding the long, downswept horns, they urged the buffalo bulls toward the ceremonial funeral grounds, goading and dragging them through the little valleys and over the hills of the grazing lands, a laborious distance of a mile or more. Probably the most difficult feat of all was forcing the buffalo through the dense virgin forest that surrounded the burial place.

Once inside the circle of trees, they continued to wrestle the bulls, pushing, pulling, riding the horns until the sacrificial beasts were totally subdued and exhausted. Then, in a tense throbbing silence, with a thrust like lightning the deathblow was struck, sending the spirits of these noble animals to join the gods. There was no torturing. It was a fair test of strength between young animals and young men with a quick release at the end.

While the men were engrossed in the outcome of the wrestling match, all the women had surrounded the weeping mother, consoling her with softly chanted funeral prayers.

A few days later, very quietly and almost secretly, I met with some of the elders of the tribe who were willing to record for me their sacred funeral prayers. The site chosen for the recording was in the open. Afternoon shadows lay purple on the rolling downs and a rosy light surrounded us.

From all directions the dignified elders, striding firmly along their mountain paths, joined us on the hillside. Morgudn had brought with him the oldest of them all, said to be ninety-six years old. He was a powerfully built man, and even at this advanced age was able to cover many miles a day in his mountains. The brightness in his eyes had not diminished in spite of the whiteness of his bushy beard, his flowing silver hair, and his slightly bent posture. After the usual salutations of foot to forehead were over and the general gossiping had died down, the chanting of the prayers began.

Their earnest voices rose in unison, bringing vividly back to life the whole funeral scene. So moving was their approach to the chants, so stirring their strong, resonant voices, even the tones of the Old One, that I realized fully why the deep intensity and feeling of their songs and poetry have been so highly praised.

For about two thousand years these pastoral people in India have repeated the cycle of greeting the sun in the morning, milking the sacred buffalo, carrying on their simple affairs until evening falls when the buffalo are again herded to the milking place for the ceremony at the Dairy Temple. And in the huts of the *mands*, lamps are lighted and, being symbolic of the sun, they too are saluted by the men with the same Dawn Ceremony, the baptism of light, which ushers in each new day.

Few people are closer to the deities which rule their lives. Almost everything the Todas do is related to worship. Even their garments suggest scriptural patriarchs, but there is more than the outward semblance: an inner radiance shines from those serene faces.

Truly, the Todas have succeeded where more civilized cultures have failed; they have found their own way to happiness by living in tune with their universe.

It was also thanks to the Maharaja and Maharani of Bhavnagar that I was able to visit Calicut on the Malibar Coast to record a large annual ceremony over which the local Raja presided. Famous exponents of music and dance in southern India were gathered here to perform a religious festival which went on continuously for three days and three nights. Processions of elephants, priests, and worshipers marched from temple to temple accompanying intricately carved carts carrying images of their deities. A large chorus of chanting priests alternated with the strident music of drums and trumpets as dancers performed unbelievably complicated steps. The most striking performance was the *Kathakali*, the greatest theater tradition in India, in which favorite episodes in the life of the Hindu deities are enacted. Spectacular dances were performed by men waving enormous plumed fans while dancing on the backs of twelve temple elephants resplendent in their brilliant trappings.

Later, at Madras, the state's winter capital and an important cultural center with a fine university, the governor arranged for me to spend a great deal of time at the School of Music and at the Institute of the Dance (*Kalakshetra*). In the latter, Rukmini Devi, one of the most famous dancers in India, hoped to bring together the highest cultures of the East and the West, for she said,

"Art and beauty are above distinctions of race, of nations, of faith."
Her motto was: "Without culture there can be no real freedom, just
as without freedom, there can be no true culture." Here pupils,
from kindergarten children to mature, talented young people
who were already performing for public, were trained in strict
Indian music, art, and dance traditions.

Indian music had its beginnings in Vedic chant. This system of
music, said to be about 3000 years old, is the most intricate of any
in the world. It is believed to be of divine origin and many legends
can be found relating music to deities, such as Sarasvati, the
goddess of learning, who is believed to have invented the musical
instrument, the vina; the god Siva, divine dancer, who animates
the universe; and many lesser divinities. From the gods, music was
bestowed upon mortals, and ruling families patronized musicians
—philosophers who not only performed but supervised musical
education for the court and country. The young were instructed in
singing prayers and praising the deities and were also taught
secular matters through melodies.

In days of old, thousands of musicians were supported by the
state to expound the mysteries of the sacred art. Temples and
shrines were filled with devotional music, and philosophers, noble-
men, and village bards sang the miraculous deeds of the gods.
Certain celebrated families of musicians have handed down their
art generation after generation, usually through the males, and a
few of these families can still be found both in northern and
southern India.

With the present revival of all ancient arts, music schools have
been founded in Bombay, Baroda, Mysore, Calcutta, and Madras,
but many of the modern students do not regard the ancient classical music with the awe and reverence given it in former days
and are unwilling to give a lifetime to acquiring a thorough
knowledge of classic Indian music's sacred lore, exacting techniques, and complicated theories.

To give you some idea of the enormous complexity of the music
an Indian musician must master, let us consider the *raga*, which
has been erroneously called a scale, for it is much more than a
scale in the Western sense. It is a group of notes consisting usually
of seven tones (maybe five or six in the oldest ragas); it is
fundamental to Indian music. Northern Indian or Hindustani music,
for example, embodies six basic ragas, and these tunes are con-

sidered to have "male" characteristics. Then each of these has five or six *raginis* ("female" tunes, sometimes referred to as "wives"), eight *putras* ("sons," or "offspring"), and eight *bharyas*, or modes. All of these, covered by the word raga, result in well over one hundred tone groups, and each has its season, time of day or night, and is connected with a definite flower, bird, color, and mood. No conscientious musician would offend his audience or the deities by playing, for example, a night raga in the daytime or a rain raga in the dry season.

Of paramount importance is the mood of each raga and the atmosphere and feeling of emotion it creates in the listener—religious, erotic, devotional, or amorous. For example, one early morning raga is called "dawn," and its mood translates as "lovely, energetic, challenging." An afternoon raga expresses "contentment," and translates as "faith, loving prayer, passive satisfaction." A raga of midnight and late night translates as "prayerful peaceful, harmonious, sublime." An example of a seasonal raga is the one for spring which expresses "bursting, awake, lively, feminine, delicate." Some ragas, however, are suitable for all seasons and all hours.

To make matters even more complex, each raga is combined with one of dozens of *talas*, or time measures. The tala is as basic as the raga and one system has 175 of them, but there are relatively few in actual use. Talas are based on a system of tabular computation and not on one of emotions or moods. Both the talas and the ragas of southern India are quite different from those of northern India, as each has its own system.

Singing is thought to be the highest form of musical expression; a beautiful voice and a thorough understanding of the demanding science and technique are required. At the School of Music in Madras special emphasis was placed on the vocal technique, which is so specialized that the Western ear may be inclined to reject it on first hearing; but as I lived with it and learned to appreciate the nuances, my ear became tuned to catch its embellishments, portamenti, and decorations. Only then could I appreciate the artistry of performance in India.

The fine singers of India may be either men or women, but the greatest I have heard were women. However, the best instrumentalists I heard and recorded were men, though I believe there is no prohibition in this matter.

The singer, like the instrumentalist, first establishes a raga, and elaborates and improvises melodically and rhythmically on its tones, often for many long hours. There were sessions when we sat enchanted most of the night by three or four soloists, all gifted musicians, and an audience that knew and understood their music. While the musician embellished the melody, the whole audience sat with closed eyes, swaying, sighing from time to time, like jazz devotees in an American jam session. But there was nothing boisterous here; it was purely religious devotion accorded a great performance.

Every song was accompanied by a stringed instrument, called the *tambura*, and two small drums, called the *tabla*. Women often played the tambura, which provides the drone, but the tabla, which often supply the rhythmic accompaniment, were usually played by men. For instance, M. S. Subbulakshmi, who was perhaps the greatest singer of all India, often accompanied herself on the tambura, with the rhythmic accompaniment of *mridangam*, the classical drum of southern India. I first heard her in the homes of Prime Minister Nehru and President Prasad; later I heard her again in Madras at the unforgettable wedding of the daughter of a wealthy Indian film magnate.

The marriage ceremony itself was fascinating, and it turned out to be a great musical event which I was permitted to record. Thousands of guests from far and near heard the greatest musicians of southern India perform during the five days of celebration; and in the ceremony itself six hundred Brahman priests chanted prayers in responding choruses, echoing each other; the effect was stupendous. It is ironic that although Indian music is changing because of films more than any other reason, I was able to record some of the purest music of India at the wedding of a film producer.

Just to the south of Madras is the city of Madurai, famous for its beautiful ancient temples and religious sculpture, where life goes on as it has for centuries. In Madurai's famous Meenakshi Temple are found the unique Singing Pillars, one of the wonders of the world. No one knows when or how these seven pillars were carved, but each pillar is made from a single block of stone and has a deep resonant tone when struck. The temple priests played several melodies on the pillars for me to record, but I found greater variety in the music of the temple musicians with their trumpets, flutes, drums, bells, and cymbals. These were typical

of the many types of folk instruments I recorded. They can always be heard, played by bands of street musicians in the bazaars,
in religious processions, at the gateways to temples (especially on
feast days), and in village celebrations.

To the great Meenakshi Temple pilgrims come for some of the
holiest ceremonies in all of southern India. The edifice is also
famous for its carved gateways on which the stories of the deities are
depicted in fine stone.

The imagination and devotion that have gone into the intricately carved details on every figure (whether gods, celestial
beings, demons, holy men, deer, or other creatures) show great
fervor, grace, skill, and delicacy. The decoration could have resulted in disastrous confusion had not the exquisite adornment of
the temple been accomplished with such singleness of purpose.

The temples are the earthly dwellings of the gods—majestic,
immense, and splendid. To the Hindu, man is "more than half
divine," and mingles with the gods not only as a worshiper but as
a brother.

Much of the religious architecture and sculpture is centuries
old, but beautiful religious art is still being produced. Some of
the finest images of gods and goddesses in stone and metal made for
temples and for private places of worship come from a small village
in the area, made by craftsmen descended from a long line of sculp-
tors. Veteran carvers have learned the art from their fathers and
have labored patiently to pass on these skills to their sons, keeping
alive a precious heritage and preserving the fame their art has
brought to certain families and villages.

The images are made from a special kind of stone, and everything is done with strict conformity to the methods and standards
explained in the holy book on Indian sculpture. The artists have no
training in art schools; they learn from their elders and derive their
inspiration from studying the remarkable works that surround
them.

The classical Indian view holds art as a means of attaining the
highest quality in personal character and citizenship. It presents
cosmic ideas in the figures of the deities. The temple arts are used
as a means of developing the idealistic side of human nature.
They depict incidents in sculpture and produce sermons in stones.
Other cultures have set high value on the use of art to express

beauty, but the content, or message, of music and art in India is devotional rather than intellectual.

To the west of Madura is the state of Mysore, a land of lofty mountains and fertile plains, roaring waterfalls, huge forests and gold mines, manufacturing towns with the most modern factories (sandalwood, perfume, silk weaving, aircraft), and vast tracts of virgin jungle with tiger, buffalo, and wild elephant. It is filled with historic interest and legendary glamor. With an altitude of three thousand feet above sea level, its climate is delightful and attracts year-round visitors.

The state of Mysore in 1956 covered an area of about thirty thousand square miles and had a population of about seven million. Mysore city, the capital since 1799, boasts the reputation of being India's cleanest and most beautiful city, thanks to an efficient municipality.

Since the fourteenth century, Mysore has been governed by the present royal family. At independence many princes lost their states, but the Maharaja of Mysore was made governor of his province because of the efficiency and care with which he had ruled. Under his leadership, old lanes and slum areas were cleared and drainage systems extended and improved. Excellent housing projects were begun and broad highways and magnificent buildings—hospitals, homes, and factories—were constructed.

The Maharaja's palace stands like a jewel in the center of the city, and is an important treasure house for Indian art. The present Maharaja is a fine musician and has a number of grand pianos, which he plays very well, and an immense collection of symphonic records. He maintained four palace orchestras of the finest musicians, one of which it was arranged for me to record. This orchestra consisted of about twenty musicians—string, winds, and percussion. The *vina* was the backbone of this orchestra, its position similar to that of the violin in Western orchestras. The vina is associated with Sarasvati, Goddess of Learning, and Narada, the Divine Musician.

The history of the Indian orchestra is found in the Vedic scriptures, the most ancient literature of the world. It is said that the deities were the virtuosos and the conductors. The highest god set the rhythm, beating out the tala on his drum, a *damaru*, shaped like an hourglass.

It is conceded that the vina produces the best expression of the science and art of southern Indian music, and of all instruments it is thought to express most completely the soul of the player. At the palace of the Maharaja of Mysore I heard one of the finest vina players of India, who produced unbelievable sounds from the instrument. He played it as though it were alive; he made it sing, talk, laugh, and cry.

If a boy wants to learn to play the vina, he comes to a great master and at first only sits and absorbs. Usually a master will take a pupil into his home if he feels he has promise. Finally, if worthy, the boy is allowed to touch the instrument and after ten or twelve years of instruction may become proficient on it. The deep reverence of the Indian for his traditional music is moving; those chosen by the masters to make the arts a profession gladly pour their whole lives into it, apparently with little remuneration of any kind.

Musical instruments in India are of infinite variety. The *sarangi, tabla, pakhawaj,* and *tambura* are generally used only to accompany vocal music. Others, such as the *vina, sitar, sarod,* and *bansuri,* are played for their own beauty of tone. Remarkable craftsmanship in metal, wood, and ivory goes into the making of these instruments, many of which are extremely ornate. There are about 200 varieties of drums and 120 of string and wind instruments. Instruments are divided into four groups: (1) those strung with brass or steel wires or with silken or cotton cords, which are plucked or struck by the fingernail or a plectrum of ivory, wood, or wire, such as the *vina, sarod, sitar,* and others; (2) those that have skins stretched over hollow circular resonators at one end and are played with a bow, such as the *sarangi, taus, dilruba,* and others; (3) drumlike instruments struck by the hand or a beater of wood such as the *tabla, dhol, nagara, pakhawaj,* and others; and (4) wind instruments such as the much-loved flutes, double-reed instruments, horns, and trumpets.

The *sitar* is probably the most popular instrument in northern India. It was perfected by Amir Khusru of Delhi in the thirteenth century, and has been made famous in America by Ravi Shankar, who played it for me to record in his home in Delhi in 1950. The name, which is Persian, denotes three strings, but now it usually has five, six, or usually seven strings. The *sitar* has sympathetic strings of fine wire attached to the side of the neck, passing under the frets and the bridge, to vibrate in unison with the notes of the same pitch and also, by sympathetic vibration, to give the upper partials, or harmonics. It is plucked by a wire plectrum worn on the forefinger of the right hand. The brass frets are movable; by changing their positions to different basic settings, the player can obtain different modes. A gourd provides the resonator. The *esar* is a modern combination of *sitar* with *sarangi;* it has four main strings but no sympathetic strings and is bowed. It usually accompanies women's voices.

The *vina,* however, is the most difficult to play. In one form it has two gourd resonators; in the southern Indian forms, only one. It has four main strings over the frets and three strings on the side which are plucked to mark the beat. By pulling a string sideways, it is possible to produce many different sounds. The frets, twenty-two in number, are at fixed intervals. The main strings are plucked by plectra worn on the first two fingers of the right hand; the strings on the sides are plucked with the little finger from time to time. The soft and plaintive qualities of tone are deeper and mellower than those of the sitar.

The *mridanga,* a drum with two drumheads, one larger than the other, is used by musicians for classical southern Indian music. The large mridanga is supposed to be the most ancient of drums, having its origin with the god Siva. *Tabla* and *bamya,* small kettledrums, are played in pairs, by the hands, and are tuned an octave apart. Indian drums are played by using the heel of the hand, the flat of the palm, and the fingers.

Beggars and fakirs use an earthenware kettledrum to attract attention as they wander from house to house, and a skilled drummer is usually well rewarded. The *nagara,* a copper kettledrum three or four feet in diameter, is often used in temple music and can be found in bands playing at the gates of forts or palaces. It is beaten with short, curved sticks. The tone is strident if heard close at hand, but when played in the mountains, with shrill oboes, the effect of the deep tones echoing from hill to hill is shattering.

Musical instruments, as musical systems, differ in northern and southern India. While some are similar but exist in different forms, many are unique to the region in which they are found. One of the most melodious instruments is the *jaltarang,* now very rare. It consists of eighteen porcelain bowls containing varying amounts

of water, placed in a semicircle and struck with two thin bamboo
sticks with cork or felt tips.

I had to leave Mysore sooner than I wished in order to be,
by early April, in Hardwar Union, haven for holy men and Hindu
pilgrims near the source of the holy Ganges River in the Himalayan
foothills, to witness the rarest and most spectacular festival in
India—the Purna Kumbha Mela. I went by car for the first part
of the journey and then by a hot, stuffy, slow-as-a-snail train
on which for a long weary night I shared my compartment,
intended for six, with eleven Indians.

The youngest of our passengers was a tiny baby whose wet
nurse, being a servant, had to travel third class. At each train
stop (it seemed every few minutes) she would run forward along
the platform to our "Pullman," nurse the screaming child briefly,
then dash back to her third-class bench just in time to catch the
train as it moved down the track. All my fellow passengers, including the baby's family of six, seemed to sleep soundly while
not engaged in loud compulsive conversation, punctuated by frequent expectoration. But with the cries of the child, who apparently
never got enough to eat, the snores of the grownups, and the
jolting of the train, I had little sleep. My sleeping bag and blankets
were stretched out on one of the bunks; the other adults slept
on the remaining five bunks, while the children huddled together
on the filthy floor.

The Purna Kumbha Mela (Festival of the Holy Urn) takes
place only every twelve years when certain constellations meet.
The date, set by the wisest astrologers of the land, was looked
forward to by the whole Hindu population, and in 1950, the Purna
Kumbha Mela was celebrated for the first time since India had
gained her independence from England. Millions of Hindus came
hundreds of miles to the holy city in the mountains. Cabinet
ministers, wealthy merchants, and other prosperous pilgrims traveled
in luxury by automobile or by train. Many hundreds, too poor
to have even a bullcart, had walked for days and nights on
end along the dusty highways of northern India and climbed
the rugged mountain roads to reach the blessed city in time
for this rare festival.

Bathing anywhere in the sacred Ganges at any time is extremely virtuous. Bathing in the headwaters at Hardwar is espe-

cially rewarding in the eyes of the gods. But bathing here at
the "most auspicious" moment during the Purna Kumbha Mela
(which on this occasion was three-eighteen on the afternoon of
April 13) brought salvation for eternity. The faithful would never
have to go through another incarnation on this earth—a reward
much to be desired; in fact, the ultimate reward. At this time
many families also performed the ceremony for six-year-old sons,
which indicated that their days of schooling were beginning. A
book was placed on the heads of the children and their ears
prepared for earrings, in this simple but impressive ceremony.

In former years there had been tragic outbreaks of cholera
during the Purna Kumbha Mela due to huge crowds assembled
from villages all over India which huddled together for weeks under
the most unsanitary conditions. Fearing another plague epidemic,
the young Indian government undertook to make the 1950 festival
a model of hygiene and orderly conduct. Thousands of police,
army men, and civilians moved into Hardwar to take charge of the
festival arrangements; extra railroad men were hired to handle
the expanded operation (more than twenty-eight trains a day
arrived in this small town); and thirty-five thousand tons of food
poured into the area. One American visitor remarked: "This is
run better than a world's fair." A supervised colony of tents
and huts was set up near the river with definite enforced sanitary
rules. Boy Scouts, government officials, and other organized
groups took charge of directing the temporary community, rescuing
lost children, distributing food, and so forth.

Barriers were set up three miles outside of Hardwar to stop
everyone arriving by train, motorcar, or on foot and make them
show the pink government paper signed by a recognized physician
that he or she had been inoculated for cholera; and hundreds of
doctors were waiting at the barriers to give shots to those without
the required pink slip. Rather than submit to the needle, some
turned homeward, but thousands were inoculated on the spot.

Before I left America, I had made careful preparations, and my
bright yellow card, showing the imposing list of inoculations I
had undergone, had impressed officials in countries all over the
world. But at Hardwar the border officials had never seen a
document like mine—it was yellow instead of pink. If I wished
to enter the city, they told me, I must line up with the weary
pilgrims, young children, hermits from mountain caves, and sadhus

(holy men) who were waiting to be inoculated. Seeing the hasty and none-too-sanitary-looking activities in the improvised health station, full of unavoidable dust and flies, I decided that I must forego this festival even though I had looked forward to it for many long months.

As a last resort, however, I went to the village doctor. After explaining my inoculation card to his satisfaction, I persuaded him to give me the required pink sheet without applying the needle again. With this magic paper I was through the barrier in no time.

The first Purna Kumbha Mela was held at some point of time far beyond the reach of recorded history. Hindu legend tells us that the 330,000,000 angels in ancient times were as mortal as men; they discovered that they could defeat death by drinking the divine nectar which was kept in the sacred *Kumbh* (holy urn). They fought a full-scale war with the demons for the possession of the urn and won. As the angels flew triumphantly to heaven with the urn, four drops of nectar fell from the vessel to the ground. Every pious Hindu who bathes in the pools formed by these drops may end his earthly cycle of births and deaths and release his soul into union with God. Hardwar is the most holy place of the four as it is located near the source of the Ganges River.

In the Sev *Ashrama*, the Ramakrishna Ashram, a permanent mission at Hardwar, where students and *gurus* come to meditate in the mountains, I was a guest during the festival. I saw firsthand the outstanding job this mission did in welfare service. The monks covered every inch of their property with row after row of tents, thatched huts, and tin-roofed sheds to protect some thousand pilgrims from sun and rain, and provide them with lights, water, and sanitary arrangements. They had also planned a steady flow of food which made it possible for the ashram to feed a thousand people a day. They inoculated hundreds against cholera and gave medical aid to thirty thousand in addition. Even minor surgery was available here. To their permanent hospital of fifty beds a temporary hospital unit was added with forty. All of them were filled. In additional hospital tents, with staff provided by the government, the mission ran two temporary dispensaries in the most crowded part of town. These were under the charge of qualified doctors assisted by members of the ashram and volunteer workers who had come long distances at their own expense to give unstintingly and joyfully of their service to patients and pilgrims.

Swami Raghubaranandaji, head of the mission, took me around to see how well managed and how well provided with medical facilities they were. Swamiji (an endearing term) and his workers told me of their deep gratitude to those in India and even as far away as America who had contributed to the fund to make this work possible. The monks, devoted to the cause of service to humanity, were eager to help make all the visitors more comfortable. I think I would be safe to say that many of the poor had never in their lives had such excellent medical attention; the consecrated work of the mission certainly did much to lift the health standards for the festival.

Essential as these physical considerations were, it was the spiritual welfare of the pilgrims that was uppermost in the minds of the monks. Every evening the Ramakrishna order gave stimulating religious discourses, and from temple services on all sides came the sound of conch shells and cymbals, of trumpets and drums. From shrines everywhere, almost constantly, the melody of chanted prayers alternated with tinkling bells and tiny gongs, inspiring and uplifting everyone.

When the busy day's activities were finished and the temple services (which I recorded) ended, late in the evening when they must have been worn out from serving the multitudes, they would assemble and discuss religious ideas, philosophic views, and music in Hindu worship, chanting special prayers and teachings for my recordings.

The excitement of the festival reached feverish heights on the all-important day of April 13. At daybreak on this day of days, indicated by the astrologers as the "most auspicious," the throngs were unbelievably orderly. But it was impossible to move in such a milling mass of humanity except with the crowd. Knowing this, the government had supplied a sure means of transportation for me and my two cameramen—an elephant, complete with a pink parasol. Since this noble, intelligent creature is revered by the Hindus, everyone made way for us, tossing coins in our path, even trying to kiss the elephant's trunk.

The morning ablutions took most of the early hours. Beginning at dawn all the men and women went to the river to bathe; first, with cupped hands, they dipped up and offered to the gods three handfuls of water to the east, and then to the other directions. After this they immersed themselves, splashed about, and some even took an invigorating swim.

About noon began the amazing Procession of the Sadhus of the many sects of Hinduism. Here was a procession to end all processions—fifteen thousand sadhus in saffron robes or loincloths; two thousand of them, absolutely nude, belonged to the sect which believes that any garment, however small, is superfluous and interferes with meditation. From noon to midnight they proceeded along the three-mile route from the center of Hardwar to Brahmakund, the sacred pool where every Hindu dreams of washing away his sins forever. The leader of each sect rode a sacred elephant magnificently caparisoned in scarlet and gold. The silver howdahs and palanquins gave a touch of pomp and ceremony which delighted the crowd. Parasols of exuberant colors shaded their holinesses from the sun. Faithful followers, colorful beyond words in their many types of national or tribal dress, trudged along the long hot road to receive *darshan* or blessing, emanating from the holy priests mounted on elephants, chanting prayers and sutras appropriate to the high occasion.

At the auspicious moment, three-eighteen in the afternoon, everyone converged on the "tank," the most sacred bathing area of the river, to cast away their sins. Although several entrances and bridges were arranged for the worshipers, and guards were stationed at regular intervals to try to restrain the masses, nothing could hold them back. As the auspicious moment approached, not even an army of Gurkha soldiers would have prevented the stampede that took place. Thanks to government permission, I was watching and photographing the scene from a square stone tower by the bridge or I would have been caught in this wave of humanity which swept by on its inexorable way to the river. Looking down on the uncontrolled fervor below, knowing the weakest would surely not survive the ordeal, I could think only of a migration of lemmings I once witnessed in the Arctic when thousands of those little creatures had dashed toward the sea to certain extinction. But here, though I was witnessing a spiritual, not a physical, compulsive urge, it also ended in tragedy for many. Thirty-five people were killed. The miracle was that it was not more.

Getting out of Hardwar was even more difficult than getting

there. The multitudes of Hindus, having bathed on the "most auspicious" day, wanted to leave for their homes all at once. In a week after the great day, Hardwar was empty and serene again. The monks of the ashrams were back to their usual routine of prayers, meditation, and temple services.

After the teeming masses had left, I was able to reserve a train compartment alone for the journey to my next destination, Calcutta. This turned out to be a terrifying experience. I had been regaled with stories about the vagabonds and thieves who lay in wait for trains at lonely stations throughout the night. It was said they crawled in through open windows at these stops and stole everything in sight. One man I knew had been robbed on trains three times in six months. Obedient to friendly instructions, I kept all windows locked and nearly suffocated, deciding no air was preferable to no sleep. I longed for my noisy companions of the journey northward.

Chapter 15

TIBETAN MAGIC AND MYSTICISM

After arriving back in Calcutta I had one of those wonderful strokes of good fortune that so often have provided me with unexpected opportunities to visit and record in remote places. Because of a devastating earthquake, causing landslides and floods, I was told it would be impossible for me to reach my goal—the lamasery on the fringes of Tibet, where I longed to record the songs and ceremonies of the Buddhist lamas. Officially, all normal communications had been cut off to Darjeeling, summer capital of West Bengal, and Kalimpong, the gateway to Tibet on the northeast border of India.

In my hotel in Calcutta, however, I met a group of Tibetans who had been delegated by the Dalai Lama to contact representatives of the Peiping regime in New Delhi, and having sat around in vain for several frustrating weeks in the Delhi heat, they had decided to return to their cool mountain homes. I told them that I hoped to reach Tibet but could not obtain permission, as all contact was broken with the north. They offered me the unique opportunity of accompanying them to the lamasery, and I eagerly accepted.

It was dawn when we left Calcutta by plane, the seven Tibetans and I, with several Indian government officials and their families. The first short stretch by air went well in spite of shockingly rough weather, and we landed with a great splash in five or six inches of water which had transformed the meadow—the nearest landing strip en route to Darjeeling—into a lake. As we sloshed and slithered through the mud to reach the modest shelter which served as a waiting room, I was horrified to see one of the porters stumble and lose his hold on my tape recorder. As it tumbled toward the mud, my heart sinking with it, another porter retrieved it just in the nick of time.

We huddled together for what seemed hours, while outside the monsoon rain fell and blew in sheets through the gaping cracks in the frail roof and walls, soaking us to the skin. Eventually Land Rovers turned up to take us on the next lap of the journey, but our ride was short indeed because we soon reached a point where the road had been completely washed away. From here we continued on foot, slipping through the debris left by the landslides until, after about five miles, we reached another stretch of road where an ancient bus was waiting. Gratefully we climbed aboard, but after a short distance even the stalwart bus could go no farther. There was no choice but to get out and start climbing up the mountainside with the soaked earth giving way at every step. A guide rope was attached to posts at intervals, and at times, post, rope, and earth beneath all gave way together, a most disconcerting sensation. Thousands of feet below the slippery ridge a raging torrent tore apart forests, fields, and plantations, sweeping trees, railroad ties and tracks, and even houses along in its turbulent course.

Up to this stage the other passengers from the plane had done fairly well. At this point, however, some were too frightened to attempt the perilous climb and entrusted themselves instead to the sure-footed Nepalese bearers. I shall never forget one wiry little woman carrying a fat Indian boy of fifteen, with terror written all over his moon-shaped face.

Had it not been for the steady, antlike procession of bearers ceaselessly making its way over the precarious mountain ridges, the Governor, the Maharaja, and their retinues—all stranded in their summer palaces in Darjeeling—and the native populace would have gone very hungry. The bearers sustained life in the city by transporting on their backs huge sacks of rice, *ghee* (the indispensable clarified butter), chickens, eggs, flour, medicines, and other vital necessities to the stricken areas.

We were beginning to wonder just how much more we could endure in our climb when a string of sturdy Tibetan ponies came into sight. These had been sent to meet us by the Raja of Bhutan, a cousin of Jigme Taring, a brilliant and fascinating man,

the only one of my Tibetan companions who spoke English.
(Jigme was later assassinated in Lhasa by the Chinese, I have
been told.) With exclamations of relief and gratitude, the seven
Tibetans and I mounted and rode off on the last leg of this hazardous trip, soon leaving the other less fortunate travelers far behind.

But for me, at least, the nightmare was really only beginning.
As we gingerly picked our way through the gullies formed by
the flood, I made every effort to get acquainted with my obstinate
Tibetan pony, but he showed no sign of understanding or even
of listening to anything I said to him. An individualist from
dripping ears to soggy stern, he showed his disapproval of the
whole business by persistently lagging behind. I imagined myself
losing sight of my companions in the rain, lost in the flood with
night coming on. My Tibetan companions seemed to have established an immediate rapport with their mounts and advanced at
a steady pace along the precarious road to Darjeeling.

Above, to the right, the mountaintops peeped out through a
shroud of trailing mist. On the left, below the edge of what
remained of the road, stretched the drenched hillsides, their deep
flanks scarred by streaks of yellow where the torrents had uprooted
the tea trees and flung them into the valleys, bringing disaster
to the planters. Every now and then the road was almost completely blocked by landslides, and we had to pick our way over
a temporary path marked by ever-vigilant patrols. Occasionally
a boulder as big as an elephant rolled down the hillside, completely
blocking our passage until a group of straining natives were able
by brute force to push it over the edge. My pony insisted,
naturally, in walking as close to the brink of the precipice as
possible, scorning washouts, soft earth, and loose gravel. Fortunately
Jigme kept a watchful eye on me, looking back every now and
then from his place in front of the file or, when things got too
difficult, turning back to ride with me.

While Jigme worried about me, the thing on my mind was my
recording equipment carried on pack ponies which brought up the
straggling rear. It is not easy to pack a two-piece Magnecorder,
weighing about one hundred pounds, with its spare parts, many
reels of tape, and three fragile microphones, over an almost non-
existent mountain road. I had brought it across half the world,
and I would have been brokenhearted if anything happened to
it now, on the very eve of my recording the songs and chants

of Tibetan priests. This music—lamentations, prayers for surcease from earthquakes, floods (ironic considering the circumstances), and the advance of the Communists toward Lhasa, sacred city of the gods—was, at this time, entirely unknown to the West.

By the time we reached the outskirts of Darjeeling the rain had stopped, and suddenly the sun broke through the low-hanging clouds, almost blinding us with its brilliance. In an instant the Himalayas were alight; from one end to the other, the ranges with their snow-covered peaks glowed with purple, orange, pink, and saffron.

Once in the main thoroughfare of the town, I was surrounded by openly incredulous Tibetans, Lepcha tribesmen, mystified Indian officials, and astonished planters, all of them acting as though I were a ghost. I was, it seems, the first European to get through since the disaster. Everyone talked at once. Stranded officials were anxious to make contact with their offices in Calcutta—how could they? The planters wanted to know when and how they could get their tea out, and the Tibetans wanted to know by what sorcery a white woman had managed to materialize in Darjeeling astride a pony when all avenues of approach had apparently been washed away. I suppose we should have been prepared for this astonishment since everyone we had talked to in Calcutta had insisted, "It can't possibly be done."

I was too tired to tell them anything much, beyond the fact that nothing short of an army of Gurkhas would have stopped me from carrying out my project. My "fellow pilgrims" were equally hungry and travel-weary and were eager to join their friends, so we rode on and they left me at the massive gray stone Mt. Everest Hotel. Here many of the climbers, about to begin the ascent of the world's highest mountain, had stopped en route to Kalimpong. In the Scottish mission chapel nearby they used to gather for a last prayer service before setting off. I, too, went there later to sit for a little time in meditation and gratitude.

When I left the hotel to call on the Governor the next day, gaping cracks across the streets left by the earthquake made it impossible for me to reach Government House by car. But fortunately I was able to get a rickshaw boy, a sturdy little Lepcha hillman, adroit enough to steer around the fissures and strong enough to pull the rickshaw up the steep, winding hills. What delighted me was that he sang all the way, seemingly quite undisturbed by the fact that house after house along the road looked ready to topple over on our heads. At one point he did pause and fling out a long-sleeved arm to indicate across a ravine the huge gash in a hillside where until recently there had been forty houses. In the middle of the night the rushing, tearing landslide had uprooted them, sweeping them with all sleeping occupants down into the valley below. Even the palatial Government House had not come through unscathed; one side was so undermined that the Governor, who was ill at the time, had to be carried in the night to one of his guest houses which was on safer ground.

After a pleasant hour with the Governor I returned to the hotel, where my rickshaw boy and several of his friends consented to record their songs for me. Later during my stay, the Governor sent Tibetans, Lepchas, and Nepalese to record for me, and it was then that I heard my first Tibetan songs. Full of vitality, at the same time very restrained, they were different from anything I had ever recorded and hinted at a great treasure awaiting me when I finally reached the lamaseries.

The journey to Kalimpong, though shorter, was almost more rigorous and exhausting than the trip to Darjeeling. In addition to the already familiar giant boulders and huge fallen logs which blocked the improvised roadway, we had to climb in the rain a mountain ridge covered with dense forest. Most of the bridges of the Tista River and its tributaries had been washed away, and we had to scramble over maksehift crossings of slippery logs, trying not to look down at the rapids boiling far below. At more than one place we seemed to be clinging to the brink of nothing.

I found Kalimpong an ideal place for my work. It was situated on one of the oldest trade routes between Tibet and India, and because it was the meeting place of caravans and merchants, the cultures of all the surrounding states met and mingled there.

I stayed in a quaint hotel which had been opened some years previously by a scholarly old gentleman of Scottish and Tibetan parentage, named MacDonald, who was then almost ninety. He gave me several excellent books on Tibet which had come from his pen. The hotel was a family affair which Mr. MacDonald's three daughters, all British-educated and widely traveled, helped run. I look back now with warm gratitude when I recall the way in which I was taken into that family circle and shown their rare treasures from Lhasa and from other strongholds of Tibet. Talking intimately with them was a wonderful introduction to the experiences ahead.

It was no more than a few minutes' walk from the little hotel to the narrow main street of Kalimpong, the trading center where Indian merchants meet the incoming yak caravans from Tibet with their loads of wool. On market days the street was crowded with hillmen from Sikkim and Nepal, with Bhutanese, Beharis, Chinese, Mongolians, Lepchas, and Tibetans, all on their way to the bazaar. Many of them led small ponies like the one which had carried me so grudgingly along the mountain trail. In the bazaar one could buy delicate Tibetan silver, Nepalese brasswork, and rugs, embroideries, leatherwork, and curious jewelry from all the neighboring countries. An array of exotic products continually passes through Kalimpong: musk on its way to France and the United States for use in perfume and medicine; yak tails which are sent to Madras to be used in wigs; bristles; tea pressed into bricks; cardamom; Peruvian cinchona bark for use in the making of quinine; and pelts of fox, lynx, stone marten, and snow leopard from Tibet. The snow leopard has especially great value for Tibetans, because it gives, so they say, protection against "sly earth currents that intrude into a meditator's thought and undo his virtue, as the termites undo buildings in the dark."

Lines of bullock carts trundle and creak over the rough roads, bringing in baskets of oranges from the warm valleys. On certain days long caravans with their loads of wool arrived from great distances over the mountains of Tibet, and on those days the marketplace was filled with noisy Marwari merchants. The wool was taken to vast, barren warehouses, where I saw tiny women sitting on the floor, their legs stretched straight out in front of them like rag dolls, braiding the woolen strands with machine-like accuracy.

It was just after my arrival in Kalimpong that I had my first encounter with the magic and mysticism of Tibet. I had lingered, fascinated, to watch the arrival of a yak caravan from the interior. I cannot imagine a more picturesque sight; the slow-moving beasts with their long shaggy coats and strangely pensive faces, laden with packs and baskets and bales of produce, were no more colorful than their attendants, a motley group of unkempt little men, almost obscured in their cumbersome cloaks, bulky with heavy padding against the mountain cold.

I was so absorbed in all that was going on about me that I almost forgot to return to the hotel for afternoon tea—an indispensable ritual in my life. Since I was so late, only one person remained in the room when I arrived: a small dark man, dressed Indian-style in the tight white trousers and long black frock coat. Recognizing me as a newcomer, he asked if he might join me. He was a professor from Calcutta, an earnest student of Mahayana Buddhism who was in Kalimpong for study.

I shall never forget, even though I still do not know whether or not I believe it, one of his stories that day. Leaning forward, as if sharing a great confidence, he said, "I was walking along the main street of Kalimpong one day when I saw an imposing lama approaching. As he drew near, I bowed and smiled. Not knowing his language, I could not exchange a greeting but to my astonishment he addressed me in faultless English, asking if I had yet inspected a *Gomba* [monastery]. When I told him that I had not, he turned and pointed to a monastery nestling high up on the mountainside, almost hidden in mist. 'Up there is where I live. Come with me and I will show it to you.'

"We fell into step and began trudging up a steep twisting path. After walking for some time, I saw the local doctor wending his way down the path, which gave me an excuse to stop and get my breath. While the doctor and I exchanged pleasantries the lama walked on a short way and waited until I rejoined him.

"I remember we entered the precincts of the monastery through an ornate archway in the eastern wall. Immediately to the right lay a building about sixty by sixty feet square, with walls of wood on a base of stone. This was the temple. The lama led me inside where we saw a full-sized statue of The Enlightened One, with a smaller figure of a Tara on either side. I was deeply moved and quite involuntarily I cried out, 'But how lifelike . . . how beautiful!'

"'Lifelike? Why, of course!' exclaimed a voice. I peered closer . . . I could have sworn those lips had moved!

"'You've been a long time in attaining the summit'—it was the same voice speaking—'and I have been waiting for you! Your path has been long and steep, full of pitfalls at times, but you have made it at last.' My first reaction was that the lama must be playing a ventriloquist's joke on me. I turned quickly and found that I was alone. I felt a cold shiver run the length of my spine and, uneasy, I departed in great haste. When I had once more reached the sunlight I hurried across to the living quarters of the monastery, thinking that the lama had gone ahead of me to announce my arrival. But the place appeared to be utterly deserted.

"I went inside and looked around. The silence weighed upon me, and it was then that I began to be afraid. With fear urging me on I was very quickly back down the road into town, and I rushed to the doctor's office. 'Tell me,' I said, 'when I met you an hour or so ago on the mountain path, did you notice the friend who was with me?' 'There was no one with you,' the doctor said, 'you were alone on the path. I'm absolutely sure.' I was beginning to feel foolish before his calm insistence, and apologizing for the intrusion on his time, I was about to leave when the doctor called me back.

"'Wait a minute,' he said, 'this friend of yours . . .'

"'He was a lama,' I said, 'a most impressive man!'

"The doctor gave me a queer look. 'So you have seen the apparition from the deserted monastery! You're only the third one in the thirty years since the abbot was murdered and the place abandoned.'" Whether it happened or not, it certainly seemed quite real as he told it.

"If you find my story incredible," he said gently to me, "how do you think I, to whom it happened, must regard it? Was the doctor sure that I was alone? Am I sure that I was not? Did the Buddha speak? Who can be sure, and above all, who can explain such things?"

I made my headquarters at the Scottish mission school in the hills near the lamaseries. Here tribesmen from many regions sang their songs for me, blending ancient, animistic exorcism of evil spirits with modern Buddhism. Even some of the seven-man Tibetan delegation which had escorted me over the mountains turned up and sang for me.

Dr. and Mrs. Duncan, the greathearted missionaries who were my hosts, extended a cordial welcome to the Buddhist priests who came to record their chants. To me this was especially gratifying, for I believe that the love of God is the same no matter what the cut of the ecclesiastical cloth. Day after day and often late into night, visiting lamas chanted the weird music of their ancient ceremonies while I recorded them. I also recorded the singing of the delightful Tibetan girls from noble families of Lhasa who were studying in the mission school.

In my recording I was helped tremendously by the Raja and Rana of Bhutan, who later were hosts to the Dalai Lama when he fled from Communist-dominated Tibet. The Rana, who comes of an aristocratic family in Lhasa, had great influence in the region. An ardent Buddhist, she had established a religious center where she published Buddhist literature; she was, in fact, a real force in fostering the revival of Buddhism in that part of the world. She most graciously sent out messengers to bring to her home singers who knew rare, old, unspoiled songs which they had brought from Tibet, Sikkim, Nepal, and Bhutan. One old man, who had traveled a long way over tortuous roads through the rain, sang for me in a quavering voice of the hard life of his people in the mountains. Another singer, a fine musician, the favorite singer of the Dalai Lama, sang ancient epics from a great Tibetan saga which ranks among the finest religious poetry of the world. He sang with moving vitality, yet with complete detachment and dignity.

From my window, in the stillness of the early morning, Kanchenjunga, which flanks Mount Everest, seemed to soar above the entire visible world; I could understand why travelers came from afar to see it and receive a benediction from the serenity of its eternal snows. No one in the Duncan household at the mission ever missed the dawn, for that was the only time at this season when one might catch a glimpse of this white-robed sentinel.

The Tibetans think that Mount Kanchenjunga is the home of the gods, and they firmly believe that the reason it has never before been conquered was that the gods did not permit it. Some little time before I was there a group of climbers had attained the summit but stopped a few feet short of the actual crest, in deference to the strong belief of the people.

The atmosphere of remoteness from earthly things, and of the awesome majesty of the Himalayas are no doubt what led the holy men of long ago to build their monasteries in their shadow. There are two lamaseries in the mountains, a short journey from Kalimpong, the smaller belonging to the Druk-pa sect of lamas, the larger founded by the late Geshe Rimpoche of the Tumbka Lamasery in the faraway Dhumbri Valley of Tibet. Thirty lamas lived here, and from their windows they could contemplate the snowy peaks of Kanchenjunga, Chomiono, Kabru, Pandim, and other Himalayan giants. (The Sanskrit "Himalayas" means "Abode of Snow.") As I approached the lamasery of Tumbka, the first thing I saw were many small white flags fluttering in the wind. Each of these flags, according to Buddhist tenets, is a prayer.

A smiling lama greeted me when I first arrived and led me through the courtyard, which is used for religious ceremonies and dramas, into the kitchens. There I shared the lama's particular brew of Tibetan tea—a mixture of tea, soda, and rancid yak butter blended in a churn and boiled. This was a very difficult ritual for me; even my stomach, which had survived monkey meat with caterpillar sauce, was affronted by this beverage.

Nearby, not far from the cremation ground of the Buddhists, was the retreat of the Hermit Lama, an oracle who could be consulted by the faithful. Other lamas lived in small huts scattered among the trees. As we approached the main building, which was surrounded by one hundred prayer wheels, a pilgrim was walking round and round, reverently touching each wheel and setting it spinning with his right hand. Every revolution represented a fervent repetition of a prayer.

Just inside the dark, cool hall, which was lighted only by altar lamps, I saw a great painting of the Wheel of Life showing the different stages in man's existence, including the seven hot hells and the seven cold ones. The wall paintings depicted the Guardians of the Four Directions—north, south, east, and west—and on either side of the great image of Lord Buddha on the altar were cupboards containing the hundred volumes of *Kangyur*, the Buddhist commandments. One of these, the ancient Chant of Difficulty, emphasized the importance of the commandments:

> To cultivate the lovely flowers and fruit
> Is difficult
> Unless we know the value of dampness.

> To understand the origin of life and thought
> Is difficult
> Unless we read and know the Kangyur.

It was hard to understand how the lamas could observe the laws of one hundred volumes when we have only ten commandments and find it difficult enough to follow them. Finally, on the upper floor were carefully preserved "the thousand images of Buddha," and in an inner sanctum were the *Cho-kyongs*, or guardians of Buddhism.

From time to time following the earthquake a procession of priests wound its way around the lamaseries. In their long saffron robes, with prayer books on their heads, they advanced at a slow, rhythmic pace, and through the still clear mountain air came the subdued monotone of their hypnotic chanting. Louder and louder grew the chanting, as they implored the gods to stop the rains and bring peace to the people and calm to the countryside.

After slowly making their march outside the lamasery, they entered the dimly lit hall to hold a service of supplication. At intervals a sudden clamor of instruments would interrupt the low throb of the chants: melodious little bells, eerie-sounding conch shells, huge strident cymbals, shrill trumpets more than fifteen feet long, and deep-booming drums taller than the men who played them. All the tones mingled together in an overpowering surge of sound.

Here in the remoteness of the Himalayas I was as far as a human being could be from occidental civilization. And here was music as far removed from our own as any in the world, music which the Western world had yet to know. Still, with all its strangeness, it did not fail to reach my heart, giving me some conception of the deep religious feeling of a people whose culture is no different from our own. It was music, even though the language was totally unintelligible, which created that moment of appreciation and oneness. And it was music, passed down through the ages since the Enlightenment of Buddha, which had kept alive his precepts and doctrines.

I was also very fortunate to come across several chants of the eleventh century which came down direct from that very holy man and great teacher, Milarepa. A wrinkled old Buddhist recounted to me how Milarepa, the poet-singer of Tibet, had traveled from place to place teaching the untutored people through songs, chanting the religious ideals of Buddhism. The caves at the foot of Mount Everest, where he spent a part of his life in meditation, are still regarded as holy and are regularly visited by pilgrims. The philosophy and idealistic teachings of this great man are simply and beautifully preserved through chant. The precepts laboriously written on scrolls by devoted lamas can still be found in eastern Tibet. One chant from the eleventh century expresses his philosophy in part and reads:

The place for meditation
Is not when you are in a crowd,
But alone in a quiet monastery
High on a mountaintop.
You may learn there
To be steadfast and firm.
To ponder in deep thought
The eight Holy Doctrines
And learn to perform
Acts of true charity.

Free then from the devils
Of possession, with the sins
Of laziness left far behind,
And all desire for earthly wealth
Forgotten, you shall see
Without distraction
The good that you should do.
Then at last, your freedom earned,
The sharp sword of sublime wisdom
Will be yours; with it you may
Sever yourself free forever
From all earthly misery.

Thus it is written.

A master yogi, Milarepa experimented with consciousness as a chemist experiments with matter. It is said that no other disciple put into practical living the precepts of the Buddha more truly. Not only the Buddhists of Tibet and other Asian countries but truth-seekers throughout the world consider him to be a "Fully Enlightened One." He made it clear that Buddhism is ever open to everyone everywhere, irrespective of religious affiliations.

This Tibetan saint was said to sustain life in the arctic climate of the high Himalayas on the most meager food and, because of the indomitable control of his physical body, sometimes with no other sustenance than that which a plant derives by an osmosis-like process from air, water, and sunshine. In his frigid cave there was no heat except that which he produced within his own body by the Yoga practice of *tummo*. For him the purpose of life was to evolve beyond the ease and comfort which create attachment to the world. In one song he taught that when desire for comfort has been transcended and freedom has been won, "Naught is there uncomfortable; everything is comfortable."

For Milarepa, as for all saints of every religion in all civilizations and epochs of human history, complete renunciation of the worldly way of life led to the attainment of the highest life here on earth. When approaching his nirvana, Milarepa is said to have counseled his disciples: "Act so that you have no cause to be ashamed of yourselves; and hold fast to this rule. If you do thus, you can be sure of never disobeying the commands of the Supreme Buddhas."

In this age of technology, Milarepa, like so many saints, is viewed with veneration by some and with indifference by others, but in the atmosphere of Tibet's centuries of devotion I was reminded of Arnold Toynbee's claim that it was not the scientists, technicians, industrial leaders, statesmen, captains, and kings who have done most for mankind, but the prophets and saints.

My glimpse of Tibet revealed great beauty, not only in her snow-capped mountains and foaming waterfalls, her blue lakes and racing rivers, but in the thoughts and the beliefs of the people. Every Tibetan wears a piece of turquoise, in a ring or fastened to a cord about his neck or on his wrist as a bracelet, to bring him happiness. The Tibetans believe that the turquoise will assume the color of the wearer. If he is good and pure of heart, the turquoise will become a pure light blue. If he is cruel, bitter, and selfish, it will grow dark and green.

Curiously enough, this does actually happen; the color does change. This is just one of those many mysteries the world can never explain. The Tibetans do not try to explain; they simply accept.

Chapter 16

THE HERMIT KINGDOM OF NEPAL

Nepal was still a hermit kingdom when I first visited it in 1950. One could enter the small barricaded country of fifty-four thousand square miles only at the invitation of the Prime Minister, Maharaja Padma Shumshere Jung Bahadur Rana. Consequently there were no hotels or guesthouses other than the Maharaja's personal guesthouse on the palace grounds.

By a stroke of good fortune I was in New Delhi when this potentate left Nepal on one of his very rare visits to the outside world. I met him almost daily at diplomatic functions given in his honor, and New Delhi was filled with chatter about the royal wedding of the Prime Minister's nephew shortly to take place in Nepal. It was at a farewell party at the Nepalese Embassy that the Maharaja, an austere, autocratic man with a flowing gray mustache in the Kaiser Franz Joseph style, invited me to attend the wedding festivities.

The only route into Nepal at that time was over two ranges of the Himalayas, a trek of several days by foot, Tibetan pony, or *dhandi,* a sloping, tilted sort of armchair slung on two cross-poles and borne on the shoulders of eight coolies. But it was arranged that I should not have to make this arduous trip with my bulky recording gear, but should be flown to Katmandu in a tiny plane owned by a cousin of the Maharaja, quite an honor in itself.

The Ranas were then still the most powerful family in the Himalayan kingdom. For over a hundred years, up to 1951, the prime ministership of Nepal was in the hands of Jung Bahadur

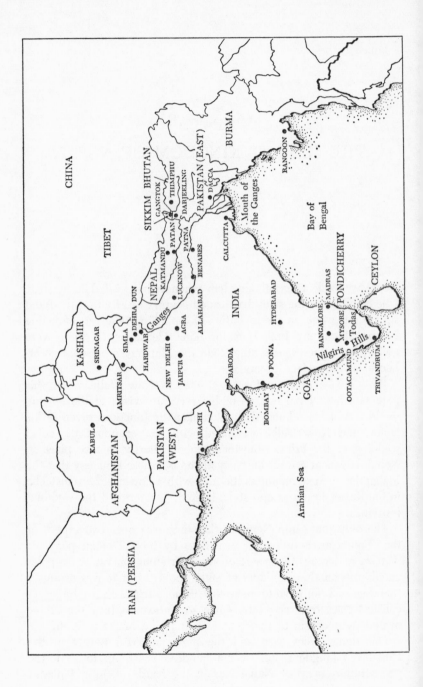

Rana, his brothers, and his descendants. The position had become a hereditary one in 1856, when Prime Minister Jung Bahadur (said to have been one of the wiliest Asians of his era) assumed the title of Maharaja, and forced the King to give the prime ministership to the Rana family in perpetuity. From that time until recently, the King of Nepal was but a figurehead.

The Ranas are Kshatriyas, the caste of warriors and princes whose spiritual home is the ancient Indian Rajputana state of Udaipur, where the twelve-hundred-year-old ruling dynasty claims direct descent from the sun. The one person in Nepal above the Ranas was the King, who represented a dynasty that had endured only since 1559. His Majesty Tribhuvana Bir Bikram Shah was held to be a living god, a reincarnation of the god Vishnu the Preserver. His duty was to propagate the dynasty and attend official functions, his divinity apparently placing him above the tedious business of ruling. It was said of this quiet man that he was a devout gardener and as completely out of touch with the outside world as was Nepal itself.

The Ranas invariably married beautiful Rajput princesses from India, thereby maintaining the purity of the Aryan blood that separates them racially from their subjects, who are mostly simple people of Mongol-Tibetan stock, speaking a variety of twenty different languages.

The office of prime minister passed from brother to brother, according to seniority, to ensure that the ruling power of the mountain kingdom would always be in mature hands (no Rana could hope to be a Maharaja until he was in his sixties). This resulted, naturally enough, in a great temptation to build up the family prosperity at the expense of the national treasury, which at this time the Maharaja controlled, having to account to no one, not even the Living God, for his expenditures.

I did not know when I set forth on this adventure that the Maharaja's government was shortly to be overthrown by the anti-Rana Nepali Congress Party (believed by the Ranas to have been guided and subsidized by illegitimate branches of their family who, barred from rights of succession by their irregular birth, had migrated to India).

We took off for Nepal in a pea-soup fog from Patna, then a shabby, rambling city, the former capital of a long-vanished North Indian empire. We flew in the tiniest aircraft I had ever been in.

This was, in fact, the only aircraft at this time that had succeeded in penetrating the clouds and mist that continuously masked the peaks of Nepal, and my pilot was the only man who had successfully risked this hazardous flight over the Himalayas to land in the tiny sheep pasture with its solitary wind sock in the Katmandu Valley. He had done it precisely *three* times before. However, this rangy young American with vivid blue eyes had an air of quiet efficiency that cheered me as he lifted the little plane into the impenetrable murk.

At an altitude of about thirteen thousand feet we came, as if bursting through a curtain, into a blaze of dazzling light. This was something more than sunshine; it was a suffusion of celestial brilliance seen only by those who had soared as high as the mountain peaks themselves. There, dazzling and magnificent, so near I felt I could touch them, were the highest peaks in the world, including Mount Everest. Never, in all my hundreds of thousands of miles of flying, have I experienced such a sensation—a feeling that sky and mountain were completely enfolding me; that for just a moment I was truly one with the universe.

"I hope we'll be able to land," the pilot said, turning to me with a grin and pointing to a tiny hole in the clouds below us. "Shall we make a try for it?" "Yes, of course. We have no alternative," I shouted back. He shrugged his shoulders, and we nose-dived through lazy clouds and plummeted down onto the tiny pocket handkerchief of grass in the valley, sending sheep racing in all directions.

The moment we climbed out of the little plane we were surrounded by children, ten and twelve year olds, wild with excitement. They were from aristocratic Nepalese families who had heard that we would be arriving and had come to the meadow to watch for us. I learned that several of them were generals, military titles being inherited in certain Nepalese families as ancestral titles are in European aristocracy. In spite of their exalted inherited rank, they acted like any other youngsters seeing an airplane for the first time in their lives.

Because of the bad weather conditions no one had been sure of our arrival and we had to wait a little time for the palace welcoming party, but what a wonderland it was! Mountain peaks towered around us, their tips lost in glowering clouds, and on their lower slopes, terraced grain and rice fields spread vivid splashes of green. The Lilliputian generals had to be repeatedly shooed away from the plane; they did their best to get inside it and would have taken it apart to see what made it fly had the pilot not been very stern. By way of giving him a little respite I opened my camera, intending to photograph the amusing scene, and at once the children transferred their attention to me. Closing in, they nearly swept me off my feet, all of them trying to peer into the viewer simultaneously. So avid was their interest we might have been visitors from another planet.

We were rescued by the arrival of the Maharaja's personal representative, a wispy, unprepossessing man named Darum, dressed in tight white pants, long, closely fitted black coat, and high black cap. Darum was to be my constant companion and guide, and I was astonished to find, awaiting me in this gleaming mountain fastness on the roof of the world, a bright red Studebaker. True, it was a little battered and slightly the worse for wear, but it was complete with chauffeur. Later another car, this time a blue touring car, was put at my disposal for use throughout my stay in Nepal. This was a great honor since, at that time, there were not more than a dozen automobiles in the whole kingdom, and those that were here had been carried across the Himalayas, partly disassembled, on the bent backs of coolies. Later, when we were returning to India on foot, we went through two mountain passes—one of eight thousand feet, another of six thousand feet— where I filmed a party of porters on the narrow, precipitous path, bearing the chassis of an automobile. Every detachable part had been removed, and as I saw the scattered pieces carried on those crawling backs strung out for miles along the rugged mountain path, it seemed inconceivable that it would ever reach Katmandu, and if it did, that the jigsaw could ever be assembled into a beautiful, brand-new Buick for the King.

Darum showed an intense desire to please me. He exerted authority over my chauffeur and dealt quite roughly with the loitering men, women, and children who surrounded the car, clamoring to catch a glimpse of the blond visitor who had dropped from the sky. Darum's knowledge of English was not really adequate for his role as guide, but somehow we managed to understand each other—in essentials, at any rate. The driver took off with a violent jerk and a crash of gears, scattering the crowd like chickens, and I all but fell onto the floor. In fact, I had a hard job remaining on

the seat at all as we careened along, bumping and jolting over cob-
blestones and unbelievably rutted roads. Wedging my feet against
the back of the front seat and hanging on with both hands, I
managed to stay upright long enough to catch a glimpse of
Katmandu as the red car tore along. In the center of the town
was a wide, grassy, tree-bordered maidan filled, as we passed,
with soldiers on their daily parade. A military review was held
every morning on this parade ground and it was said in Nepal
at that time, "Every man is a soldier."

Nepalese titles of nobility are modeled on Western military
rank, and this accounts for the many generals in such a small
country. The Gurkhas (their name derives from the onetime kingdom of Gurkha, now a minor Nepalese town) are famed for their
love of fighting and for their ruthless ferocity in battle. They are
possibly still the best-known export of this tiny Himalayan kingdom.

The Gurkhas were first sent by the great Nepalese Prime Minister
Jung Bahadur Rana, to help the British army put down the 1857
mutiny in India. In gratitude, the British ceded back to Nepal the
lands appropriated in 1816 in the Terai, jungle slopes that slant
down from the Himalayan foothills to the present Indian border.
(The *kukri*, the chief weapon of the Gurkhas, has an ivory bone
handle and is carried in a stout leather scabbard slung from the
belt at the small of the back; its thick blade, about a foot long and
curved downward instead of up, has struck terror in the heart of
the enemy in all the main theaters of war ever since. Arms of various
types from past ages to the present formed the principal exhibit in
the Katmandu museum.)

On one side of the maidan I noticed fairly modern office buildings: the Chandra College with its impressive clock tower in front,
and hundreds of students crowded on the lawn. On the other side
were the bazaars and the old town. The narrow, twisted streets
were lined with two-storied houses of many-colored bricks and
wooden crossbeams, and a flood tide of humanity surged noisily
around the open-fronted shops with their stacks of soap, cooking
pots, candles, tea, umbrellas, mats of an endless variety of colors
and designs, sugar, matches, cheap cigarettes, spices, and rice.

Everywhere, rising admonishingly—sometimes, it seemed, right
in the middle of the road—were Hindu and Buddhist shrines.
Leaving the center of the town, we bounced along dusty rutted

roads, passing strings of coolie women wood-carriers, doubled under their enormous loads, carrying baskets almost as tall as themselves and held to their backs by leather or woven bands
stretched over their foreheads. I caught glimpses of little family
groups clustered in doorways, children with bunches of bright-
colored flowers in their arms, and workers stooped at work in the
rice fields and cornfields, all of them clad in gay-colored homespun
wrap-on garments. No matter how much one travels, these first
glimpses of the people in a strange country seem to stay fixed in
the mind forever.

At last we turned into the road leading to the Maharaja's
guesthouse, which was not far from his own palace. My bedroom
and living room were spacious but sparsely furnished. Had I not
coped many times with the austerities of the old-fashioned pitcher
and washbowl and other meager toilet facilities in remote countries, the bathroom might have dismayed me. It was a triumph
of inconvenience. But I missed few of the conventional comforts
so dear to Westerners, since a whole retinue of gentle, courteous
servants had been assigned to see to my well-being. They kept
reappearing and looking at me appealingly, awaiting instructions;
they seemed almost offended when I could not find something for
them to do.

In the garden in front of the guesthouse, among the trees and
shrubs and brilliant flowers, was a small marble statue of a Hindu
deity, and floral offerings to this god—exotic blooms of brilliant
colors and strong spicy fragrance that floated on the soft breeze into
my Spartan quarters—were daily renewed by my cheerful personal
maid, Lakshmi, a devout Hindu. There was another lush garden
at the rear of the house, and on the other side of this lived the
palace servants and their families, in much less grandeur.

The conscientious Darum hovered about outside my door while
I refreshed myself, and seemed impatient to whisk me off to
the Maharaja, who he said was awaiting my arrival. The senior
members of the Rana family—the commander in chief (civil affairs), the senior commanding general (military affairs), and General Kaiser, G.B.E., formerly Nepalese ambassador to London—
all had grand palaces, but they were no match for the Singha
Durbar, a vast colonnaded structure covering many acres where
the Maharaja lived and from which he ruled the kingdom.

As we drove under a lofty white arch iron gates were swung

open by saluting soldiers, and we entered a wide carriageway encircling a beautiful formal garden. It was here that I had my first glimpse of the Maharaja's small grandson, wearing an immaculate replica of the long white frock coat and tight white trousers of a high-caste Hindu gentleman, pedaling his way along the drive on his tricycle, while a uniformed *syce* (groom) walked solemnly beside him holding over his small royal head an enormous fringed umbrella.

On the broad terrace steps the master of protocol greeted me in excellent English and led me through lofty halls filled with hunting trophies of every kind. We threaded our way between many tiger-skin rugs adorning the floor, all of them just a little too realistic with their great heads and snarling red-rimmed jaws. Rhinoceros heads and other fierce trophies glowered from every wall, all of them bagged by royal Rana hunters of the past in the mountain jungles that slope down toward India. Even the paintings and photographs were of hunting scenes, including one of the youthful Prince of Wales, now the Duke of Windsor, standing proudly beside a tiger he had just shot.

The rooms were vast but packed with massive and ornate furniture of every period, and *objets d'art* from all over the world were crammed into every available nook and cranny, some of them amusingly opposed in taste. For instance, exquisite French crystal chandeliers glittered overhead, while the austere dignity of the royal meeting room was decorated with floor-to-ceiling distorting mirrors. These "fun house" mirrors had caught the fancy of the former Maharaja Chandra while in Europe in 1908, and he had had them carried over the mountain passes and installed in the palace for the amusement of guests. Catching sight of my reflected image as I passed in the wake of my escort, I was astonished to see myself in turn a dwarf, a giant, a beanpole, and a circus fat lady. They certainly did little toward building up one's confidence when approaching the august presence at the farthermost end of the long room.

In this vast conglomeration of antiques nothing was more impressive than the enormous carved chair in which the Maharaja awaited me. When Padma Shumshere stood to receive me, he seemed not so tall as I had remembered; perhaps the vastness of his surroundings, even of the chair he had just vacated, tended to dwarf him. On the other hand, as he stood very erect in spite of his sixty-seven years, his manner, now that he was on home territory, seemed more compelling than it had been in New Delhi. Even while he held my hand, smiling cordially, I sensed ruthlessness behind those cold dark eyes. Like his little grandson, the Maharaja wore the customary long white frock coat and white trousers of a high-caste Hindu, but his flowing gray handlebar mustache lent him a deceptively Edwardian drawing-room appearance, in spite of the black military cap with its Rana seal of crossed *kukris*. These were made entirely of diamonds, framed by three larger diamonds, one the size of a pigeon's egg.

Since he was about to leave to take part in an annual religious festival at a neighboring village, my host asked me if I would like to see it and suggested that Darum should escort me there. Off we went, bumping and leaping along the appalling roads in the old blue touring car, into the very heart of Katmandu Valley. Vibrant colors permeated the entire scene—the blue sky, purple mountains, green forests, and terraced rice fields. Even in the poorest streets of the villages, the color of the aged stones in the half-timbered balconied houses seemed to soften their shabbiness. All these colors—soft pinks, rust, bluish gray, and a variety of mauves and purples—blended with the scarred, brown wooden strips that latticed the leaning, tilted fronts of the houses. In the pitted, dusty road, amid the dull garb of the Nepalese men with long open-necked shirts worn trailing over once-white trousers, the women, however poor, moved like flowers, their brown bodies swathed in intense blues and crimsons.

The soft indeterminate shades of fuchsia, mauve, and violet seemed to be achieved only by the Eastern races with their unique age-old processes of dyeing. Throughout the lush countryside we came upon vast squares of dyed cloth drying on the grass beside the road, strung out on balconies overhanging the narrow streets, or spread on rocks and pool edges bordering the endless shrines and fountains.

Nowhere was there a place without temples or shrines. As one of the earliest writers on Nepal has said, "There are nearly as many temples as houses, and as many idols as inhabitants, there not being a fountain, a river, or a hill within its limits that is not consecrated to one or another of the Hindu or Buddhist deities."

These shrines and temples were always alive with activities. To their nearby pools and fountains, women bring their household washing, banging and bashing it against the stonework or standing in the water to wash their bodies or their long blue-black hair. One woman I filmed was washing her hair in the fountain before an ancient shrine; she was wrapped about with a deep purple skirt, patterned in a scattered wine-colored design. Combined with this were a deep blue underskirt, a pale blue blouse, and a vivid scarlet sash. The whole effect against the rich brown skin of her shoulders and arms and black hair, tousled and soapy though it was, would have delighted the eye of Gauguin.

The festivities had already begun when we arrived, and the small village was swarming with humanity bent upon enjoyment. An elaborately carved "cart," laden with symbolic figures towering into the air, tier upon tier, was being jolted over the cobbled streets on its great wooden wheels, drawn by twenty or thirty willing worshipers. White-clad priests were milling around the guardhouse under its precariously wobbling dome.

Even in all this excitement, I was still a center of interest as I was escorted through the crowd to the royal enclosure. At that time I was the only Western woman, apart from the British ambassador's wife, in Nepal (only five American women, I was told, wives of our ambassadors based in New Delhi, had ever entered this remote hermit kingdom). With unconcealed pride in his family, the Maharaja introduced me to his attractive grandchildren and to his son, Major General Bijaya Shumshere Jung Bahadur Rana, the young and handsome Director General of Foreign Affairs. Then the Prime Minister went to officiate in the religious ceremony taking place at the holy cart, while the crowd, surging and jostling in the brilliant sunshine, waited for the supreme moment of acclamation.

When at last one of the priests came to the edge of the cart and held aloft the brocade holy vestment, the people chanted and bowed, and then became completely silent for a moment, while the statue of the god was put on view for the thousands to gaze at with rapture, receiving a benediction from the divine countenance.

With the return of the god to the sacred precincts of the temple, the decorated cart was left forlorn and forgotten in a side street; then the festivities really began with three days of gambling. This popular religious festival marks the one time in the whole year during which the Nepalese are allowed to indulge their delight in this particular pastime. All along the narrow streets, booths had been set up as gaming houses, and within minutes of the sacred moment of awed silence these little canvas houses were bulging with a mass of people, scrambling to make the most of the three days, hoping to get rich quickly. In the warm, spicy air there arose a new sound, the rattle of wooden counters, mingled with staccato exclamations of anger or dismay, murmurs of delight or disappointment: all the sounds of frustration and exuberance of a voluble population, recently blessed and now free to enjoy itself to the full.

In the early days of my visit, I was always rushing outside into the streets at the sound of music, and usually it was a bridal procession passing. Spring in Nepal is the propitious time for marriages as well as for other religious festivals. A Hindu wedding is full of the poetry of human life, with special songs sung at each of the many stages of the ritual while magical verses are continually chanted. Preparations, of course, extend over many months; in fact, they begin years before the marriage, with the betrothal. During this time the giving of gifts of cloth, a symbolic coconut, and the anointing of the would-be bridegroom with a mark of *sandhur* (red oxide of mercury) on the forehead make the contract almost as final as the ultimate vows.

The bridegroom's parents begin by asking an astrologer to find an auspicious day for the marriage, and this worthy, after consulting the horoscopes of both boy and girl, sets a day and a season suitable to the parents of both parties. Then a representative comes from the bridegroom's house to the bride's house with the offer of the date on which the wedding should be celebrated. Since the astrologer's word is law, the date suggested is always accepted.

Spring is the preferred season, with its association of bursting buds and renewal of life. Almost every day in the streets of Katmandu or Patna I saw a bride, with her face demurely veiled in red, carried along in a *dhandi*. Her groom followed close behind in another dhandi, trailed by dozens of children and an admiring crowd busy assessing the caste, status, and wealth of the bride and groom by the quality of the colorful umbrellas carried over the dhandis. The number of bearers following behind and the extent to which their baskets were loaded with gifts also indicated the social and financial status of the couple.

I cannot recall having seen a smiling Indian bride or groom, although Hindu brides in particular certainly have more to smile about today than in earlier days when widows were burned on their husband's funeral pyre. In Nepal, Hindu practices in general prevail, but it was sensibly decided long ago that this terrible custom should be abolished. In order to avoid the practice of *sati*, the word for this form of sacrifice, and yet follow the spirit of Hindu law, an ingenious plan was devised in which girls were first married with all the elaborate ceremony of a ritual marriage to a beautiful flower. When the "del flower," as it was called, wilted and died, it was given a proper funeral and with due ceremony sent floating down the river on a little barge. The girl's ultimate marriage to another bridegroom was counted as a second, so the question of her having to be sacrificed when her husband died never arose.

So many peoples and religions mingle in Nepal that there is considerable variance in the marriage customs, though almost everywhere divorce is rare. In one district, divorce was carried to a point of absolute simplification. All a woman had to do was to place a betel nut under her husband's pillow. This was a definite indication that she was about to leave him.

The wedding of the Maharaja's nephew, for which I had journeyed to Nepal, was an elaborate embodiment of wealth and glamour, with all the color a festooned, flower-garlanded city could contribute: elephants in gold trappings, troops in ceremonial uniforms, flags, banners, coaches drawn by prancing black horses, royalty in headdresses of bird-of-paradise plumes and ornate regalia, glittering silver- and gold-ornamented dhandis, and a dozen or more orchestras, sometimes all playing different tunes simultaneously.

The actual ceremony took place in a pavilion of silk erected in the palace gardens, but the festivities continued for days. In the bridal chamber, to which I was invited, I was dazzled by the glorious jewels and the rich silk of the many saris in magnificent colors, woven in silver and gold thread, into which the bride changed so frequently during the long series of ceremonies. It was small wonder that she looked exhausted before it was over. At the end of the rituals she emerged in a dazzling gorgeous red sari with a spangled veil over her face. She was carried in an ornate dhandi, while her prince, wearing a uniform of gold cloth and the inevitable peaked cap denoting his rank and nobility, was carried on the shoulders of his aides.

It was the music at the royal wedding that thrilled me as much as the brilliant spectacle, and I sat at my recording equipment day and night in order not to miss the sequences of ritual music, some of it music never before heard in the Western world. Music throughout Nepal varies in type with different tribes and districts. The Nepalese classical orchestra acquired much of its music from India, and the songs heard in the Rana palaces were usually accompanied by the harmonium and the *tabla*, both Indian instruments. The Nepalese harmonium is a portable organ, similar to the *regal*. Like the regal, it is an instrument in which tones are produced by forcing air, by means of a bellows, through freely vibrating metallic reeds. The singer plays on a keyboard with his right hand while he pumps the bellows with his left. The instrument carries the same melody in unison with the voice.

In Nepal, as in India, the tabla, two small copper drums tuned similarly and always played in pairs, are essential to the music of palace musicians. The difficult art of playing the tabla requires long years of study, and the player uses the wrist, the heel of the hand, the palm, and the fingers. Each drum has two heads, which are tuned to the tonic and fourth or fifth as required. Pieces of wood, attached under thongs connecting the two drumheads, serve in tuning the instruments. The tabla are absolutely indispensable to Indian music because they set the tempo and maintain the rhythmic flow.

The palace orchestras that I recorded in Nepal included, in addition to the harmonium and the tabla, clarinet (they call it clarionet, the medieval terminology, a word Sir Thomas Beecham always used), trumpet, cornet, bass clarinet, flute, euphonium (a small base saxhorn), xylophone, violin, tambourine, clybell, *medal* (large drum), castanets, and saxophone (which my interpreter insisted on calling "sexaphone," something he had in common with the Dean of Women at the University of Chicago when I was a student).

The Nepalese brass bands in attendance during the wedding festivities played familiar marches on the same instruments as are used in our Western bands, although they were of more ancient vintage. They created enormous excitement with their exuberant performances, and just as in our own country towns, swarms of little boys ran along beside them beating the tempo on sticks. The Gurkhas, trained by the best Scottish pipers during service in the British Army, contributed color and sound to the show. Hearing once again, in this little mountain kingdom, my favorite Highland tunes, which I had recorded while in Scotland, caused my heart to skip a beat or two.

But my favorites of all the orchestras and bands at this spectacle were the little groups of ragged children and men in drab and tattered homespun who took up their position at the entrance of the driveway just inside the palace gates, blowing primitive trumpets, clanging cymbals, and beating drums. Let no one underestimate the importance of this cacophony: they played a certain primitive melody required for every Nepalese wedding, no matter if it is in the royal palace or in the tiniest village hut. Whether the musicians were there from respect for the ceremonial, for love of music, or for the food that would follow as a reward for their labor, does not matter. Everyone present knew that the ceremony could not go on without this ancient, strident performance which has come down through the ages. These musicians could always be found at a temple entrance on a special feast day, at the gates of any house where a wedding was in progress, or accompanying a wedding party through the streets. Among all the many types of primitive and classical musicians I recorded in Nepal, these unprepossessing, shabby bands with their raucous but appealing music remain most deeply rooted in my affection.

In Nepal two worlds meet. The towering ranges that shelter Nepal from the outside also shelter a living Hindu god, the King, and a living Buddha, the Grand Lama of Boddhnath. In temples of unrecorded antiquity, two great oriental religions thrive. Fantastic Hindu idols and Buddhas with their inscrutable smiles mingle everywhere throughout the little kingdom.

The founder of Buddhism, Prince Siddhartha, later called Gautama Buddha, was born in Nepal of a noble family twenty-five hundred years ago. Today the Nepalese are almost equally divided between Buddhism and Hinduism, although in many parts of the country Hinduism has become so mingled with Buddha's Creed of the Middle Way that the two are almost indistinguishable, and there are many shrines sacred to both. The two most famous Buddhist temples, visited by pilgrims who come on foot from far-off lands across the difficult Himalayan passes, are enormous monuments. From the eight-thousand-foot Chandragiri Pass, the tall golden spire of Swayambhunath, glittering from a hilltop, catches the pilgrims' eyes like a challenging tongue of fire. This is the ancient and widely renowned temple to Adi, the Essential Buddha, the Eternal and Self-Existent One.

Boddhnath, one of the oldest temples in the Buddhist world, houses the Living Buddha, the Grand Lama of Boddhnath or, as he is sometimes called, the China Lama. The shrine itself is awe-inspiring. At the base of its immense golden spire is the rounded dome or stupa that enshrines the relics of the Buddha. The dome is encircled by a frieze of startling erotica in bas-relief, representing, not licentiousness, but the positive and negative forces of nature in eternal embrace, and from the four sides of the spire four enormous blue-rimmed pairs of eyes gaze across the city with the serene stare of the Enlightened One.

On arrival at Boddhnath, the Grand Lama received me, wearing the headdress denoting his rank and a beautiful brocaded gown of gold. He was a cheery, rotund little man in his sixties and he seemed delighted to have an excuse to display his fluent though deliciously ungrammatical English. Conversation bubbled out of him, and when I asked him about his title of China Lama, he said with a twinkle: "My grandfather came from northern China one hundred years ago." But it is claimed for him that he is the reincarnation of the Buddhist saint Padmasambhava. When I asked him about this the chubby China Lama, "The Living Buddha," beamed: "He was born in a lotus! He came from India and introduced Buddhism in Tibet in the seventh century." The China Buddha liked to meet foreigners and talk with them; he believed he could do more good in this way than by retreating to endless contemplation of the higher mysteries and tried to show it by doing lucrative business in selling Tibetan art. He went on to explain to me that in tantric Buddhism priests may marry, wear ornaments, and mingle freely with worldly people. I had to keep reminding myself that this chatty little man was the bearer of such an august title.

My visit to Nepal yielded many musical treasures, but it was an unexpected privilege when the China Lama offered to let me record for the first time the moving music of the services of the visiting lamas from the great lamasery of Lhasa in the heart of Tibet, and to film their Devil Dance. Spring in Nepal marks the

annual pilgrimage of these Tibetan lamas to pay tribute to the
lamasery of Boddhnath, and recording their chants and the over-all
cacophony of sound—the throbbing drums, the blaring trumpets,
and the tinkling bells—was tremendously exciting for me. The
sonorous voice of the huge conch shell and the enormous cymbals
clashing from time to time, marking musical episodes, might have
been the meeting of meteors in the whirling galaxies of the universe.

The rhythmic chants of the lamas were sometimes solo, sometimes ensemble, but through all the chanting I felt the strange,
compelling power of antiquity and reverence for the sacred doctrine passed down by devotees over two thousand years. One Lhasa
lama in particular stirred me with the intensity and vitality of
his singing. His sustained falsetto was a miracle of technique. Having grown up with singers and having studied voice production
for years, I was amazed at the breath control and the perfection
of every note. The mental focus and spiritual concentration required for this performance were almost incomprehensible to a
Westerner. This was a high moment. While unable to understand
a single word of the strange language, the impact of the music
brought immediate communication.

Suddenly "the Living Buddha" opened a bronze chest, brought
out a horn, and blew a solitary deep note. The small golden
Buddhas on the marble altar seemed alive in the glow of the
flames emerging from the large brass tubs of clarified butter,
and the silver bowls of uncooked rice, offerings to the idols, glittered
in the flickering light. Beside the idols on the altar were copper
bells decorated with silver, and three-foot bell-mouthed trumpets
studded with turquoise and coral beads.

At the blast of the trumpet the China Lama came to me and
said: "Come—we go outside for the ritual dance!" The masked
dance of the lamas to drive away the evil spirits was one of
the most impressive, colorful, and fantastic I have ever seen. The
late-afternoon sun shimmered on the golden spire of the stupa,
casting its shadow across the eyes that kept eternal vigil over the
encircling mountains and valleys. Silence seemed to enclose the
little village; it lay wrapped and enfolded as by a shawl, in a
mood of timeless serenity. Even the occasional barking of a dog
or the crying of a child that floated up from the streets seemed
muted.

The China Lama seated himself with the musicians of the

22. Sam Coles, "preacher with a plow"

Blackstone-Shelburne Studios, New York, New York

23. Woman seeing her own face for first time

University of California

24. Ovambo initiates dance at Coming-of-Age ceremony

25. Efundula drummers, Ovamboland

26. Initiates ceremonially "transformed into men" efundula (Ovambo Coming-of-Age ceremony)

27. Bushman playing musical bow

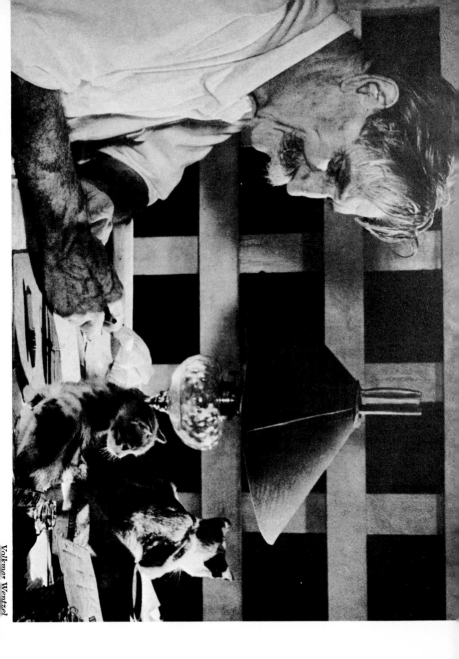

29. Albert Schweitzer's orderly playing primitive harp

30. Procession of holy men during the Purna Kumbha Mela (Urn Festival)

31. Millions of Hindus at Purna Kumbha Mela

32. Nilgiri Hills, Todas

33. Vina players in Mysore orchestra recorded by author

34. The author with her unpredictable Tibetan pony

Laura Boulton Collection

Laura Boulton Collection

35. Jigme Taring, Tibetan interpreter, and the daughter of the Raja of Bhutan

Mohen
1950

36. Maharaja of Nepal

37. The Prince and his bride, Nepal wedding

38. The author recording the Yellow Lama and Tibetan lamas

39. Tibetan lamas' Devil Dancers

40. Royal musicians and dancer, Angkor Wat, Cambodia

41. Mai-Sai, Thailand

42. Thai dancers

43. Balinese prince, host of author

44. Author with Dyak chief, Sarawak

45. The author in Korea with head of International Red Cross

46. On a glacier at Pt. Barrow

47. Peterhead in Hudson Bay

48. Eastern Arctic Eskimos on walrus hunt

49. Eevaloo making drum

50. Author recording Eskimo Drum Dance on Southampton Island

51. Sid Wein and passengers, Alaska

Laura Boulton Collection

52. Eskimo drum orchestra, Point Barrow, Alaska

temple orchestra under the spire's searching eyes and the music began. He lifted his hand and rang a temple bell vigorously, the signal for the start of all ceremonies. With the other hand he set in motion a small drum which then beat out its fast rhythms. This tiny drum has two little balls attached by cords which automatically beat the two drumheads as it is turned rapidly from side to side in the hand.

A droning chant now rose and fell, building up to a powerful climax which engulfed me in a wave of incantation and then, with dramatic suddenness, ceased. In that suspended moment an unbelievable clangor broke out. The strange quality of the tones of the instruments and the transport which swept over me made me feel as if this were all happening for the first time in the experience of man. As though born of this emotional tumult, there suddenly emerged from the bowels of the earth a fiendish and terrifying demon's head. Gradually the rest of the body appeared, garbed in a flowing brocade robe with voluminous sleeves almost touching the ground. This apparition was followed by other dancers in equally grotesque masks and similar brocaded garments of magnificent multicolored fabrics. Before I had fully recovered from the shock of the first arrival from the underworld, all the actors had assembled and the dance was in progress.

Standing in a circle, one by one, with a plunging step, they thrust themselves toward the center, throwing out their long-sleeved arms in a surging wave of color. They returned to the precision of the circle for a brief second only and then repeated the plunging step outward, flourishing their trailing sleeves to catch the last rays of the sun. Stepping back into formation, they pivoted again, a kaleidoscope of color and motion.

Suddenly I came out of my trance and started the tape recorder, realizing just in time that I had almost missed the chance of my lifetime to capture on tape and to share with the Western world this unique music. Fortunately my Indian cameraman, who had arrived on foot over the mountains to join me a few days earlier, was more accustomed to Eastern spectacles than I and had filmed in color all that I had seen. In the gathering purple dusk, while the orchestra was still playing and the dancers were slowly vanishing into the earth whence they had come, the camera panned up over the musicians, then to the eyes of the shrine, and upward to the tiptop of the golden spire.

I saw that the China Lama was beckoning to me to come and sit by him. It was an effort to rouse myself from the spell of this experience, but joining him I asked him to explain the chant that had opened the ritual, and this recording has preserved his exact words. His English may be, at times, difficult but the information, especially relating to musical instruments is interesting:

"These are the manifestations of Buddha. There are six parts. First, world of God; second, world of demons; third, land of man; fourth, world of beasts; fifth, world of birds of prey; sixth, in hell. He who remembers 'Oom-mani-patme-oom,' he will cross the world and attain to the paradise of Arialugishora. The man who remembers all instruments, flutes and cymbals and shells, he may, hard by himself, attain to the paradise of Arialugishora. And human being all happy and not to be sorrowful when they hearing of these instruments, of flutes, all for the Buddha's purpose. These are all given in the instructions by the Lord Buddha.

"And there are in Hinayana Buddhism no necessary of these human flutes and instruments. No necessary, even the rosary and beads, no necessary. Always with meditation for them. And whatever they act, they got to at the time of leisure, he may be always in meditation. That is the beside of Hinayana Buddhism.

"But these are the instruments of flutes and cymbals and bells and trumpets of Buddhism, all necessary for the Mahayana Buddhism. He was a reformer—as a secular to the whole world. [He meant someone who comes once in centuries.] Of north side, of even in India, and west side, and east side, all reform his religious perfectly. One who believes in the mind of Buddhism, he may get the heaven life in the seculars of time. [He meant ages.] All whatever he do, he done, he did the good actions for other peoples."

After this deeply serious interpretation, the China Lama became less the priest and more the host, and it was with very real dismay that I saw the large bronze Tibetan teapot approaching, in the hands of the China Lama's attractive daughter, Jigma, who had recently returned from her studies in India. She chatted with me in excellent English while pouring the tea, and then returned to the house across the compound, leaving us to our informal conversation and our tea.

How can I describe this strong Tibetan tea grown on the slopes of the Himalayas and brewed over a fire of yak dung? From previous experience I knew the unappetizing contents and the horrible clinging taste and aroma to which courtesy would commit me when the moment came.

I looked up to the spire and asked, partly to delay the drinking of the tea, "Tell me, Venerable, what is the message in those huge questioning eyes, and why the question mark for a nose?"

The China Lama turned to me seriously and said: "Maybe there is double question here, of the Buddha to you, and from you to yourself." And then, with sudden change of mood: "How you like our tea?"

In spite of the objections of my stomach and my conscience, I tried to be polite.

"This brew of tea is a new and fascinating experience. I've consumed large quantities of tea all over the world . . . and I love it . . . everywhere."

I thought my poker face had covered the situation, but my friend, with a twinkle in his eye, persisted.

"You think butter improves the flavor?"

"Well . . . I certainly think it makes it more interesting."

At this we both laughed heartily, but whether for the same reason I'll never know. Pointing to the rice terraces in the distance, I commented on their beautiful patterns. The China Lama appeared to be very pleased with this, and entered into a long discussion with our interpreter. Apparently what he wished to say was beyond his optimistic but not entirely adequate English. Finally Bahadur, the interpreter, explained in his more than adequate English: "When the wasteland on the mountainsides comes under cultivation, it is rent-free for ten years. The China Lama is very happy that you admired these rice fields because they are new ones and already they not only add to the beauty of the mountain slope, but they are producing heavily this year. Our people will eat well."

My eyes came back to the golden spire.

"Here in this land of temples, peacocks, and pagodas, this is the most impressive shrine I have seen. I have heard it is the oldest temple in the Buddhist world."

I could see the China Lama swell with pride.

"Why, it's old as Buddha himself!" And there followed another prolonged exchange between the two men before the interpreter

said: "Venerable says everybody in this happy valley has a pilgrimage spirit. There are twenty-seven hundred shrines and temples scattered over Nepal, and each one has its own days of ceremonies and worship and sacrifice. Holy days are holidays here.
The astrologers, who are everywhere, consult the stars and read
horoscopes to decide the best days for pilgrimages, ceremonies,
business, marriage, for every undertaking, great or small."

Now I knew why, wherever I went in this land of mysterious
yellow idols, I met so many cheerful travelers, all of them no doubt
urged on by the merit of happy pilgrimage, much as in Chaucer's
day of merrie England.

Their day began, as one author has written, "as soon as the tiles
could be counted on a roof or a cat's whiskers could be silhouetted
against the dawning light."

Often, as I watched them joking and gossiping on their way to a
shrine, I was reminded of the ancient Nepalese proverb: "Laughter
cleans the teeth."

It had been a hair-raising experience getting to Nepal in that
tiny plane, but how fortunate I was to have known the hermit
kingdom in those early days. I made a collection of Nepalese
music that will stand for all time. When I returned to Nepal, again
by invitation, for the coronation of the young King in 1956, change
was already at work. They had built a road so that people could
motor up over the mountains from India. A beautiful Rana palace
had become The Royal Hotel. They had opened an airline from
Patna to bring in the King's guests, and, of course, a regular air
service has been established now and every tourist who goes to
India can fly to Katmandu as easily as to Benares.

Perhaps the most significant indication of the rapidity of this
change is the fact that quite recently when a dancer from Nepal
was in America presenting special dances of his country, he had
to come to me for tapes of special Nepalese music. When a
country becomes part of the world and too accessible, it pays for
this status by losing part of its cultural heritage.

Chapter 17

CAVE COUNCIL IN BURMA

While studying and recording music, the most vital expression in the lives of people everywhere, I realized that much of it was an emotional outpouring connected with sacred rites. As there are no people without music, so there are none in the world without some form of worship. Since the beginning of time, man has felt an urge to pour out through prayers, hymns, and chants his innermost feelings to some Power (or Powers) greater than himself. It is a means of closer cooperation with the Spirit (or Spirits) that rule his universe. This is born in man, and I have observed it in all my travels. It is a psychological as well as spiritual necessity, a universal tendency of human nature. Since the dawn of human consciousness, religion has been the most vital force in man's life, and music has provided the most demonstrative means of expressing it.

Men everywhere are essentially religious; even among the so-called "primitive" people, religion is a powerful expression. I have found all kinds of godheads from the lowest to the highest "Unnamable and Boundless One." This spiritual and mysterious power, called by many names, is worshiped by many forms of ritual. But even among preliterate peoples who offer praise and supplications to numerous gods and spirits, there is often a firm belief in a Supreme Being who can be reached through the intercessions of lesser gods.

Man is born with the inner voice. It speaks to him and through him. He spends his whole lifetime constantly searching, through that divine spark within, to adjust to his total environment, to become at home with his universe.

His spiritual and psychological experiences have much in common with those of his fellow men the world over. Although in different geographical areas the beliefs of people may be affected by historical events, outstanding influential personalities, certain climates or temperaments, and other factors, still men everywhere are to some degree conscious of things spiritual and supernatural.

Religions are living things, involving deep human emotions, provoking strong human reactions, and prompting very special human behavior. They grow and expand, or they lose their power and die. In every religion most of the followers accept with blind faith the precepts taught by their fathers and forefathers. They do not question. They do not wonder about ultimates. However, in every culture there are a few reflective souls who begin to speculate, who begin to search for the One Force behind the Universe. As vistas open, not only for individuals but also for social groups, as the needs change, new leaders rise up who believe that they have the *true* interpretation of their faith, the original meaning of the God of the Universe, and that they are his *true* prophets. Thus new religions are born, and new hymns of praise or supplication are sung.

In the beginning, my interest in music was academic, but midway in my career, as my horizons widened, my interest became concentrated on music in worship. I decided to undertake the study and recording of it in all twelve major religions of the world, a project until then neglected. On earlier expeditions I had recorded ritual music with the so-called primitive peoples. Now in the Near and Middle East I began this project in earnest. In India I found the hymns and chants of the Hindus, which grew out of primitive ritual; the music of Jainism and Sikhism, which grew from Hinduism; and that of Zoroastrianism, which came to India from Persia. On India's northern borders I glimpsed the mysticism and magic of Tibetan Buddhism, while in the interior I recorded a moving ceremony under the Bodhi tree where Buddha is said to have preached his first sermon.

Buddhism had its historical beginning when a princely ascetic, Siddhartha, in northern India, attained Buddhahood which is regarded as the supreme status of a thinker and teacher. With this mental awakening and profound vision began a movement whose strength lay in the deepest personal conviction as to the nature of truth, gained through direct experience and internal perception.

Rationality, tolerance, moral purity, fortitude, friendliness, and humanism are some of the important features of the religion. Even as a form of mysticism its appeal is great. Buddhism is still the ancestral faith of many people in Assam, Chittagong, eastern Bengal, Darjeeling, Nepal, Bhutan, Sikkim, Simla, and along the spurs of the eastern Himalayas. The half of Indian thought that is Buddhism is rational, critical, creative, directive, and progressive.

Buddha is said to have been born and attained enlightenment and nirvana on the Full Moon Day of Kadon, the first day of the first month of the Buddhist year. This most sacred day of the Buddhists' calendar occurred in 1954 on May 17, the twenty-five-hundredth anniversary of Buddha's birth, and marked the beginning in Burma of one of the most important gatherings in the history of Buddhism. This was the Sixth Buddhist Council, a meeting of the faith's world leaders which would run for two years. I planned my arrival in Rangoon to coincide with this historic Sixth Synod, then in session.

It was held on the Siri Mingala Plateau—that is, "The Most Glorious and Most Auspicious Land," where the World Peace Pagoda had previously been built. The main purpose of this council was, like the five previous ones, to re-edit the teachings of Buddha in order to preserve their purity and make their precepts easily accessible to the general public by means of contemporary translations. The Synod was held under the patronage of the President of the Union of Burma, Dr. Ba U; Prime Minister U Nu; the Buddhist Sasana Council; and all Buddhists of the five Theravada, or Hinayana, Buddhist countries.

The opening ceremony, which lasted three days, was conducted with great pomp and splendor. It was attended by many thousands of Buddhists, many non-Buddhist foreigners, and the complete diplomatic corps in Rangoon. Representatives, both lay and ecclesiastic, attended from India, Thailand, Ceylon, Cambodia, Nepal, Malaya, Vietnam, Assam, Indonesia, Laos, Pakistan, Germany, and the Cocos Islands. The proceedings followed the same lines as were adopted at the First Buddhist Council, which was held on the first year of Sasana, 483 B.C., shortly after the death of Buddha.

The Synod was held in the Great Sacred Cave of the Sixth Buddhist Council, created and modeled on the cave in Bihar Province

of India, where the original great Buddhist Council was held
twenty-five hundred years before. On arrival at the Cave one of
the head priests told me the history of this impressive structure. I
could scarcely believe that it had been built in only fourteen
months. It was a tremendous project which required hundreds of
thousands of cubic feet of special sand and stone, thousands of
tons of rocks and cement, hundreds of tons of structural steel, and
vast quantities of valuable timber, such as teak, as well as other
woods. Four hotels had been built near the main edifice to accom-
modate the *bhikkus,* or monks. There was a dining hall with fully
equipped kitchen big enough to feed fifteen hundred bhikkus at a
time, an international Buddhist library, a sanatorium and dis-
pensary with forty beds. Another building contained huge presses
which printed the Tipitaka and texts in Pali (ancient language of
the scriptures) and Burmese. Dominating the whole scene was the
impressive World Peace Pagoda.

Long before I reached one of the six entrances (to symbolize
the Sixth Synod) I heard the resonant chanting of thousands of
voices of the Great Recital, which sounded at first like the humming
of a giant beehive. As I drew closer, the melodious and rhythmic
chanting of monks repeating their sutras rose in an overwhelming tide of sound. Entering between the high rocky walls, I proceeded through a dark passage and into the Sacred Cave, and was
dazzled by the sight of hundreds of orange-robed monks ranged
against brilliant blue walls. The Cave resembled an amphitheater,
the floor of which was crowded with foreign visitors, high dignitaries, and worshipers from many Buddhist lands.

The monk who was guiding me said, "We are approaching where,
at the opening session, the King of Cambodia, the Crown Prince
of Laos, the Prime Ministers of Siam and Ceylon, and other distinguished visitors entered. They took their places before the high
platform, facing the northern end where the presiding Sangha Na-
yaka of the Sixth Synod was enthroned. Behind them row after
row of devout worshipers sat Buddha-fashion on the floor."

He pointed out the platform and showed me where the saintly
patriarch, the late Nyaung-yan Sayadaw, had sat when he presided
over the opening session.

"At that first session," he said, "they completed the recitation of
five books of scriptures of two thousand two hundred sixty pages
each. The recitations were made one hundred sixty-nine times.

There were five sessions in all, each of which lasted forty-six days. Throughout two full years leading priests from the entire Buddhist world have come here to study, compare, and correct the scriptures. Now for the closing sessions, three thousand of the greatest men in Buddhism are assembling in Rangoon to close the Synod."

On the highest tier of the platform sat the head bhikku, Maso-eyein Sayadaw. I was awed to see this holy man before whom royalty from many countries had knelt, and who was the head of the whole *sanghayana* assembly of monks. Later I was to have the privilege of meeting this eighty-three-year-old saint and talking with him about music and worship. On a lower level were three priests, *mahanayaka,* or patron saints, who blessed the whole gathering. Nine priests sat below them.

On three sides of the Cave were tiers of hundreds of priests sitting Buddhist-fashion, facing the high priest.

"Why are only the priests on the left side chanting?" I asked my guide.

He explained, "At certain hours of the day only the head priests chant; then those on the left or on the right take their turn, each group chanting scriptures at certain hours of the day. Sometimes the entire congregation chants in unison."

He pointed out to me the *pucchaka* (Questioner) and the *visaj-jaka* (Replier), both of whom bear the title "Venerable" and are among the most learned men in the Buddhist world.

Question-and-answer periods were an essential part of all six great councils; the purpose was to interpret and explain the true significance of the teachings in the light of the great wisdom of the leaders. Every evening for the benefit of the entire populace this section of the chanting was broadcast throughout the land over Radio Burma, allowing the most humble Burmese to participate in these rare meetings. The Questioner was the Venerable Aggamahapandita Bhadanta Suvhana (Mahasi Sayadaw) and the Replier was the Venerable Tipitakadhara Dhammabhadagarika Bhadanta Vicittasarabhivamsa (not the least of my problems was trying to remember the names of these dignitaries).

I joined the worshipers, and as I sat on the mat in the central portion of the Cave and looked around at the rows and rows of chanting monks, I was extremely impressed by the earnestness of these men in their labor of devotion. Here they were, for two years, dedicating all their efforts toward correcting, modern-

izing, and translating into many languages the scriptures as part
of the movement to revive Buddhism throughout the world. Sitting
with closed eyes I was overpowered by the chanted, almost
hypnotic repetitions.

Later, when I was able to record on tape the massed chanting
of the priests, I tried to picture how those early monks of the
First Synod (483 B.C.) would have marveled if they could have
gazed into the future at the miracle that made it possible to
preserve voices for all time.

Chief Justice U Chan Toon, one of the most colorful notables
of Burma, paved the way for the Sixth Synod. He went in person
to various countries which practice Theravada Buddhism to negotiate with political and religious leaders and persuade them to
join in accepting the responsibility for initiating "a spiritual
shake-up," as he put it.

My first interview when I arrived in Rangoon was with this
energetic and inspiring person. He received me in his own home,
and I was surprised to be ushered into a completely European
drawing room. What struck me most on entering were two handsome portraits, nearly life-size, of him and his beautiful wife. He
greeted me so cordially that I felt I was with an old friend.
Having been educated at Oxford, he spoke faultless English, and
his command of the language was impressive. A small man, like
most Burmese, he was perhaps in his early fifties and clothed in
the conventional dress of his country.

It was this dynamic, helpful man who made all arrangements
for my visits to the Synod, who made it possible for me to
record, and who set up one of the most interesting and rewarding
conferences I had in Burma—the inspiring interview with the
Venerable Masoeyein Sayadaw.

In my conversations with U Chan Toon I learned more of the
history and development of Buddhism than I had from dozens
of books and innumerable meetings. With his precise and logical
mind, he summarized and vitalized the story of Buddhism.

"In the days of Buddha," he told me, "some monks took the
yoke of meditation and others the yoke of learning; they actually
learned by rote, and they still do. A short time after the death
of Buddha the first great council was called. Some monks wanted
to relax the rules, and they formed groups of reciting monks; to
each one was allotted a portion of scripture. They recited their

sections daily, from time to time checking with other groups the same portion of scripture. These groups were like communities— young men came into the group when the old ones died, as new cells take the place of old ones in our bodies. These same groups continue even today."

He went on to tell me that the Mahayana sutras of northern Buddhism were made up a thousand years after Buddha's death. With a twinkle, he said, "Buddhists are taught respect for Christ or anyone in the right, but they do not respect wrong teaching, even from a Buddhist."

He touched on the fact that Burmese Buddhism began in middle Burma, and referred to the remarkable religious sculpture still to be found there. "King Anoraoha in the middle of the eleventh century was responsible for the Buddhist revival and established the religion throughout all Burma, Thailand, Ceylon, Laos, Cambodia. The King sent a mission to Ceylon and established there the son of the Emperor of Cambodia, who became a great scholar." When Islam became powerful, U Chan Toon also told me, it jumped over Burma with its southern Hinayana Buddhism, but "swallowed Indonesia because their northern Mahayana form of Buddhism lacked inherent strength." He emphasized the fact that Buddhism in Burma has remained true to the original Buddhist teachings.

In this connection he said, "Tibetan Buddhism, its language and scriptures, stress mysticism, magic, wheels, incantation. In China Buddhism is mixed with Taoism and Confucianism. In Japan Buddhism is mixed with Shintoism. In all these transitions the spirit of independence has been wiped out, and man has become weak, reliant on outside beings. We all started with the same tenets, but some of them have toppled over."

He went on to expound his views further. "Islam," he said, "teaches blind faith; spiritual faith is not enough; and Islam emphasizes economic and political matters.

"The old economic view was to develop without limit. The Buddhist view is that there are three economic positions: one, poverty and want; two, sufficiency; three, surfeit. The first emphasizes the inner fortress of the spirit, the second develops the outer fortress of economic and social betterment, but at the same time develops the inner fortress of the spirit. This is the one to follow. People must be helped to sufficiency, but not to surfeit."

He told me of the effect his plan for the Synod had had in various Buddhist countries and how their leaders had one by one caught "the Rangoon fever." Ceylon, Thailand, Cambodia, and Laos combined with Burma in support of the Sixth Synod.

He told me some of the details involved. Twenty-five hundred monks had to be fed, and during the final period more than three thousand. Women organized volunteers and everyone worked hard, including the Prime Minister's wife, cabinet members' wives, and common laborers. All contributed their utmost. Thirty thousand women were organized in two weeks—they undertook the entire problem of preparing, cooking, and serving meals for all the monks. They worked in groups of from one hundred to four hundred day and night.

As the Synod was about to close, there was a feeling that Prime Minister U Nu would be pleased with the results. This dedicated man had even resigned his office for a time in order to give his whole effort to the meetings. Paraphrasing the exhortation of King Ajatasattu, who opened the first Buddhist council, U Nu at the beginning of the council had said:

"Reverend Sirs, please give a righteous decision with regard to the good and correct form of scriptures, while the Union government will protect you with legal authority. May I most respectfully request you, Reverend Sirs, who are virtuous, fond of discipline, well versed in the sacred scriptures, and devoted to religious practices, and who belong to the noble lineage of holy arhats, to give a recital of the scriptures without any fear or hesitancy."

The highlight of the session for me was when I was privileged to interview Masoeyein Sayadaw, President of the Supreme Sangha Council of Burma. He received me in his private quarters adjacent to the Cave. This gentle old man of eighty-three years seemed much too frail to have the responsibility as the head of this great council which had required so much organization. He wore the orange robe of the bhikku. As he greeted me, his smiling face was a network of wrinkles out of which shone eyes so intelligent and wise that I felt he was looking through all the years of the past as well as into the far distant future. Around him was an aura of serenity. Although we had to speak through the interpreter, I was intuitively aware of a warm and sympathetic understanding between us. In introducing me, my guide explained my mission. The bhikku talked to me about the message which

Buddha has for us today, and I suggested that he prepare a message for the Western world. I give it in part:

"The message of Buddhism proclaimed by Gautama Buddha twenty-five hundred years ago is a message of peace and hope that inspires millions of hearts in Asia and is addressed to all men, irrespective of race, nationality, and creed, throughout the world. It is not impaired by the lapse of time, nor affected by changing conditions; as it was given by the Buddha, and as it survived the centuries, so it speaks to us today in terms that deal directly with our modern life and its problems.

"In his teaching the Buddha, moved by compassion for a world in spiritual darkness, showed why it is that all sentient beings are subject to old age and death, grief, lamentation, suffering, misery, and despair, and he pointed out the way by which we may be released from these sorrows. They are self-inflicted hurts, the result of ignorance leading to evil actions in life after life, a train of cause and effect which the teacher perceived by his enlightenment [insight]. To bring them to an end and attain lasting happiness and liberation man has to cleanse his heart of defilements and make himself pure in thought, word, and deed. For as the *Dhammapada*, the most oft-quoted of the Buddhist scriptures, says:

> To put an end to all evil,
> To cultivate all that is good,
> To purify one's mind—
> This is the teaching of the Buddha.

"The only way that man can achieve enduring peace and happiness, therefore, is by strenuously exerting himself to eradicate these dark and downbearing tendencies, and cultivate in their stead the noble and positive virtues: generosity, love, and wisdom. These constitute the basis of the good life, and they are our salvation. This is why Buddhism teaches the absolute necessity of developing a heart of boundless love and compassion toward all beings. Again and again throughout his teaching the Buddha emphasizes this vital truth, the very core and substance of the way of life he laid down for us. The highest wisdom is only to be reached through restraint of the passions, the curbing of self-interest, and the continual practice of loving-kindness to all living creatures. Buddhism teaches us to have regard for all beings as for ourselves, without distinction of high or low, large or small, near or distant; all alike are to be cherished with thoughts and acts of the purest disinterested love. . . .

"The moral law is supreme, the only unchanging thing in this universe of change. It is not a human invention, to be altered and adapted to the convenience of any particular group of mankind at any particular historical period. The Buddha showed that it has always existed as a scientific principle of cause and effect, and it is as such that it wields an inescapable sovereignty over all life. To go against it is to bring misery upon ourselves and others; but to harmonize our lives with its goodness in thought, word, and deed is to find the greatest happiness here on this earth, in this very life. It is within the power of each of us to bring blessings upon ourselves and all around us by the unconquerable virtue of purity and love. That is the message which the teaching of the Buddha has for us today.

"The Buddhists of Burma bless all beings with thoughts of loving-kindness. May the hearts of men everywhere in the world be purified, that hatred and suspicion may cease and peace and good will germinate and flourish in the light of wisdom and truth."

While working with the music of all the major world religions, I have been amazed to find that the basic teachings of all their scriptures have much in common. Unfortunately it is the differences that have been overemphasized. Of all my collections of religious chants and songs, I regard among the most valuable the historical chanting recorded at this great Synod.

Chapter 18

SOUTHEAST ASIA: INDOCHINA AND SIAM

In 1950, when I first visited Indochina, Cambodia, as well as
Laos and Vietnam was still a part of the large territory of Southeast Asia that was under French rule (it has now become four
countries). I flew from Bangkok with a group of friends who had
chartered a plane to see the ruins of the great cities and temples
of the remarkable Khmer civilization that flourished a thousand
years ago, and which have been covered with the encroaching
jungle for four hundred years.

The cities and monuments of the Khmers were abandoned
when in the late fourteenth and early fifteenth centuries they
were defeated by the Siamese and fled into southern Cambodia.
The full tragedy of Angkor is felt in the huge ruined temple of
Prah Khau which the French had left much as they found it
more than a hundred years ago, completely imprisoned by the
jungle. Wild fig trees emerged through broken roofs, their immense roots twisting and crawling into crevices and breaking
down the walls, covering amazing sculptures, and destroying beautiful façades. When I saw the writhing jungle on all sides of
Prah Khau, it was clear that as soon as the French gave up their
vigil, the forest, monkeys, and leopards would soon take over
again.

Angkor Thom (Great City) in the days of its triumphant splendor was the heart of a powerful and gifted civilization. Here
the Khmers lived magnificently and built their palaces and temples. In 1860 French scholars became interested in reconstructing

these splendid ruins and gradually they freed Angkor Thom from the relentless jungle that had engulfed it. The huge ruins, and the surrounding roads and canals cover hundreds of square miles. From the hotel in Siemréap, a small town four miles from Angkor, I first visited the ruins in the golden afternoon sunlight. Music and dances were performed for us then and later when a moon flooded the temple with mysterious light.

The immense Hindu temple of Angkor Wat with its commanding façades and more than fifty carved towers has an outer wall that is almost three quarters of a mile long. The moat that surrounds it and mirrors the towers brilliantly served as military protection. We crossed the moat on a causeway as wide as a four-lane highway, paved with huge stone blocks. Acres of bas-reliefs depict Hindu religious and poetic epics, with thousands of dancing girls and hundreds of goddesses in graceful movement. (It is thought that the temple once held more than five thousand dancing girls and concubines.) The entire structure is a chronicle of civilization and of oriental pageantry. Angkor Wat, a giant among more than nine hundred masterpieces in stone, could enclose all the monuments of Greece, it is said. It was built about the same time as Notre Dame in Paris (during the twelfth and thirteenth centuries), but great cities had flourished here as early as 880. Angkor Thom had a population of one million, and according to the report of a Chinese traveler, the royal processions were magnificent with jeweled elephants, brilliant parasols, and custumes of great beauty.

The pomp and splendor of ceremonials in Cambodia are still magnificent even today, as evidenced in March, 1950, when King Norodom Suramarit and Queen Kossamak were crowned. Their son Norodom Sihanouk (aged thirty-four) had succeeded his grandfather to the throne in 1941 and abdicated in 1949 to become active in politics as the prime minister of his country. The coronation week of elaborate, colorful rituals reached its climax in a parade of ancient pageantry. The court astrologer, who draws up the country's calendar and forecasts the weather, led the proceedings. On Sunday of that week sixty-two Buddhist monks (one for each of the King's sixty-two years) ate a traditional breakfast of soybeans and salad in the palace. Although Buddhism is the dominant religion of Cambodia and the King himself is

Buddhist, there is still considerable Hindu influence and Brahman priests officiated at the ceremonies.

For the coronation the new rulers were clothed in golden costumes and sat on golden thrones. In the climactic procession, floats of beautiful Garudas (half man, half bird) represented the favorite figure of Hindu mythology. Royal elephants carried the thrones through the streets, but as the Queen was not feeling well the royal pair changed to a carriage drawn by white horses. According to tradition, as a symbol of family happiness, a young pregnant woman carried a blue-ribboned cat in the procession.

The Queen, a very musical and artistic person, has encouraged all the arts, especially music and the dance. She was very much interested in my work and arranged for me to record the royal musicians in the palace. This was a rare privilege and it provided more varied material than the recordings I had made earlier at Angkor Wat.

Since Vietnam was still a part of Indochina in 1950, I was able to go to Hanoi for my work and to villages even farther to the north, but those were dangerous and tragic days for that war-torn country. While I was staying in Hanoi, it was impossible to go out to the villages before eight in the morning because all the roads out of Hanoi had to be checked for mines before a car could venture forth. I was told that many of the same natives mined them at night employed by the Communists and demined them in the morning for the government. When I started out with recorder and cameras, always in an armored car, soldiers went before and brought up the rear, and in our car soldiers were on guard with rifles ready, watching for ambush at any moment. At that time I was sometimes during the day in a village or a French military outpost which that very night fell into the hands of the rebel troops. In one of the small French military outposts I had a marvelous luncheon—a more delicious one could not have been had in the heart of Paris. The conversation was as witty and as carefree as it might have been back home. The soldiers said, as they sang and toasted, "This is all we have left. We're here today; tomorrow we may be dead." And that night their post was taken by the enemy.

In a village near this French post one of the most prized instruments in my collection was given to me—a small drum, carved in the form of a fish with its belly slit. It was one of the signaling drums that hung in the center of the village to call the people together and warn them of danger from the enemy.

Here I recorded charming women's and children's songs only, as all the men of that area were away fighting with the French. I captured much exotic old music throughout Asia but there were also new militant sounds of a very different kind. These new songs of freedom and nationalism were neither modern Western nor an adaptation of old traditional music, but because they were composed by a group, out of its experience, they can be called folk songs. In Borneo the children of rubber tappers were singing "The Cry for Freedom." Even in isolated Nepal when I was first there just before the uprising against the Maharaja—Prime Minister, some of the songs reflected discontent, and young men were singing complaints of poverty. Freedom was in the air everywhere, a well-organized movement, and many of the songs were indications of the great tidal wave that was flowing across Asia.

One of the songs of liberty I recorded in Indochina in 1956 had been sung, I was told, by the Vietnamese people during ten years of resistance to the French. Here are the words:

You and I,
Let us hold hands and dance and sing
So that life will glow under the winter mist,
So that our blood will burn more ardently by the side of the campfire.
Tung tung tinh tung
Binh bung binh bung
Tang tinh tang tinh tinh

We are fighters, born in war and ready to sacrifice ourselves for our country.
Forever we pledge to make our heroes' names resound
Going everywhere in the four directions, in the woods and on the waters.
The more we brave the cold night dew,
Let the fire burn and burn to make your determination firm.
Let us sing loud (o ho o ho),
Hand in hand dancing around a fire (o ho o ho).
Tens of thousands attack (o ho o ho).

Listen to their souls filled with hot blood.
Let us unsheathe our swords and pledge to defend our land.
Let us eliminate all injustices.
Let us kill all the greedy and cruel enemies.
Let the fame of the Vietnamese resound till eternity.

Among the most interesting melodies I recorded in Indochina were those performed by a Mr. Ba in Hanoi, a master of several instruments, especially a stringed instrument which is related to the Japanese *koto*. So dedicated was this artist that he plucked the strings with his bare fingers, refusing to wear a plectrum because, he said, "it would interrupt the flow of music from my heart to the strings."

Mr. Ba was very anxious to preserve the national traditional music of his country. As he said, "To collect the musical materials left from times immemorial is a sign of respect toward one's ancestors and is also full of many other sacred meanings." His attempt to restore the heritage of the forefathers through national melodies included an effort to introduce Vietnamese culture to foreigners through music, since, in his words; "nothing reflects the cultural level of a nation more than its music." He was especially interested in making the study of the instruments more scientific as he felt that some extremely rich and profound instrumental music had lost its prestige because of inadequate means of transmitting it from generation to generation.

Through the years much of the old music has been lost or has changed greatly as each musician added individual variations to create a new effect or to display his own particular talent. Sometimes the variations were quite incorrect, applying the technique of one instrument to a different kind of instrument, or applying vocal technique to instruments. Even the same person may play a melody quite differently on different occasions or according to his mood. One may want to hide his special techniques, thinking that his playing is unique and fearing others may copy or even excel; thus, music may become a traditional secret, making it all the more difficult to investigate.

The musical instruments of Vietnam are varied and numerous. Of the stringed instruments, one of the most melodious is the sixteen-stringed "zither," the *dan tranh*, related to the Chinese *tchen*. The strings of this three-foot-long instrument are usually of steel with wooden or ivory pegs. The musician plucks the strings with the thumbnail and the nail of the index finger of the right hand. A moon-shaped lute called the *dan kim* has two silk strings. (The old form has two pairs of strings.) The *dan tam*, a three-stringed lute that sounds rather like a banjo, is very popular and is found in most orchestras of the traditional theater in South Vietnam, and in trios or groups of five or more instruments in central and North Vietnam. A very interesting instrument which I acquired for the collection is the *dan nhi* (*nhi* is a Sino-Vietnamese word meaning "two"), named for its two strings. The strings, which are tuned a fifth apart, are divided in the middle and a bow of horsehair passes between them. The resonator is a small wooden cylinder covered at one end by snakeskin. The musician usually sits on the ground supporting the open end of the resonator with his left foot while playing, but in processions the resonator rests against the left hip. In North Vietnam this instrument is often played by wandering blind minstrels. In South Vietnam it is a very important instrument in ceremonial orchestras.

There are various forms of drums. The *cai trong manh* is probably of Chinese origin and is an important instrument in court, for popular orchestras, and for ritual music. The *mo* is a small hollowed-out drum which can be found in numerous shapes, even in the form of a fish. In some areas it is used to accompany prayers. In pagodas and temples the big bell called the *bac chung* is used in ritual music. It is struck with a suspended beater which is moved by pulling a rope; it is often beautifully decorated with dragons. The *chieng*, a gong of copper, beaten with a wooden stick, is used to call the people for religious and military ceremonies, to announce deaths, and occasionally for giving other signals.

About the time of my first visit to Vietnam, a fascinating discovery was made that indicated the region had formerly been populated by a race of Stone Age men who had a well-developed ear for music. A prehistoric lithophone was discovered in the hill regions of Indochina. At a place called Ndut Lieng Krak (Village of the Protruding Stumps) a French scientist heard the natives talking about big gray stones they had unearthed in making a road. He visited the place and found eleven stone plates or keys; the biggest was forty inches long, six inches wide, and two inches thick, and weighed twenty-five pounds; the smallest was about twenty-six inches in length. He accidentally discovered that they produced musical notes and vibrated strongly. Seven of them were pitched to produce a complete Eastern pentatonic scale. Three other "keys" which formed part of a second scale, were at first thought to be remnants of another instrument. Back in Paris these plates were found to be fashioned from a special rock formed by earth pressure and ancient lava into a "ringing" or phonolitic material. Musicologists assembled the stone keys across two narrow wooden supports (in the form of a xylophone) as perhaps they were originally placed, and were delighted to be able to play melodies ranging from Debussy to the latest modern tunes. I played this instrument recently in Paris and was amazed to find tones very similar to those produced by the "singing pillars" of southern India.

In the early 1950s two more lithophones were found (also in what is now central Vietnam). It is now thought that the "keys" of stone found together probably did not belong to a single xylophone-type instrument, but were perhaps played singly. However, authorities do not all agree on this subject.

Because of the manner of chipping the stone it is thought that the keys were fashioned by a people known as Bacsonians, a tropical race of Stone Age men who made crude tools out of the same type of rock at least four thousand or five thousand and possibly eight or nine thousand years ago. It is believed that the lithophone plates were hewn from solid rock and tuned to accuracy of tone by a process of chipping or flaking. The longest and heaviest plate does not give the lowest tone as might be expected; and it has been decided that the pitch and sonority resulted from a complex relationship of weight, length, method of chipping, and even curvature—as some of the plates are slightly bent like a banana.

If the prehistorians are right, these would be the oldest known musical instruments in the world, more ancient than the neolithic flutes found in Swiss lake huts and the famous Sumerian lyres unearthed by Sir Leonard Woolley in Chaldean Ur.

Siam, unlike its neighbors, was never a part of any empire but has been strongly influenced by the West. At some period India, Burma, Indochina, China itself, Indonesia, the Philippines, and Malaya have all been under outside domination, but Siam, although very tempting to the Communists, having the world's largest surplus of rice and booming rubber and tin production, has remained free.

This small country has a fascinating past ruled well by a royal family which has one of the most complicated genealogies in history. There are an unbelievable number of nobles, for most of the kings had scores of wives and a great many concubines. King Mongkut (1851–68) of *Anna and the King of Siam,* who had eighty-two children by thirty-five wives, learned Western languages and democratic ways and became the reform ruler who led Siam, now Thailand, away from medievalism toward the modern world.

The present dynasty was founded in 1782 by General Chakkri, who fought the Cambodians so well that he was chosen to succeed King Phya Tat (called the savior of Siam for defeating Burma and Cambodia). Chakkri called himself Rama I and established the capital in Bangkok. The title Rama, from the legendary Indian god, has come down with his ruling descendants to Rama IX, who became king in 1946.

Phumiphon, the present king, was born in Cambridge, Massachusetts, in 1927 while his father was studying medicine at Harvard. After a few years in Brookline, Massachusetts, he moved with his mother, sister, and brother Ananda to Lausanne when his father died. Six years later his uncle, the childless King Prajadhipok, abdicated in favor of his nephew Ananda.

When Ananda was mysteriously shot on June 9, 1946, Phumiphon was desolate. When, two months later, he left to study in Switzerland, two million Siamese in tears cast flowers under the wheels of his car. In Lausanne, Phumiphon developed a passionate interest in photography, music, and fast cars. He read law but much preferred organizing orchestras and composing dance music, both Western and Siamese. Princess Sirikit Kitiyakara, in the court that developed around Phumiphon, was also very musical and was chosen to be his bride. For four years the King spent his days in studies, organizing a swing band (he is a great jazz enthusiast and a fine musician) and playing with his many cameras.

At last word came that the young King was coming home. Bangkok was busy for weeks preparing to welcome him. Soldiers, sailors, princes, and workmen rushed through last-minute preparations. Along the broad King's Walk five thousand soldiers marched in rehearsal while others joined hands to hold back imaginary and expected crowds on the sidewalks, and on the parade grounds carpenters worked to complete the tower that would serve as a funeral pyre for the late King Ananda Mahidol. The country was eager for the return of Ananda's brother, Phumiphon Aduldet, to light the pyre and take the throne.

Five royal relatives in addition to Phumiphon's brother had died, and only the King could light their pyres. The coronation was most important, and there was to be a royal wedding as well. In late March, 1950, the thin, bespectacled young King with his pretty seventeen-year-old fiancée arrived in a jubilant Bangkok which was dancing to the hit of the week, one of the compositions of the Siamese royal jazz expert:

> The little bird in a lonely flight
> Thinks of itself and feels sad.

Eighteen million excited citizens eagerly awaited his arrival. The news had been proclaimed throughout Bangkok's crowded streets, passed from sampan to sampan in the traffic-jammed canals (*klongs*) of this Venice of the East, and up the great rivers and over the plains the news traveled with wandering merchants.

Everywhere in the ancient temples yellow-robed monks prepared to welcome their young King (the Great God on My Head Phumiphon Aduldet, The Power Coming from the Strength of the Earth). Every temple bell in the country rang a greeting when he stepped on Siamese soil. Thousands of sampans rushed out to meet his ship; radios blared recordings of his musical compositions; the crowded landing stage at Memorial Bridge on the Chao Phraya River collapsed and a hundred people were drenched but no one was drowned. Giant paintings of the King and fragrant incense candles were ready for his arrival. Royal guards in red coats, black pants, and striped helmets stood stiffly, but occasionally in the heat a soldier closed his eyes and swayed. Then water boys nearby rushed up with a dash of water and a whiff of smelling salts.

As the King came ashore airplanes circled overhead, dropping flowers and puffed rice (a gift of greeting) in little parachutes. In a pavilion nearby the Prince Regent turned over the powers of state; the King took up the sword of state, walked over and exchanged a few words with the British and United States ambassadors, and left for the palace.

The next morning the King gave rice to the beggars, and followed by nobles and officers of the guard, went to the Temple of the Emerald Buddha to receive the Candle Blessing. Three Brahman priests entered to the accompaniment of music on conch shells. Phumiphon bowed before the Emerald Buddha, touching his forehead to the floor, and lit fifteen candles as flutes joined the conch shells and the Brahman priests chanted softly. One by one the candles were lighted and incense filled the air. Drums joined the triumphant music while the lighted candles were passed in a chain around the group of men and women and back to the table where the priests extinguished them. To end the ceremony the chief priest anointed the King's shoes with scented water, wiping them off with a silken scarf. Then Phumiphon drove back to the palace in his Daimler to prepare for the long-awaited cremation ceremony.

It is impossible to imagine a more colorful or impressive ceremony than the Buddhist ritual that surrounded the cremation of King Phra Paramendr Maha Ananda Mahidol Sayamindradiraj. An auspicious date for the cremation was chosen by the court astrologers since practically everything in Thailand, as in most of the Eastern countries, is planned by astrologers. (I myself went to the famous astrologer of the Prime Minister, and in a colorful ritual he predicted a glowing future for me.) Dates for all public events from the opening of a bank to the wedding day of the King depended on the auspicious position of the planets. There are many lesser astrologers operating all over the place, telling fortunes for the equivalent of a nickel apiece, but the most important astrologers are learned members of the Astrological Society of Siam who work for the government by day and practice astrology by night.

On the morning of March 29, 1950, at four o'clock, I left the Oriental Hotel with the correspondent of the *New York Times*. I had worked all night long on a black dress, with long sleeves and a high neckline, for the occasion. The day before, I had found out that I could appear at the cremation ceremonies only in black from top to toe, and I did not have such a dress in my wardrobe. I decided the only thing to do was to take a pedicab and go in search of suitable material. The search took me through many fascinating shops, and back at the hotel I tried to arrange the material I had selected so that I would not have too many seams and hems to sew. Finally, just before time to take off for the first phase of the ceremony, I wound myself into this costume, which to my surprise turned into quite a successful creation.

We managed with great difficulty to get an early cup of tea at our hotel, and this was all the sustenance I had until nearly midnight. Armed with still and movie cameras, we took off in the direction of Ducit Hall, where the Buddhist monks had been chanting since dawn. Even though it was scarcely light, the streets were so full of people that we had trouble finding a pedicab and ended by walking most of the way. As we were with the press, we could move more freely than those who were confined to definite locations. At seven o'clock, the sermon and chanting finished, the meditation group started on the long ceremonial procession from Ducit Hall toward the Royal Cremation Stand in what was called the Royal Field.

King Ananda had died four years before, and a board of regents had governed the country since then. For these four years the remains of the King had rested in a royal urn in a temple on the palace grounds, and I had earlier been invited to go with Siamese friends to kneel in front of the lighted altar and pay our respects.

Under Siamese Buddhist rites the cremation of a king or any high-ranking member of the royal family must take place within a specially built pavilion or temple called the Golden Meru. (Meru, in Buddhist legend, forms the axis of the world.) This huge pyre, only a temporary structure with a wooden frame covered with brilliant cloth, was very beautiful; skilled artists who hold hereditary posts required three months to build the Meru. It combined the regal splendor of a royal edifice and the inspiring beauty of a sacred pagoda.

Long flights of steps on each side of the square pavilion ascended to the small, central platform where the funeral urn was placed. The terraced roof rose sharply into a tall spire and the whole structure glowed with color, gold predominating. Nearby, other pavilions were constructed where the royal mourners, persons of high rank, and monks would be seated.

The royal urn was made of copper, with a detachable sheath of gold heavily embossed and studded with priceless jewels. For the procession it was conveyed to the Phra Meru grounds on a royal carriage which was drawn by hundreds of mourners and attendants. The carriage with its high-terraced platform was delicately carved and covered with gold.

The ritual called for a nobleman to ride in state in front of the procession, scattering rice as an offering to the spirit of the dead. Then came the Prince Patriarch of all the Buddhists of Thailand, a very old man, reciting stanzas of the sacred scriptures. His seat was connected to the urn by a broad white ribbon. Bands of red-clad musicians accompanied the march with ancient wind instruments and drums. The music was shrill, eerie, and funereal. The whole population, dressed in severe black, except for the saffron robes of the monks lined the route and flocked to the cremation ground to watch the procession. In 1950 there were no shaved heads, but until 1870, when King Chulalongkorn abolished the practice, every man, woman, and child was shaved as a symbol of mourning when a king died. Even though the economy program had eliminated the royal elephants on which the princes used to ride, it was still a thrilling spectacle. While the procession moved very slowly along Rajadamern Avenue past the Temple of the Emerald Buddha toward the parade ground, a canon roared a salute every minute.

Large detachments of soldiers with medieval-style helmets, spears, and shields wearing the ornate dress of former Siamese armies, with the skirtlike *panungs,* the traditional Siamese substitute for trousers, which fitted like loose diapers pinned up in the back, were followed by countless mourners in black, both men and women. The golden urn containing the King's remains was borne on a royal chariot 195 years old and weighing forty-two tons, pulled by soldiers and sailors. Royal attendants crouching on the side of the chariot guarded the urn and protected it from the sun with a leaf-shaped fan and a royal umbrella. The royal caisson was decorated with gold and jewels which glittered in the sun. Those with royal rank were shaded by five- and seven-tiered silk umbrellas resembling tall wedding cakes. The Prince Patriarch, aged seventy-seven, grandson of King Mongkut, officiated for life as head of the Buddhist church.

At the cremation grounds the procession marched with the royal urn three times around the high gilt tower, the Golden Meru, symbolizing heaven, where the King would be cremated. The fragrance of incense and the chanting of the Buddhist priests filled the air.

The King in white dress uniform, shaded by his umbrella of orange satin with gold thread, followed the caisson as it circled the Meru. The Prince Patriarch, highest priest of the land, was carried in a palanquin by soldiers in medieval costume. He delivered a brief sermon, led the meditation prayer, and accepted from King Phumiphon traditional gifts.

At the foot of the pyre, the urn—shaded by the nine-tiered umbrella denoting the King's rank and guarded by the chief attendant —was moved into an inclining elevator manipulated by hand cranes which raised it to the high platform. At the top of the tower the urn was placed inside the pyre with gold and scarlet draperies enclosing it on three sides. The screenlike doors of the pyre were opened and the draperies drawn back, the cremation fagots properly placed, and the urn was ready to be viewed.

Alone and walking slowly, the King left his royal pavilion, crossed to the stairs which only he could ascend, leading to the high place where the urn reposed. At the foot of these stairs he was given a few sticks of incense and a torch of scented wood which had been carved to resemble lovely flowers arranged on a central stem. He lit the torch, and after reverently ascending, placed it among the fagots of gilded and varnished wood under the urn. The flame was extinguished after a brief moment, as the actual cremation would take place much later.

As this youthful, solitary figure descended the stairs with measured steps and quiet dignity and resumed his place in the royal pavilion, I tried to imagine what was going on in his mind. This young man, who had spent practically all of his life in Switzerland, had been uprooted from the surroundings which he had learned to love, from Western friends and schoolmates, from European studies, sports, dress, food, and ways that had become his own. I knew well his keen interest in Western music, his ability as a composer, his prowess as a performing musician on many instruments. Suddenly he had been catapulted back into the land of his ancestors, and thrust immediately into these age-old formalities which were overpowering for me to witness, and certainly for him must have been completely overwhelming. He must have realized at that moment more poignantly than ever how completely he had given up his life of free choice and independence for a life in which every action would be dictated by centuries of traditional beliefs and ceremonies. Involuntarily I felt a catch in my throat and tears came in my eyes.

Following his example, other mourners, close relatives of the King, approached the pavilion, and at the foot of another stairway priests gave them similar flowerlike torches, and they wound their way up the stairs, adding their torches to the pile of fagots underneath the urn.

In the late afternoon, with the Golden Meru gleaming against the sky, heads of governments, members of the diplomatic corps, and other distinguished visitors ascended a third stairway and approached the urn to add their torches to Ananda's pyre. It was up this stairway that the princes and princesses climbed, carrying tapers which they placed in tribute. Close friends of mine in this group invited me to join them in this act of reverence. When I received the delicately fashioned torch in my hand from the priest at the foot of the stairs, I became a part of this moving ritual. I ascended the stairs as though I were in a dream; the reality seemed to transcend reality. Nearing the altar, I was awed by the beauty of the urn in its golden, bejeweled casing, by the form and color of the hangings, and by the rapt earnestness of the attendant priests.

Returning to my place I watched almost hypnotized as thousands of monks in their saffron robes, who had come from far and near to participate in this touching ceremony, moved slowly up and down another stairway in what seemed to be an endless river of molten metal in the glow of the afternoon sun. For hours I sat, too fascinated to leave, long after the royal family and diplomats had left, while quiet dignified students in mourning proceeded in a steady stream up the stairs to add their torches to the growing pile of fagots. Then the populace came, thousands of them, and although there was no outward sign of grief, one could sense their deep-seated love and respect for kingship and tradition and a kind of awe for this ceremony which had been performed again on this day with the same reverence for the ancient practices that their forebears had shown.

All this torchbearing was purely ceremonial. The flames were quickly extinguished by the priests who presided over the urn. There was a tense moment at one point when the gold and scarlet curtains, blown by the breeze, caught fire, but fortunately, the blaze was put out at once. Had the entire tower burned, it would have taken another three months to prepare a tower for the cremation of the other members of the royal family.

Late, near midnight, with only the members of the royal family and closest friends present, the actual cremation took place. The next morning the ashes were placed in a small, decorated urn to be kept in the Grand Palace with those of former kings. The young King could then prepare for his wedding and coronation.

After the cremation ceremonies, I was free to turn my attention to Thailand's music. I knew that during the nineteenth century, in the early part of the reign of King Chulalongkorn, a fusion between Siamese and Western (European) music had begun when military bands were equipped with Western instruments, and that later Siamese melodies with Western harmonization were introduced and for a time were very much in vogue. At a reception for German and Russian princes who visited Siam in 1890, a quadrille was played which still exists. Since the introduction of jazz, a hybrid music has become popular in Thailand for dancing and popular singing. However, I found that traditional Siamese music had fortunately not disappeared.

The *Ramakien* (as Thais call their version of the *Ramayana*, the well-known Indian epic about the legendary Rama and his consort, Sita, and their famous monkey warrior, Hanuman) has had a great influence on the traditional Thai music, especially dance music. The Ramakien has also had an extensive influence on Thai painting and all other Thai arts.

Thai music is derived from Indian sources but differs from Indian music considerably. In 1929 Prince Damrong Rajanubhab, disturbed by the disappearance of traditional music through the death of Siamese music masters, started a movement to preserve the national music. A system of notation was devised based on Western notation to write down the melodies so that they would not be lost forever. Even though the scales are different, with special signs written above and below the notes, arrangements were prepared which could be played by Western instruments. The Thai scale is composed of seven full tones within its octave distributed in equidistant steps, so there are no semitones. By placing accidentals above or below the notes, a workable notation evolved. Thai music is polyphonic and contrapuntal. It is in simple duple time only, and the compositions are without changes in dynamics.

There are six melodic instruments in the orchestra called the *piphat* band. The woodwind section is represented by a single instrument of the oboe type, called the *pi nai*. The percussion section is divided into two groups, six melodic instruments (xylophones and gongs) and rhythmic instruments (three kinds of drums, and sometimes rhythmic gongs, and metal gongs of indefinite pitch). The pi nai is made from pieces of seasoned rosewood about sixteen inches long with six holes for fingering. The high tones are piercing and shrill, the low tones grunting and rough, but when played by an expert it produces enchanting music. In a piphat band, the pi nai doubles the principal melody and embellishes it with many variations. A pi nai player has to exhale and inhale automatically, a special technique which must be acquired for this instrument. The xylophones are made with resonant bars from seasoned hardwood (sometimes bamboo) on a body which acts as a resonator. They are often richly carved and inlaid with mother-of-pearl or ivory, and are tuned by sticking under each bar a composition of scraped lead and beeswax. The *ranat ek* has twenty-one resonant bars or keys and is built on a curve, or boat-shaped. This instrument produces variations on the principal melody in octaves, splitting each beat into sixteenth notes. The *ranat thong ek* also has twenty-one graduated resonant bars, but they are of steel and the instrument is flat rather than curved. Both are played with two beaters with knobs. The *gong wong yai* is nearly circular and the performer sits within the circle. Each of the sixteen resonant "keys," made from a special metal alloy in the shape of discs or kettles with a knob in the center, has a different pitch. They are arranged consecutively according to the scale. The performer strikes with two beaters on the top of the knobs of the discs. This instrument carries the principal melody and is indispensable in the piphat band. The *gong wong lek* is similar to the *gong wong yai* but smaller. The *ranat thum* is similar to the *ranat ek* but has deeper tones; and the *ranat thong ek* has deeper tones than the *ranat thong thum*.

In Thailand there were many opportunities for recording numerous types of music. Thanks to Prince Thani, whose guest I was on numerous occasions, I recorded some very beautiful music by the palace orchestra, and Prince Prem of the University of Chulalongkorn also found unique and interesting material for me. In the villages outside Bangkok I recorded indigenous folk music so different from the palace music that it was hard to believe that they both belonged to the same culture. In Thailand, as in all of Southeast Asia, everything makes music—even the kites—and most activities are accompanied by music, including the wrestling matches.

One of the favorite pastimes of the Thai is boxing. Before a bout of Thai boxing each contestant engages in a performance that combines shadowboxing, dancing, and praying and represents both a demonstration of technique and a ceremonial salute to the teacher. This also provides (hopefully) some sort of insurance against injury. The insurance was clearly not enough on the one occasion when I went to see the boxing match and record the accompanying music, for, in the most important bout of the day, one of the opponents crashed to the floor with a crunching sound and was carried out dead. Thai boxing is supposedly governed by strict rules, but to me, an uninformed observer, it seemed that everything goes—kicking, biting, terrific punches with elbows, knees and feet—and the action more often than not ends in a very bloody knockout. The fury of the pugilistic spectacle is enhanced by a ringside orchestra of flutes and drums, which furnishes loud mood music throughout the fighting.

Thai dance, which represents stories from the life of Rama, must be performed in traditional style and requires a long and strenuous training of the whole body. The boys and girls who wish to dance start their studies in the dance academy as soon as they have finished primary school. Practically every muscle of the body must be trained. As in Indian dancing, the smallest movements of the hands, head, eyes, fingers, or torso have profound significance, and the whole audience, as well as the dancers, understands and appreciates their meanings. I spent long hours watching the performers in their traditional masks and costumes and also the even more ancient form, the *nang* or shadow play.

Sometimes a poignant human story is uncovered in the search for a country's music. In Chiengmai, capital of the northern province of Thailand, the United Presbyterian Mission has a fine hospital with a nurses' training school, and on an island in the river which flows by the city, they have built the McKean Leprosy Hospital. My interest in the rehabilitation of lepers has taken me to leprosy colonies in many countries of the world, and the McKean Hospital is the most beautifully situated colony I have seen, surrounded by lovely tropical trees, gardens, and fields. Here the patients live as families, or in dormitories if they have no family, and not only raise their own crops, keep their herds of buffalo for milk, raise poultry, do simple tailoring, and run the community efficiently, but have also been encouraged to pursue the arts. Some of the finest carvings in Thailand have been made by badly crippled hands of patients on this island. They have a special pride in their work, because they have risen above a terrific handicap and in spite of it have produced beauty. The inhabitants learn to earn a living as productive members of their community. Through the miracle of medicine disabled hands are reconstructed and collapsed noses restored; even paralyzed eyelids and lost eyebrows have been replaced by pioneering work in reparative surgery for those in whom the disease had progressed too far before the modern cures had been discovered.

Leprosy is no longer the dreaded disease it was formerly, and I have long ago overcome the hopelessness I felt when I first visited a leper community in Angola in 1931. Nowadays, when diagnosed in time, it can be completely cured so that patients are not without hope as they were during the Middle Ages and a long time afterward, when indiscriminate and compulsory segregation was the only treatment. Many types of cures have been tried and for some time chaulmoogra oil, a native remedy in Asia, was the main treatment; but the drug's effectiveness was limited. Now with new sulfa drugs, a safe and effective remedy has been found. The disease can be arrested and with a follow-up of regular examinations a tendency to relapse can be halted in time. With the general rise of standards of public health and with calming of public prejudice and the compassionate work of dedicated trained doctors, ministers, and staff, total rehabilitation is now possible to many thousands of lepers who might a few years ago have been completely helpless.

It was at the McKean Leper Colony that I met Mah-Sai. The story of this lovely young girl, a celebrated dancer and favorite of the Queen in the old court of Chiengmai, had become a legend in Thailand. I had heard it first on an earlier expedition, and now I had come again to learn the complete story. Here it is as I heard it from her.

Mah-Sai was sixteen, confident in her beauty, with lovely almond eyes, blue-black hair and a supple body. She was assured a long life of security and comfort at the palace, and the rhythm of her days was as smooth as the dances she performed each night for the pleasure of the royal household.

One night, while removing her long curled fingertips of gold with which the Thai dancer extends her slender hands by as much as ten or twelve inches, Mah-Sai saw, near the base of her thumb, a small dark mark. She scrubbed it with soap and water, but the smudge would not go away. She tried not to think about it, but her eyes always kept coming back to it. As the days passed, the smudge grew; it darkened; it spread. Soon Mah-Sai knew that the other dancers had noticed the blemish and were whispering about it while they sat together in the dressing room waiting their call to the Royal Presence. She began to sit apart from them; their gaiety and laughter became almost painful for her.

At last her fear drove her to take a pedicab to another village where a kind army doctor examined her hand and gave her some salve.

"It is nothing," he said. "It will go away."

Mah-Sai went daily to the temple to give thanks, prostrating herself before the Buddha, praying with the monks in their saffron robes, grateful that her fears were ungrounded. Joy returned to her dancing, the light to her eyes. Patiently at first, and then with mounting desperation, she waited for the blemish to disappear. Instead it was spreading, and her hand was growing numb. She returned to the army doctor. This time he looked more closely at the mark, and when he lifted his head she saw doubt in his eyes.

"I cannot be sure," he said. Mah-Sai walked out into the sunny street, chilled with apprehension.

Now she no longer dared mingle with her companions at the palace. She knew there was only one thing she must do. On the outskirts of the city, across the narrow bridge that led over the river to an island, there was an American mission.

When the doctor saw the young girl coming toward him across the garden, saw her rich garment, the flowers in her hair, the bright sunshade, he went quickly to meet her. No one crossed the bridge to his leprosarium without real cause.

He was gentle as he examined her hand, but he knew that to give her least pain he must be brutally honest. When he spoke the dreaded word, Mah-Sai sprang up and stood before him, trembling, her eyes filled with tears. The doctor watched her walk away from him, proudly, swiftly, bravely, as he had seen so many go. Tomorrow, the day after, maybe, she would return.

The girl's feet were leaden as she crossed the bridge and she paused for a moment, as perhaps others had paused, having just heard the death sentence pronounced upon them, to look down at the waters flowing serenely below. It would be so simple to end her life in this way, instead of by means of the seeds of destruction within her. But she lacked the courage to jump from the bridge. The parasol fell from her hand. Leaning against the rail, she watched it bobbing away downstream until it was no longer visible. With it went all she had ever known and loved: of beauty, laughter, and joy. The next time she crossed the bridge she knew she would be going away to die, not gently, not with dignity as other people might, but to disintegrate slowly, pitied in the eyes of all.

That night Mah-Sai danced as never before, but she could scarcely see through her tears the long curled fingers of gold on her weaving hands. The other girls knew now. She could tell by the way their eyes rested on her—eyes full of sadness and questioning. She must go quickly, before open disclosure drove her to the step she dreaded.

While the girls still rested next morning, Mah-Sai wrapped a few of her precious belongings in a little bundle and slipped away to cross the bridge for the last time. She walked quickly; she did not look back. A young doctor greeted her as she left the bridge and stepped into the island garden; a nurse put a blindfold over her eyes, while they gave her the first test: a gentle touch in various places on throat and arms to measure the sensitivity of her skin Each time Mah-Sai was able to indicate the exact spot that had been touched, but when they touched her hand she sat still, waiting, unaware of even a heavy contact with the dying flesh.

The doctor made a quick entry in his book: the blindfold was removed from her eyes; and Mah-Sai was led away by the housemother, a gentle old woman in a long black robe, to her quarters in the neat wooden house across the garden. Walking beside the old woman, Mah-Sai in her grief felt infinitely older. Alone in her room, the girl sat on the bed and for the first time gave way to the full force of her grief. From time to time the old housemother would come to the door to stand silent, her brown wrinkled face creased in deep lines of voiceless sympathy, lending the girl the comfort of her presence. Her understanding had no need of words.

For a long time Mah-Sai lived in a world apart, but gradually she became aware of the change at work in her mind as well as within her body. Life could never return to her hands, nor the beauty she had known be restored to her world, yet beauty of another kind existed here in the mission; a strange, prosaic beauty of cleanliness, of kindness and orderly service, beauty that in the beginning she mistook for pain, beauty in proving herself bigger than her affliction.

There was always plenty to do; everyone was kept busy. The little colony grew its own rice and sugar cane, papayas, and bananas, raised its own water buffalo, and made beautiful objects in spite of maimed and twisted hands. There were the houses and gardens to be tended, the weekly rice ration to be collected—a very small ration but all the mission could afford—and endless ways in which the patients daily proved themselves bigger in spirit than the disease that had begun slowly to consume them all.

Mah-Sai loved to walk alone in the cool banana groves or watch the papayas ripening on the trees, marveling at the miracle of growth, the ritual of spring, absorbing the things of nature she had been unaware of before.

One day when she was walking beside the river, she saw on the other side a youth pursued by a crowd of men with long sticks. They were yelling and hurling stones at him as he came stumbling across the shallows. Seeing the girl standing on the bank, he sank exhausted at her feet. Mah-Sai helped him to his feet. As his fingers closed about hers, his eyes filled with gratitude. She knew why he was being chased by the mob. He was an outcast, like herself.

Slowly, silently, they walked together to the mission. Perhaps it was in this moment that she realized that her life could still be useful. She would teach the girls to dance; she would pass on to them the graceful movements in which she had been, and was still, so highly skilled. Even she had some special work to do, something no one else could contribute. She no longer fought to forget where she was but threw all her energies into reviving her broken spirit through the beauty of dance. Though she was not yet a Christian, the teachings at the mission had brought to her a spiritual serenity in which she could love rather than be repelled by her brothers and sisters in sickness. She was no longer alone, and would never be.

The most baffling day of Mah-Sai's life came when she learned that she was cured, that she could once again cross the bridge and return, after years of absence and isolation, to the outside world. Freedom suddenly brought a greater loneliness that she had ever known.

The nurse, overworked and very tired, had no time to help this poor creature in that moment of overwhelming crisis. "You're quite cured, my dear," she said. "Free . . . you can go any day you like. . . ." She climbed on her bicycle and rode away to other duties; Mah-Sai covered her face and wept.

For some time she wandered about the colony seeking any excuse to put off the terrible decision that must soon be made. Is there anything more terrifying than freedom when one is alone with it and does not know how to use it? What was there for her on the other side of the bridge? The doctor understood her anguish: to be looked at always with suspicion, healed but bearing forever the scars of a loathsome disease. He would be grateful for her assistance in the laboratory; there was always plenty of work to be done.

Mah-Sai had been in the leprosarium more than twenty-five years when I met her, and through an interpreter she told me her story. Her illness had made her an old woman, although she was barely forty. Her body, in the typical dress of the country, wrapped skirt and overhanging blue blouse, was shrunken; her once graceful fingers were now twisted. But the eyes in her creased face were infinitely gentle and filled with light. She herself was now a housemother, welcoming and sharing her silent sympathy with bewildered newcomers.

"As my body grew weaker," she told me, "my spirit seemed to grow stronger. My mind and heart are sometimes full to overflowing. . . . When I agreed to remain here forever and work I shed the net that had enshrouded me for so long. It is true I am free now, but it is freedom of which I am no longer afraid."

When I asked Mah-Sai if some of the girls she had taught to dance would dance for me, her face broke into a radiant smile. At once the young girls were assembled in the open pavilion in the garden, and three musicians came hurrying with their instruments. The girls performed the intricate dances with a beauty and grace one could scarcely believe possible, with such crippling disability. They had been meticulously rehearsed, but this was more than mere movement; it was an expression of something deeper.

The small orchestra—a xylophone, a drum, and a flute, played by musicians so maimed that I marveled they could hold the instruments at all—was a poor substitute for the twenty-one-piece orchestra which I had already recorded at the court, but they played with such pride in achievement that I was moved to tears.

Dancers and musicians were overjoyed when I suggested I should come across the bridge again the next day with my camera and recording equipment. And for as many days as I was a guest in the doctor's house on the mainland, I crossed the bridge daily to film the dances and record the music of the bravest little orchestra I have ever known.

One day the doctor came to me. He was a shy man, reserved, but I could sense about him a kind of excitement. Looking sternly at me he said in what I took to be tones of reproach: "Well, you've certainly started something!" "Oh dear!" I said. "What have I done wrong?"

He laughed. "They have come asking—no, demanding politely—all the instruments of a full orchestra! They said you thought their music fine enough to record, and now that they have heard it played back to them they have taken a new lease on life!" He smiled. "You have unwittingly done something for them which medicine could never do."

Not long ago I learned that they now have a splendid orchestra on the island. Every day they bring fresh magic, color, beauty, and happiness to the life of the colony. The recordings of that little three-piece orchestra are still among the most prized in my collection.

Chapter 19

SOUTHEAST ASIA: FROM BALI
TO BORNEO

It is a gift of the gods, I believe, to be in the right place at the right time. The two years of my first sojourn in the Orient were a very eventful period for that part of the world. I celebrated the first Independence Day in India as the guest of Nehru; I was in the Himalayas at the headwaters of the Ganges for the Purna Kumbha Mela; I was invited as the guest of the Maharaja of Nepal for a royal wedding; and I was in Indonesia before, during, and following the transfer of sovereignty from the Dutch to the Indonesians.

The morning after I attended the impressive ceremony at the palace when the Dutch turned over the government to the Indonesians, I woke up in my hotel and found there was no service. It seems that Premier Sukarno had told everyone, "You won't work for the white people any more; they're going to work for you now," and they had taken this literally. The manager of the hotel went to the kitchen and did his best to provide breakfast for the guests. His wife tried to do maid service while other members of their family took on the telephone and miscellaneous duties. It was practically impossible to go anywhere; the taxi drivers could not find addresses since the names of all the streets, as well as the names of cities, had been changed overnight. The capital, Batavia, was suddenly Djakarta and the Dutch airline KLM now became Garuda Airways, named for the bird famous in Indonesian legends. Life was very complicated and difficult; in fact, for a short time it was bedlam for visitors and especially for those Dutchmen who had been persuaded to remain to help the new government in its gigantic task of running its own affairs with few trained personnel. Although some of the Dutch had stayed in good faith and had been promised complete cooperation, the promises frequently were not kept.

The first night I arrived in Batavia, prior to the transfer, a friend took me to dinner in a restaurant where he said there would be not only excellent food but wonderful musicians, minstrels who wandered from place to place. It is true that the food was delicious and the musicians did come, but imagine my dismay and disappointment when they started out with a charming Indonesian rendition of "Give Me Five Minutes More, Only Five Minutes More." This was hardly the music I had come in search of. What I particularly wanted to record was the gamelan music of Bali. I proceeded to that enchanting island where I was guest in the palace of the Anak Agung, a Balinese prince who liked to think of himself as a link between the East and the West. He spoke some English and loved having American visitors. In addition to the palace in which he lived, there were two smaller ones in which he had prepared a few rooms for guests. When I was there, there were also professors from Harvard and from one of the midwestern universities.

This Balinese prince was a delightful, warm person, always laughing and joking, most hospitable, full of information about his people, and very musical. At his side usually was his favorite young son, the offspring of one of his numerous wives. The Anak Agung was related to a very highborn family which formerly had been very rich and had owned large tracts of land. Much of their income had come from rice, but the mountain streams which had once furnished irrigation had been diverted for a dam and the fields had dried up. He was very composed but had that nervous habit I have often observed in the East of pulling out each finger systematically until the bones click, first the right hand and then the left. No doubt he had his worries. It was well known he had squandered his money on his dancers and musicians and even on much less worthy things such as fighting cocks.

His financial state doubtless had something to do with his decision to entertain paying guests, and he seemed to prefer Americans; probably they were the most generous. He loved having his picture taken and Americans always had good cameras. The large rambling palace was in need of repair. The courts were impressive but overgrown with plant life. The older buildings behind the wall, although beautifully carved and often gilded, had been damaged by beetles and rats. In what were formerly sedate gardens, hibiscus, gardenias, and jasmine now bloomed in great confusion, and orchids hung from the trees.

As all princes did, he maintained a *gamelan* (a gong orchestra), a *gamelan angklung* (instruments of bamboo), and a group of young dancers. The dancing span in Bali for a girl begins when she is about six years old and is over by the time she is fourteen. When she reaches puberty she marries and has her own little girls. During the period I was there the girls danced every evening, accompanied by the gamelan, rehearsing the gestures and dance movements of secular and religious dances, many of which re-enact legends in the life of Rama and the gods that surrounded him. The Anak Agung's gamelan consisted of the usual twenty-odd instruments: gongs, xylophones, and drums, with at least one wind instrument and one string instrument. His fine angklung orchestra produced lovely liquid music that to many people is even more attractive than that of the classical gamelan. The Anak Agung played the drums very well, and he used to say, "How could there be music without drums?" The drumbeat to him was like the heart beating, like the blood coursing through the body.

About a million and a half people lived on Bali when I first went there—mainly Balinese, attractive, handsome people with a delightful sense of humor. Most of them followed their own brand of Hinduism, although a small portion of the population was Buddhist. The two religions existed happily together and at important feasts there were usually both Hindu and Buddhist priests presiding in snowy white, the holy color, even brighter than gold. Beside the great chief deity, Ciwa (Shiva), there are many lesser gods—important village and family deities as well as sea, wood, and mountain gods. Ranged against them are many wicked spirits which have to be appeased by elaborate rites, and many of the dances have originated with these propitiation ceremonies.

There are four castes, but the caste system is much less rigid than in India. The priests must be of the Brahman caste. To the second caste, Ksatrias, belong the princes and rajahs: Dewa Agung, Anak Agung, and Tjokorde. The ordinary people without titles belong to the fourth caste, Soedras, but any caste may practice trade.

A man may marry a lower-caste woman, but never vice versa. (The Balinese often have more than one wife.)

Rice growing was the most important occupation and the rice fields of Bali are perhaps the most beautiful terraces in the world. The Balinese are masters of constructing these fields and experts in irrigation. Cattle raising is the second most important means of livelihood. The Balinese cattle with their small graceful feet—bearing only a small resemblance to the ordinary cow—are not raised for milk, but only for slaughter. Pigs are raised widely, and the Balinese coffee is world-renowned. The arts should perhaps be listed as a means of livelihood, for Balinese carvings, paintings, metalwork, and weavings have been in great demand for many years by outsiders. In Bali, art is not for a chosen few; everyone is artistic, even the poorest village woman preparing her exquisite arrangements of fruit and flowers for the temple ceremonies.

When in the middle of the fifteenth century Islam spread throughout Java, important Hindu-Javanese families fled to Bali. Bali became independent and was never again under Javanese dominion. After World War II, Bali became one of the autonomous regions of the state of East Indonesia. Eight kingdoms were federated into one area governed by a council of eight rulers, the Rajas' Council, assisted by a representative body chosen by democratic methods. The office of the Raja's Council was in Denpasar. From my hotel in the center of town I could go easily to temples, palaces, beaches, and fascinating villages where I recorded and filmed splendid ceremonials. On one of the most attractive beaches, Sanoer Beach, lived the well-known Belgian artist, Le Mayeur, and his exquisite Balinese wife, Polok, the most photographed lady in the Far East. We became good friends and through them I learned a great deal about Balinese culture.

Hinduism dominated the cultures of both Java and Bali from the first century until the thirteenth century, but Java today is ninety percent Mohammedan. In Bali a fusion of the indigenous culture with Hinduism made a strong religious life which is still basic. Much of the art, music, dance, drama, literature, and sculpture is inspired by religious beliefs and legends. In Denpasar I went to a remarkable series of dances, plays, and shadow plays. The dances were drawn from religious ceremonies or from the secular theater; it is difficult to separate them as they are so interwoven. Among the most important ceremonial dances are the *baris,* including many different ones for men, danced with weapons. The special costume for the baris consists of long trousers, a sarong pulled up through the legs, and a sleeveless vest with a leather collar. The *sanghyang* are trance dances and all the dancers are girls, generally not more than twelve years old. They are put into the state of trance, possessed by various gods. They dance with closed eyes and can walk through fire without being burned or perform on the shoulders of men in a manner that defies the laws of gravity. These trance dances take place when the evil spirits of sickness must be expelled from a village. The *Ketjak,* or monkey dance, performed only by men, belongs to the trance dance group. This is one of the most fantastic performances I have ever seen. The singing men sit in concentric circles with an oil lamp in the center whose flickering flames cast an eerie light over the concentrated, ecstatic faces of the singers and dancers. The singing is very dramatic, building up to an almost unbearable excitement with the guttural, growling *"Ke-tjak-ke-tjak-ke-tjak"* continually repeated. The *Ketjak* forms an integral part of many trance dances but it has been developed into a play and, as theater, is included in the secular dances. This spectacle holds everyone spellbound.

The *barong*, a holy object which has power to suppress evil spirits in the village, consists of a huge animal's head with body attached, which is very costly, belongs to the whole village, and is kept in the temple. For the barong dance the head is carried by two men, invisible except for their legs, in a procession accompanied by special ritual music. A variation of this is the *barong landoeng* with two or four doll-like figures, larger than life, telling stories through singing and dancing. The *kris* dance is part of temple services and is performed after the priests—always in white, the holy color—have completed their temple ceremonies. A group of men shouting and gesturing wildly run through the temple while holding a kris, a short Malay dagger, against their chests. Some of them are in trance but are seldom wounded seriously. If they become too wild for safety, the kris is taken from them.

The theater plays and secular dances are extremely popular, especially the *legong*. The dancers, always very young girls, are clad in magnificent costumes and headdresses. They dance a story and although they may take several different roles which continually change, the audience gets the full meaning through the *dalang,* who sits behind the orchestra and provides a running explanation.

The charming little dancing girls who played the leading roles in the legong danced at the Anak Agung's palace were especially lovely. At the beginning the two main dancers performed as "a double projection of a single image," from the fingertips and the tilt of the head to the position and angle of the feet. Suddenly they would break away dancing in opposite directions, only to return quickly to reflect each other as in a mirror. As the story continued, the characters emerged with the greatest delicacy; every gesture, however dramatic, was highly stylized and done with great restraint. In the tale of Lasem and the abducted princess, Lasem was killed with only the tap of the fan and a slight shove; sorrow and weeping were indicated by a fluid motion of the hand. But a great contrast was produced by the *chondong* who became a raven by donning a pair of gilded wings. The drumming was turbulent as she danced violently as a bird battling the storm against the wind. The chondong, a brilliant, wild beauty, was slightly older and graver than the others, and in another year she would no longer be a child and her dancing days would end. Anak Agung was relentless during the rehearsals, which were held each day and every evening. He corrected every movement of the fingertips, the tilt of the head, and all their gestures with patient, exacting authority.

Even the most elemental instruments and primitive melodies of Southeast Asia are very interesting. Although it has been the tendency by some who approach this area of music for the first time to place the primitive and the theoretical art music in the same category, actually they are drastically different. The music of the gamelan has its own definite system and form, although it grew from the theoretical systems of Hindu and Chinese art music.

When the Moslems arrived in Indonesia from India about the thirteenth century the emphasis on temple and festival performances was shifted to court ceremonies and entertainment except in Bali, where the Hindu culture, combined with the indigenous background, was firmly established. The gamelans developed in Java and Bali, not by planned evolution, but as a response to beauty and a desire for expression. The concept of the music, the kinds of instruments, the color of the sound, and the rhythms give the Balinese instruments a positive and individual sound that seems to express perfectly the outgoing nature of the Balinese, and the people participate; while in Java, the people are the audience for a refined Javanese gamelan that was associated with the elegance and power of the Sultan's court.

In Java I had spent considerable time with the orchestras, but I found Balinese music quite different, although the instruments are similar in many respects to those of Java. It is more varied and to the Western ear more appealing than the Javanese gamelan, which on first hearing sounds somewhat monotonous. In Bali there are at least thirteen types of gamelans and no two gamelans are tuned exactly alike. A few archaic ones are tuned to the seven-tone *pelong* from Java. The *slendro,* the five-tone system, and the pelong are found in both Javanese and Balinese music.

The angklung is made of five or more tubes of bamboo, cut at the ends like the barrels of an organ. These are graduated in length and placed in a frame in such a way that they can move and vibrate when the frame is shaken. These instruments have been described by Sir Stamford Raffles as being played in the Lesser Sunda Islands by a troupe of ten to fifty mountaineers, accompanied by small drums for festivals. The upper parts were decorated with feathers. The liquid music was simple and gay. The angklung is thought to be an early improvement on the bamboo tube hanging in a tree which produced music as the wind blew through it.

I photographed in Bali a tall bamboo pole with carved openings which let the winds blow through it; the tones were amazingly sweet. In Southeast Asia the people make music out of everything. They even fasten little whistles to certain birds so that they make music during flight. Today, in remote parts of Bali, the angklung instruments (limited to four) are played with one or two xylophones, ever-present cymbals, drum, and gong. It was formerly used in ceremonies for the cremation of the dead, and only in recent times has it been used for temple festivals and other religious ceremonies. During the cremation rites, the angklung orchestra performs for three days preceding the actual burning. According to the caste and financial state of the family, other gamelans are assembled to fill the air with glorious sound during these three days. The angklung is in most cases purely ritualistic; it may be played in the procession or may accompany the rites following cremation, when the ashes are carried to the sea, or it may nowadays take part in other religious ceremonies. It is used to accompany dancing in very few villages. The tone of a good angklung orchestra has a sweet, chimelike quality in the upper registers with mysterious, throbbing lower tones. Its tuning is different from that of the classical gamelan. Each instrument has a well-defined part to play, but all function together like the parts of a well-adjusted watch. This music has a marked individuality and a simplicity of outline that places it closer to folk music than that of other gamelan orchestras.

Malaya is just across the Strait of Malacca from Indonesia and racially closely related. In 1950, when I was there, the British were trying desperately to clear the country of Communist guerrillas who were bleeding the people. The guerrillas appeared in the night, demanded money from those who were affluent, and they demanded food from the poor. Since life itself was at stake, everyone complied with their demands. It looked as though this situation could go on forever with the people actually supporting their enemies until a plan was devised which finally cleared the country of guerrillas. All the people were moved into government-built villages surrounded by barbed wire. During the daytime the people went forth to their fields, but at night they slept in the enclosure carefully protected by efficient policemen. I went to the first village that was functioning under this system and found that the people seemed delighted with the arrangement, because for the first time for many years they could sleep without fear of unwanted night visitors. But it seemed to me that the system would take too much time to implement, and time was of the essence if the marauders were to be checked.

I saw evidence of the guerrillas' handiwork when I visited a rubber plantation near Penang in the north of Malaya. It was a rather harrowing experience. The walls of the manager's house were dotted with bullet holes from a recent all-night attack. He and his wife, who was pregnant, had spent the night on the floor hoping to survive until morning. It was dangerous even to travel the road to this plantation in those days, but it was such a beautiful spot and my hosts were so cordial that it was more than worth the risk involved. Fortunately the British worked more quickly than I could have imagined and the guerrillas were eventually defeated.

Singapore, then a part of Malaya and under its capital, Kuala Lumpur, was a bustling, progressive port full of business activity and a charming, attractive city with fine beaches and a pleasant social life. The famed Raffles Hotel had not then been attacked, destroyed, and rebuilt. Though there were troublesome episodes with storm clouds on the horizon, all still seemed peaceful.

The journey from Singapore by Malayan Airways to Labuan, North Borneo, was a six-hour trip. The island of Borneo, the third largest in the world, is divided by the equator but in the mountainous regions has a healthy climate. Two thirds of the island belong to the Republic of Indonesia; the northern third is British Borneo and consists of the colonies of Sarawak, North Borneo, and the Sultanate of Brunei. The entire island is roughly two and one-half times the size of England, Scotland, and Wales together.

Borneo is surrounded by the Java Sea to the south, the South China Sea to the west and north, and the Sulu and Celebes Seas to the east. It is the best-watered island in the world with many rivers, but most are navigable only with a *prahu,* or local canoe; the larger rivers have so much silt at their mouths that seagoing vessels cannot enter safely. The rainfall ranges from a hundred inches annually on the coast to two hundred inland. During the rainy season, October to March, there are heavy rains, strong winds, and rough seas, and the streams may rise as much as fifty feet above their normal level. A flood of rain can rage for six or seven hours, registering as much as six inches in one rainfall. But when the skies are cloudy and sunless and the trees hanging low over the river drip with mist, it is a happy time, for it is the season that fruit pours in from the jungle brought in boats by tribesmen living there. The temperature is in the eighties by day, but the nights are cool and delightful. I found the native people most attractive; and the Europeans, a relatively small community, were happy and extremely well adjusted, and apparently enjoyed their work in this healthy, picturesque land.

History tells us that fifteen hundred years ago Chinese and Hindu civilizations existed in Borneo. By 1291 there was considerable trade by junk, the small Chinese sailing ship, between Borneo and China. In 1292 the Emperor of China sent an expedition to Borneo which is no doubt the origin of the present prosperous Chinese colony. The Moslems invaded and their religion persists today as the religion of the Malayans of Borneo. Finally, in the fifteenth century, Portuguese and Spanish navigators came and wrote eyewitness accounts of the glories of the Sultan's court in Brunei. By the middle of the sixteenth century the Portuguese had established several trading posts to deal in spices, rare woods, gold, and precious stones. Dutch voyagers appeared and in 1602 the Dutch East India Company was set up and ruled most of Borneo for two centuries until the company was dissolved in 1798; until 1949 Dutch Borneo was governed by Holland, and since that date it has been under the Republic of Indonesia.

When Kubla Khan invaded Borneo in 1292, the beginning of a province of the Chinese empire was established. Rivers and mountains still have Chinese names, and Chinese objects—jars, beads, and coins—have been found. The highest mountain in North Borneo is named Kinabalu, from a Chinese word meaning widow. There is a legend that on top of this mountain a precious stone guarded by a dragon was coveted by the Emperor of China, who ordered his ministers to get it. Great numbers of Chinese were devoured by the dragon before the stone was acquired through a minister's successful strategy. He made a glass box and put a lighted candle in it. When the dragon went out to eat, the minister seized the precious stone and put the lamp in its place. Thus the dragon was deceived. Deciding to go to Brunei with his precious stone instead of to China, the minister married a princess there and became the Sultan Ahamat. Then the legend says that his beautiful daughter married a visitor from Arabia who became Sultan and established the Mohammedan religion. The Sultan of today is theoretically a descendant from these people.

In 1522, when the Italian, Pigafetta, visited Brunei, he found a hundred thousand people living in the city. The Spaniards and the Portuguese, who gained power for a time, were replaced by the Dutch, who reported that by 1770 the population had shrunk to forty thousand. Early settlements were destroyed by pirates who infested the seas and whose powers were so great that Brunei Town in 1840 was reduced to fifteen thousand souls.

It was then that James Brooke, who became "The White Raja,"

came to Sarawak in his yacht *The Royalist*. In the rebellion that was going on, he took the side of the Sultan of Brunei. The Mohammedans were contemptuous of the other inhabitants of the country, the Dyaks, Kayans, and Murut. They bought from these inhabitants, on their own terms, all their goods—rice, birds' nests, wax, jungle products, boats, even clothes—and seized their women and children to sell into slavery. The Sea Dyaks angrily turned pirates, so the Brunei princes furnished them with boats and weapons and made them work for them. When Raja Brooke first visited Sarawak, he found the inhabitants rebelling against their Brunei oppressors. The Sultan of Brunei offered Raja Brooke the country of Sarawak and its government if he would help put down the rebellion. Raja Brooke put down the rebellion for the country's good and offered it to the British government. It seemed such an unpromising and dangerous land at that time that it was not then accepted. Brooke set about to bring peace and prosperity to his new country. He and Captain Keppel cruised the coasts of Borneo in 1843 and faced pirate fleets of as many as two hundred vessels with brass guns and double tiers of oars —some of the oars were as much as nine feet long. These pirates, descending on the coast, sacked and burned the villages, killed or carried off the men, women and children and sold them into slavery. Most of the natives preferred death to the tortures which awaited them if they were captured. After the pirates were suppressed, all the adjoining countryside begged to come under his prosperous rule.

In his headquarters in Sarawak, Brooke set up a paternal and humane system of government and made himself completely accessible to the local people. He established a just rule in which both the rulers and the ruled did their portion of the work with full cooperation. He learned the manners and methods of the people and was devoted to their welfare and interest. He was so much loved that it was no wonder that his nephew who succeeded him was wholeheartedly accepted by the people.

This second white Raja, Sir Charles Brooke, was an able, enlightened man and a true friend to the Malays. His government, administered by Englishmen of the best type, was a model to the civilized world. The taxation was light and taxes were spent on the country itself. The Raja, although he owned a rich country nearly as big as England, drew for his personal expenses only two or three thousand pounds a year.

After Sarawak became a British colony in 1946 it was difficult for the British government to find a governor who had the same firm but fatherly approach to the native population which had held the people together and had kept the peace. When I was the guest of the government in Sarawak I found that Governor Anthony Abell was such a man. He came to Sarawak in 1950 at an awkward moment to succeed a governor who had just been murdered by a remote tribe in the interior; he did a superb job and in a very short time had won the hearts of the people. Under The White Raja the local population had felt free to come and sit down in the Raja's palace whenever they wished to discuss their problems or just to visit as with a friend. This continued paternal attitude was the secret of the success of Governor Abell.

When I revisited Sarawak in 1956, as in Singapore, I gave several radio programs about other peoples of the world, their customs, and particularly their music, and collected fascinating music including paddlers' songs. I experienced the thrill of watching the annual regatta of the huge dragon canoes, each with about fifteen paddlers, that had come from the whole area to compete. I was delighted that the canoe of the Sultan of Brunei won the regatta because by this time he had become a good friend, and his beautifully carved canoe was my favorite in the race.

A journey through the jungle and along the river took me to the Dyaks, the head-hunters of Borneo. By the time of my visit the days of wildmen and head-hunters were past, although I was told that some groups in the interior occasionally carried out the practice. When I visited them in their long house (the whole group lives in one house, almost the length of a city block, which shelters as many as a hundred families, possibly a thousand people) I felt so at home I couldn't believe the many bloodcurdling tales I had heard. Later, however, in the ceremonial cave, with skulls hanging above, nearly touching my head, the stories seemed more real. I had heard that the fingers were considered great delicacies, and as I could not sit on my hands and record at the same time, I hoped for the best. Actually they were charming, friendly hosts and I soon felt no fear.

My only attendant when I went to visit the Dyak villages was my young Chinese guide and interpreter. Recording in the long house was one of my most thrilling experiences. Each family's house is called a "door," and one long house might be the home of a whole tribe. Dishonesty is unknown among the inhabitants. They all work willingly on communal tasks, and the authority of the elders is never questioned. The sanitation may be somewhat primitive, but it is not unhealthy, as one might imagine, and actually is a very sensible solution to the needs of these people. The long house, built on stilts, keeps the people high above the swampy land. A notched log provides an adequate ladder for going and coming, and the space under the houses takes care of the needs of pigs and chickens. I was not very comfortable on this notched-log ladder at an angle of forty-five degrees but I managed not to disgrace myself by falling into the swamp below.

British Borneo is an oasis of peace surrounded by the troubled world of Southeast Asia, Communist China, Hong Kong, Macao, and Formosa to the north, the Philippines to the northeast, Indonesia to the south, Malaya to the west, and Thailand, Cambodia, Laos, and Vietnam to the northwest. There was very little infiltration from outside when I was there. It was true that on a few occasions troublemakers slipped across the border from Indonesian Borneo but there was no serious problem.

The background story of the colony of North Borneo until 1872 was much the same as that of the sultanate of Brunei. In 1872 a syndicate of traders negotiated with the Sultan of Brunei and secured a large territory for their company. In 1881 the British government granted a charter to "The North Borneo Provisional Association, Limited." The charter provided that the company should always remain British, that there should be no transfer of land without British approval, that there should be no monopoly of trade, and that the activities, including the appointment of its chief representative in Borneo, would be supervised by the British government. Slavery was then a thriving institution and there was an active pirate community. The company undertook to abolish slavery and administer justice with due regard for the local customs, laws, and religion. In 1888 the British protectorate was created. In 1890 the island of Labuan was placed in the jurisdiction of the British North Borneo Company and remained there until 1906, when it became a British colony. The little-known regions of the interior were gradually brought under control. Areas not included in the original territory were added from time to time, and by 1900 North Borneo had reached its present size. In January 1942, North Borneo was invaded by the Japanese and was governed by them for three and a half years. During that period it was the location of some of the worst prisoner-of-war camps and the scene of a notorious death march in which the occupants of the several camps were marched across country and died like flies along the route.

The local people, loyal to the British, often paid for their loyalty with their lives. When the military administration was set up by the British after the area was liberated, they found a state of appalling devastation with many towns completely destroyed or nearly so by fire or bombing. Many of the former employees of the company had been killed in the great massacres. Rehabilitation measures, first aid, and medical assistance were begun on a large scale to assist the local population, as practically no town or village had escaped the wanton destruction by the Japanese. In 1946 North Borneo became a colony.

As soon as possible after the basic needs of food, shelter, and social services had been taken care of, the reconstruction and development program began, extending medical services, restoring lighthouses, building and repairing the colony's roads and railways. When I was there the last time in 1956, the rubber estates and timber workings employed a large number of the local population and North Borneo was a growing and prosperous community. The oil fields were functioning again although the Japanese had burned them and had undone most of the great work that had been done since oil was discovered. The oil field at Miri and the refinery at Lutong in northern Sarawak were active again, and the Seria oil field about thirty-five miles away in the British-protected sultanate of Brunei was expanding rapidly.

North Borneo was so stable and comfortable that the British in Brunei considered the island of Labuan in North Borneo, forty miles away by launch, almost as a holiday resort where they could find a doctor, a telegraph office, a golf course, tennis courts, a race course, shops, and clubs, signs of "civilization." The bungalows at Port Victoria are on top of a small hill where the evening breezes are very refreshing. When I was visiting British North Borneo, I stayed in one of these charming bungalows with one of the British officials and his family surrounded by all the charm and comfort of a palace. I was there over St. Andrew's Day, and that was a night I shall never forget. The young doctor and his wife and many of their friends were Scottish. We danced reels all night, and although I had one Scottish grandmother, I never before felt so properly initiated into Scottish rites.

I arrived in Brunei on the government launch with the British Resident, Sir Eric Pretty, and his wife. The trip was full of beauty and interest. The estuary was busy with native canoes paddled by Malays with flat, wide noses, their thin lips stained with betel nut, the whites of their eyes yellowed, their scant clothing dirty and ragged. Beyond the smooth estuary, low grassy hills rose gently from the shores and the distant mountains rose high, jagged, and blue in the brilliant sky. Occasionally we passed a sandy cape with old, gray coconut palms and straight, spruce betel palms. Fleets of canoes, with masses of brown fishing nets protruding, were paddled by many fishermen naked to the waist, laboring at the paddles to get their catch home before darkness fell. The sun was sinking rapidly below the hills and the flaming sky was thickly strewn with powdery puffs of clouds. Brunei Town used to be called "the Venice of the East," and I had been impatient to see this town built almost entirely over the water, which, it is said, was the largest Malay city a hundred years ago.

Brunei, the ancient capital of the Mohammedan sultanate of Brunei, was famous in early days and attracted visitors from distant lands. From Turkey and many Arab countries came those hoping for favors from the court; the Chinese, shrewd businessmen, came to establish trade. The Portuguese navigators described Brunei as a rich and glorious city surrounded by a prosperous land with gardens and plantations, ruled by a Sultan descended from a very long dynasty—with an alluring court and a harem of hundreds of beautiful women.

Much territory had been taken away from the Brunei Sultanate for British North Borneo and Sarawak so only a tiny state remained and about two-thirds of the entire population lived in the capital. I shall always think of Brunei as I saw it from afar, a fairy city perched on stilts in the middle of a large, gleaming lake surrounded by ranges of low, graceful wooded hills. "Daru'l Salem" the natives call it: "The Abode of Peace." Shortly after my first glimpse of the town, we rounded the island and I saw to my disappointment a very ordinary jetty, corrugated iron roofs, a few modern bungalows, and to my amazement a little factory belching smoke. But not even these signs of "civilization" could destroy the peace and charm of the place.

Brunei was probably the only town in the world where household arrangements, family life, town government, everything in fact had to be adjusted to life on the water. How the people survived through so many generations is a mystery, with the damp, the lack of exercise, the germs in the filthy mud under the huts, the epidemics, and the high infant mortality. They doubtlessly drank a lot of tea, with enough tannic acid in it to arrest even cholera. The first British Resident of Brunei had asked in his report that a clean, dry village be built, and that building on the river be discouraged; this has now come about.

The natives of Brunei are Mohammedans and most of them with their dreamy, idle nature are rather mild about it. But I was told that in some cases they might become mad fanatics. They believed in charms and omens and were very courageous. The average native of Brunei was industrious, and usually had only one wife with a large family. He wore a sarong, and when not working wore a coat over the sarong. When he worked he took off his coat and rolled it up into a sort of loincloth.

The people of Brunei are very skillful in weaving, brasswork, and silversmithing. In a separate part of this city on stilts, the trades were carried on. The moneylenders (Sikhs from India or Chinese) lived quietly and did a very good business. Their huts were in the Water Village, clustered together with a private causeway leading directly to the palace and the houses of the ministers of state who held hereditary offices. The usual home owned by a rich noble of Brunei was a square wooden central house with a long front veranda built out over the water, and grouped around this was a huddle of thatched huts, smaller houses, women's quarters, and slaves' huts, the whole surrounded by a heavy bamboo fence. The silversmiths, the most skilled tradesmen in Brunei, lived next door to the moneylenders and formerly made their silverwork from old dollars melted down—new Straits dollars from Singapore —but later discarded them for strips of silver, which were easier to beat into shape.

I loved my visits to the silversmiths and gongmakers. In a small canoe with children splashing all around us we paddled to the favorite silversmith of the Sultan and scrambled up a little bamboo ladder placed precariously in the canoe to lean against the hut made of reed walls with thatched roofs of palm leaves. Inside, squatting on the matting which covered the split palm floor, we found a small, thin, brown man with all the implements of his craft around him—silver, resin, hammers, punches, and numerous wooden blocks. The intricate patterns were put on with punches and required much thought and patience as well as genuine hard work. I marveled that tools of the most elementary form could produce patterns so delicate and beautiful.

I had been invited as guest on a British plantation. Although we were ten thousand miles from London, all the amenities were observed there as at home. The factory on the plantation made cutch, a substance used for tanning leather and dyeing cloth khaki-color from the bark of the mangrove tree. The bark is ground, extracted in vats, boiled down in large copper pans, run into molds, and allowed to settle. Large shipments of cutch were made to Europe.

The manager's bungalow was elevated on palm-trunk stilts and was comfortable and charming. The nights were deliciously cool but we had to sleep under mosquito nets. Some of the servants were Malay, other Chinese. I think they considered me very stupid that I spoke no Malay, and if I had stayed longer I would have done something about it. I learned a few words quickly and was told that I could master it in three months, but unfortunately I had only a few weeks left in the country. The manager was more progressive than most in providing neat little houses for the tappers, a school for their children, and other advantages lacking on many plantations.

As always when visiting an area, I asked to visit the school, and the manager came with me. And, as always, I asked the children to sing. Imagine the consternation of the manager when the little brown "cherubs" burst forth with the "Internationale." It had certainly never occurred to him or to British government officials to ask to hear their music, and little did they dream that the young were being indoctrinated right under their noses. The teacher was fired, but no doubt much damage had already been done.

There were other signs of Communist infiltration. The arrivals in the ports could be checked but it was impossible to guard the borders and prevent natives stealing through the forest from Dutch

Borneo—now Indonesian Borneo. From time to time disturbing things happened on the plantation: The machinery was sabotaged from time to time; a new type of quarreling and minor agitation had begun. But for the most part, life was very peaceful.

The Sultan of Brunei, Sir Omar Ali Saifuddin, was a modest, cordial, charming host. Dinner in his palace was a delightful occasion with much interesting conversation and music provided by the court orchestra of ancient gongs—which he later presented to me and which are now in New York. The young Sultana, the mother of six, was as shy as a young maiden. They posed with the children for numerous photographs, but the Sultan had to use a great deal of persuasion on the Sultana. She did not enjoy social occasions and, of course, never traveled with her husband. He was greatly admired in London when he was a guest at the coronation of Queen Elizabeth. But his elegance and charm were somewhat overshadowed in the stately procession because he was placed in the carriage with the statuesque seven-foot Queen of Tonga. The Sultan was a very progressive young man who had only recently come into office. Sultan Sir Hamed Tajudin had ruled the country for twenty-six years until he died in June 1950 at the age of thirty-six. A succession of vigorous and far-seeing British Residents had given firm guidance and helped with the colossal rehabilitation problems in the first years following the Japanese occupation, which had, as everywhere, tragic results: They had destroyed property, burned the oil wells, and decimated the population.

During and following the Japanese occupation, the Sultan was not in good health and could not be active in governing the country. His younger brother, Sir Omar Ali Saifuddin, had served as First Minister of Brunei since July 1947. Educated in Malay College, he brought modern, enlightened ideas back to his country. When Sultan Sir Omar Ali succeeded his older brother in 1950, Brunei's annual revenue was about a million pounds, and the cost of administering the country was about half that amount. About that time a tax on the oil company was introduced which brought a big increase in revenue in addition to increased oil royalties so that by 1953 the revenue had increased more than ten times. The Seria oil field was expanding rapidly, and Brunei could have splashed its money about on rash, new expensive "toys." Instead, the Sultan with the British Resident, Sir Eric Pretty, and their advisers worked out a five-year development plan which served as an orderly blue-print for the future of the state of Brunei.

When I returned in 1956 I discovered that this plan had worked very well. This tiny sultanate had become a model welfare state; the income from oil, rubber, and other large industries goes for the welfare of the people. Oil fields which had been working from 1925 until the war were functioning again, and new rich wells had been dug under the sea. By helicopter I flew out in a gale to see one and landed on a minute, heaving platform. On this tiny man-made "island," the workers were both Mohammedan and non-Moham-medan. Not the least of the problems was that they had to have not only two cooks but also two refrigerators, and two quite dif-ferent menus, all this in the smallest galley I ever saw.

Since my previous visit, the Sultan had announced his desire to give the state its first written constitution and broaden representa-tion of the people on the state council. He with his advisers had provided pensions for all subjects over sixty years, to blind persons, widows and orphans, and to all people who through sickness or deformity were unable to support themselves. He arranged for thousands of families who had been living in Brunei's picturesque but unsanitary Water Village to settle on land. Widespread irri-gation and land reclamation with agricultural research and develop-ment were under way to make Brunei self-supporting in food and other supplies, and to increase rubber and other raw materials for export. The plan included improved port facilities; new air-fields and roads to the hinterland; a radio-telephone system to con-nect the larger towns and villages; piped water supply and elec-tricity for the larger towns; the building of many new schools, teacher training, and overseas scholarships; an education plan that included school meals to be served in all state schools; and a great increase in medical work to include training new staffs, controlling and eradicating diseases like malaria, and providing a large new hospital. Brunei had the will and desire to put this plan through and brought experts from remote countries to help use the wealth to rehabilitate the state.

On my second visit, the town of Brunei was not so picturesque as in former days, but it was a model for the rest of the world, not only as an example of rehabilitation and political peace but in a broader sense. It was heartening to see the tranquillity of people of many racial backgrounds and interests living and working in harmony and mutual toleration although completely surrounded by an uncomfortable circle of unhappy, restless countries, either war-torn or enjoying a very uneasy peace. It is uncertain how long it can escape the discord of the rest of Southeast Asia.

Chapter 20

TO THE FAR EAST

When I left the music faculty of the University of California in 1949 to spend two years pursuing music in the Orient, that flight from San Francisco across the Pacific held great thrills for me. This tight-packed two-year schedule was under the joint sponsorship of the East-West Association (of which Pearl Buck was president) and the American Museum of Natural History, for which I brought back musical instruments and anthropological material.

In the Hawaiian Islands I recorded chants from the only living Hawaiian singer who knew the ancient ritual chants. Our stay at Guam, the southernmost and largest island of the Marianas archipelago, was to have been very brief; however, we were caught by a typhoon and were grounded there. I was delighted. While my fellow passengers in the Pan American Rest House fussed and fumed at the delay, I took my recorder to the native quarters and collected some fascinating material, both instrumental and vocal—recordings which I undoubtedly would never have had otherwise. How many times I have found the reminder that there are no people alive without some kind of music, and whatever happens, shipwreck or any other possible vicissitude, there is always someone who will sing a song for you.

In the Philippines, as well as recording music, I was lecturing at the University in Manila, and as friend and guest of our American ambassador I was given many opportunities to visit remote villages, including a small inland town which boasts the one and only bamboo pipe organ in the world. I was allowed to record and play

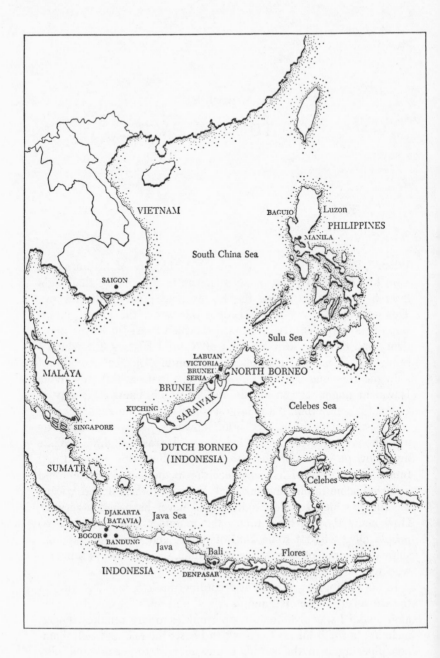

the instrument, a very great thrill to me as an organist. It was built by early Spanish fathers and had been in use ever since. It is a beautiful little instrument with a surprisingly appealing tone. Another unexpected adventure was being taken into the mountains to record the Ifugao tribal songs.

But a shadow fell over this happy period while I was still in the Philippines. Two young American anthropologists whom I knew were killed by the Ifugao tribe in the mountains of Luzon. The primitive does not always understand the way of outsiders; these two young anthropologists went into Ifugao territory wearing sneakers and sweat shirts, taking with them no food, living off the land, and trying to act as if they were natives. They had the mistaken idea that this was the proper way to make friends and influence the locals; it did precisely the opposite. The Ifugao chief was brought to trial for questioning and said simply: "We did not believe them when they said they were proper Americans. They did not live or dress or behave like Americans. We thought they were just bad people come to do us harm." This kind of tragic situation must have arisen many times before through the over-zealousness of the visitor. It is vitally important that anyone going to work with primitive tribes in any part of the world preserve some of the amenities expected of him; certainly he must follow and respect the etiquette of the tribe whose privacy he is invading, but at the same time, preserve the ethics and manners of his own culture.

I left the Philippines with the greatest regret; I had made so many friends among these charming, hospitable people, including many congenial musicians who helped me in collecting very valuable material. I was entertained royally by President Quirino in the palace and in peasant thatch-roofed huts, and every aid was given to make my work easier and more fruitful. When I said farewell to brilliant government functions, delightful embassy parties, and gay village festivals, I took off by plane to Okinawa en route to Hong Kong.

Okinawa to most Americans is a reminder of some of the bloodiest battles of World War II. All of us remember with regret that Ernie Pyle, one of our most loved newspaper correspondents, was killed there. Since August, 1945, the Okinawa prefecture, which includes all the southern Ryukyu Islands, has been placed under U.S. military government. I was in this mountainous island—

the largest of the Ryukyu Islands—only briefly but I had time
to record some lovely songs and to realize my great wish to see
the Teahouse of the August Moon, made famous by the novel
and the play of that name. The flight from there to Hong Kong
was fairly uneventful, but looking down on the unbelievable view
as we approached Hong Kong, I felt as though I were entering
a kind of fairyland.

Probably few people know that the official name of Hong Kong
is Victoria. This British crown colony (391 square miles), which
had a population of nearly two million in 1956, is adjacent to
Kwangtung Province of China and comprises Hong Kong Island
(thirty-two square miles), Kowloon Peninsula (three square miles),
and the New Territories, an adjoining mainland area with an
inlet of the China Sea called Mirs Bay. What is ordinarily meant
by Hong Kong is the bustling city on the northern shore of the
island. The superb natural harbor makes Hong Kong an important
naval base and the principal distribution center for southern China.
Victoria Peak, which rises 1825 feet behind the city, is the highest
point of the granite range which covers much of the island. Large
crops are raised on the mainland, and flourishing industries include
tobacco growing, rope and cement manufacturing, sugar refining,
cotton spinning, and shipbuilding. The colony was surrendered
to the Japanese in December 1941, but since the end of World
War II it has remained under British control in spite of repeated
Chinese demands for its return. Since 1948, refugees from Communist China have swelled the population of the colony to the
bursting point.

The influx of thousands of refugees from Communist China
created terrible problems for the British government of Hong Kong.
There was absolutely no housing for them. The flimsy shacks that
were thrown together on the hillsides could not stand heavy rains
and on occasion were washed down completely. There was no
sanitation and no piped water, and the health problem seemed
insurmountable. There was a great fear of cholera or other epidemics. As fast as possible the government built blocks of housing for
the refugees, but they continued to come in such numbers that
they have never been able to abandon completely the cluttered
shacks on the hillsides. When the Chinese Communists decided
to hold back only the most useful people, they practically pushed

across the border the old, infirm, and unskilled so as to avoid
having to feed more mouths. The problem is still unsolved.

Another difficulty which faced the British was that the "have not"
Chinese began to have pride in their own people, because they
had at last got rid of foreigners in China. They were not Communists but they were agitating for China for the Chinese. But
this was a small group. For most of the Chinese poor, life goes on
and on. Wars and political changes have always been and will
always be. They are born philosophers.

A serious problem for the government came from the fact that
all the night-club dancing girls, gamblers, and unsavory characters
from Shanghai rushed into Hong Kong. At first the government
tried to resist them, but finally decided that rather than allow
them to operate by clandestine methods, they would recognize
them and allow them to function under strict government supervision. So a very exuberant night life sprang up in Hong Kong.

Many of the richest Chinese, when they fled from Communist
China, already had money in Hong Kong banks, and at first they
hoarded it, hoping for the collapse of the Communists. When
this did not happen, and as they were good businessmen who
wanted to make money, they decided to take a chance and invest
heavily in real estate on a basis of four to five years only. They
built hotels and apartment houses on the Peak which looked fine
from the outside but were cheaply built and now are practically
slums. But they got back their capital during this period. When
it appeared that the Communists would not invade as was feared,
but rather wanted to keep Hong Kong as an open door to the
outside world, some of these financiers began to show a limited
confidence.

With the capital from this short investment they reinvested in
longer-range projects, and Hong Kong is now in the midst of a
tremendous boom, with skyscrapers taking over the city and great
new hotels like the Mandarin and the Hilton doing excellent business.

But when I was there first in 1950, no one knew if or when the
Communists might attack. There was an air of excitement that
comes with the threat of physical danger, a subconscious apprehension. Everyone was saying to himself, "I hope this holds until
I get out of here." For the British, many of whom had been born
and brought up there and were too old to go back to England to

start a new life, it was simply a matter of hoping for the best.

In Hong Kong the days were too few and much too short for me. I visited friends on the Peak and marveled at the breathtaking view from its heights. I ate the delicious rare foods of the city's fabulous restaurants. I spoke on the Hong Kong radio and at the University of Hong Kong, a coeducational institution under government control which was opened in 1912 and modeled on British universities. I met with musician friends and recorded both folk and art music. But especially I did what everybody does visiting Hong Kong—I shopped. Many rare and beautiful antiques had come in with the refugees from the mainland since the Communists took over China; I found paintings, carvings, and other art treasures. And I had clothes made. What every traveled woman knows about Hong Kong is that the expert Chinese tailors there, who seem to work around the clock, can copy the latest Dior model or absolutely anything in twenty-four hours. A dress, a suit, and two coats complete with buttons and buttonholes were ready for me in two days.

When I went to Macao in 1950 the short voyage from Hong Kong was much more precarious than today. Chinese bandits had taken to the seas and waylaid small craft that plied the waters along the coast. (It was about this time that two men I knew, one a reporter for the National Broadcasting Company, were seized as they were cruising not far from Hong Kong. They and their yacht completely disappeared. The men were released from China two years later.)

At three in the afternoon I left Hong Kong on an attractive little coastal steamer. I found a spotless if minute cabin for the night's voyage. I was horrified to see as soon as I came on board that the captain on his bridge was enclosed by iron bars; it was as though he were prisoner on his own ship while the passengers were free. Actually it was for his protection and to prevent bandits from taking over the ship, crew, and passengers, not to mention any valuable cargo that might be aboard. When I wanted to interview the captain he got out a huge key, opened up the iron door, and locked it securely behind us. From there we could watch the activities on board and were safe from marauders. They had formerly tried to take over his ship but luckily he had eluded them. The captain told me fantastic tales about pirates. They were so brash that they once stole the undersea cable to Hong Kong and at another time boarded a seaplane that was transporting gold and murdered the crew and twenty-two passengers in flight.

After a beautiful voyage down the coast we approached the port, teeming with everything from a sampan fleet to the most modern small ships. It was exciting to see the rhythmic ballet of fishing nets thrown to the accompaniment of bells from shuttered convents near the sea.

Macao is the oldest colony in the Far East. Settled by the Portuguese, Macao has an area of six square miles, is adjacent to Kwangtung Province of southeastern China on the estuary of the Canton River, and comprises Macao Peninsula and two islands. When I was there, it had a population of about 315,000. The settlement was begun in 1557, and in 1887 a treaty with China confirmed the present holdings. The city of Macao is on Macao Island, and until the rise of Hong Kong in the nineteenth century it was the leading port for foreign trade with China. Today it is the center of fisheries and small industries, but most of the revenue comes from the licensed gambling establishments; in fact, it is often referred to as "the Monte Carlo of Asia."

Very early in its history it became a center of learning, medicine, and Christianity. It has been considered for centuries not only one of the most exotic and intriguing spots in the Orient, but also a refuge for every race and type—persecuted Christians, destitute orphans, lepers, British fleeing the Chinese, Chinese fleeing the Japanese, Nationalists fleeing the Communists.

It used to be called "the City of the Name of God," but it has not always been such a godly city, for the sale of opium was a government monopoly. The Chinese still call it "the Mirror of the Sea." When I was there, there was constant traffic across the border—a sort of "chain-gang" activity, by which the traders in Macao outwitted the original intent of all custom regulations. Their dealings in gold made Macao for a period the world's busiest center for the transfer of that precious metal. From Communist China constant lines of thousands of coolies crossed the invisible border daily into Macao with products for export to the Western world, to be sent out under a Macao label; and returned in the night, each carrying his legal quota of some desperately needed commodity from the West which could not be purchased through direct trade with certain non-Communist countries. The fleet of heavily armed junks taking gold or cigarettes to Hong Kong and the China coast was referred to as "the Golden Chain."

A picture was taken of me standing near the border with the Communist Chinese flag waving behind me. I took great care not to touch the border even with one foot, for I could then have been seized by a Chinese soldier, as happened not infrequently on this dangerous border.

Some shipbuilding still took place in Macao, but it was mainly small industries that kept the natives occupied as makers of matches, fireworks, incense sticks, pottery, and beautifully woven mats. The flute makers had a thriving business, too, but I believe it was the fortunetellers who perhaps had the most successful means of livelihood, for the picturesque marketplace was crowded with all kinds of people wanting to know what fortune held in store.

In Macao the inhabitants varied from delightful aristocratic Portuguese officials, sleek merchants, and cultured monks to international spies, Communists, anti-Communist resistance workers, and pirates. The population lived in everything from modern housing projects for the refugees to the crowded sampan fleet, many of whose population had never set foot ashore. The aristocrats, government officials, and other leaders in the community had beautiful homes, and one could eat in elegant restaurants where girl runners took bets to the gaming rooms as an electric board flashed the winning numbers. Or if you preferred, you could go to dingy spots where panting rickshaw coolies ran between fares to place their bets. In this city of contrasts one could mingle with the native throng in the marketplace or rest in the sanctuary of Buddhist temple gardens whose serenity has remained undisturbed since before the days of Vasco da Gama. As guest of the Governor I met an amazing variety of people. He helped me to locate musicians, and the recordings from Macao are unique.

Macao plays a role in the Orient somewhat analogous to that of Switzerland in Europe; her strictly observed neutrality gained for her the friendship of the Chinese and fairly continuous prosperity until the shadow cast by the United States embargo on Communist products. Macao is considered by some as a symbol of the possibility of understanding and reconciliation between the East and the West.

To the east of Macao lies the island of Taiwan. When the

Portuguese navigators viewed for the first time its green meadows and high mountains, they exclaimed, *"Ilha formosa,"* which means "beautiful island." It is one of the most breathtaking places I have ever seen with its unspoiled natural beauty and its 4000 magnificent Buddhist and Taoist temples. Now it is prosperous, stable, free, and booming in industry, thanks to foreign investments, with modern-minded leaders and a streamlined fighting force of 1,200,000 (army, navy, and air force) with probably the best morale, equipment, and training in Asia. With American help, technical training is being given to young people from many countries, including Southeast Asia and more than twenty countries of Africa. Formosa's forty-one universities and colleges turn out about 17,000 graduates annually, and free compulsory education from the age of six is providing a very literate society. Cultural life is dynamic, with the finest Chinese opera—a mixture of acrobatics, drama, and singing—that can be seen anywhere. Their cuisine is superb; the Chinese love to eat, and Taiwan is the world capital for Chinese food. It was here that I learned one of the secrets of Chinese living: Something is always left for those in the kitchen. It is a commandment of Chinese eating and their way of life not to be greedy.

When I first went to Taipei in 1950, it was shortly after the Communists had taken over the China mainland. It was not then the bustling city that it is today with modern hotels and every facility. Even with the difficult problems facing Nationalist China, the proverbial Chinese hospitality was the warmest imaginable. There were no visitors on the island except those who were present for military, technical, or diplomatic reasons or with the press, of which I was a member representing the National Broadcasting Company. The only comfortable place for me to stay was the Press Club. Even it could not be called luxurious, but it was in the center of all activities.

For a time in Taiwan I was the guest of the Generalissimo and Madame Chiang Kai-shek. Everyone was working desperately, as they anticipated direct conflict with Communist China in the very near future. All the men who could possibly be considered of military age were training in camps; even the small boys were in camps being taught by the soldiers and officers, both school subjects and simple military exercises. The women were doing magnificent work seven days a week, around the clock, making all the uniforms, including caps, pack bags, even shoes, for both the young and adult armies.

Madame Chiang Kai-shek directed the women's work and she herself was indefatigable in her labors. Very few people had time to record music for me in those days, but as I was representing NBC, I met and recorded interviews with citizens and military officials, and while visiting training camps I was also able to record soldiers' and children's songs.

However, I still had uppermost in my mind the work which I wanted to do with world religions and their leaders. With this in mind, I made arrangements to meet with "the Living Buddha" who had escaped from Mongolia when the Communists took it over. He lived as an exile in Taipei until his death a few years ago. He received me cordially and through an interpreter discussed Buddhism and recorded a wise and extremely thoughtful message for the world.

I was also eager to reach the man who was the head of the Confucian religion, Dr. Kung Teh-cheng. To meet him, I had to proceed to Taichung in central Formosa, where I was invited as the guest of the director of the State Department Chinese Language School. The only way to get there was by train, and as all express trains had been fully booked for ages, I had the questionable pleasure of going on the local farmers' train. Old and young men and women in many kinds of garb with howling babies carried rice and all manner of foodstuffs, even squawking chickens and grunting pigs. We stopped at every watering trough while everyone got out and drank tea.

It was nearly midnight when I finally arrived at my destination. My host, who was giving a big dinner in my honor and could not leave his guests to wait for this much-delayed train, sent a local messenger who had considerable difficulty finding me in the mass of humanity that poured out into the station. When at long last I arrived the guests were enjoying the final course, so I had a good deal of eating and drinking to catch up with.

The object of this arduous journey was at the dinner party in person, Dr. Kung, seventy-seventh lineal descendant of Confucius. The name Teh-cheng, which means "Virtuous Completion," is derived from his illustrious ancestor. Confucius himself, born in 551 B.C., was a descendant of Emperor Tang who founded the Shang Dynasty almost four thousand years ago. Dr. Kung has the longest genealogical tree on record, more than four times longer than that of Queen Elizabeth II, who traces her descent from Alfred the Great (A.D. 871).

Dr. Kung, born a duke, gave up the dukedom which was conferred on his family by Emperor Hsuan Tsung in A.D. 717, 154 years before Alfred the Great was born. But even in 1912, when the revolution overthrew 4609 years of monarchy in China, the new republican government made a sole exception of Dr. Kung when abolishing all titles of nobility. However, in 1925, when Dr. Kung was eighteen, the Nationalist government dispensed with this last title and appointed him "Hereditary Keeper of the Confucian Shrines," a duty that will remain forever in his family. Chüfou, where he was born, is the birthplace and burial place of Confucius and was, before the Communists overran the country, a mecca for the Chinese people. Confucianism is an ethical system with a mixture of ancestor and nature worship, and the Chinese of all religions, including Christian and Moslem, find nothing strange in paying homage to the great sage. In 1934 the Nationalist government by decree made the anniversary of the birth of Confucius a national holiday called Teachers' Day.

In 1948 Dr. Kung gave China his estates in Shantung (1,560,000 acres) to be distributed to the populace, especially to those who till the land. In gratitude for this property, which had come into his family through grants from various emperors, the Nationalist government gratefully provided $250 a month for the upkeep of Dr. Kung as Hereditary Keeper of the Confucian Shrines and his staff of thirteen people.

Dr. Kung was a moon-faced man with a quick smile and a very jovial laugh. Our first meeting at the dinner party was rather hilarious, since everyone had drunk a good deal of beer—including Dr. Kung, as this was his favorite drink. He was five feet eleven inches tall, weighed 175 pounds, and smoked a pipe or cigarettes almost constantly.

In 1948 he had spent a year at Yale University doing special research in Chinese history and literature. Since the documents he studied were in Chinese, he got only a scant knowledge of English, but he developed a taste for hamburgers, hot dogs, and ice cream. Although he did not remember enough English to carry on a conversation, he used the words he did know very amusingly and laughed loudly at his own jokes. As everyone else at the party spoke

Chinese, they translated for me, and I, too, found his sense of humor delightful. During the next two or three days I saw a good deal of this young man (he was then thirty-six), and I was much impressed by his knowledge and philosophy. He was a national assemblyman and one of President Chiang Kai-shek's twenty-four senior advisers—for which he received twenty dollars a month.

Dr. Kung lived with his family, his wife, and four children attending school in Taichung, a bustling railway town on the west coast of central Formosa. The heir to his title, Kung Yi, who was sixteen when I was there, will be the seventy-eighth in the unbroken lineal descent. He wanted to be a pilot but his destiny offered him little chance of fulfilling that youthful ambition.

Although Dr. Kung had grown up in a ducal palace and been educated by private tutors, renowned scholars, in Formosa the family received no special favors and lived like any other average middle-class family. Dr. Kung was preserving in Formosa the Confucian teachings which are abominated by the Chinese Communists (all works relating to Confucius have been banned), who regarded him as a feudalistic reactionary. Confucius was an ardent advocate of the family system and considered filial piety one of the most important human virtues. As the Reds wanted to eradicate the family system, they wiped out all vestige of filial piety. (How could a son practicing filial piety betray his parents for the capital offense of listening to the Voice of America?)

In Chinese society Confucianism set the social pattern, the conventions, the system of laws, the ethnic and social principles by which men live together. The Confucian way formed the unquestioned mores of the people of continental eastern Asia. Man lives in the world where a rational social order based on ethical concepts means that the individual, the family, the state, and the world are ordered in a harmony of good manners and propriety. The world is a unit in which these relationships should be adjusted with regard to moral obligations. Man must order himself. When the members of a family are orderly, the family is harmonious. When the families are orderly, the states are at peace. When the states are in proper relationship, then the nations and all of nature are in harmony. In Confucian literature the rules of *li* are like the tablets of Moses, not man-made but discovered by the wisdom of man. Those who follow *li* shall be preserved; those who violate *li* shall be destroyed. An endless ladder extends from the lowest to the highest with a place for everyone, and everyone must find and acknowledge his place and responsibility.

Dr. Kung was also a recognized expert on ancient bronzes, earthenware, ancient calligraphy, and musical instruments, and was attached to the Committee for the Joint Administration of Museums and Libraries. He took me to the underground vaults in a rural hideaway in the foothills of central Formosa where I saw the hidden art treasures that had been brought out of China when the Communists took the country. This great collection of Chinese art treasures had been assembled over the centuries and had been housed in the Peking Palace Museum and Nanking's Central Museum. Four hundred thousand invaluable works of art—many of them still in packing cases—were stacked in three concrete warehouses and in a large tunnel. Most of them had never been outside of China before. I was especially interested in the exquisite paintings, many of which showed musical instruments being played.

By 1957 with the opening of a small museum in Peichou a few of the treasures were chosen and put on display for the first time in a generation. The rest remained locked away, the unseen legacy of a very rich culture, until 1957, when the Metropolitan Museum in New York held a splendid exhibition which included some of the most outstanding examples. I was very happy to see them again, especially when displayed in my country.

Now there is a new museum on Formosa, opened in November, 1965. Here some 300,000 of China's most priceless art treasures have become accessible to the general public—admission twelve and one half cents—in the Sun Yat-sen Museum in suburban Taipei, at the foot of the forest-covered Grass Mountain. This $1,500,000 four-story structure follows the traditional palace style in architectural details and interior decoration. The Chinese-style roof is covered with glazed tile which fits beautifully into its scenic location. The U.S. paid half the cost of the museum, which took three years to build. A thousand treasures at a time are displayed in constantly changing exhibits. The paintings, jades, bronzes, tapestries, calligraphs, lacquerware, enamelware, embroidery, sculpture, and carvings make up the world's greatest collection of Chinese art and cover a span of 6000 years. There are great paintings from the T'ang, Sung, Yüan, and Ming Dynasties, covering the first 600 years of the Christian era, and stone rubbings of the work of Wang Hsi-chih, described as "flying as a dragon and dancing as a phoenix."

One of the most frequent sights as I moved through Formosa was the huge flocks of geese piloted by young boys who kept them in line by the skillful use of a long pole like a fishing rod, with numerous little streamers. One of the characters I shall never forget was Foo-li. His family had been able to escape from mainland China, torn by civil war, in one of the last ships for Formosa. All of Foo-li's young friends had gone to army camps to train in military exercises as soldiers in a junior army. When I visited the army camp I was much impressed by these boys and by their disciplined performance of duties. I recorded their spirited songs, sung with true patriotic fervor, as well as many songs of freedom which the grown-up soldiers were singing.

But Foo-li was needed at home since all of his brothers as well as his father were with Chiang Kai-shek's army. However, he was proudly doing his duty for family and country and was thrilled with the sense of power and importance that went with his work. Although he was only eight years old, he was general of an army which numbered several thousands, and the responsibility that had been thrust on him weighed him down. Although his army consisted mainly of ducklings, he was well aware of the fact that their welfare was completely in his hands. He supervised their comings and goings to and from the mudbanks where they cleared everything that was edible and a great many things that were not. He disciplined their parades and their feeding like a tough little sergeant. This tiny boy seemed the very embodiment of the firm will and determined efforts of the Chinese people deprived of their homeland.

I was in Formosa when the Korean war broke out, and since I was traveling with four tape recorders, I was asked by NBC to send back recorded assignments from Korea and Formosa. It was arranged that I should fly across to Korea from Japan in a United Nations plane. At this time our soldiers had been pushed almost into the sea; all we had left was the Pusan beachhead. All European women and children had been flown home, and the only place for me to be housed was with eighteen refugees from the capital, Seoul. These included the Mayor of Seoul, his wife and two children, the head of the Ewah University for Women, the Minister of Education, and the Prime Minister, who was also Minister of Defense, whenever he came from the front.

As is usual in a crisis, everybody cooperated; under the calm direction of Dr. Hwal Lan Kim, our hostess, a tiny Korean woman who was head of the girls' university in Seoul, the jam-packed little establishment ran as smoothly as possible under the strain of overcrowding, acute shortage of food, and all the tensions of desperate warfare. It was, in fact, a fascinating household. Everything happened from there; when the delegation for the United Nations left for New York, the farewell dinner and briefing were held in our house; when bombing planes flew overhead, as still happened occasionally, everyone, including the Prime Minister, emerged in various (and sometimes most bizarre) night attire and huddled together against the one dependable wall of that frail house in an entirely illusory bid for protection. Had there been so much as a near hit, that little dwelling of sliding doors and rice-paper windows would have crumbled like a matchbox about our ears. I always felt that what we were doing, in fact, was propping *it* up against possible bomb blast.

When I think of this little house, I remember first the *otami*, (mats of woven grass) which were treated with something akin to reverence. There was always a row of silk slippers ready at the entrance for use by anyone coming inside. When the army cameraman assigned to work with me came barging into the house in his heavy army boots, I remember with what firmness and authority Kim dispatched him and ordered him to remove them. No blustering army colonel could have withered him so completely as did this tiny woman with a few quiet, well-chosen words. Cheerfully he set about unfastening the boots' long laces; and since none of the little Korean embroidered slippers would fit his enormous feet, he clumped about the house in stockingfeet.

When the advancing American army under General Walker, who was later killed, moved from Pusan to Taegu, the correspondents also moved, and there we lived in an empty schoolhouse. On free evenings we gathered around the piano in a missionary's comfortable house, then occupied by the UN contingent, and sang old songs from home and new Korean songs we had just learned. "Home" meant Australia, Canada, El Salvador, and other remote lands, and from what I observed these particular military representatives appeared to be doing very little work. Although none of them was American they had only the very best rations—big steaks, fresh lettuce and tomatoes—all the comforts of home provided from the U. S. Officers' Mess and PX. As one of them said to me: "You don't think we're going to be in a hurry to leave. We know when our bread is well buttered!"

At this time Seoul was in the hands of the Communists, and as there was no direct cable or telephone communication for the correspondents, it was necessary for us to fly across to Japan with our material and air-mail or cable it from Tokyo or one of the seaports nearby.

I have had many memorable flights, some of them hair-raising. For example, when the antenna of the plane in which I was traveling from New York to the Bahamas was struck by lightning and a ball of fire ran along the side of the plane, I thought I had seen everything. But this Korean assignment provided some unforgettable flying experiences. The cargo planes were the only route open for us at this time, and one day when several newspaper correspondents took off into the sunshine from Japan the plane nosed over and plunged into the sea. The verdict was that it had been too heavily loaded. The next day four of us, three men and I, were lined up to fly back into Seoul and we were, quite naturally, on edge from the previous day's tragedy.

When we went on board we found that our load included a complete Bailey Bridge—an invention of an Englishman during the war which could be shipped in sections and quickly set up where needed. The parts were so long they had to lie diagonally across the plane from corner to corner. In addition there was a complete post office with thousands of dollars' worth of stamps and other essentials all ready to start working the moment it was lifted out at the Seoul airport. My colleagues looked over the load and walked out of the plane. I said to the pilot: "The others aren't sure this plane is safely loaded. . . ."

He shrugged. "We think it's all right, and we value our lives, too."

So I stayed on board. Instead of the customary bucket seat I would have had in this C-57, I was given a stool up in the cockpit with the pilots.

No words could adequately describe that flight as we took off and flew right into a blazing sunset. Clouds of crimson and gold enfolded us so that we seemed to be floating on a flood of celestial light. And then, as we approached the airport, there below us lay Seoul, on fire. Great bursts of red and orange flame spurted skyward, pillars of black smoke spiraled and curled, and as we flew in lower we could see the flashes of gunfire pinpointing the fighting that was still raging.

Our army had taken the airport but the city was not yet in our hands. Nothing remained of the airport but the bombed-out concrete shell of what had been the main building. Here I spent a very cold night with a wonderful Scandinavian couple—both husband and wife were correspondents—who had flown in from the south; my equipment was one army blanket and a small navy raft blown up, for which I was deeply grateful since it served as shield between me and the icy concrete floor.

Another night I flew into Tokyo in a hospital plane; nurses were so few and hard-pressed that any two hands were useful; although I had no training I was able to help with oxygen masks and other routine things. It was one of the hardest ordeals of my life to see those wonderful young American boys, some of them basket cases, so stoically accepting the fate that had uprooted them from their homes and pushed them into this political maelstrom.

Another assignment had to do with the rescue and care of wounded soldiers. In connection with these reports, I flew with the team in a helicopter into no man's land to rescue the wounded, return with them to first-aid posts, on to a hospital plane or hospital ship, and eventually to the base hospitals in Japan; then eventually I visited them in hospitals in America.

An assignment much closer to the work I had originally come to do in the Far East before the Korean war broke out was to record the songs the Korean soldiers were singing and the songs of the Chinese troops who had just escaped from the mainland and were training in large camps in various parts of Formosa. Everywhere they sang of freedom.

The Koreans organized a kind of USO to entertain the troops. I attended one of their performances for the servicemen. The little Korean girls were lovely to look at, the boys were sprightly, the singing and dancing were excellent; but in the whole evening's performance there were only three true Korean songs; the others were all mediocre performances of popular American songs. On another occasion I went to the performance given for American soldiers by Al Jolson. He was so great in his relationship with the boys: cheerful, warm, quietly sympathetic but not over-sentimental, pouring out in his inimitable way "Mammy," "Sonny Boy," and other much-loved songs that had come to be his personal trademark. He was tireless in his efforts for the troops and in his heartwarming conversations with all of us. He poured out a glow of friendliness and warmth although he was already struggling under the fatal illness which began as a severe cold picked up on this trip during these arduous labors of love. The whole Western world mourned his death.

There are no words strong enough in my vocabulary to describe the horrors of war. Yet I was amazed to find a brotherliness, a comradeship, a great kindness and thoughtfulness that seemed to exceed anything I had seen in times of peace. I have often wondered why it required a war to bring out the best in people.

Chapter 21

JAPANESE SOJOURN

Life began at five A.M. in my Buddhist temple. It is strange how quickly I came to regard the Shokokuji Temple in Kyoto as my own. My visit there had been made possible by the extremely intelligent and understanding cultural attaché at the American Embassy in Tokyo while General Douglas MacArthur was military governor of Japan following World War II. I had also been privileged to know the General and his lovely wife. I first met them during a difficult period in their life, in the years of the political tug of war between MacArthur and President Truman. I was at a loss to understand, as certainly the Japanese were who worshiped MacArthur almost as a deity, why Washington felt that it was better equipped to deal with oriental problems than this great man who had spent most of his life in the East and understood it and its ways as few Americans have.

Through the cultural attaché, who spoke Japanese perfectly and knew everyone from royalty to the man on the street, it was arranged for me to meet with Japan's leading religious and musical leaders. When I suggested to him the idea of an extended stay in a Zen temple in connection with my work on music in worship in the religions of the East, he readily agreed to help me, for he was anxious to demonstrate to the Japanese that America had a genuine interest in their cultural heritage.

In my temple I discovered a serenity and peace not easily found in the Western world.

Shokokuji Temple is really a group of twelve temples—one

large main temple and eleven smaller ones. Each temple has a priest, and each priest has his own congregation of certain families who look to him for spiritual help. He conducts his own temple ceremonies and assists at all services of the large chief temple.

Sohaku Ogata, the priest of my small temple, was genial and friendly; when he laughed, which was often, his eyes would disappear into cheerful little slits. He had a beautiful wife, petite, smiling, extremely hospitable, and three charming children, two bright young lads and an enchanting daughter. I do not remember in all my travels ever knowing such well-behaved children. They were so quiet that I was there for days before I realized there were any children in the family.

As a boy, Ogata had come from a village on a smaller island of Japan to study at this temple, and when his studies were completed, he was honored by being invited to remain as one of the permanent priests. Since the Zen sect permits marriage, Ogata sent word to his family to choose a bride for him and make the necessary wedding arrangements. According to the old Japanese custom, a bride was found with suitable qualifications. She was the lovely daughter of the local doctor. The young priest returned to his home village for the wedding, brought his bride back to his temple, and a happier pair would be hard to find. No wonder that they disapprove of the modern trend in Japan toward what they call "free marriage" in which young people consider themselves wise enough to choose their own mates and all too often end in divorce.

In Japan everyone is industrious. Wherever you go, you see people walking rapidly to their jobs or working seriously. I do not recall seeing idle people. In America we work at a terrific pace, but I have never lived anywhere before with people who are so consistently busy. In my temple I was often up and on my way to a ceremony by five in the morning, but I was never the first astir in the household. Until far into the night my temple family was occupied with some useful activity. This in itself probably contributed much to their happy frame of mind.

Reverend Ogata, who was also a professor at a nearby university, was always either at his desk, preparing for a ceremony, translating for a temple guest, or helping with some household arrangements. His wife seemed never to sleep; the first to rise and the last to retire, she was always concerned with her domestic duties. When I saw the children's rooms, where they spent their days and nights, I found them, too, always quietly busy—with schoolwork, with art work of some kind, or with household tasks.

Professor Ogata had spent considerable time in America and Europe; he spoke excellent English, and was eager to do all he could to bring the East and West together in deeper understanding. He liked to invite occasional guests to stay at the temple, but only those who for some good reason wanted to learn more about Buddhism. During my visit there were four guests: a brilliant Englishman from Oxford University who was studying Buddhism, a Fulbright professor of art from an American university, and another professor who approached the study of Buddhism through poetry. My own purpose in being there was to learn all I could about music in Japanese Buddhism.

Our temple was built very much like a Japanese house around a small garden, compact and typical, and completely surrounded by venerable pine trees, many flowers, and a great variety of shrubbery with exotic foliage. It was a landscape in miniature, dotted here and there with traditional stone lanterns; viewed from my veranda in moonlight, it was silvery and unreal. My quarters were on the sanctuary side of the temple, the family quarters were on the other side of the small garden. As in all Japanese houses, space was not fixed and finite; paper walls moved at the touch of a finger, and this was what happened in my quarters whenever there was a ceremony in the temple. The sliding screens were set for a small space around the altar on ordinary occasions, but for a special ceremony they were slipped back to provide a larger area and seemed to vanish as if by magic.

For example, there was the day when the Onichi family came to honor their father, who had died seven years earlier. Small ceremonies such as these are performed in the temple at the time of death, and also one year, three years, five years, and seven years afterward. The more impressive rituals are those performed on the twenty-fifth and particularly on the fiftieth anniversaries of the death.

On this particular morning my soft bedding had been rolled up and put away as usual, to leave the floor space clear; my walls disappeared to enlarge the temple space, and the priest prepared the altar, which had its own alcove. I had permission to record this simple ceremony commemorating the seventh anniversary of the death of the head of the Onichi family. Only close relatives participated; in this case it was the eldest son, his elder sister, his wife, and their small son and daughter.

The family, having requested the ceremony, arrived. According to custom, all removed their shoes on entering the temple, lined them up in a row, and stepped up on the otami-covered floor, where they put on soft slippers, proceeded into the sanctuary, and took their places on the floor near the altar.

Reverend Ogata appeared on the veranda in his priestly robes and struck a big bronze bell of great antiquity. Every day while going to and from my quarters I had admired its beautiful design and lovely tone, and whenever I passed I had gently tapped it and been thrilled by its muted voice. But this was the first time I had heard its full, resonant peal.

The ceremony began when Reverend Ogata seated himself before the altar, where he had earlier placed offerings of fruit and other foods in finely carved bowls. The fragrance of the burning incense drifted over us, creating an aura of intimate worship, as we sat Budda-fashion on the soft grass mats that carpet every Japanese house.

The priest chanted in a deep voice the prayers and sutras required by the occasion, and accompanied his chanting by ringing small temple bells and beating a little sacred drum. From time to time he tapped the carved dragon drum, and at the end of the chanting the members of the family went, one by one, and stood before the altar, each dropping three times a pinch of incense into the burning bowl. Even the small children performed this act of veneration, the little son with his father and the little daughter with her mother, both looking proud and pleased to be participating in this ritual. We then proceeded to the ancient graveyard in the garden nearby, where the priest chanted and the family again offered food and drink to the spirit of the departed. After this we all returned to the same temple area and had tea and delicious cakes served by the priest's wife. While the grownups chatted over their teacups, the little children scampered about, and they were all intensely interested in hearing my recording of the service.

I remember thinking that this was the way a temple should be used: loved, lived in, enjoyed, and, at the same time, deeply revered.

One of the many privileges of living at the temple was that Reverend Ogata made himself available at any time of the day or night to discuss Buddhism in its many aspects. He had dedicated himself to becoming a bridge between East and West, and spared no effort in trying to explain Eastern philosophy to the Western world. I recorded many of our conversations about Buddhism. In discussing the history and meaning of Buddhism, Ogata spoke of the two forms, northern and southern divisions: Hinayana, which is practiced in Southeast Asia, Ceylon, Burma, Thailand, Cambodia, and Vietnam; and the northern branch, Mahayana, which is preserved in Tibet, China, Korea, and Japan.

Buddhism was introduced into the Japanese court in Nara by a Korean king, about A.D. 552. A little later, around the end of that century, Prince Shotoku became a devout scholar, and while acting as regent to Empress Suiko, his aunt, he made Buddhism the religion of Japan. In his celebrated edict of the year A.D. 604 he said: "Sincerely reverence the Three Treasures: the Buddha, the Law, and the Order." He built many Buddhist temples in Nara and its vicinity, including Horyuji, which I later visited with great interest. It is the oldest wooden building in the world, more than 1400 years old. Prince Shotoku is regarded as the father of Japanese Buddhism and of the culture and art techniques which were brought with Buddhism from China to Japan.

Asked about education in those early days, Ogata explained that by royal edict temples and nunneries were built in every state and that the temples were not merely places for worship; they were schools, hospitals, orphanages, refuges for the aged. The monks were schoolteachers, doctors, nurses, and engineers as well as spiritual mentors.

It seemed to me that Buddhism with its many divisions (Mahayana Buddhism has many sects and subsects) was even more complicated than Christianity. Ogata told me there were in Japan about seventy thousand temples, a hundred thousand priests, and fifty million adherents belonging to a wide variety of sects. I told him that in America many people were particularly interested in Zen, and for the first time I heard this sect clearly explained.

"Zen is a Japanese word. It has come from *Ch'an-na*, which is a Chinese translation of the Sanskrit *dhyana*. Dhyana means meditation, contemplation, or concentration of mind. It is the common factor in all Indian thought. Bodhidharma, who came from China by sea from India in about A.D. 520, is regarded as the founder of Zen, which is differentiated from dhyana by being called Patriarchal Zen. In Buddhism, dhyana is regarded as one of the three vehicles of learning the teachings, the other two being *sila* and *prjna*. But Zen has quite a different meaning from the Sanskrit dhyana.

"The spirit of Zen is generally expressed by the term *mu*, which literally means 'nothing.' It is in a way identical to *wabi*, or *sabi*, which constitutes the Far Eastern mind. It is affirmation after negation. It is the new way of looking at things after experiencing the oneness of individuality and universality, or the identity of subjectivity and objectivity. Here life and religion are one . . . we can practice the religion of no God."

To me, this implied that Zen is a form of atheism, and with this Ogata agreed but he qualified his agreement with:

"But it should be differentiated from the material atheism. Zen is a sword for killing man and at the same time a sword for giving new life to man. Zen would prefer to define religion as follows: 'A religion is life, and the religious life is to live in transcending oneself.' Self-transcendence is not a mere idea, but an experience, and the experience of self-transcendence is the destination of religious journeys. There is nothing to worship, nothing to be worshiped at the self-transcendence or the last station of spiritual pilgrimage. Thus, it may be reasonable to say that a religion without God is possible and that a religion is life."

I was sorry to disagree with my friend, for I do agree with the abbot of the great Nishi Hongonji Temple, who said to me: "Some say that Buddhism is a 'way of life,' but I feel that Buddhism is the way to attain our highest ideal, and the highest ideal of all mankind. There is no religion without a God or gods, or supernatural beings. Some Buddhists revere their many Buddhas as gods and pray to them for spiritual attainment and thank them for earthly blessings."

Reverend Ogata was very generous in arranging for me to record the music of other religions, and it was a testimony not only to his liberalism but to his lovable quality as a human being that he was more than welcome everywhere, even among groups where one might have expected jealousy or antagonism of some kind.

One morning very early we drove about five miles across the city in the dawn light to the Nichiren temple where we were guided through the private quarters of the monks, winding our way into the inner sanctuary. Here temple attendants helped me to install the recording machine beside the altar, so that I was in the midst of chanting priests, bells, drums, clappers, and gongs. This was a very large temple of a sect which was rather new but was growing rapidly. No doubt, it caught on quickly primarily because of its emotional and demonstrative form of worship.

I was absolutely amazed to find at this early hour—actually the "crack of dawn"—men, women, little children, nursing mothers, old and infirm, all ages and types, some in kimonos, some in Western dress, seated on the floor of this large hall, each one rattling his wooden clapper and chanting with the priests, shaking and swaying to the rhythm of the chanting, and all apparently in a state of ecstasy.

The effect was completely overpowering. The vibrant intoning of the chants, accompanied by the clappers, played as one instrument, from time to time was suddenly stilled while the head priest chanted solo from his high place at the altar, punctuating his chant occasionally with small temple bells, drum, and clapper. At other moments every priest, about twenty of them in all, participated in the chanting. Then, without any signal visible to me, the entire congregation would break out in a flood of sound. For me not only was it a tremendous emotional experience to witness all this, but it also posed a problem in engineering while working with my highly sensitive tape recorder. I had no warning at all as to when these blasts of concerted sound would send the meter needle soaring beyond the red danger area which would produce only distortion. Here again I was more than grateful for my splendid equipment, which made possible the difficult recording of this fantastic ceremony which had never been recorded before. I thought on that particular morning that there must have been unusual fervor. But I was told that with the noisy Nichiren sect exactly the same thing occurs every day at dawn.

I marveled at the stamina of these people who could start every day with a dawn ceremony so emotionally overwhelming, so physically taxing, and yet have enough energy to carry on their arduous tasks in the long hours ahead. Surely they must have some driving force not evident in other sects? Such a noisy demonstration came as a surprise because I had always thought of Buddhism as essentially serene. Here was but another aspect of the myriad forms of worship which link men to their universe.

It was from the Patriarch, Kosho Ohtani, head priest of the Shin sect temple of Honpa Hongwanji, one of the largest and most influential in all Japan, that I was given a complete and fascinating introduction to *gagaku* music which I recorded there as well as in the Imperial Palace in Tokyo, one of the first Westerners ever to be invited to record the court musicians. For my special audience with this revered man, I was formally received at the Great Gate by two associate priests, one of whom spoke English and served as our interpreter during the interview. Without guidance one would have been completely lost in the maze of small temples, living quarters, lesser shrines, and gardens. I was escorted with ceremony past the main temple with its many incense altars and priceless art treasures, through gardens of exquisite beauty, to the Patriarch's abode. This was set in its own glorious garden with a lily pond flanked by irises of many colors, miniature pines, and a great variety of shrubs. The house was a typical oriental building. After removing our shoes we were ushered into a spacious audience room, furnished with Western as well as oriental furniture, where we were seated on chairs rather than on the floor.

The Patriarch entered. He was an impressive figure, of middle age, tall for a Japanese, and his gracious manner immediately put me at ease. He was wearing a priest's plain black robe reserved for informal occasions, and his highly intelligent face expressed complete serenity. His domed forehead and close-cropped hair added to his priestly appearance, and the rimless glasses he wore seemed to accentuate his innate scholarly dignity. When he smiled, his eyes crinkled with kindness. Through the interpreter he stressed how happy he was that I should be in his country making this special study of music in worship, and I quote here his eloquent summary of the basic relationship between the two:

"When a mind overflows with spiritual emotions, it seeks an outlet in the stream of rhythm and melody of music; then we have sacred music. The sacred music in turn, being played, stirs up the sense of truth, beauty, and holiness dormant in human nature. Interacting in harmony, both religion and music take fundamental roles in building up and formulating the spiritual culture of humanity."

He spoke at great length of music in early Buddhism, of the *gatha*, or hymns, dedicated to the praise of Buddha's virtues, that were being brought into ritual first as chants in a simple musical scale, later accompanied by musical instruments. Out of the musical legacy inherited from Chinese Buddhism, Japan produced two kinds of sacred music: *sho-myo*, a kind of hymn, and gagaku, an ancient form of instrumental music. The sho-myo has been refined and polished throughout the ages by many sacred musicians, and has exerted a great influence over the musical realm of Buddhism, even extending into secular life. If a tourist is lucky enough to be invited into a laborer's home, for example, he would hear the sho-myo that the countryfolk perform in a small chorus composed of the members of a family in a morning service, or at vespers, before their household altar.

Gagaku is said to have been introduced from China into Japan in the eighth century. It was played first in the imperial court by the court musicians at ceremonies and festivals. Then the world of Buddhism adopted it for its services and ceremonies, because, the Patriarch told us, "the tone colors of the gagaku instruments produced exotic and mysterious sounds which incited a sense of sublime beauty from the depths of the heart. . . ." It is no wonder that Buddhists occupied themselves with tuning the gagaku to the feelings of Japanese Buddhism.

When I told the Patriarch I was very interested in the modern music being composed for Buddhist services, he assured me that Buddhist Japan was eagerly searching for new creations in the field of music. Since the restoration of the Meiji era, Western culture and science reached Japanese shores and in their wake came their music. This produced such a new musical climate that the archaic music, sacred and secular, could hardly live in it, "except in a windless corner of conservatism."

"By the painstaking efforts of progressive Buddhists," he said, "a new sacred music is being created. It should not be a mere adaptation or graft of the form, tone color, and melody of Western music to the time-honored one of theirs. Nor is it to be a synthetic conglomeration of Western music and its Eastern counterpart. It must be a new creation out of those parental strains; herein lies the pain of birth of a new Buddhist music."

When I told him I had recently heard some such selections in one or two concerts in Japan, he said he eagerly looked forward to the day when the whole world would listen to the truly new creation of sacred music produced by the progressive and devout Buddhists of Japan. This encouraged me to inquire whether it would be possible for me to come with my equipment and record his temple musicians. To my great joy he arranged for me to return at ten o'clock on the following morning.

The temple grounds were enclosed by a high wall with numerous gates which greatly confused my driver. After taking me to a gateway blocks from the temple where we were to make the recordings, we had to return, in despair, to the Patriarch for directions. He came with us to the very gate and personally advised the driver where to go, even sending an emissary with us to ensure our safe arrival.

After arrival at the temple itself we still had to go through a labyrinth of halls and corridors, up long flights of stairs, and through more halls and corridors which led us eventually into a small upper temple of exquisite beauty. Here a special ceremony had been arranged for me, with twenty-two monks, some of the finest musicians in Japan. We lost no time in setting up the equipment; and then the Patriarch, who had arrived by some private labyrinth, came to welcome me formally and to introduce me to the musicians. There were to be some chanted sutras, but the ceremony was to comprise mostly gagaku music. After turning me over to the director of the temple music, with a smile that was a benediction, the Patriarch departed and the director then took me about and introduced me to the musicians in his orchestra, speaking about each instrument in turn.

"As you see, the *sho* is a gourd with its top cut off and a flat cover cemented on it. There are twenty-one bamboo pipes inserted around the cover, but four do not sound, and are only for convenience in holding the instrument. The seventeen that sound are provided with small brass reeds. The varying lengths of the pipes are purely for appearance. The actual lengths required are established by slotlike cuttings in the pipes, not seen in front. Seventeen pipes are played, but there are only fifteen notes, as some of the pipes are mute, and they are played in chords."

I was surprised to learn that the sho is played by breathing in, instead of blowing out, in this respect following the principle of the organ. The sho might be considered the original pipe organ.

We then moved on to another musician.

"This is the *biwa*," he said. "You see it is a lutelike instrument in the shape of a divided pear, which becomes narrower toward the neck. The body is about thirty-four inches long, and seven and a half inches of that constitute the fingerboard. There are four frets on the fingerboard; it has four strings and is played with a six-and-a-half-inch-long *bache*, or plectrum, made of horn, wood, tortoise shell, or ivory."

The next was the *hichiriki*.

"This is a kind of primitive oboe. It is a conical pipe with a double reed inserted in the larger end. Because of this, the instrument sounds an octave lower than a pipe that is cylindrical. The hichiriki is made of bamboo, and the interior is heavily covered with red lacquer. It has seven finger holes and two thumb holes at the back."

I inquired about its scale.

"The scale is diatonic with the occasional insertion of a sharp fourth. This interval is frequently heard in Chinese music when there are ascending seven-note scales. The disc which is suspended at the top of the pipe is adjusted when the hichiriki is played in order to protect the player's lips. This precaution is necessary because of the shortness of the metal reed."

Holding up the *samisen*, the director said: "The Peking musicians used to call this *sen-tze*. It has no frets, no definite pitch, nor are its strings always tuned in the same manner. The drumlike body is covered on the upper part with snakeskin; the underside is left open as in a tambourine. The strings are plucked by two plectra extended like artificial nails, beyond the ends of the fingers. The scale is pentatonic.

"But it differs from the Chinese pentatonic scale and from the tonic or five-note one used in Java called *salendro*. In length the samisen is about thirty-seven inches. It has a resonant membrane of parchment stretched over a nearly square wooden body, seven and a half inches high, six and a half inches wide, and three inches deep. There is a knob on the underside to hold the strings, and the upper side and underside of it are covered with a special part of a cat's skin. The value of the instrument is set by the little black spots on this skin. Four give the highest value, two mark ordinary instruments, and those without any spots are very cheap. The size of the samisen is determined by the size of the singer's voice. A good singer requires a smaller one; high voices are regarded as the good voices. For carrying the instrument, the body and neck can be separated. It has three strings of silk. Although the samisen is used in the temple orchestra, it is also used to accompany the dancing and singing of the geisha girls. It is, in fact, the most common Japanese stringed instrument.

"An instrument very like the samisen in construction is the *kokiu*, which is generally thought of as a woman's instrument but now is rarely played by them. The kokiu is a kind of fiddle about two feet long over-all, the body being five inches long and five inches broad. It is two and a half inches deep and is covered like the samisen. The bridge is long and low, with notches to receive the strings. Three are equally spaced, but the fourth is very near the third. It is played with the *kiu*, a bow nearly four feet long, which is made in four lengths so that it can be taken apart for easier transport. It is strung with white horsehair, fastened with a silken knot to a silver holder, and the instrument is played with a rotary movement of the bow; double stops are very rarely used."

At last the director talked about the *koto*, speaking at length about this important instrument, a member of the zither family.

"The koto is a thirteen-stringed instrument—sometimes it has seventeen strings, but the original is supposed to have had six. As in all Japanese instruments, the strings are made of silk drawn through wax. The strings are equally long and thick, and are stretched to the same tension. The notes are obtained by means of movable bridges, as many in number as there are strings. The second string is the lowest tone, while the first and third strings, tuned alike, are tuned at the interval of a fifth above the second. Tuning is done by ear, note by note, the player pitching the instrument to his voice. Both classical and popular music are pentatonic, and this instrument follows that system.

"The koto player wears on the right hand, plectra-like wire thimbles, terminating in small projections of ivory. With these he touches only the shorter division of the strings. With the fingers of the left hand he can press the longer and sounded lengths of the string, or he can pull them toward the bridges and thus increase or decrease the tension, and this way sharpen or flatten notes to get intermediate tones. The koto is usually about six feet two and a half inches long, around nine inches wide, and nearly two inches deep at the sides. The instrument is made of strong

kiri wood and has two openings on the underside. Often it is beautifully ornamented."

The percussion instruments used in this temple recording were
the familiar *taiko*, a large bass drum; the *kakko*, a small kettledrum; the *san-no-tsutzumi*; and the *shoko*, a small gong. The many
gongs and flutes completed the orchestra. My priest-guide had
interesting words about each of these also. I was pleased during
this visit to find on their home ground all of these instruments,
which I had known quite well prior to this visit in Japan.

It was also my very good fortune during this first visit to
Japan to meet Michio Miyagi, the internationally famed blind
koto player, the musician who had probably done more than anyone else to make the koto the favorite instrument of modern Japan.
After many years of untiring efforts he had reached the highest
possible standard in koto music and his compositions held first
place in the hearts of the Japanese. The chief example of this
was *Kara-Ginuta*, in which he drew from reminiscences of boyhood
in Korea, where he lived for many years with his parents. This
music represents the sounds of the *kinuta*, or clubs, used by
Korean women in washing during a Korean night. Another favorite
was *furin* (wind bells). The Japanese love the tinkling sounds of
small wind bells hung in the windows on hot summer days and
Miyagi's house was filled with wind bells. His music opens with
the sounds of all the bells suddenly starting their clinking in a
merry wind, and then he depicts the different notes ringing one
after another. This piece requires the highest technical achievement
in koto playing.

Born in Kobe on April 7, 1894, Michio Miyagi became blind when
only seven years old. At the age of fifteen he composed his
first modern piece, "Variation on Water," which is loved throughout
all Japan. He was a member of the Japan Art Academy and
professor of Tokyo's Art University's music department. One of his
primary achievements is the fact that he introduced the technique
of Western music into Japanese classical form to create a new
style in koto playing. He also created modern Japanese music
for other traditional instruments, and composed more than six
hundred pieces, including the far-famed "Sea at Springtime" and
"Variation of Sakura," which have been played often by traditional
and Western musical organizations.

One of the things I most looked forward to on my return to

Japan in 1956 was renewing my acquaintance with this remarkable man and I had an appointment to see him during the first week of my visit to Tokyo. Just before our appointment, I received the news of his tragic death. While en route to give a concert in Osaka, an overnight journey from Tokyo, Miyagi met with a fatal accident. It is thought that, being blind, he had opened a wrong door and fallen from his railroad compartment during the night. He died of head injuries four hours after being found.

On the day we were to have met, I attended his funeral. There were throngs of people, not just his pupils and colleagues from the University and the Conservatory but thousands of Japanese who had come to feel through his music the warmth and glory of the man as a human being. His influence and individuality will never die in the affectionate memories of the people of Japan.

On arriving at the Buddhist temple where the service was held, we passed through solid lines of people, many with tears flowing down their cheeks, quietly paying tribute to this great man. We joined the slow-moving mass of people wending their way down the long approach to the temple. Inside were banks of fresh flowers and wreaths, and above them a photograph of Miyagi, smiling. On the right, sitting on the floor before their kotos, were nearly a hundred colleagues and students of the master, playing his compositions. I added my three portions of incense to the votive bowl before the shrine, and moved on past a long line of mourners and Miyagi's students. All were robed in black and as we passed, handed us beautiful chrysanthemums to carry away in memory of their master.

This was a unique funeral. There was no chanting of the scriptures, no prayers, nothing but flowers and music. Here again it was music that lifted the spirit in reverence and exaltation, an experience which I have relived many times and each time with the same poignant sense of its power.

As planned, I recorded the entire concert at which Miyagi was to have played the following night in Tokyo. Members of the orchestra had placed his famous koto in position in the center of the stage. It was very moving to see the beautiful instrument standing there, silent and alone. In the program a square of rice paper had been placed over his photograph.

Section III

THE AMERICAS

Chapter 22

TO THE EASTERN ARCTIC IN CONVOY

In the summer of 1942 I was on board the S.S. *Nascopie* when she made her two hundred seventy-third voyage, the longest she had ever made, on her annual round of the Hudson's Bay Company posts. I was directing a government photographic-recording project for the Canadian Film Board; the next phase was to be devoted to Eskimo life. The trip took 135 days largely because of war conditions (sailing in convoys, which meant delays and much slower travel), bad weather, and many other interruptions of the regular schedule. The *Nascopie* was under the command of Captain T. F. Smellie, who had built up this annual resupply service for the comfort and convenience of government and Hudson's Bay Company employees and missionaries in the eastern Arctic. This was Captain Smellie's last trip. On his return to Winnipeg, this witty, delightful Englishman was given a dinner by the company celebrating the twenty-fifth anniversary of his taking command of the *Nascopie* in October 1917.

The little freighter has now been taken out of service. But when we sailed on her, the *Nascopie* was registered in the romantic term "Trading into Hudson Bay," and carried on her annual trip only those who had essential duties in the Arctic. Among my shipmates in 1942 were a medical officer, a dental officer, as well as a Roman Catholic and an Anglican bishop whose lively sniping at each other across the captain's table lent a sparkle to every meal. My shins, I recall, were black-and-blue from the kicks of my companions who were greatly amused by the ecclesiastical exchanges. Bishop Fleming, the Anglican, was making his ninth episcopal visitation and his nineteenth voyage into the Arctic, this time with his bride of a few months.

I would not have been aboard the *Nascopie* or even alive to tell the tale of our voyage had my original plans to travel north to King William Island—about a hundred miles from the magnetic pole—materialized. I had been working on the film program in Manitoba province and in Winnipeg had met "Paddy" Gibson, a name famous throughout the Arctic. He was home on one of his rare leaves from King William Island, where he headed the local Hudson's Bay Company trading post. An Irishman—calm, capable, a natural-born philosopher—Paddy possessed remarkable inner resources. He had remained a splendid human through many years of complete isolation at his post at Gjoa Haven, one of the more northern points where human life could be sustained for any length of time. Once a year the Hudson's Bay Company plane flies in with mail and supplies from Winnipeg to Coppermine, then a last outpost of civilization. From here it is hundreds of miles north and east by dog sledge to Gjoa Haven.

Paddy had regaled me with many arctic tales, but always he made light of the rigors of his lonely post—even those bad years when the supplies could not get through at all. The resupply ship was sometimes unable to reach even Fort Ross for as many as three years in succession. All arctic posts carry ample staple foods and staple supplies to tide them over such emergencies without undue hardship, but it is impossible for anyone who has not known the rigors of this arctic existence to have any conception of what the arrival of the supply ship means to these isolated communities scattered over the roof of the world—with its mail from the outside, new magazines and periodicals, fresh foods, and little extras and luxuries which embellish the tedious winter menu.

It was January 1942 when Paddy and I discussed plans for me and my cameraman to accompany him when he returned to King William Island in February and produce a film on Eskimos. I was very disappointed that my schedule could not be altered in time to fit in with the plane's departure. Instead I booked passage on the *Nascopie*, which was to sail from Montreal. Before joining the ship, I stopped in Ottawa, the home base for my work in Canada and also the home of the Canadian Film Board for which I was a producer. Here I learned that on Paddy's return flight, the one on which I had been invited to join him, his plane had crashed and burned in the arctic wastes. Paddy and his pilot had perished.

In his book *Kabloona* (material for which he collected while living with Paddy at King William Island) Gontran de Poncins probably spoke for many white men and scores of inarticulate Eskimos who loved and admired Paddy when he wrote: "He had been one of those men whose fine spirit and sense of brotherhood were for me, and are for me more than ever in this troubled world, the best example of human relationship. He was a *man—Inuk* (Supreme Man) as the Eskimos would say; I cannot say better of any human being!"

The *Nascopie* left Montreal at night, in a convoy of six ships, sailing in complete blackout throughout the three weeks' journey to Southampton Island, entering Hudson Bay the day the ice broke in July. At every big trading post we unloaded supplies for several days—Newfoundland, Labrador, Baffin Island, and the smaller posts as well. At each, from the shores, raced little sealskin canoes, the age-old kayaks of the Eskimos, skimming swiftly and silently through the blue-green water among the drifting ice floes, double-bladed paddles flashing in the dazzling sunshine, and upturned brown faces wreathed in wide, welcoming smiles.

Our ship hardly nosed her way to shore and anchored before groups of Eskimos scrambled on board for the mugs of sweetened tea and cookies sent up from the galley, a feast which had apparently become an annual ritual. They streamed about the decks, shaking hands with everyone over and over again, their impassive brown faces suddenly transformed by radiant smiles; all of them as simply, as openly delighted with the little ship's arrival as a child opening gifts on Christmas morning.

I liked them on sight. It is impossible not to like an Eskimo. I loved the strange primitive clatter of their consonants, that awkward pigeon-toed gait, the shy women giggling together in clusters, and the cheerful, staring children—sturdy little roly-poly bundles in their parkas of skin. If they all smelled just a little of seal, it was at least a friendly, homey smell.

While the ship was unloading in Labrador, an Eskimo "band" from the famous Grenfell Mission came on board with an assortment of battered instruments and gave us a concert. Their favorite item, played with enormous gusto and repeated several times, was

"Nearer My God to Thee." In view of the need for convoy and total blackout, this was more appropriate than they could have guessed.

Southampton Island first appeared to me as a broad brown strip astride the green water of Coral Harbour with the trading-post buildings, white with red roofs, huddled together behind a rocky promontory. Just beyond them I could see the spire of the Roman Catholic mission jutting upward like an admonishing finger in the dazzling glare. All around us was immense activity, the chugging of a few little motorboats, the clank and jangle of hoists being made ready for unloading, and on shore a tremendous buzz of excitement with Eskimos shouting and laughing and running to and fro like jubilant children.

When we landed, there was more handshaking; the visitor from the outside quickly realizes that this habit, introduced by the white man, is now something of a ritual with the Eskimo. But he has enhanced our mechanical hand-pumping action, changing it to a gentle lifting of the proffered hand to the level of his face, much as a courtier might raise the hand of a lady to his lips, and over the top you receive the full impact of the Eskimo smile, a mixture of naïveté and frank curiosity as to just what manner of person you may be. When you arrive in a camp, you must shake the hand of everyone: man, woman, and child. If a woman should hold back, you must take her hand, and she will beam with pleasure at the courtesy you have extended her. Babies in the mothers' hoods are soon taught to reach out in greeting, or perhaps a mother herself will take a little hand and place it in yours. This courtesy is valued to such an extent that I was told no matter if an Eskimo's beard and eyebrows are hung with icicles, and he meets you in the heart of a blizzard, he will ceremoniously remove his fur mittens before shaking hands.

One is accustomed to thinking of Eskimos only as being clad in snow-encrusted skin parkas with their faces framed in the deep fur of their hoods. But it was summer and here they were, some of the men in baggy slacks, bright checked shirts, windbreakers, and sweaters, smoking their pipes and cigarettes, a few even chewing gum. Some of the women and girls wore gingham dresses under heavy pullovers or parkas of duffel or fur, their hair tightly braided and sometimes tied with crumpled ribbons. Shoes ranged from high sealskin boots to canvas slippers. But I quickly realized that the people wearing this strange assortment of foreign clothing had changed very little, if at all, in many centuries.

During our stay on Southampton Island my cameraman and I were billeted with the trader in the post house and therefore had an excellent opportunity to study the Eskimos who came in to the store to trade their skins or simply to sit for an hour or two immobile and expressionless as statues on the benches in the outer room, thinking or just not thinking—an art I believe the Eskimo has perfected.

In 1670 while America was still very young indeed, "The honourable the Hudson's Bay Company Gentlemen Adventurers of England" (to give the full title) began to trade for white fox skins with the Eskimos in the eastern Arctic. The Eskimos no doubt considered it odd that the white men should value so highly an animal which provided neither good meat nor useful fur, but they gladly trapped great numbers and brought them to the trading post to exchange for goods. In some far northern posts, and on Southampton Island, the skins were paid for by wooden "sticks"— value about fifty cents each—which could later be spent and which were, no doubt, the Eskimo's first taste of currency.

In 1942 the Hudson's Bay Company was giving ten groups of five "sticks" in exchange for three fox skins. It seemed a small fortune since the white fox fur is not popular for making the fur ruff around the face of the Eskimo parka since it mats too easily; the long soft hair becomes moist from the breath and freezes hard. The fur of the wolverine, wolf, or dog is used chiefly for this purpose and is apparently the one worthwhile attribute of the wolf family, which is hated by the Eskimos and invariably emerges as the bad character in their folk tales.

As early as the seventeenth century a few good fur trappers earned enough sticks to buy from the white trader guns, ammunition, and traps. Now such luxuries as tea, sugar, flour and tobacco, woolen coats and sweaters, and summer cotton dresses to wear with parkas and pants of sealskin have become necessities. Small wonder the arrival of the yearly supply ship is the biggest day in the Eskimo's year.

A good trapper could trap as many as fifteen hundred foxes in a year and some had saved enough sticks to buy small powerboats. Amundsen in his notes referred to Eskimos traveling hundreds of miles to barter for a few nails. One tried to imagine how these primitive people must have felt when the stores were first set up in the Arctic with their glittering arrays of kettles, cooking pots, and knives hanging from the walls, warm clothing, and eventually canvas for canoes and tents. It was easy to understand why an Eskimo with a bag of skins to trade would come into the store laughing and swaggering and acting as though he owned the world. It is not easy for us to appreciate the Eskimo attitude to the value of property. The value of a thing appears to be measurable only in terms of his own desire to have it. I heard of an Eskimo who traded half a sack of his precious flour for one crayon pencil he fancied. The next day the pencil lay in the snow abandoned, forgotten. But he did not bemoan the unequal bargain. He just as quickly forgot that, too. He had got the crayon and that was all that he wanted at the time.

When we were on Southampton Island, the population was approximately 150. These nineteen thousand square miles of rock, lying to the north of Hudson Bay directly west of Cape Dorset, are known as Southampton Island only on the white man's maps. The native people were wiped out in a mysterious epidemic— probably smallpox—in 1902, and the two groups now living here, the Aivilingmiut and the Okomiut, were brought from Repulse Bay and Baffin Island by the whalers and by the Hudson's Bay Company in the first quarter of the century. To them the island is still *Shugliak,* "The Island-Pup-that-is-suckling-the-Continent-Mother-Dog."

For days after the *Nascopie* left, the post still buzzed with life, as Eskimos from camps far and wide had come to help with the loading and unloading. After their work the men and women played a strenuous ball game among the boulders, while the younger boys played their version of football, which seemed to consist of hitting one another with the ball as hard as possible. The balls they tossed about and threw at one another were made of sealskin. And, in other games, they imitated grownups: hunting, fishing, harpooning, and even in rare cases a game of "graves," when stones were laid around the body of a child who pretended to have died. The Eskimo version of playing "families" is a more frank interpretation than that given by our children, for there is little room for modesty within the cramped tent or family igloo. The cleverest children's game we saw was an Eskimo version of the jigsaw puzzle which involved putting the bones of animals together all in their proper places. Everything, even the simple game of hide-and-seek which is played by grownups, involved noise and boisterous laughter.

During this time in World War II, America was building landing strips across a part of the Arctic every five hundred miles so the fighter planes could be refueled on their route to England. The strip on Southampton Island was just about to be built, and the first construction ship came in from the U.S.A. shortly after the supply ship had left. Since there was no dock, she had to stand well offshore, and unloading called for all the ingenuity of the commander and crew. The drums of fuel were simply thrown overboard and floated in to shore. For carrying the heavy equipment, several kayaks were bound together to form rafts. During the unloading of heavy equipment, there was an accident in which a young sailor of nineteen was killed. He was a Lutheran and a Protestant burial was required, but at this time there was neither Protestant cleric nor a Protestant prayer book on the island.

From my years as a soloist in an Episcopalian choir while studying voice, I knew enough of the burial service to help the trader, who was Anglican, put a Protestant ceremony together, and he officiated. Looking around at those boys who had just landed on this barren waste and were confronted with a long, lonely year of work, I found it sad to think their very first job on the island was to dig a grave for one of their own. The grave was covered with heavy stones to keep the huskies from digging in it, and a little white cross was placed on it which no doubt still reappears from the snow for a few short months every summer as a sad reminder.

Groups of Eskimos stood around in silent clusters watching the white man laid to rest, paying their respects by being present, absorbed as usual in anything the white man does.

The Eskimos of the eastern Arctic readily attend church services and many had learned to read prayer books printed in syllabic Eskimo, a sort of alphabet invented by a missionary to the Indians decades earlier. They enjoy the hymn singing, but what they seemed to like best was the hot sweet tea and biscuits that always followed. At Chesterfield Inlet the Catholic mission had a pool table which was almost as great an attraction as the tea.

In untold centuries of isolation these people have developed a dignified culture with a religion well suited to their grim environment, and certainly they have the appearance of being serenely content. Nominally they are, of course, Catholic or Protestant depending upon which missionary had reached them first, but I feel sure they did not know the difference. The basic religion of the Hudson Bay Eskimos has numberless supernatural beings: some harmless, a few helpful, and a great many with the power to do considerable damage if they are inclined to. The most feared of all is Sedna, goddess of the sea, for it is she who controls the weather and the supply of seals. The souls of animals are still conciliated, especially those related to game hunted for food, and the souls of dead Eskimos are propitiated by the observance of ancient rituals and taboos.

Sitting up there on top of the world, far above the tree line in the arctic wastes, the Eskimo's chief concern is still, as it has always been, with the preservation of life under conditions in which no other human beings have been able to survive. Their territory, the largest habitat of any primitive people in the world, stretches from Siberia in the west to Greenland in the east, and in this almost limitless space they number fewer than 50,000.

Descended from the same Mongoloid stock that predominates in eastern and northern Asia, they are distinct in appearance, language, and customs from the American Indian tribes. In the Canadian eastern Arctic they still pursue a nomadic existence just as when they came across the Bering Strait from Siberia thousands of years ago, traveling across the frozen lakes and tundra from camp to camp by dog sled in winter and by the kayak and umiak—the larger family canoe—in the open water during the brief summer. They live, as they lived then, in igloos built of blocks of hard snow in winter and in summer in tents of canvas now, formerly caribou skin. The sea mammals are scarce or abundant depending on the movement of the sea ice; therefore the existence of the nomadic Eskimo is never wholly secure. The Eskimos of the Barren Grounds in the interior west of Hudson Bay rarely visited the Bay to hunt sea mammals but depended almost entirely on caribou for everything—food, clothing, bedding, and tents. They eke out a precarious existence, always in the shadow of possible famine when the great herds migrate south; then, except for an occasional musk ox, they must live only by fishing or by spearing seals. They have no herds of reindeer to depend on as in Alaska, where the United States government has introduced them. Since I was in the eastern Arctic, intensive acculturation and widespread changes with government aid have altered Eskimo life considerably.

Although one of the most ancient peoples in the world, the Eskimos are very loosely organized. A "tribe" meant simply small communities of families who live together, wandering as a group from one hunting ground to another, their movements completely controlled by an environment which makes the struggle for food never-ending. The natural resources of this icebound territory are so limited that the men spend all their time and energy hunting and fishing in an effort to eat and store away food against the months when the fierce arctic blizzards make movement of any kind impossible.

The Eskimos appear to be vigorous and healthy enough, but they live in such tightly packed communities that an epidemic such as influenza can sweep through a whole encampment; the child mortality rate is particularly high. They have no immunity to outside disease. An attack of measles is usually fatal, and even the common cold is terribly serious. Always after the supply ship sails away, the camp rocks with coughing, even among grown men, whom I have seen prostrated on the ground shaken with coughs.

In certain areas it was a serious problem to keep a balanced population to avoid extinction of the race altogether. At Port Burwell the Canadian Government found there were far too many women, most of them widows. On Southampton Island there were not enough women to provide wives for the men, and nowhere in the world is a woman more essential to a man than in Eskimo land. I was on hand to join in the general excitement when a large group of Port Burwell women, transported by boat with their belongings over a thousand miles, arrived on Southampton Island. It was a wildly joyous day; all the women immediately found husbands and began making plans to leave for their summer encampment.

We were able to film the whole of this journey to the fishing area and the building of the Eskimo "summer" colony. How the Eskimo must long to hear the first geese honking in the sky on their northward flights, for this is the sound that heralds the long-awaited summer. Everywhere there is the creak and crash of ice breaking up in the warmer air; the winter igloos begin to melt and slowly daylight replaces night. Inland herds of caribou once more dot the snow-patched, moss-covered tundra; out in the open water whales blow from time to time, seals pop up their heads amid the ice floes, and schools of fish swim upriver. The cries of nesting fowl fill the air. All these sights and sounds spell paradise for the Eskimo.

There is no private ownership of land but particular hunting and fishing grounds are regarded by mutual agreement as the domain of certain groups. This communal principle, an absence of our fixed "mine and thine" attitude, is one of the outstanding characteristics of these people. Bound together in a mutual struggle for survival against an environment that for the greater part of every year seems bent upon destroying them, they share everything. Hoarding by an individual could not be tolerated when there is often so little to go around.

But on Southampton Island many of the white man's machines had already given the Eskimo his first taste of private ownership, and for several years motorboats had begun to replace the family umiak, made of canvas, and the skin kayak is giving way to canoes bought from the trader or to small boats with outboard motors attached. When I was there, a few successful hunters had even earned enough sticks to acquire small schooners with auxiliary engines. (I am told that the umiak and kayak have now disappeared in this area.)

The Eskimo is fascinated by machinery. I am told that on acquiring any mechanical device the first thing he does is to dismantle it entirely, removing even the smallest bolt and screw in order to determine how it operates. There is a practical reason behind this: he pulls everything apart so that he will know how to fix it when it goes wrong—which needless to say it does very frequently, for the mechanism is never quite the same after these exploits. Sometimes before reassembling the white man's mechanical device he himself drills another hole in it just to show he is superior.

One of my Eskimo friends had even ordered a bicycle through the trader, but was saved from riding the thing on the rocky, slushy tundra because after he had finished dismantling and boring extra holes the wheels never turned again.

Kooshooak and his brothers, my crew for the brief summer, all successful hunters, had saved two thousand dollars, enough to buy between them an arctic schooner, a thirty-eight-foot Peterhead, strongly built to withstand ice, with sails and an auxiliary engine that worked sometimes. It was in this that my cameraman and I sailed to various islands hunting white whale, polar bear, and even walrus, and to the fishing grounds of our arctic friends, where we lived aboard during our stay.

After crossing several miles of open sea, we had scarcely landed at the fishing grounds before the women were clearing rocks and pitching tents on a dry spot free from melting snow and ice. The young boys unloaded their weighted fish nets from the boats and went off to the mouth of the river. The men moved upstream, each carrying a three-pronged fish spear with a handle about eight feet long. We had watched and filmed an old man named Eevaloo (which means caribou sinew) making these primitive fish spears which had been used in the Eskimo technique of fishing long centuries before traders ever found their way to the eastern Arctic.

Eevaloo's hunting days were over, but he had once been so successful a hunter that he had been able to buy a splendid tool kit from a trader. He never allowed it out of his sight, and this expert craftsman was forever working at something. Caribou antler and whalebone were used for the two flexible outer arms of the spear with a bent nail firmly set into each prong. The prongs were scraped until shiny smooth and needle-barbed, then nailed and lashed securely to the long spear handle and given added strength by a final tying with caribou sinew. These primitive weapons were deadly when in action.

At the fishing ground where we had docked, the men built a dam of rocks across the stream from bank to bank, leaving an opening just big enough for the fish swimming with the tide to enter. Upstream from this, in the shallows, were laid circular stone traps into which the fish swam.

Once the traps were filled, the Eskimos jabbed the fish with their pronged spears, pausing only long enough to toss them onto the shore. In twenty minutes the traps were empty except for the smaller fish which were picked out from under rocks. The next day and the next the traps would be refilled by the tide and the harpoons would go into action again. To the Eskimo the hunting of food has none of the element of sport about it. In the short weeks of summer he must store up as much food as possible for the long arctic winter. From every hunt some meat is cached in stone cairns for future use, and a great deal of this catch—arctic salmon trout, *ichalook,* a bright red-fleshed fish that can weigh as much as twenty or more pounds—was dried for use in the winter months.

Back in the camp the tents were up and the seal-oil lamps were heating big pots of water for tea. Only the Eskimo woman knows how to make a proper wick for this ancient stone lamp, and patiently gathering the special moss from the rocky tundra is another of her important summer tasks.

In winter the primus stove is now often used in the igloos, but for the outdoor summer camps the moss wick smoldering in the traditional Eskimo lamp is doubtless more reliable in the constant violent wind.

The lamp is no more than a hollowed-out lump of soapstone from a foot to eighteen inches long. In this indentation floats a little precious seal or whale oil, which has to be replenished from time to time by a piece of blubber from the storage barrel, the blubber melting slowly as the flame warms it. Along one side of the stone the women deftly shape a saw-toothed fringe of the gray-green moss, letting it protude just above the rim. Each time it is needed the oil lamp must be specially prepared all over again, and it seems to need constant trimming to prevent it from smoking. When the wick is well trimmed and saturated, it is ignited and (given time!) will heat water for tea, to which the Eskimo has been addicted almost ever since the first white man came to the Arctic.

I am told that Eskimo children often wake in the early hours and howl for their mugs of sweetened tea; the mother will roll out of her fur sleeping bag in the icy igloo and go through this whole tedious task in order to make the children this brew.

Heating snow water over the seal-oil lamp can take up to two hours. Water is never boiled for Eskimo tea. The leaves are put in the cold water and brew as the water heats. Even so, the mugs of tea are always allowed to cool, as the Eskimo cannot take liquid or food very hot. Tea leaves are never removed from an Eskimo pot; those that do escape into the mugs with the thick black liquid are solemnly eaten when the mug is empty and are considered a rare delicacy.

The heating of water is in fact practically all the Eskimo woman needs to know of the culinary art except for occasional stews, since the main diet, fish and sea mammals, is very often eaten raw (the raw flesh and internal organs provide their vitamins). But the making of tea goes on endlessly, and therefore matches from the trader are at such a premium in Eskimo land that each match is carefully split into two pieces. This is a very difficult thing to do but the Eskimo woman with her indispensable *ulu,* a crescent-shaped knife first fashioned by the primitives in stone, does it expertly. This razor-sharp steel blade is used constantly and for a large variety of jobs. It is ideal for use in the crowded igloo since it requires only movement of the wrist, not even the elbow. A child still young enough to be carried in the parka pouch on his mothers' back is soon skilled in the use of the *ulu,* wielding it in his tiny hands with bloodcurdling skill. Ability to handle the ulu is the one really necessary art of good eating in the Arctic, and during the feast that followed the day's fishing, we saw it put to most efficient and alarming use. Even tiny children ate like the elders, holding great chunks of raw fish in their teeth as that sharp curved blade flashed against their lips with each bite but never cut them. While filming the meal we were able to observe at close quarters the primitive method of eating and the uninhibited manners of the group.

The artic trout lay in a blood-red heap beside the host, in whose tent the feast was held. He selected a fish, one after another, and sliced it from head to tail. After biting into it and cutting a piece from it with his ulu, he passed it to the Eskimo sitting next to him, who in turn passed it on. Fish after fish went the rounds, always clockwise and with a kind of grim haste, to the accompaniment of smacking lips, appreciative gulps, and an occasional rumbling belch. In no time the red flesh had disappeared. At other hunts in which we participated, music invariably followed the feast; here, while the men sat smoking their pipes, the rest of the trout were slit open by the women and girls, the precious oil pressed with the ulu into the storage bladders of sealskin, and the fish was hung out to dry in the brilliant sun on guy ropes of the tents.

Because his whole existence in this vast territory has always depended in the summer on fishing and hunting from the water, the Eskimo long ago evolved the small kayak, a craft ideal for his particular needs. On nearby Baffin Island we filmed the making of one of these ingenious canoes from the laying of its first rib to the ceremonious launching.

Of all people in the world the Eskimo is said to have the art of making a completely watertight skin boat. The Eskimo cannot, as a rule, swim, but by securely tying his waterproof clothing to the opening of his watertight kayak the man makes himself one with his craft.

The kayak has no keel to steady it; even stepping into and out of it requires long practice and is an art taught by father to small sons with infinite patience. Frail as his craft appears, the Eskimo has been known to cross more than a hundred miles of open sea. Even if in very heavy swells the boat is overturned, and takes the buffeting of a rough wave on its rounded bottom, the hunter rights himself again with a deft roll. It is claimed that one Eskimo paddling his kayak can travel much faster than three men paddling a canoe.

As well as being employed for the pursuit of water fowl, seal, bear, walrus, and even the white whale, during storms the little craft can provide shelter on land, the Eskimo using it much as a snail uses its shell. In most of these arctic communities during the summer, someone is bound to be busy building a kayak or an umiak.

In the old days whalebone or driftwood was used for the skeleton of these swift skin boats, but already in 1942 we saw wood being bought from the traders for making the ribs. However, these were still being bound together in the old fashion, with strips of sealskin, soaked and chewed into pliability, which tightened as they dried. Making the frame of a kayak is the men's work but the covering process is entirely in the hands of the women; only they can be trusted to sew the sealskins for covering the boats, carefully patching any spot that shows signs of weakness, and "chewing down" the seams to make them soft enough to sew. When the skins were finally sewn and pliable enough everyone came to help in the task of stretching the covering over the frame, and at the launching the kayak was taken to the water's edge and ceremoniously given a drink to ensure its good fortune in the hunt.

In the short summer of six to ten weeks, the white whale, a member of the porpoise family, is a rich source of food hunted by these diligent people, and much of this is also preserved in stone cairns for the hungry winter. The Eskimo learned many short cuts from the white whalers who hunted in Hudson Bay about a hundred years ago. Once the Eskimos drove the whales ashore and harpooned them in shallow water; today they shoot the whale immediately when he surfaces, using the harpoon with detachable spearhead and float simultaneously with the gun, and towing the whale to shore by means of nets or, as we did, taking him on board the schooner by means of an ingenious pulley. Once this huge mammal is freed from the net everyone has a part to play in the cutting of the meat.

The crescent-shaped ulus flash in the women's hands; the children, too, crowd around for their favorite morsel, the three-inch-thick spongy skin called *mukluk*, which they slice so expertly with their ulus, gobbling it down raw with the same relish with which an American child devours candy. Again I was amazed at the frightening dexterity with which they used these razor-sharp knives. I waited breathlessly to see a nose disappear, but never saw a child so much as scratch himself.

The mothers' concern is with the whale blubber, so necessary for heating and light when their world will be blanketed in semidarkness for much of the year. The blubber is chopped into small pieces and stored in barrels. The most valuable blubber is that provided by the winter seal, the *netchek*, pursued among the ice floes by the Eskimo in his kayak for countless centuries, or harpooned through the ice in winter. It has always been a mainstay of life for the Eskimo of Hudson Bay.

The patience of the hunter in pursuit of the winter seal is quite remarkable. The husky is a great help in locating the seal's winter shelter under the sea ice by finding the seal's breathing holes in the covering snow. After cutting three or four large blocks of snow and placing them as a windbreak, the Eskimo makes a round hole in the snow and ice with his snow knife and takes up his position with his harpoon, with its detachable head, in hand. Because of the seal's acute hearing, the hunter must remain absolutely still while he waits for the mammal to pass under the hole. An Eskimo has been known to stand in this stooped position, indifferent to the passing of time, for days, if necessary.

Netchek, the seal, has another indirect use in the pattern of Eskimo life. He is also the favorite food of the polar bear (*nanook*) which is a great delicacy in the Eskimo menu and prized above all for the thick warm fur that covers his three- to nine-hundred-pound bulk. The polar bear travels alone covering great distances while hunting seals around the edges of the sea ice. He is regarded as the gourmet of the arctic regions since he prefers only

the blubber of the seal and often leaves the rest. In his wake
pads the canny fox to eat what the bear has discarded . . . and
behind the fox comes the Eskimo with his traps!

The Eskimo now mostly hunts the polar bear with guns where
once he killed nanook face to face with a spear after his dogs
had brought him to bay. On land, dogs are still used to corner
bears, and although the modern methods have now replaced the
spear and the ancient bow and arrow, the old rituals still apply
to the slaying of polar bears. Everything the Eskimo does has
some basic practical principle, and rituals to propitiate the soul
of a slain bear are designed to ensure that other bears will be
captured.

The Eskimo eats his bear meat raw but we, living aboard the
little schooner, boiled ours on the primus stove. I was delighted
with bear meat at first tasting. It has a faintly sweet flavor and
perhaps it is that that palls after a short time. It is not a diet I
would choose, but we had been without meat for some time and
it came as a great treat.

Other delicacies I tried in Eskimo land included venison and
walrus heart; seal liver and caribou tongue; whale steak and
mukluk, the skin of the white whale. Arctic trout with its sweet
red flesh was also very good both frozen and cooked. Indeed,
all arctic foods were infinitely better than some of the food I had
to eat out of courtesy in Africa.

The seal provides the most waterproof skin of all arctic animals
for clothing, boots, harpoon cords, and floats. Preparing the skin
is a never-ending chore, and in an Eskimo community every
woman and young girl seems to be forever chewing on a skin
of some kind. Even tiny girls go about not with a lollipop but a
piece of skin in their mouths.

The sealskins are first treated by scraping off surplus fat, and
intensive rubbing provides a form of "friction" tanning. Tanning
as we know it is not used, although some skins may be scalded
and others frost-dried, but all have finally to be "chewed down"
into pliability before sewing. It is not surprising that the teeth
of most Eskimo women appear to have been filed down to the
gum. (My dentist tells me they do not suffer since the nerve
recedes as the tooth wears down.) Even the seams of the tough
caribou hides used for the large summer tents have to be chewed
down to make them soft enough to be sewn. When we were

there, these were being replaced by the less bulky, more easily transportable canvas tents. I noticed some of the women still using the primitive thimbles of thick skin worn on the index finger; others had fancy ones bought from a trader. The whalebone and old ivory and bird-bone needles were fast being replaced by steel but the women still preferred the thread made of a split sinew from the back of the caribou because it is durable and swells when wet.

Using a special lock stitch—from which our own lock stitch is thought to have derived—the women make their hunters' clothing so completely watertight that it prevents even the snow, much more penetrating than water, from seeping through the seams.

The making of boots never ceases. The *kamik*, the knee-length boot of the hunters, has an upper part of *netchek* sealskin with hair left on, and a lower part of *ugjuk* sealskin with the hair scraped off. The everyday boots for use in the rocky, mushy terrain have soles of walrus hide for which the women appear to have one basic pattern. After the leather is soft enough to take the needle, the edges of the soles, which have been beveled with an ulu, are carefully crimped over the boot top, fitted together, and so closely sewn that the whole boot is completely waterproof and snowproof. The woman ranking highest in the Eskimo community group is the one who keeps her man and her family safe in all weather by providing them with the strongest clothing. Hunter or small child must be able to fall into the icy water and emerge as dry as possible, merely shaking the water off himself like the seal whose skin he wears. "The man is the hunter his wife makes him" is a saying in Eskimo land, and we from outside soon understood why. A man's very life depends on the skill and integrity of his woman's work. Every morning an Eskimo woman begins the day by chewing her husband's boots to make them soft enough to wear.

Since the Eskimos have very small feet, it is almost impossible for a white man to get kamiks made in the right size. One bootmaker took a look at my feet, grunted, smiled, then went off and cut a pair for me by the basic pattern she used for her family. They were much too small but were beautiful, completely waterproof, and made wonderful souvenirs along with my sealskin parka, which did fit.

In winter two parkas are worn, one with the fur next to the body, and one with the fur outside, from which snow and sleet can be easily shaken. In the doorway or small "porch" of a winter igloo, beaters are kept for removing snow and water before one comes inside. It is quite common, particularly with the women, to see parka sleeves hanging empty and the owners' arms clasped across their chests for added warmth.

On Baffin Island a few wives of the most prosperous Eskimo hunters were wearing summer parkas of white duffel with bead embroidery. The art of bead embroidery was borrowed from the Indians to the south, who had used beads long before the Eskimos had thought of adding anything decorative except fur designs to their clothing.

Eskimo women too old or ill to go out on long hunting trips with the group, were taught the intricate art of finger weaving by the French nuns in the hospital at Chesterfield Inlet. (Early French Canadians had learned from the Indians how to weave broad woolen bands on their fingers.) These woven bands added splashes of color when used as slings under the babies carried in the pouches of their mothers' bulky parkas.

It is impossible to think of these cheery people without their dogs, and most Eskimo legends feature the husky in some way. There is a delightful fable associated with *kingmik*—the Eskimo word for a husky. Kingmik's real trial of strength and worth, indeed the peak of his career, is his ability to hold a polar bear at bay, or better still, to do battle with nanook himself. The Aivilik Eskimos tell a story of a man on Shugliak a long time ago who was so poor that he had only one dog. He was devoted to his kingmik, but one day in battle with a huge bear the faithful animal was killed. The hunter was so stricken with grief that he crouched down on the ice and wept.

The bear, seeing the man's sorrow, lay down beside the dog's carcass and his spirit entered into the dog's body. At once kingmik sprang up with a joyous yelp and ran back to lick his master's hand. Together they went to where the bear now lay dead and skinned it.

The sound of a dog team howling in chorus is chilling and absolutely unforgettable. One author has described it as the national anthem of the north country.

One of several things can set off a husky chorus: a raised

voice in the stillness, a fight over a scrap of food, even the ringing of the mission bell. But for most people visiting the Arctic for the first time, the sound is probably more often associated with the blazing, unbelievable beauty of the aurora borealis.

Here one finds the old phenomenon of dogs baying at the moon magnified a thousandfold. Is it the sudden sizzling and crackling above them in the clear cold sky that provokes that first whine within the pack, a thin plaintive sound that swells into a skin-shivering cadence as every dog and puppy in the settlement adds his voice? Or could this wailing incantation be the wolf dogs' primeval acknowledgment of some power that spins and whirls overhead in gigantic dazzling splendor?

The Eskimos believe that the spirits control these fiery darting northern lights, and that when the aurora is most brilliant, the spirits are playing a game in which the skull of an Eskimo recently dead is tossed about the sky.

It is not easy to describe the awesomeness of this dazzling cascade: the mysterious lights, flaring and flashing, writhing and wavering across the sky, shooting and showering their pinks and purples, yellows and greens like celestial bullets. So overpowering was the majesty of this display of heavenly fireworks that I cannot to this day determine whether the experience was more spiritual than physical. I only know that I felt myself deeply moved as by some mystery not of this earth, and that the lonely, long-drawn wailing of the huskies seemed an inseparable part of the blazing panorama.

When they are working during the winter the huskies are fed every other day; in summer they are not fed at all and must scrounge along the fringes of the ice for any edible refuse washed up by the waves; it is pitiful to see them hanging hopefully around the doorways of the tents, ready to gulp down anything that might be hurled outside. I often saw them gnawing away at an old skin boot or a fur mitt. After every hunt they were kept at bay until the meat had been evenly divided. Then they rushed in like mad creatures scratching for the smallest bit of flesh or blood. They even carried off bloodstained stones and licked them until their tongues were raw. I was told that they would eat another husky too weak or ill to defend itself.

Just before I had gone North, there had been a tragedy at one of the posts which made the ravenous hunger of the huskies even more horrifying to me. A young Mountie had left his post with one of the dog teams for a routine tour of his area, which could have involved anything from aiding an Eskimo with a broken leg to rescuing a hunting party trapped on an ice floe which had broken off from the mainland. In his absence his young wife had the responsibility of the remaining dogs. Although the husky appears to be subdued and brought under control through intensive training, his wolf ancestry and savage instincts are easily stirred; the pack instinct has never been bred out.

The young woman was on her way to feed the dogs one day when she slipped and fell. In a flash the entire pack was upon her. The wild commotion of the fighting, hunger-crazed dogs attracted the attention of the trader, but his help came too late.

Chapter 23

ESKIMOS OF THE EASTERN ARCTIC

It was a stormy morning in Hudson Bay when we set sail aboard Kooshooak's Peterhead from Southampton Island for an uninhabited stretch of rock called Coats Island where, with luck and the cooperation of the sea goddess, the Eskimos hoped to get enough walrus meat in one week's journey to supply their families for months to come. (Walrus hunting in Canadian waters has long been forbidden to white men since it is such an essential food of the Eskimos and their dogs.)

This was the great hunting event of the year—Coats Island and nearby Walrus Islands were the hereditary mating ground of huge walrus herds and without calendars or clocks, the Eskimos, through experience as skillful hunters and perhaps some mysterious seventh sense, knew the time to begin their hunt.

This was no pleasure cruise! Although it was arctic summer, I was never warm in spite of my fur parka and three layers of wool under that. The winds were icy and seemed always to blow with gale force. When we went to sleep at night, we were never quite sure whether we would find ourselves in the morning on the east or west shore of turbulent Hudson Bay. On one occasion, in the middle of the night I awoke at a most uncomfortable angle. Crawling out of my sleeping bag, I sought Kooshooak. Apparently we were stuck on a reef and would have to remain in this awkward predicament for a few hours, until the tide rose.

There were no kitchen or bathroom facilities at all on board— unless you counted the one-burner primus stove or a rusty old

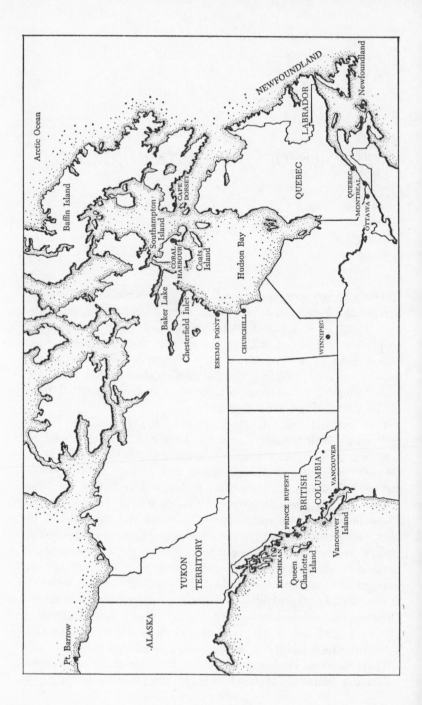

bucket, hardly luxury conveniences. No doubt I was the first white woman who had sailed with these Eskimos and such things as my comfort or modesty never entered their minds. But their good cheer and enthusiasm for the hunt were so contagious that it never occurred to me to complain. What was foremost in our minds was whether the walrus would be there and whether we would have a successful hunt. In addition I was concerned about whether there would be enough light to take the pictures I had come so many thousands of miles for.

The morning we sighted Coats Island with our telescope, there came a welcome burst of color and warmth as the sun broke through stormy clouds above, one of the ten days during my whole arctic summer in which there was sufficient light for color photography. Gradually the sun climbed, and we sailed into Coats harbor on a glorious bright but still a brisk day. From the first ray of light the excitement on board was intense, with everyone preparing for the great moment when we would sight the prized giants of the sea. The crew was huffing and puffing, blowing up sealskin floats, vigorously chewing the harpoon lines to soften them, and checking harpoon heads.

Such aids to hunting as the white man's telescope and rifle have long been in use among the Eskimos throughout the Arctic. But even when the animal has been sighted and shot, Eskimos still must use the age-old harpoon with its attached float to prevent the prize from being lost. The making of these floats calls for expert craftsmanship in skinning; the seal's skin is drawn intact from the animal, like removing a glove, by means of slits at head and at tail flippers. It must then be dried, softened by chewing, and carefully made watertight and ready to be blown up for the hunt. Working in pairs, one man shoots the walrus while another throws the harpoon. The tip of the harpoon lodges in the mammal, and the float, attached to the harpoon line, shows where the prey has sunk.

"*Aivik!*" Kooshooak shouted the Eskimo word for walrus. The engine was switched off and we glided silently toward the shore. What looked at first like great dark rocks suddenly came to life! The island bristled with life, with hundreds of walrus spread out, basking in the warm sun. Suddenly there was a slow roar, and then the beach erupted in movement and sound; brown bodies heaved and scrambled, tumbling over one another in their flight to gain the water. Only the biggest bull remained, bellowing defiance from his rock, as unyielding as a captain on the bridge of a sinking ship. Only after seeing all the herd safely away did he slide down into the sea.

Surrounding us in the water was a churning mass of heaving gray-green-brown bodies rolling about, shouldering one another in their confusion, blowing through their coarse whiskers and bellowing and grunting like angry elephants. Their thrashing flippers and flashing ivory tusks provided excellent targets, and simultaneously with the first staccato rifle shot we began filming Kooshooak wielding his harpoon. Out went a long line of softened hide; another shot, another streaming line, and yet another. Time after time the bullet and the harpoon struck home. The wounded animals turned savagely, reared high out of the water, splashed, and slowly plunged like rocks to the bottom of the sea, leaving only a red stain on the surface below the bobbing harpoon floats. Gradually the deep blue of the water around our ship turned to an equally deep crimson.

I am not a hunter at heart and deplore the taking of life except when necessary, but it was stirring to see men fighting an age-old battle, as the elements raged against them, for the food that meant their survival.

The hardest part of this hunt was the beaching and cutting up of the catch. At low tide the bulky, cumbersome bodies were towed into shallow water and everyone frantically set to work in an effort to get the meat cut before the tide came in again and covered the bodies. One wounded bull crawled onto the rocks from the sea and was pursued and killed, for the Eskimos have such a high regard for animals that they try never to leave one wounded at the end of a hunt.

The waves curling over the rocky beach returned to the sea colored with blood as the men hacked away at these huge two-ton bodies in order to get them on board our craft. As they worked feverishly they laughed and called gaily to one another. The hunt had been successful; their childish joy was unbounded.

What conservationists these people are! Not a sliver of that meat was wasted; every morsel might mean the difference between life and death for them, their wives, and their babies.

Before leaving the island, as after every hunt, they built a high cairn of rocks and much meat was stored there to freeze for future use. When the winter closed in and home supplies ran short, the men would return by dog sled across the frozen waters and this cache might well save them from starvation. The rest was loaded into the boat by means of an ingenious Eskimo pulley —mounds of it steaming and trickling red, all the small boat could hold. There is no danger of the walrus being exterminated by the Eskimos, for out of this great herd of thousands only seven were killed and carried away.

The six exuberant Eskimos sang gaily and took turns at the helm of the boat or slept on deck. The hold, which had on the journey out served as parlor, kitchen, and bedroom for the crew, was now storage space for the walrus meat and skins. How infinitely grateful I was for that calm, clear, cold weather that kept unpredictable Hudson Bay peaceful for a few days and made possible a most successful hunt and a beautiful sunlit film called *Arctic Hunters*.

When at last we got back to the settlement, women, children, and dogs joined in the general bustle and noisy excitement as the great mounds of meat were unloaded, and almost at once a feast was under way. During our absence the women had gathered enough driftwood, a rare commodity, to build a fire. This was the first time I had seen Eskimo women actually cooking their food. The walrus meat was made into a kind of thick, mushy stew in a pot over the little fire. When it came to the meal itself, the traditional pattern still applied. The men ate first, then the women and children had what was left. Very few scraps remained for the dogs.

While traveling around Hudson Bay in the Peterhead, I learned that Kooshooak and his friend Harry had recently exchanged wives. Even before visiting the Arctic I had heard tales of the Eskimo host offering his wife to a guest as a matter of traditional courtesy, but this is not, as it is with some South Sea islanders for instance, just a token of hospitality. Even in the South Seas, however, barter of wives is not unknown: one man I knew was offered a chief's youngest wife in exchange for the immaculate tailored white shorts he was wearing!

Formerly, the Eskimos might freely loan or exchange wives but this is rarer now. With Eskimo hunters, exchange of wives is almost automatic and, I am told, comes as a relief from the monotony of existence.

This does not always make for happiness in the snow house. The wife, who is never consulted about the matter, may be very put out if she happens to be fond of her husband; sometimes she prefers the exchange and wishes to remain in the other man's igloo permanently. When wives find the exchange to their liking, it has led on occasion to violence and even murder.

The offer of an Eskimo wife to a white man, I was told, might take days of contact, many visits in which the Eskimo will sit in igloo or tent or post hut silent, his impassive face breaking every now and then into a wide, ingratiating smile, his half-closed eyes watching every move of the newcomer, speculating as to what such an offer might be worth. Sometimes the wives are sent without bartering. If the courtesy is accepted, the husband will call the next day to collect his reward. Should the woman be rejected, he will no doubt call just the same to inquire what was wrong and to offer a daughter or some relative as substitute. Should a child be born from this swapping, it does not bother an Eskimo husband, for he often borrows or adopts children from other families.

In the Arctic the exchange or sharing of wives among Eskimos —especially among those not influenced by missionaries—was apparently an integral part of the ancient pattern of communal living among groups, and no doubt arose from the age-old struggle for survival. There are no fixed rules of ownership; there are careful, sometimes elaborate rules of sharing. Everything is shared —food, igloo, sleeping bench, snow knives—so why not a wife, who becomes married simply by moving herself with her possessions into her prospective husband's igloo or his father's igloo.

Missionaries in this vast tract of icebound territory have more than ancient taboos and superstitions to fight in trying to win the Eskimos away from their primitive pattern of behavior. Our standards must appear bewildering to them and complicated in the extreme—that is, if they think about them at all, which is unlikely.

Another problem facing the missionaries is the manner in which Eskimos deal with their old. No one is more solicitous of the elderly than the Eskimo. When traveling in the crowded boats he sees they are comfortably settled; bumping overland by dog sled he is constantly running back to see if the old ones are still wedged comfortably among the paraphernalia on the sleds; and in the igloo, help is given the old in every possible way. But finally a stage is reached when the situation becomes impossible.

Sometimes, as with many primitives, the old ones can die simply by deciding to do so, but failing this, a family conference is held and the old people are told that it is their time to die. They agree—after they suggest it first—to be taken out into the blizzard or left in an igloo to freeze.

Suicide is especially welcomed by old men who can no longer hunt or who feel themselves displaced by those who are younger and stronger. After days of brooding, an old man may order his wife or some relative to prepare a sealskin rope and, with his family carrying on their normal life about him, will, without fuss or farewell, hang himself. This is the signal for the group to strike camp immediately, load the sledges or the boats with all their belongings, and move off, out of reach of the evil spirits that had claimed the man.

On rare occasions an Eskimo will journey long distances to seek the help of a priest or a post manager when a suicide is pending in his family or within his group. If the old man or woman wishes it that way, then it is for him or her to decide.

When the time came for me to leave Southampton Island I sailed down the western side of Hudson Bay in the Peterhead to Churchill. On arrival I walked in on the American officer in charge of the U. S. Army camp there. He looked up from his desk and stared in amazement at me, in my Eskimo parka with white-fox ruff. Knowing full well that no ship or plane had arrived he exclaimed: "How on earth did you get here?"

I pointed to the Peterhead bobbing in the harbor. "On that!" I said.

I explained to him that my project was jointly for the United States and the Canadian governments, the filming of various phases of the building of airstrips in the North as well as Eskimo life. In that difficult muskeg terrain near Churchill our officers were most cooperative in my enterprise; but afterward, back in New York when the war was well over, one of them I had met there invited me to dinner with his wife in their apartment. He laughingly told me that at Churchill he had been assigned not to assist me in my work, as I had thought, but to keep an eye on me (suspected as a spy, due to my unheralded arrival).

It was this same officer who had first asked me, "Do Eskimos have music?"—a question I have been asked many times since.

It is a joy to me to realize that there are no people without music; everywhere people sing when they are happy or sad; they praise or placate their gods; and they are born, marry, work, play, and are buried to some form of music.

The Eskimo is no exception. It is true he does not sing at his work like many primitives; his lungs would probably freeze if he did. In the winter, at fifty degrees below, the very breath he emits freezes instantly into a thick fog before his face. Most of his work involves the hunt for food, and in the Arctic, where a whisper can become a shout, silence is deeply ingrained in his nature.

However, the Eskimo welcomes any excuse for a celebration, and this always means music. After a summer feast, or during the long arctic night, a dance song may continue for days. Nothing refreshes the spirits of the group more than dancing, drumming, and singing—or, as the traders put it, "whooping it up."

At the feast following the big walrus hunt which we filmed, it was old Eevaloo who began the dance, striking a few beats as if testing the drum. The *someak*, or drum, is the only musical instrument of the Hudson Bay Eskimos. In one of our films *Eskimo Summer* we showed Eevaloo in every step of making a drum while his wife, Tuktoo, sat beside him singing songs and telling folk tales for me to record. While she sang and talked, she was scraping with her ulu the hair from a caribou skin that would soon form the drumhead, and carefully storing away the hair for use on some later day, perhaps for stuffing a pillow.

The frame of this someak, which I acquired for my collection, is a hoop about two inches wide and twenty inches in diameter. Once it was made only from whalebone or wood from the tiny willow that grows sparsely on Southampton Island; today it is more often made of some light, pliable timber bought from a trader. Over this the scraped wet skin is stretched tightly (a new membrane is fitted for every special occasion), and it takes several men to hold the skin taut enough over the frame while another draws a sinew cord around the rim, securing the membrane to it.

The handle is a short, stout piece of wood notched at one end to fit the rim and lashed to it with strips of chewed-down sealskin.

The wooden drumstick is bound at the end with sealskin which has been softened to mellow the tone, and the drummer, holding the drum by its small wooden handle above his head, turns it from side to side and strikes, not the fragile drumhead, but the wooden rim, first on one side of the handle, then on the other, producing a deep resonant tone as he beats a slow persistent rhythm.

As Eevaloo drummed the feast music he danced around the ring of women singers, swaying with closed eyes as though entranced by their singing. He balanced first on one foot, then on the other, keeping time with the music. From time to time he lowered the drum, usually near the end of a refrain, and then raised it again as he began the next verse. When he was tired from dancing, or perhaps from holding the big *someak* against the wind, another drummer stepped in to take his place. One can imagine that in the long winter of darkness and blizzard there is plenty of time for such songfests and dancing.

One of the favorite songs recorded following the walrus hunt was sung by my Eskimo friends Polly, Mikusha, Atitah, and Billy Boy, all excellent singers. Each man has his own special songs and most of them, with the exception of incantations and children's songs, can be used for dancing. Many of the dancing songs recount the experiences of the composer, usually the exciting events of a hunt during the brief summer.

One such, the "Johnnie Bull" song, is the sad song of a very old man who was once a successful and famous hunter; now his hunting days are over and he can no longer keep up with the hunters when they go out by dog sleds in the winter. Always he must remain behind, but he has his memories and proudly recalls the great hunts and the good days when he shot seal and caribou.

> I must think of what to put into the song
> That I should have out here in the wild.
> I have not much to tell.
> I gave a piece of lead [a bullet]
> To what will be a boot bottom
> [A bearded seal used for making boot soles].

In the same summer I gave a piece of lead
To a big horned animal [caribou buck].
Though I go no more, I remember them, for
Now I cannot leave the camp, even in the summer.

In Eskimo music there are found certain distinct influences of
northeast Asiatic and American Indian music, and in later years
increasing evidence of the whites' music as well. In Alaska and
Greenland the music is more developed than in the Hudson Bay
region, where there has been less contact with the outside world.

Among the Eskimos of the eastern Arctic many songs—for example, play songs, lullabies, and story songs—have no accompaniment at all. The melodies are extremely primitive, the text meager
in the extreme, and nonsense syllables such as *aayaa, yaayaa,*
and *yaiyaa* recur again and again, especially in the refrain.

Besides these, there are the conjurer's songs for healing or
weather incantations, hunting songs by the score, songs of tender
sentiment such as that I recorded from a sick old man who is
begging his wife to find another husband quickly who will be
her refuge, and animal songs in which all the creatures of the
Arctic are imbued with human characteristics, suffer the same
hardships, deride, torment, flatter, and woo one another endlessly. Children as well as adults act out these folk tales about
animals; they are all born mimics.

The art of imitating sounds is no game for the hunter, it is a
serious business. On Southampton Island I made some fine recordings of Harry, one of the crew on the Peterhead, imitating the
calls of the Canada goose, the snow goose, and the swan, which
brought the birds close to us. He could imitate with great accuracy the grunts of the seal and walrus, sometimes well enough
to bring the curious animals within shooting range.

In a very unusual game song that I recorded, two girls about
fifteen years old placed an open kettle on the ground and used it as
a resonator; they bent down and breathed words or syllables into
it. Their rhythmic, aspirated breathing cleverly imitated the sound
of tools, among them the saw and the drill, which they had heard
on a trip to the Hudson's Bay Company Post.

This music of Eskimo women and girls is probably the most
primitive type of music in existence. The songs I recorded were
in a fast, even duple rhythm, so regular and driving that to my
ears they resembled the chugging of a train. This panting music

is also known in certain South Sea islands but it must be among the rarest musical effects in the world.

Storytelling, like singing and dancing, helps pass the time when the Eskimos are confined to their igloos. Sitting around on the skins spread over the *iglerk*, the sleeping bench of packed snow about one foot higher than the floor, the men smoke—one pipe sometimes passing clockwise from mouth to mouth. The women nurse their babies or chew skins, and the children sit on the blanket of skins listening intently. The elders are strict in insisting that the stories be told and learned correctly.

The storyteller, usually a respected older man, tells his tales with great deliberation and with many gestures and grimaces to suit the narrative: big eyes when the owl talks, peeping around among the rocks when the lemming is chatting to the weasel, showing wild excitement for the walrus hunt. All the birds and animals have their own story songs, so that it takes many days and nights to sing and talk through the whole cycle. From the men's hunting experiences and accurate observations the habits and customs of the animals—the clever ones, the strong ones, the stupid ones—are explained and taught by means of story and song to the children.

Ashivoo, a great singer of hunting songs who belonged to the Caribou Eskimos, lived at Baker Lake in the Barren Grounds, west of Hudson Bay, where an old Eskimo culture was well preserved. It is believed locally that the hills west of Baker Lake were the favorite meeting place of the aboriginals. There were, until recently, four groups of Barren Grounds Eskimos and they literally live from one hunt to another, depending entirely upon caribou and fish for food, clothing, bedding, and tents; when the herds are frightened away from their ancient migration routes, the Caribou Eskimos face starvation. This barren country is wide open. The hunter has only scant cover behind which he can hide when pursuing his prey. Nowadays he uses a telescope, which has become almost as essential as a gun. When he sights a caribou, however, he resorts to primitive stalking methods despite his modern weapons. He will spend hours imitating the grazing motions of the caribou, crawling along on the tundra with arms and gun raised in imitation of the animal's horns until he is within shooting range.

Starvation conditions are so common in these regions of the

Arctic that the people have developed a stoic calmness in the face of almost continual privation; it is small wonder that so many of their songs have to do with hunger, like this one:

> We were very hungry, our voices were weak,
> We were too weak to go out on the hunt
> But we went hunting.
> We shot two large caribou with much fat on them.

I found this song as well as the other music of the Caribou Eskimos to be even more primitive than that of the Hudson Bay people.

The religion of the inland Eskimos also differs from that of the sea people. Since the very precariousness of their living and the harshness of the continual struggle for survival allow them little time for anything else, there are fewer taboos to be observed here; even the customs regarding birth and death are much more simple.

The Barren Grounds Eskimos are far from the sea. However, when we were there, we found stories and songs of the sea that clearly indicated some contact with coast Eskimos. There was, for instance, the song about the polar bear that tried his strength against a bull caribou . . . and the girl who married a whale . . . and many others.

Although there are no tribes among Eskimos, there are distinct dialect or linguistic areas but no powerful chieftains as with most American Indians. The shamans or angekok (medicine men) appear to be the nearest thing to public officials in an Eskimo group. They are both priest and physician. Through the help of the spirits shamans, usually male, but sometimes female, are thought to bring aid to unsuccessful hunters. The shamans also diagnose the causes of misfortune and illness and intervene between the people and the spirits. They intercede directly with the spirits when bad weather prevents the hunters from getting seals and other game and when starvation threatens.

The usual procedure is for the shaman, in a trance, to utter phrases and produce songs that influence the gods in the desired way. Beside the much-feared sea goddess, who must be kept constantly appeased, the god of the winds and the god of storms are all-powerful. The gods of the sun, Venus, and the moon are also vitally important to these people—especially that of the moon, which is believed to bring luck to hunters and fertility to women.

Even on Southampton Island, where the outside world has brought changes to his pattern of living, the Eskimo still cherishes amulets. One boy we saw was wearing no less than eighty charms, including miniature whips to drive away evil spirits, the claws of the white owl, the front teeth of caribou to bring luck on the caribou hunt, and a musk-ox tooth for luck during salmon trout fishing.

The Eskimo also had charms for his songs. For example, the skin of the Lapland bunting, fastened in the neck of a coat, is thought to inspire good words for the composition of harpoon songs. One of these charm songs for hunters was translated for me as:

> How shall I do it?
> The animals were not influenced
> By my song when I sang it.

On Southampton Island the shaman recorded for me a conjurer's song which dealt with the intrusion of outside religion into the Eskimo tradition. The shaman made this song just after he had emerged from a trance.

> Before they came to this religion
> They used to meet with strange things
> Not seen by ordinary people.
> The land moved . . . the rocks moved . . .
> They used to meet with strange, strange things. . . .

Music and the primitive poetry expressed through it are an important form of Eskimo art. Because their song texts are so meager, the audience is expected to be familiar with the subject and to fill in most of the meaning. Difficult though it was for me sometimes to grasp their meanings, the songs I recorded frequently contained profound and beautiful poetry, expressing the deepest thoughts and moods of these isolated people when traveling, while hunting in solitude in the icy wastes, or when back once more in the warmth and safety of a tent or an igloo.

The dance songs were sung not only as a pleasant diversion, as an expression of joy, or as gratitude for a successful hunt, but in adversity were sung and danced as consolation for the sorrowing, to bring hope to the downcast, and as supplication to

the gods. The longer one remains with the Eskimo the more one
realizes the power of his basic religion. Among some Eskimo
groups there is always a moment of mute thanksgiving after the
hunt. Ravenous though the hunters may be, the group will crouch
about the body of the dead animal, and the one who killed it
will make an incision in the body, draw out the liver, and offer
a silent prayer of gratitude to whatever god blessed and rewarded
the hunt. Only then is this delicacy, believed to house the soul
of the animal, shared equally among them.

The Eskimo is not by nature voluble. Despite his ever-growing
contact with the outside, his motorboats, his cigarettes, and his
windbreakers, he is still a nomadic hunter and an unpredictable,
charming creature.

Only when he sings do we learn something of what goes on
in his mind; only through his rhythmic recounting of personal
experiences can we gain an insight into his stoic life, into his
inner feelings which he would be totally at a loss to express to us
except in song.

Of all the music I recorded throughout the Arctic during the
course of three journeys, none was more revealing to me than
the Eskimo's songs of rivalry. These songs of derision are extremely important, acting as a form of contest between men who
have become enemies. They perform a vital social function within
the group by providing an outlet for pent-up anger. The men
speak their minds in texts that are completely ruthless, abusive,
and rude, but ridicule always predominates and the singer is required to be entertaining and amusing. As far as I could see,
friendship was usually restored in the end. How enlightened it
is to settle disputes by song!

It is not uncommon for a wrestling match to begin between
rivals in the middle of a song dance, and this quickly becomes
a formal contest—a primitive form of jujitsu brought with the
Eskimos from Siberia. It lasts until one or the other of the com-
batants has fallen and been pinned to the ground, but more
often until both are too exhausted to continue any longer.

The Eskimo has a wonderful word, a phrase really, which seems
to embrace his attitude to the whole of existence in this vast
white expanse which shuts him off from the rest of the world.

"*Kooyannah ayornamut!*"

So complex, so tightly condensed is the language of these people that only a loose translation is ever possible. "*Kooyannah ayornamut*" was explained to me as: "It doesn't matter" or "It cannot be helped." This phrase seems to cover their inbred resignation to the overriding elements which always have the final word in anything they do.

"*Kooyannah ayornamut!*" covers a hunting accident, a drowning, the death of a child (buried in the snow under heavy stones to protect it from the ever-ravenous huskies), and even the rifling of some precious cache of food by an unknown traveler (a rare occurrence). If an Eskimo is the equivalent of our ne'er-do-well or sponger, he will rarely be criticized by his own kind; he merely "did not hunt or trap this year." When there is no food or clothing for his wife and children, some group member will sooner or later take them in.

Eskimos may be considered primitive by many, but I wonder . . . It seems to me that any people who have evolved a culture in which personal disputes, jealousies, and angers can be solved through song reveal a richly civilized attitude we might do well to study.

I remember one incident on a morning during the summer of 1942. Whenever we were at a post between stints of filming or collecting material, we would gather in an inner room for the eagerly awaited two hours each day when the post was in touch with the outside by radio. The war was then at a crucial stage, the battle of Stalingrad.

In the big community room beyond, Eskimos were coming and going, and one or two of the more curious stood in the doorway, fascinated, as always, by the white man's behavior. At last one of them, unable to contain his curiosity, inquired what it was that held us all there listening so intently to a voice from the outside.

With infinite patience the post manager began to explain. There was a terrible war going on; many men were fighting each other with guns, many guns. Many people were being killed, and we listened because we wished to know how the fighting was going.

The Eskimo's impassive brown face was a picture of bewilderment. We looked at one another, vaguely self-conscious. How could anyone explain the malignancy of civilized warfare to one of these placid, naïve people, whose only battle in life was against the elements? How could we explain this hideous, organized orgy

of violence to men who for untold ages had settled their disputes
in lusty song, more often than not re-establishing friendship in
the last verse?

The post manager was doing his best, but when his voice
ceased, the Eskimo still lingered outside the door, his face clouded
with an effort to understand, his eyes studying each of us in
turn, seeking some sign that might make some sense of the whole
matter.

Suddenly, after he had exchanged a few quiet words with a
friend, he turned to us and we knew that he was about to speak
for the other.

It was a question at once so simple and so complex that everyone in the room knew there could be no really adequate answer.
He said simply: "What do men fight about?"

Chapter 24

FLIGHT TO THE ALASKAN ARCTIC

In 1946, when I went to Point Barrow on the Alaskan Arctic Ocean to work among the Eskimos there under the auspices of the U. S. Department of the Interior, I was thrilled to feel that I was with fellow Americans. I found western Eskimo life quite different from that of the eastern Arctic: in the Alaskan Arctic I found a more complex social organization with formal partnerships between individuals for mutual aid, well-organized whale-hunting crews, and inherited obligations among families. Life is more rugged in the east, where the Eskimo lives much as he did when he came across the Bering Strait from Siberia thousands of years ago.

Alaska was bought in 1867 by the United States from Russia for $7,200,000. It was referred to as "Seward's Folly" or "Seward's Icebox," since it was through the determined energy of the Secretary of State, William H. Seward, that the purchase was made. As early as the 1870s missionaries had considerable influence on the arctic dwellers and it was due to one of them, Sheldon Jackson, that reindeer were introduced to help provide an adequate food supply for the Alaskan Eskimos, whose livelihood had been in jeopardy due to the wanton destruction of the fur seals. The United States government built frame houses for the Eskimos, and schools and churches where they taught them the customs and lore of the "outside." However, Eskimo culture is so deeply ingrained that outside influences were, I felt, only skin-deep. Their language remained intact, although great numbers of them spoke

some English since they had been under the care of our government for many years. They still made kayaks and umiaks for summer travel, built igloos when hunting in the winter months, and
depended on dog teams for moving about on the snow and ice
that covers their land for so much of the year. It was interesting
to see the old and the new side by side, the sledge and dog team
drawn up beside a small airplane on skis on the frozen tundra.

I had been lecturing as the Walker Ames Lecturer at the University of Washington in Seattle. A wealthy man had, in memory
of his wife, set up a fund which permitted the university to
invite visiting professors from abroad; I was not from abroad, and
I was apparently the first woman to be invited by this foundation;
it was one of my happiest experiences. From Seattle, I proceeded
to Point Barrow on the Arctic Ocean with a young assistant on
a series of fantastic plane journeys on the Alaskan project.

John Klebe, my assistant, was a very talented young man who
had been in my class at the University of Washington and was so
fired up with enthusiasm for the type of work I was doing that
he begged to go with me when I was leaving the university
for the Alaskan Arctic. I told him that if he could get his professors
to agree that the field work would be more beneficial to him than
staying in Seattle and pursuing his classes, I would be delighted
to have his assistance as my cameraman. Permission was granted
and he turned out to be not only an excellent cameraman but
the best secretary I have ever had.

Our northbound flight on McKinley Airlines from Seattle to
Anchorage was a spectacular experience. We flew among dazzling
snow-capped mountains which stretched out in every direction,
with that proud giant, Mount McKinley, the highest point on our
continent, towering above the other peaks in all its beauty.

We were sandwiched in the plane amid huge dogs sleeping on
piles of bananas, boxes of frilly dresses and high-heeled shoes,
and bunches of cut flowers, the latter ordered by a prospector
who wanted to please his girl. There were also celery, beans,
onions, greens, carrots, butter, and eggs for appetites weary of the
normal diet of reindeer meat, and such furnishings as lamps, tables,
and chairs.

Anchorage, although then much smaller than it is now, was
very lively and full of vigorous, adventurous men and women who
foresaw the great future Alaska held. These stalwart souls were

excited by the challenge of frontier life where every enterprise—economic, social, or cultural—was a tremendously thrilling undertaking. Fortunes could be made overnight with a little imagination and a lot of hard work.

We flew on to Fairbanks, practically on the Arctic Circle, where I spoke at the young University of Alaska, three miles west of Fairbanks on College Hill, an elevation which commands a magnificent view of the Tanana Valley, the center of Alaska's agricultural and mining teaching activities, and Mount McKinley. Now it has become a large accredited university, but even then, while still an infant institution, founded in 1915, the sizable catalogue (1946–47) indicated very active departments in many fields—not only mining, agriculture, aeronautical engineering, medicine, anthropology, and other scientific and practical subjects, but also liberal arts courses that were well designed to provide a richer life after graduation. The young people came from many states, and I learned of the healthy and happy enthusiasm of the students through one of them, the daughter of my friends, General and Mrs. Simon Bolivar Buckner. The General, during World War II, had played an active part in the war in the North Pacific and Alaska, and had become so inspired by the vision of the great future in store for Alaska that he had bought large holdings and planned to spend much of his future life in this fast-growing and stimulating part of the world. His early death prevented the fulfillment of that plan. When I lectured in the university's music department, I was delighted to discover what an excellent curriculum was offered. I spoke also at the splendid radio station which had been built by the oldest active citizen of Anchorage. Very early he had envisioned a great future for this land and had built several very successful business enterprises, a good hotel, and the excellent radio station, perhaps at that time the only one practically on the Arctic Circle.

In planning this project Oscar Chapman, Assistant Secretary of our Department of the Interior, had wisely arranged for the most famous bush pilot in the Far North to fly us from Anchorage to Point Barrow. Noel Wien was a remarkable man. He was sky messenger for all Alaskans and was highly respected by everybody. One might not guess from his smiling blue eyes and his youthful expression that he could land or take off on any spot of land, ice, or water. His manner was imperturbable and reassuring. Everything about him made me feel that here was a responsible man who could be completely depended on no matter what the situation. His movements were deliberate and exact. His small air service later grew into the major airline in the Far North—no wonder, for he was an excellent businessman as well as the best pilot in the Territory. When we met Wien in Anchorage he told us with his characteristic shy smile that there would be several stops en route to Point Barrow on the Arctic Ocean as he was the only link with the outside world for most of that area, especially inland communities of the north. I was delighted with this news and thoroughly enjoyed meeting the Eskimos who rushed out to meet our small plane, even when the stop was only long enough to leave a mailbag and a few boxes of necessary supplies.

I knew that there would be stops at Tanana, Bettles, and Wiseman en route to Point Barrow, but I little realized what actually lay ahead. There was one stop that not even Wien had anticipated. He received word by radio that a tiny plane carrying a new schoolteacher and a postmaster to Point Barrow had had to make a forced landing on a remote sandpit on the Koyukuk River. Fortunately they had been able to radio their plight to Anchorage, and we were requested to pick them up and take them to Point Barrow with us. It never occurred to me, with Wien as my pilot, to worry about landing on this tiny spot completely surrounded by towering spruce trees where it seemed that nothing but a helicopter could take to the sky again. We not only landed safely on this pinpoint of land, but by some miracle, we also emerged from the forest. We flew in the direction of Bettles, named for an early prospector who was among the 80,000 people who had stampeded into this area at the time of the 1898 Klondike Gold Rush.

It was late afternoon when we left the sandspit and headed toward Bettles, where one lonely soul manned a weather station. He was obviously not expecting his mail that day, as this was an unscheduled call, and we found that his housekeeping left much to be desired. He was a cordial host, however, and we had an extremely pleasant night at his small post. When the trim young schoolteacher saw the pile of dishes covering the sink, stove, and shelves of the room that served as kitchen, dining room, and sitting room, she looked at me aghast. In unison, without a word, we rolled up our sleeves and started washing dishes and cleaning up the place while our host stirred up the fire in the big stove. In no time we were seated around a shining table with steaming pancakes and coffee. He regaled us with amusing tales of his life alone in the Arctic and seemed perfectly content with his lot.

The town of Bettles is thirty-eight miles by trail and ninety miles following the bends of the Koyukuk River from the nearest post that has outside contacts. Where the river joins the John River there were about a dozen houses on a small flat space eight feet above the river, with a tiny store which is the social center of the town. There were few people and there was very little activity while we were there.

The most entertaining stop on our journey to Point Barrow was eighty-five miles farther up the Koyukuk at Wiseman. I am told that about a hundred people came to this post to do their trading, but most of them were living miles out in the bush and the settlement was very lonely. The nearest doctor or hospital was 150 miles away and not even the steamboats could proceed the distance from Bettles to Wiseman.

Wiseman is within that imaginary line known as the Arctic Circle and there are thirty-one consecutive days when the sun can never be seen, from December 7 through January 6. In midsummer, when the midnight sun should be visible for at least two weeks, the high mountains that completely surround the town block its direct light and warmth. Even so, when the sun is shining, the Eskimos who come and go for trading chant cheerfully about the joys of summer, and the children especially are full of excitement when the arctic winter ends.

Around the old Wiseman roadhouse, at the mouth of Wiseman Creek, the little mining town had sprung up. Food, clothing, and whisky for the miners were brought into it and there was a boom for a short period. The old-timers told me that in those booming years hundreds of thousands of dollars' worth of gold poured out, and fortune seemed waiting for everyone. Whisky flowed like water and the miners squandered thousands on prostitutes. By 1916 the richest claims had been worked out, prohibition went into effect, and World War wages attracted many energetic men to the outside. The last prostitute left in 1919, and only a few sturdy souls remained in the Koyukuk area, half of them foreign-born. They had come in search of gold from Ireland, Germany, Norway, Sweden, Herzegovina, England, Austria, Wales, the Shetland Islands, Finland, Poland, Lithuania, Dalmatia, Serbia, Montenegro, Greece, and Canada.

This tiny community regarded Noel Wien, the first aviator to land in the Alaskan Arctic, as one of the greatest heroes of the world. Since we were traveling with him, we had an immediate and most cordial welcome. When we arrived most of the miners were prospecting. Aside from the postman and his wife, who had been sent from Washington, D.C., the remaining inhabitants were thirteen old miners whose ages ranged from eighty-five to ninety-six, but they were the lustiest old men I have ever seen. I always thought of this ghost town when I heard the song made famous by Dinah Shore; ". . . there were thirteen men and only one gal in town." That these men had survived the rigors of life within the Arctic Circle was a miracle to me, but they were still going out with pick and screening pan whenever the weather permitted, still hoping to strike it rich—the dream that had brought them from faraway lands long ago. From time to time they found a nugget or two which kept them supplied with food for a few weeks or months. One tall handsome Virginian had preserved a kind of elegance. His snowy-white hair and mustache were carefully trimmed and brushed, and he wore his somewhat ill-fitting clothes with a kind of swank style. He was very cordial but his friendliness did not include, or permit, allowing his picture to be taken. I have always wondered what personal tragedy had kept him in this frozen isolation. He was also the only one who, although fluent in conversation about the North, seemed to balk at any mention of the past. On the other hand, an old German, Carl Frank, ninety-two years of age, was extremely talkative and created for me, through salty reminiscences, a wonderful picture of his frontier days and of his early life when he played in the band of Emperor Franz Josef in Austria.

While I was interviewing these intrepid old miners, John was at my elbow taking down in shorthand their unbelievable tales, colorful jokes, and philosophical conversations. John could type as fast as I could talk, so we were able to keep up with the notes of the journey—a rare achievement. On previous expeditions the notes, cataloguing, labeling, and compiling of essential information mounted up to such a degree that even by working far into the night I found it almost impossible to keep abreast of the paper work involved. I must say, in this Arctic "ghost town" I was very glad to have John's protective presence to divert the attention of these lively octogenarians who had probably not seen a young blonde for more than twenty years.

From Bettles to Point Barrow the flight was without incident. It was summertime when we arrived, so the weather was comfortable. Two-thirds of Alaska lies below the Arctic Circle and has temperatures that compare with other parts of the United States. For example, the weather bureau has reported a summer temperature of ninety-nine degrees Fahrenheit at Fairbanks. Even though the winter is longer at Point Barrow on the Arctic Ocean the lowest winter temperature is slightly above the lowest records of North Dakota, Wyoming, and Montana. The summer heat in the Arctic is usually humid, and much to the surprise of some visitors, the mosquitoes are a real plague. Actually, the mosquitoes survive in spite of the fact that the temperature goes to seventy degrees below zero in the winter. But anyone who has visited the Adirondacks, where it can be fifty degrees below zero, knows that the mosquitoes can be bad there, too.

En route we had been observing Alaskan Eskimos and their houses—modern frame buildings, log cabins, or sod houses which when covered with snow in the winter look like igloos. Around Point Barrow in the old days the Eskimos built the frames of these earthen houses from driftwood, and the covering earth made them comparatively warm. The ventilating hole in the roof assured a constant circulation of air through the house, but with three seal-oil lamps the temperature could be kept at eighty degrees in the daytime, dropping to possibly sixty degrees at night.

The Eskimo's own type of house was much better suited to his environment than the modern frame houses that became the fashion after white men introduced them. The new ones were larger, draftier, flimsier, and let the cold in more readily than the warm, cozy sod houses. Whether the Eskimos lived in the old-type houses or modern ones, they all lived in tents for the summer, formerly of skins but later made of canvas. When I was there, some of the sophisticated people were beginning to live in houses all through the summer, which was believed to be the reason for the high tuberculosis rate.

All Eskimo activities centered along the beach. It was from the beach that the hunters took off in their kayaks to hunt seal or, from where in winter, the family started off over the ice by dog team. The umiak in Alaska was thirty-five to forty feet long and could carry as many as sixty or seventy people. This large canoe took several families when they wanted to move about by sea. When the sea was frozen the sleds were essential, pulled by Eskimo dogs which are related to the chow and Siberian husky.

Early missionaries and schoolteachers planted small vegetable gardens for their own needs and gradually interested the Eskimos in agriculture. The growing season is short, reckoned by weeks, but it is sufficiently long, reckoned by hours of sunshine. In June there is daylight for twenty-four hours a day. Since plants grow according to the amount of sun they receive, rather than the number of days they are growing in the ground, the vegetables and flowers flourish. There are records of an eighteen-pound cabbage, a seven-pound cauliflower, a twelve-pound turnip, a three-pound head of lettuce, a two-pound potato, and peas that grow as large as cherries. More than a hundred species of wild flowers and at least fifty varieties of cultivated flowers thrive in the brief, hot summer. Although the favorite food for the Eskimo is caribou, seal, or fish, vegetables are standard diet now.

The walrus and whale hunts are still important to the Eskimos, and they still use the harpoon, but now instead of hurrying after the harpooned animals in kayaks, the modern Eskimos go in pursuit in motorboats. They still wear high boots, *mukluks* made from sealskin, and the Eskimo women must spend a great deal of time chewing and sewing the skins as in the eastern Arctic. Reindeer or caribou hides provide warm mukluks, parkas, and mittens, and, of course, their meat is very much prized.

Point Barrow at the top of the globe is the northernmost point in Alaska. It is five hundred miles northwest from Fairbanks as the planes fly. It was named after Sir John Barrow, a great patron of exploration, but is still known as Navuk, meaning "the point," to the natives. Point Barrow is twelve miles north of Barrow, which has a post office, a settlement, and an important trading post. An excellent store was run for many years by Charlie Brower, who resided there from 1884 until his death in the early 1940s. His son David took over the store and was doing an excellent job when I was there. Charlie Brower was one of the most famous men in Alaska and a warm friend of everyone who ever visited Barrow. Many explorers tell affectionate stories about him.

The few trading vessels that called at Barrow when the water was open were unloaded on to lighters or barges, and the store at Barrow was well equipped to supply the needs of whites and Eskimos throughout a large area. Formerly all travel around Point Barrow in winter was by dog sled, but when I was there the chief means of travel was the airplane.

Barrow stands on subsoil that is permanently frozen; storage chambers are dug that will keep meat fresh for years. The summer thaw goes down from six to eighteen inches into the tundra; this topsoil is extremely fertile. The meadows of grass, that formerly supported vast herds of caribou, supported growing herds of reindeer. When I was there, Barrow had three herds, owned locally and supervised by the Department of Indian Affairs. The waters were rich with animal and plant life.

The United States government school at Barrow was the northernmost school of the United States, Canada, or Greenland, although the Soviet Union was said to have some schools farther north. The Presbyterian mission was well established, and the government hospital, built in 1939, was doing an excellent job.

I had missed the coming of spring to Alaska, which is pure magic. The snow melts and disappears practically overnight, and you can actually smell the thawing things. But I was fortunate that winter found me still at Point Barrow, and I watched the ocean slowly icing in our world. It was there that I had my first experience riding on a sled behind an excellent team of huskies. It was marvelous. After I learned how to stay on, I had time to admire the delicate technique of the driver, with his hand full of skin lead lines that went out to every dog, and the skillful handling of the walrus-hide whip with which he could flick the ear of the lead dog far out in front, or, for that matter, of any dog that got out of line.

As I had been in the eastern Arctic during Eskimo summer, that glorious period of relief from the rigors of the long winter night, winter life at Point Barrow was new and exciting to me. This was the time for music and dancing.

The music of the Alaskan Eskimos, like that of other Eskimo groups, is almost entirely vocal. In 1946 they had only one kind of musical instrument, a tambourine-like drum that was similar to that of the Hudson Bay Eskimos. But the Point Barrow drum was smaller, with a diameter of about two feet. In the Hudson Bay region one drum only was used, and was played by the dancer, but in Alaska as many as five drums might be played together to accompany group songs and dances. The musicians moisten the membranes to tune them, but when two or more were played as an orchestra, there was apparently no attempt made to tune them to each other.

In spite of the fact that missionary hymns and popular songs picked up from traders, soldiers, and government men have been brought in from the outside, these northern people had preserved much of their own music. There was a large repertory of secular songs, especially game songs, but the songs of magic had almost disappeared. Many songs were about birds, animals, the aurora borealis, and subjects connected with their everyday life. The game songs accompanied cat's-cradle games and ball games, and had been handed down generation after generation apparently with little change.

There were many dance songs but they were composed, flourished temporarily, and often died within a year or two, much like our own popular music. Sometimes the tunes were old with new words added for a special event or person. Occasionally there were words with meaning, but more often nonsense syllables were sung, like "ai ya yanga," which might be sustained on the same note over several successive beats, ending with a staccato "ya!"

Most singers had their own songs with lines they themselves had composed. One man, when asked how many songs he had, answered: "I have many. Everything in me is song. I sing as I breathe." Another singer said: "Music makes the old young, and the drum is the beating heart." Another old Eskimo said: "To stop the Eskimo singing and dancing is like cutting the tongue out of a bird."

One night at a dance in Point Barrow I recorded the best drummers of the settlement with the picturesque names of Joe Sikvayunak, Otis Ahkivigak, Guy Amiyuruk, Willie Silak, Alfred Koonaloak and Leo Kaleak, who was the leader. Their drums were different from Eevaloo's on Southampton Island. Some had reindeer skin stretched over a wooden hoop; others had whale liver for drumheads; and one had a walrus stomach. The drum handles were made of wood, reindeer antler, or walrus ivory. All of them produced deep resonant tones and insistent rhythms that were very exciting to both listeners and singers. Indeed, Point Barrow's whole population of 120 families tried to get into the little dance house for this boisterous occasion. Dancing appeared inseparable from drumming and singing.

The vocal technique is the characteristic which gives any music its individual quality, and among the Alaskan Eskimo singers at Point Barrow we heard the forceful mode of attack and the pulsations on a single note—held through several beats—that are also characteristic of the music of the American Indians of our Southwest. Research workers in Greenland have found that a definite connection exists between the music of Alaska and Greenland. The conclusion is that the musical culture moved from Alaska to Greenland and that the various different local styles of Eskimo music throughout the Arctic have their origin in the same basic style. Much of the shared culture is explained by a west–east population drift that began from northern Alaska about A.D. 900.

Joe Sikvayunak was one of the best singers in Point Barrow and was always accompanied by a good drummer. The titles of the dance songs he recorded for me might easily be from our "top ten": "I Am Lonesome," "When I Feel Like Singing, I Sing," "I Am Waiting for the Boat to Come," "I Will Show You the Way," and "It Was a Very Lovely Day When the Water Was Calm."

I was fortunate, too, in being able to record songs from one of Point Barrow's rare festivals: the Inviting-in or Messenger Feast, so-called because messengers were sent to invite other villages to be present. This was held in the *kazgi* (in Point Barrow called the *karigi*) which in a few places still served as the communal house of the settlement: clubhouse, town hall, sweat bathhouse, and dancing pavilion all in one. It was the center of Eskimo life. It had one entrance for the shamans and the dancers and another for the public.

About forty years ago this was the procedure. The principal host of the Inviting-in Feast had to save up for years for this privilege, for it was his responsibility to feed the whole crowd for the first day of the festival. The spirits, too, were thought to sit about and enjoy the dances given in their honor, and offerings of meat and drink were placed especially for them. The host was often quite impoverished at the end of it, but he had gained much fame and prestige, and all his guests were forever obligated to him. It was apparently a voluntary gesture; the host or head simply announced his intention to hold a feast and sent messengers out over vast distances with invitations to other Eskimos of other settlements. Before the guests arrived, songs and dances were rehearsed. In some villages the songs belonged exclusively to one old man who "sold" them to different dancers, as well as teaching the people proper dances for the festival. Weeks were spent in learning the songs; every intonation had to be exact. The chorus consisted of five or six men led by an old man; everyone joined in after the song began.

At the feast each group presented its best performers who tried to outsing and outdance one another. Masks were worn, some to amuse the guests, some to honor the spirits of the animal for which the dance was being given. Dances varied from the comic dances of the first day through others more serious, impressive, and graceful. The dances of the third day were devoted entirely to portraying animals. Finally the shaman danced until he fell down in a trance. When he came to, he announced that the spirits had been placated. The ceremony ended with offerings of meat, drink, and tobacco given to the spirits through a crack in the floor. Now a very abbreviated form of the old ceremony takes place, for some objected to it as too "pagan." But fortunately the songs remain and these I recorded.

Chapter 25

THE QUEEN CHARLOTTE ISLANDS AND
THE NORTHWEST COAST INDIANS

In 1942 on my first trip to the Northwest, I worked on a project called "Peoples of Canada" for the Canadian government during which I recorded and filmed several Pacific Coast Indian tribes—primarily the Haida. Close relatives of the Tsimshian and Tlingit tribes on the mainland, most of the Haida live on the Queen Charlotte Islands off the coast of southern Alaska about forty miles northwest of British Columbia, of which they are a part. Actually my work with them nearly came to an abrupt end when the Japanese war planes swooped down on the Aleutian Islands not far away. Everyone thought they would keep on to invade not only the naval installations on the Queen Charlotte Islands but also the West Coast of Canada. The admiral in charge was reluctant to let us remain in the islands, but I persuaded him to allow us to finish our project there. Fortunately the Japanese came no nearer—no one knows the reason; perhaps they were getting too far from their base of supplies.

One hundred and fifty years ago, before the advent of the whites, the Haida and neighboring tribes scoured the coast on war or trading expeditions in canoes fifty or sixty feet in length, carved from trunks of giant cedar, spruce, or hemlock trees. The vessels were beautifully decorated. One canoe could carry a huge war party strong enough to conquer a whole village. The canoe was to the Northwest Coast tribes what the horse became to the Plains Indians. In their boats they fished for salmon in fiords and rivers, traded with friendly people, and raided the settlements of hostile tribes.

They were called the "Vikings of the North Pacific," and tales of their prowess were used to frighten little children into being good. Those days of dueling and raiding are over and the Pacific Coast Indians are adapting themselves to a new era. Now all the timber is in the hands of large companies, and their canoes no longer skim through the waters. The sea is still teeming with fish but now the Indians have to share the catch with Scandinavians, Finns, and Japanese, whose large seines scoop up fish for canneries and for producing oil and fertilizer.

In the old days the Indians fished not only for salmon but for halibut, which they sliced and dried on large racks. The fish eggs of the herring and seaweed were dried for winter use. In the autumn when salmon cohoe and humpback choked the streams, they were either speared or trapped in great quantities to be dried for later consumption. In the summer and early autumn the women gathered berries, which they cured and stored in boxes. Wild roots were eaten, and after 1791, when white fur traders introduced the potato it was added to their diet. Although on the Queen Charlotte Islands there was no game to hunt, ducks and geese were plentiful as well as seal, sea lion, and porpoise. Hunting, wild-berry, and fishing territories were strictly owned by families, even the deep-sea areas.

Today the Indians work with the whites in the canneries at Massett and Skidegate or on the mainland, and the patience and thoroughness of the women make them especially reliable. The men have become good mechanics; they build houses and boats, operate engines, and have uncanny ability as sailors.

Originally the Haidas lived in rows of houses of red cedar that lined the beaches. In front of each house a fifty-foot totem pole stood, and at its base was an opening four feet high which provided an entrance into the one large room where the dwellers worked and slept. There was a fireplace in the middle, and a hole in the roof, which could be opened or closed with a trap door, served as a chimney. Twenty or thirty similar houses with their totem poles made an imposing picture as one approached the old Haida villages from the sea. In former days many canoes lined the beach, and people were busy making canoes, paddles, long spears, bows and arrows, and fishing gear. But when we visited these deserted villages, the beaches were abandoned, the dilapidated houses were gray with age, the totem poles were in a sad state of disrepair.

53. Navajo "yebitshao" (night chant) musicians with the medicine man at

54. *Los Voladores* Flying Pole Dance

55. Yaqui Deer Dancer

56. Houngan making the *vevers*

57. Author recording Haitian singers

58. Recording peasant harvest songs

59. Zoltàn Kodàly

Rudi Vig

60. Author with the King of the gypsies

61. Ancient monastery near Trabzon, Turkey

Ara Güler

62. Author recording Easter liturgy in the patriarchate

63. Emperor Haile Selassie

64. Dance of David
(sistrums in left hands)

65. Author recording Ethiopian orchestra

Wayne Fox

Wayne Fox

66. Musician playing "harp of David"

There were formerly many small towns, but most of these have long been abandoned. Out of the twenty-five important towns once occupied by large populations, only a few were inhabited when I was there. According to their own tradition their oldest towns are around the eastern shore of Moresby Island. After the discovery of the Queen Charlotte Islands in 1774, many expeditions came to trade for furs. Through smallpox and other diseases introduced with the coming of the white man, the native population was reduced to one-tenth of its former numbers. Haida villages have intriguing names like Skidegate, Massett, Uculelet, Tanoo, Skedans, and Cumshewa.

A few Indians still had houses in Uculelet, a typical village, when I visited it. The houses were large and squat, made of thick hand-hewn cedar planks held together by wooden pegs; the walls were of driftwood; bark weighted with stones made the roofs. Every house was separated from the next, and the wind roared through the narrow spaces between. The houses, like the people, were soaked with wind and rain and sometimes sunshine. Several families lived in each large house. They shared one door and one smoke hole, but each family had its own fire with its own possessions around it. The Indians seemed not to notice the smoke that filled the dim interior as they squatted on the earth floor, the men smoking, the women weaving cedar fibers into mats and guarding the papoose from the fire.

We visited Tanoo, Skedans, and Cumshewa, abandoned villages on Moresby, the southernmost large island of the Queen Charlotte group, to film the fascinating totem poles. Tanoo was typical of the old villages. All the houses lined the beach and had disintegrated, with only the corner posts and great beams remaining, and inside, where people had lived, elderberry bushes and scrub trees grew luxuriantly.

Many totem poles still stood to tell the stories that had been carved on them. One pole, which had at its base the figure of a man on whose tall hat a raven was perched (with many small figures of men climbing up the hat), told the story of a man who had adopted a raven as his son. The raven was wicked and brought a flood on his foster family. When the waters rose, all the man's relatives climbed up the rings of his hat and were saved from being drowned. It was expertly carved, bleached of all its former color, but covered with a beautiful yellowish-green mold.

Skedans was more open than Tanoo. The trees stood farther back from the houses in luxurious groves which in the rich moistness made a dense thicket. The wide beach was covered with driftwood and seaweed that had floated in from the sea. A row of totem poles circled the bay. Many were mortuary poles with coffin boxes on top carved with the crests of the chiefs of the Eagle, Bear, or Whale clan. They were often broken, and skulls were peering out through the cracks. The tall carved poles were of equal interest. Some bowed forward, others tipped back sternly, but no matter what the wind and weather had done to them, they never lost their dignity. They still sincerely expressed the strong feelings the Indian carvers had put into them.

Not many houses were left, but breaking through the growth we found the remnants of one. Stones blackened by fire were lying on the earthen floor. Sleeping benches ran around the wall.

All the villages have the West Coast wetness, but Cumshewa was always blurred in mist. Another typical village, it had only one street, where all the houses had faced the beach. A very impressive pole still stood mounted by a great carved raven, his wings flattened at his sides. His mate had sat on a pole a few feet from him, but she had rotted away and he sat alone, moss-covered and dilapidated. Strong young trees sheltered him from the winds that tore through the islands. He seemed to express a great lonesomeness. In spring, with the gay, brilliant blossoms about, one could imagine that these villages had been quite beautiful when filled with vital, cheerful Indians. Most of the houses had long since disintegrated, little streams ran under the planks, and weeds poked up through every crack, but the power and tremendous force behind the carvings of the totem poles were still present. The old-type houses were abandoned nearly a hundred years ago and now the Haidas live in modern houses, and the change from large, well-ventilated community houses to airtight modern ones has apparently not improved the health of the people.

The artists who had enriched the bare poles with carvings told things about the creatures, their relation to each other and to the families who erected the poles. Birds, animals, and fishes were linked together and made "strong talk" for the people. Through the totem poles the creatures and man were linked with supernatural beings. The animals were accepted as ancestors, but the supernatural beings were feared and had to be propitiated.

The totem poles were not pagan gods to be worshiped. Rather they were coats of arms like those of European nobility. The stories of the origins of the coats of arms were formerly chanted in tribal festivals; they explain how human-like animals appeared in a vision and then were depicted in the heraldry of the totem pole. The carvings on the memorial poles and house posts recount memorable events of past generations. The myths explain the origin of the family emblems.

Later in Vancouver I was fortunate to meet Emily Carr, who was one of the best artists in Canada. She gave me a whole new concept of Indian art. As a very young woman she had traveled in small Indian boats through the Queen Charlotte Islands to preserve through her art the amazing carved poles which had even then fallen into disrepair. When I met her she was about seventy years old and, although not well, insisted on bringing out dozens of her original paintings of Indians and totems because she was thrilled to find someone devoutly interested in "her" Haida Indians.

Klee Wyck (Laughing One), as the Indians called her, was a serious person, but she knew how to laugh, which always creates an immediate bond between people. She was born in Vancouver of English parents and loved Canada with deep loyalty. She always painted Canadian subjects with sincerity and courage, but it was only late in life that the indifference, and even at times hostility, of her friends and fellow Canadians was overcome and her distinguished work gained the recognition it deserved. Her paintings of Indians and totems have found their way into large museums, and her individual and distinctly personal style of presenting them have brought vivid attention to the vital art of the Indians.

Haida society was divided into two main clans, Raven and Eagle, with numerous subdivisions. Every clan and individual had a particular emblem, and the totem creatures were believed to help those who were of their emblem. When you saw a man's pole, his coat of arms told you who he was, whom he might or might not marry, and what sort of person he was since he tried to be like the creature of his symbol—fierce, brave, wise, or strong.

The Haidas are regarded as superior to other coast tribes in the arts as well as in war and trade. All of the Indians of the Northwest show remarkable imagination in their carving, weaving, and goldwork and silverwork. The Haidas, however, are the best carvers and painters; their designs have great power and their bold, exotic art is as fine as that of any primitive people in the world. (They earn considerable money by selling carved objects of wood and slate to traders.)

Totem poles, house posts with heraldic designs, names, myths, songs, and valued privileges were individual possessions owned by men of great wealth and they were passed on by blood lineage. The greatest of these were the nobility titles which were used as personal names and were said to come down "since the beginning of the world." When a person ceremoniously took such a name and the privileges that went with it, he assumed all the greatness of his ancestor. Great men owned immense quantities of goods—canoes, shells used as money, copper plates, goat's-hair blankets, mats, etc. These possessions might be loaned (100 percent interest was usual), but at the ceremonial feast called the Potlatch, they were distributed as gifts; etched sheets of native copper, for example, were valued as high as 10,000 blankets and more. The most frequent Potlatches were those given when a man took on the name and position and privileges of his deceased predecessor. This involved raising a totem pole, building a house, and the dramatization of his wealth and status in the tribe.

The Inviting-in Feast of the Point Barrow Eskimos is similar to the Potlatch ceremony, but the Northwest Coast Indian culture is unique in that the society was based on the public disposal of individual wealth through the Potlatch. The ceremony is characterized by the giving of gifts, especially copper plates and goat's-hair blankets, and custom demanded that a gift be accepted and an even larger and more valuable gift be given in return. The Potlatch, usually a series of feasts, was a public ceremony at which all the host's property was given away; this novel economic system in a primitive way kept the wealth of the tribe distributed. In his Potlatch a chief or important man dramatized his coat of arms, displayed his wealth, and gave names to his nephew. Whether the Potlatch was the occasion of the coming of age of his grandchild, or a marriage, a funeral, a demonstration of religious powers, or an intertribal challenge to a rival chief, the host used the occasion to assume a new name and all its prerogatives.

When a copper shield was bought or sold, the transaction was the occasion for a great formal Potlatch. In the days of tribal wars, a man who wished to organize a war party gave a Potlatch, and the acceptance of the gifts by the guests was a pledge of their support in the war. The Potlatch was even used at times to impoverish a disliked person. A chief could shame his rival by giving him more gifts than he could return with the required interest, or he could even destroy his own property—for example, his valuable copper pieces—to demonstrate to his rival his great wealth. In both cases a return gift was called for. A chief could not destroy property to the impoverishment of his people, however.

When a man decided to have a Potlatch he sent messengers forth to invite his tribe and neighboring tribes just as in the Inviting-in Feast. The host not only had to feed everyone for days and nights on end, but also had to give extravagant presents, heirlooms. Throughout his whole life he had saved blankets, copper shields, and so forth for this occasion and after the feast he was impoverished. But he had gained tremendous prestige and soon someone else would hold another feast and this time he would be on the receiving end.

At a Potlatch a family announced new claims to an increased social standing; the greater the rise and status, the greater the number of guests required as witnesses. The size of the Potlatches varied from small ones given for the first ceremony for naming the child, and confined to the mother's relatives, to those in which a man became chief of a large village—to which ruling families of all neighboring tribes were invited.

Great importance was attached to acquiring a name. These ceremonies continued throughout life and were held when children received ancestral names, when a son came of age and assumed the name of an ancestor on his mother's side, or whenever a man decided to take on the name and privileges of an ancestor. For the naming of a child, relatives and friends gathered and called on the great powers of the spirit world to give their blessing to its name.

At every Haida Potlatch the host was required to raise a totem pole, and the pole-raising might be the main event of the feast or only a part of it. A Haida nobleman would set up a pole to commemorate his predecessor on taking his name and privileges, and this Potlatch would end his period of mourning for the relative. The carved figures on the totem pole showed the lineage of the owner and the exploits of his ancestors. The pole was a tribute to them, and the birds and animals carved on it were creatures that tradition said had had a part in their adventures. As with all their paintings and sculpture, the totem had a purpose: It was an historical record and a means of communication and represented tribal myths as well. When the pole was raised, stories were told, songs were sung, and dramatizations of the traditions and history of the owners of the pole were performed. Only a wealthy man with many relatives to help him could undertake the raising of a totem pole, as it was expensive. The pole stood as a constant reminder of the wealth and prestige of the owners.

There were definite duties for his tribe and guest tribes to perform. The rough tree trunk was supplied by the owner, but it was highly improper for members of his lineage to do the carving. A skilled outside carver worked under the direction of the owner. When the totem pole was completed the host sent out invitations to the Potlatch. Neither the owner nor any member of his clan could take part in the digging of the hole or lifting it into place. This had to be done by guests who were not related to the owners. As the setting of the pole progressed, the host explained the figures on the pole, boasting of his and his ancestors' prestige, wealth, and brave exploits. In the former days a copper shield or a slave might have been placed in the hole, but more usually they were given away. Once a pole was in position it could not be repaired, repainted, or moved without a formal Potlatch with all its expense. Thus many poles have been allowed to decay and fall. This, however, does not affect the owner's reputation. In some cases the Canadian government has stepped in to preserve the beauty of these poles.

No large Potlatches are given at present. Today the Potlatch is a skeleton of the old procedures, and takes place only in name-taking and death ceremonies, and the whole village is invited regardless of tribe.

The economic contest began in childhood and continued throughout life. When a child was given his first important name, the elders of his family gave him blankets to distribute among his relatives. No one could refuse a gift and everyone who received a gift had to repay promptly with a larger gift (exorbitant interest). At the Potlatches which he gave or took part in as he grew older, he took greater names which indicated his family connections.

The ultimate reason why Northwest Coast Indians cared about the nobility titles, the wealth, the coat of arms, and so forth was that they used them in a contest in which they sought to shame their rivals. With age they chose more and more formidable rivals. "We do not fight with weapons, we fight with property," they said. A man who had given away a copper had overcome his rival as much as if he had defeated him in battle. A man called out in songs the names of the rivals he had vanquished by the distribution of property. To maintain his own status he gave out in song insults and ridicule to his enemies "to break their names."

The object of the host to show himself superior found expression in songs and speeches of self-glorification and ridicule of the guests invited to the Potlatch. For instance, he sang: "I am the great chief who makes people ashamed," or: "I am the only one among the tribes; I cannot find one chief among the guests with greatness like mine." Songs of self-glorification were sung on all great occasions. In song the host ridiculed and publicly scorned the guests for their poverty, their insignificance, and their inability to give back gifts as great as his.

My contact with everything and everyone—for information, photographs, songs, and dances—was an Indian named Captain Brown, and through him I learned about Haida life. He held a very important place in his tribe. He was a huge man and the most jovial Indian I ever met. He had worked with white men on boats and in the canneries; he spoke English fluently (his peculiar brand of English), and had an excellent voice. He knew the ritual songs and the old dance melodies, which he sang very correctly and with fervor.

It seemed that Captain Brown's word was law and whenever he asked anyone to sing and dance they appeared with great alacrity. It was Captain Brown and his family who sang the best songs. His wife knew beautiful lullabies, and his daughter had a large repetoire of love songs. Captain Brown explained to me the lore of the tribe, the meaning of their art, and the important function of music in their lives.

He also explained why most of the religious ceremonies as well as social activities took place during the winter months when the tribes gathered in their permanent winter villages. The hunting season was over, the food supply was stored away, and the trading trips were ended; they were free from work until the fish began to run in the spring. In these winter months the initiations of the secret societies took place because the natives believe that the spirits are very close to man during the winter. They call this season the "Time of Taboo," the time to acquire spirit powers and "power songs," which were very important in these ceremonies. The songs were dramatized by the owners of the songs assisted by special musicians. Power ceremonies for children gave them prestige and stronger spirit powers, but certain powerful spirits were acquired only by adults. In the secret societies the professional artists, composers of songs, and organizers of the dramatizations were men who had received special supernatural powers in the winter ceremonies.

Northwest Coast Indian songs are quite different from the songs of other Indian tribes: they are vastly more varied, more highly developed, and more poetic. The scales are more exotic, the melodic range is more extensive, and the themes richer. There are usually some meaningful words as well as nonsense syllables; this provides interesting historical and literary material, so they are valuable for their texts as well as for the melodies. They are often reminiscent of Asia and comparisons can be made with songs from Siberia. To quote Dr. Marius Barbeau, eminent authority on Northwest Indians: "Some of them resemble Chinese cradle songs or the songs of Chinese workers. The mourning songs like the Chinese dirges, often end with the refrain 'hayu, hayu' (alas, alas)."

This similarity is not surprising when we remember that the native tribes on our side of the Bering Strait are recent arrivals, having crossed the strait either in canoes or on the ice less than a thousand years ago. Around the twelfth century thousands fled eastward over the barren grounds, chased by Mongolian hordes. They crossed the northern waters, bringing with them their simple culture, including their songs and myths.

They had songs for lively games, manly war songs, Peace Dance songs, love songs and lullabies full of tenderness, fishing chants to charm the fishes into the nets, and lamentations and dirges for the dead. Among the most interesting music was the body of songs for the Potlatch, the house building, and the raising of totem poles —all winter festivals performed when they dramatized their coats of arms.

The fascinating Haida Potlatch dance songs which I recorded were accompanied by wooden drum with skin drumhead, sometimes whistles, and rattles—pieces of metal attached to the women's skirts in such a way that they clinked in rhythm with the dance step. The Haida were passionately fond of dancing and singing in connection with every ceremony, but they also had a large repertoire of songs performed for pure pleasure with no ritual or dancing involved. There were two classes of songs: community property, free for anybody to sing, and exclusive family possessions inherited and jealously guarded for the use of the rightful owners. An example of a song that was common property of the tribe was sung to me by Charlie Thompson, a fine singer. Charlie explained that the song was often sung when people gathered for amusement, while drinking and gambling—favorite pastimes of the Haidas. Charlie also sang some beautiful love songs—pleasant, graceful melodies sung by either men or women and distinctly rhythmic.

The most common songs belonging to families were war songs, property songs, cradle songs, and songs for making peace. Captain Brown and his wife sang a very old war song which included the words "Let it go, let it go," meaning the arrow. The Captain explained, "This is the war song I sing now. It was sung a hundred years ago. No guns at that time. The Indians in the north, you know, used the arrow. White people got guns but Indians got arrows. There were two or three hundred Indians—two or three hundred enemy. When time come to fight, they start song—war song they call it. Other people [the enemy] looking, looking— they lost their heads. Then they kill all other people, other side. That's the kind of song they call war song. We had wars before the white people come to us from the east. They taught us something good that we follow today. Today everything is well for all over the world. No trouble." Would this were true for our world as well as the Haida world!

Power songs were sung at a Potlatch to bring about a special result: for example, success in warfare, good hunting, or the proper weather for an ocean voyage. The war parties starting out in the large canoes always took a medicine man along to bring luck to the fighting or hunting or trading.

The songs of the Haida secret-society dances apparently came from the Tsimshian on the mainland, for they usually had Tsimshian words. The Haida also had a particular type of song sung with Tsimshian words composed to ridicule a man of low standing who tried to take the attitude of a chief. (There was a caste system: high, low, and slave.)

The Potlatch dance songs, an essential part of all Potlatch ceremonies, are probably the most interesting of all Haida music. The Potlatch called Si'ka, given only at the raising of a chief's grave post by the man inheriting his position, had particularly interesting dance songs. Captain Brown described to me the wild dancing which followed the feasting on the occasion of a Potlatch when a big house was built. The dancers dressed in fantastic apparel with beautifully decorated, fringed blankets around their shoulders and great carved headdresses of wood; some had painted faces, some wore carved masks. They danced with frenzy for long hours around the campfire until they collapsed. Whenever a Potlatch for erecting a house was given, there was much singing and dancing. Only a very wealthy man could afford to give this great feast with many guests. The cooperation of a large group of men was required to finish the house, so it was very expensive business. One of the most interesting songs I recorded was a part of this ceremony called "March into the House." Another interesting one was "The Young Man's Dance," part of the "Spring Dance." This spirited, vigorous music was among the most interesting I have recorded. It began, as is frequent in primitive music, on a high note and slowly descended a chromatic scale. The accompanying rhythms were produced by drum, rattles of deer hoofs or large puffin beaks, and pieces of metal attached to the skirts of the dancing women.

Dorothy Edgars, a fine Haida singer, recorded for me some melodious love songs and tossed in a few English words, indicating that these songs probably have developed since contact with English-speaking people. In one of them, a farewell song, she sang "Dear sweetheart" and "Good-by, my dearie" and closed with the English "Farewell, good night." From Captain Brown's wife I learned Haida lullabies which were charming and often set to lively melodies. Indian parents have deep affection for their children and they take great pride in their heirs, especially in the case of the chief. The lullabies, private property belonging to individual families, are inherited like the coats of arms and the carved totem poles.

I also found extremely interesting songs among other tribes of the Northwest, especially among the Tsimshian on the coast of

British Columbia and the Gitksan Indians at Hazelton, British Columbia. The Indian name for Hazelton, situated at the junction of the Skeena and Bulkley rivers, means "The People Who Spear Salmon by Torchlights." When gold was discovered there about 1890, many whites arrived and called it Hazelton because of the abundance of hazelnuts in the locality. The Gitksan (Carrier) Indians here belong to the Athabaskan group, so are related to the Navahos. It was extremely interesting to find riding songs which were reminiscent of riding songs I had formerly recorded with the Navahos in New Mexico. These lyric songs belong to a type known as the mountain love song on the upper Skeena River. One of them was sung for me by Abel Oaks, a Gitksan Indian who had also sung the same song for Dr. Marius Barbeau more than twenty years previously. Most of the syllables of the text are meaningless. The only meaningful words are in English: "Will you come?" and "You come back, my sweetheart." Others said that it was introduced into this region by packers who sang it while driving their horses up from the Fraser River valley about 1860. It is an excellent example of the broad melodies with wide melodic range of the people of the interior.

The Indians on the Skeena River are among the most musical tribes on the North American continent. The singers' voices are lyrical and often rise to a high pitch, vibrating with feeling, before descending suddenly to the tonic sound. These songs cover a wide range of subjects and many of them belong to everybody, a common heritage.

One of the best singers I recorded was Watserh (Otter) or Andrew Wilson, a member of the Kisgagas tribe. Kisgagas is one of the uppermost villages of the Gitksans about 225 miles from the seacoast. Watserh belongs to the Athabaskan stock of the interior. He is of the Frog-Raven clan and was blinded while young from an accident. Dr. Marius Barbeau recorded his songs as early as 1920 when Watserh was twenty-three years old. His voice was still remarkably high and clear when I recorded him nineteen years later, and his singing technique, as well as his songs, is typical of the Indians of the interior, quite different from coast Indians. In addition to the songs to bring success to the fishing, he sang songs to celebrate the return of plenty when they have successfully speared or trapped the salmon in the swift streams. Most songs have broad melodies and may be accompanied by a skin drum, but the charm chants have no accompaniment. These songs often have the refrain *"Hone, knoe, kaw."*

Among the Gitksans, as with the Haida, the office of shaman was hereditary in certain families. Both the Haida shaman and the Gitksan shaman wore special insignia pertaining to the spirit that possessed them, and their long hair was never combed. There were both men and women "doctors." Their principal duties were to cure illnesses resulting from the "loss of the soul" and the entry of an evil spirit into the body. They could cast a spell on the enemy, could bring sickness to those who did not believe in their powers, and could cure the ill, especially those who could pay well.

Every doctor had "soul hunters," which might be the head or feet of a mink, owl, eagle, or hawk or the tooth of a wolf. These objects were brought out of their bag and laid around the head of the patient while the medicine man sang their songs and played the drums, thus "hunting the soul" and bringing it back. If the patient died, it was because the soul could not be caught.

Andrew Wilson also sang medicine songs required for healing ceremonies, and talked about the strenuous training of the conjurer while learning these songs and practicing with the special round rattle required for this "medicine" music. The young medicine man, trained from early youth by the one whose power he would inherit, had to endure long periods of fasting and bodily privation in order to receive the "spirit powers."

The songs of chiefs were very important in the tribal repertoire. They were inherited and guarded jealously and became the property of a new chief when he gave a Potlatch to take on the name of his predecessor along with the coat of arms, certain privileges, the totem pole, etc. Among the ancient chiefs' songs Andrew and Abel sang for me to record was the chief's Chant for Peace, a part of the Peace Dance. When there was a dispute or fighting, the chiefs called the warring people together, danced before them, scattering eagle down over their heads and chanting a song "to cure trouble." The chief declared after this song that peace was established and anyone causing trouble again would be punished severely.

A Peace Dance was always held after warfare but also at certain other times. In the spring at the time of the *oolachan* fishing when the Tsimshian were in their fishing camps on the Nass River, a Peace Dance was held. The Tsimshian would invite the Nishgas and entertain them for several days. It was recognized by all the coast tribes that the Nass River belonged to the Nishgas, but during the oolachan fishing it was opened to everyone; even Alaskan Indians came. A big feast was given, a Peace Dance performed, and all agreed to live on friendly terms and settle their disputes by arbitration. The peace songs were passed down from father to son. The Tsimshian have very few, and they generally concern peace with the Haida Indians. They all have Haida words which usually have to do with peace finally restored after warfare when many canoes met and a great feast was held.

Taboos were numerous, and essential rituals were carried out to honor the spirits of the sources of food. There were taboos in connection with the hunters' preparation for the hunt and taboos following the hunt; for instance, slaughtered bears were treated with great ceremony and special hunting songs and mourning songs were sung—as with the eastern Eskimos. Songs and ceremonies were performed with the first fish of spring, especially the salmon.

Great excitement filled the camps along the river the first day the oolachan appeared, and everyone chanted, "Now our time of danger is over; these fish are our salvation." The name for the oolachan means "savior." The first cooking of the oolachan involves special ritual; before eating it everyone shouted *"Lowaa,"* which means, "Great honor to the oolachan." This fatty fish provides grease that is considered a great luxury and is eaten with berries, seaweed, fish, clams, or potatoes (like olive oil to the Mediterranean people). It is as essential to the Indians as butter to the white man. During the time of the annual oolachan fishing, the Peace Dance is performed.

Abel Oaks knew songs of every type and was very familiar with all the ceremonies in which they were used. He sang funeral songs for me which were a part of a great Potlatch ceremony. (The Gitksan ceremonies were similar to the Haida.) Death was regarded as an insult to the tribe and required the distribution and the destruction of much property. The Indians took this long-established method to restore the well-being of the tribe by wiping out the shame of having lost a member of the tribe, as in funeral ceremonies of Africa and other areas. All the expenses of the funeral Potlatch fell on the lineage that had lost someone.

As with the Haidas, the eldest man most closely related on the maternal side to the deceased inherited the names, privileges, and use of territory of the dead man. When there was a dispute as to the heir, the relative who could get his wealth together first was the most apt to be recognized, but he had to have the support of most of his relatives since very few were rich enough to assume these responsibilities and expenses alone.

When Abel Oaks sang these mournful songs he imitated the singsong mourning of the women, which continued several days following a death, a custom that resembled that of the Chinese. Also the refrain "*hayu*" (alas), which was used in Chinese dirges, was often used in the songs of mourning of the Eagle and Wolf clans, recent invaders from the north. (The Eagle clan still remembers its migration down the West Coast.) Dr. Barbeau reports another custom similar to that of paid mourners in China: following a death in the village, the old women crouched on the ground in front of their houses and beat the ground with their foreheads.

The coast Tsimshian songs are, generally speaking, less melodious than the songs of the Skeena River; they are often somber, and their range is far more restricted. While the singers on the Skeena River seem to be tenors, the Tsimshian voices are deep and throaty, even harsh at times. This again is reminiscent of the Indians of the Southwest, where the Navahos are tenors and the Pueblo Indians are basso profundos. On the coast the singing is usually confined to rituals and ceremonies, and most of the songs are the exclusive property of definite clans and families. Like the coat of arms, they are heirlooms, and if their ownership were challenged, quarrels and probably bloodshed would follow.

The coast drum sometimes accompanied the songs. It was quite different from the drums of the interior. Made of a thin slab of red cedar, suspended by a short cord from the roof of the house, it gave a deep and muffled tone. The drum of the interior consisted of the skin of moose, beaver, or caribou stretched over a circular frame. When struck with a drumstick held in the right hand, it produced a clear and vibrant tone.

The Tsimshian are divided into four clans, Eagle, Raven, Wolf, and Blackfish (or killer whale), which are divided into subclans, people who have the same myth of common origin. The subclans are divided into "houses," large households including relatives, adopted members, and slaves in large dwellings. Each household inherited personal names, coats of arms, privileges, songs, dances, and myths, and also special hunting, fishing, and berry-picking territories. A village consisted of a number of "houses." The coast Indians are the most conservative in preserving the ancient customs.

William Pierce was my best informant with the Tsimshian at Prince Rupert, an important coast village of British Columbia. He belonged to the Eagle clan by birth and the Blackfish clan by adoption. When he sang these clan songs for me he was eighty-four years old but still knew very many songs, which he sang well. He remembered the huge high-bow red-cedar war canoes made to attack enemy tribes on the sea, and actually recalled the last war between the Haida and Tsimshian tribes. He told me: "The warriors don't eat much, nor drink much water: only thirst for victory, and they get it. The wives stay behind and go through the exaggerated motions of fighting the enemy. They do not eat much or drink much. They go from house to house aiming to win the war. During that last war the Tsimshian warriors crossed one hundred miles of open sea to the Queen Charlotte Islands, killed many Haida men, and took their women and children.

"When the war is over they sprinkle eagle down over their heads for peace. The ones that win give something to the brother of the enemy that was killed—a gun, canoe, copper, a black fox, sea-otter hide, a daughter, or a brother. Those from the enemy tribe dance in a straight line, and if they are not satisfied with the gift, they dance with bowed heads. A peacemaker than has to negotiate. Now we go to magistrate; no more war."

I recorded some myths and found that, as in Africa, many things are explained through these tales. Here is one that explains why their highly valued halibut is white on one side and black on the other:

"There was one time when a Wonder Man was going from place to place to find out what kind of a people he meets. So one day he went to a little fish house and there he saw two or three families in the house drying halibut.

"And the Wonder Man said, 'Where you get your halibut?'

"'Oh, we fish outside every day and we dry this for our winter food.'

"So this Wonder Man said, 'I like to go out with you and see how you fishing.'

"So one day both of them went out. So as they cast in their hooks, the Wonder Man says to the other, 'What is your name?'

"'My name is Kushken.' [That means gum.] 'All right.'

"Later on this Kushken began to call, 'I want to get to shore. I'm too hot, too hot!' The sun was beating on him; and the Wonder Man say, 'No, we are making good time fishing.'

"So at last the Gum Man says, 'I feel so weak.' The Wonder Man says, 'Well, there's a net here. Take it as a cover.' And the Gum Man covered himself at the bow.

"After while the Wonder Man called, says, *Kushken!*

"'Ooooh,' getting smaller [fainter].

"Bye'n bye the Wonder Man begin to see that the Gum Man was melting until there is nothing left. And all the gum covered the halibut in the canoe—covered one side—the upper part of the halibut all covered with gum.

"And that is why the halibut today one side is white and one side is black!"

Chapter 26

INDIANS OF OUR SOUTHWEST

The oldest music in America is the music of our American Indians. Even though the Indians have been under cultural influences of the white man for about four centuries, they have retained, and are still developing, a great body of songs which reveal their artistic and spiritual strength. Moreover, these are gradually being recognized as a vital part of musical America.

Through music and dance the Indian worships his gods. By singing and dancing, the spirits are propitiated; sickness, famine, and drought are driven away; and the people are blessed with plentiful food, good health, and many children. Thus the Indian has kept what many more progressive civilizations have lost and are striving to recover: a rich, intimate, and natural use of music and art in their ordinary lives.

There are many types of songs. A great number are connected with healing the sick, bringing rain, and other sacred practices. There are also war songs, hunting songs, and work songs, such as the corn-grinding songs, which are still connected with certain ritual observances. Secular songs are numerous: gambling songs, riding songs, songs for social dancing, lullabies, and love songs. Among certain tribes in which the earlier culture has broken down to a great extent, songs from ancient myths are now used for purely social dances, although at one time they had great religious significance.

The poetic texts of the songs are beautiful in their imagery: rain, clouds, lightning, thunder, rainbows, the directions, as well as the colors associated with the directions, are often mentioned. Beans, cornmeal, pollen, and squash blossoms are also dealt with in the poetry.

The words are often obsolete, and the sacred chants are too obscure for the uninitiated to understand. Indeed, nonsense syllables are common in Indian songs. A great many have no actual words, and simple syllables without meaning are used to articulate the song. Yet they may have a very definite place in a ceremony and the singers are as careful of the accuracy of the syllable order as they are when using words which convey meaning.

There is a general downward trend of Indian melodies with a definite tendency to end on a low tone. This is true of sections and phrases as well as of the whole song itself. The intervals are small—even fractional tones are used—and the phrases short and well balanced. Broken rhythms and elaborate rhythmic patterns are employed, especially in the drumming, and the rhythm of the drumbeat varies with the character of the song. In certain tribes the drum and song rhythms are seldom synchronized but go along in more or less independent parallel lines, a sort of horizontal music—or rhythmomelodic counterpoint, if you will—in contrast to conventional harmonized music, which is perpendicular.

Indian music is pure melody, and there is no fixed scale in our sense. The manner of singing is the characteristic that gives the music its individuality, more so probably than any other trait. The singing technique of the Indians is peculiar to their race. The Indian sings with his jaws only slightly open, and there is very little change in the position of his jaws or lips while singing. The tone is forced out and has remarkable carrying qualities. The stress on the throat produces a special timbre, and sometimes special tone qualities are reserved for certain kinds of songs. For example, in the Navajo *Yebitchai* (night chant), a healing ceremony, the singers use high falsetto to represent the voices of the gods.

Indian music is almost completely singing, and musical instruments are limited in use and variety. Percussion instruments, drums and rattles, usually provide the only accompaniment. The rasp, a notched stick rubbed with a smooth stick, is widely found in the Southwest and is used for ceremonial songs. The bull-roarer, a flat, elliptical piece of wood which when whirled produces a weird, whirring sound, represents the voice of the spirits in certain chants.

A flat basket can be converted into a musical instrument by beating it as a drum or by rubbing it with a stick. I recorded this among tribes very far from each other culturally and geographically, in the Navajo corn-grinding songs of northern New Mexico and in Papago medicine songs of southern Arizona. In addition to the many types of percussion instruments, whistles of bone, wood, or quills, and flutes of wood, cane, and pottery are found.

Music, both instrumental and vocal, is primarily a man's profession among the Indians. In certain tribes it is very difficult to hear a woman's song, although every tribe has some singing by women. Customarily, ritualistic songs are sung by the men because they are thought to bring more power to music when calling for rain, imploring the spirits, or attempting to heal the sick. But medicine women are sometimes to be found.

Indian music is a communal, tribal outpouring. Even when a soloist performs it is not because he has a beautiful voice and wants to give aesthetic pleasure, but because he has a song which has particular value or power. He may have bought it from someone or received it in a dream, as the Plains Indians do. But it is not the individual that counts in the singing or even in the composing, it is the tribe. As there is no written notation, it is through the songs and ceremonies that the beliefs and traditions of the tribe are passed on.

The Indians of Arizona and New Mexico can be divided into pueblo dwellers (for example, Hopis and Zunis); sedentary people who live in community dwellings, cultivating fields of corn, beans, and squash; camp dwellers (Navajos and Apaches), nomads who wander about securing their food; and village dwellers (Pimas, Papagos, and Mohaves), living in one-family dwellings which are grouped into fairly permanent villages.,

The Pima and Papago Indians of southern Arizona and northern Mexico belong to the same group in culture and language, and they regard themselves as one people. They are the southernmost group of this southwest area and in many respects they are closest to the tribes of Mexico.

Papago-Piman music is more melodious than most Indian music. The attack, instead of being forceful, is gentle. Instead of pulsations on every tone, accents are rare and tones are repeated or held. Many old songs trail off at the end with "m-m-m. . . ." There are no shouts at the beginning or end of the song, and calls are rare. The tones are fixed rather than vague. The melodies are varied, and the melodic movement is generally downward. There are often two definite tonal sections, and the vocal range is limited. Instead of sharp contrasts in the rhythm there is an even flow of short rhythmic figures. The songs usually have meaningful words, rarely nonsense syllables. Accompanying instruments used are gourds, rattles, notched sticks, and a basket drum, beaten or scraped. The Papagos are said to have a flute, although I have not seen it played.

Their medicine men have power to bring rain, foretell the results of war and races, and cure the sick. In curing he sings all night—often for many nights—beside the patient, accompanying the song on a gourd rattle and brushing the patient with eagle plumes from time to time. One of their medicine songs I recorded tells of a fly who found an eagle feather and put it on his head. He then went into the west and returned with a beautiful diamond which he invited all the people to see. This is part of a long cycle of songs.

The girls' Coming-of-Age ceremony has many important songs which the medicine man sings all night for four nights, never repeating the same songs. One which I recorded was the Coyote Song describing the sun setting in the west and how the mountains there against the sun look like leaves of an oak tree when they have turned red. The Papagos have a special manner of playing the rattle which produces a continuous, pulsating accompaniment.

On the Pima reservations only the older men sing the old songs. These songs, which formerly had great power, are now used for the Social Dance, a circle dance which is the last remnant of tribal social gatherings, inherited from the ceremonial rites. In this cycle of songs the composer tells of his experiences—in his dreams—when he went to war and came back exhausted. Maidens greeted him and fanned him with burnt feathers. One particular song of the cycle I recorded described a trip into the sky to bring help to the maidens.

The Mohaves belong to the Yuman-speaking people who live in western Arizona, and the lower Colorado River Valley. They are closely related to some of the tribes of northern Mexico. They have well-defined tribal lines, live in settled villages, and practice agriculture, growing corn, beans, pumpkins, and melons. Their adobe homes have cottonwood supports and are roofed with thatch.

Their musical style is very distinctive. Mohave songs are sung in a cycle that requires a whole night to perform, with special songs for each part of the night. Each series is a definite unit with a distinctive style. They are learned by listening and later singing along with an old man all night for several nights. The songs are often used with legends, sometimes embodying a part of the narrative. It is very important that the correct order of songs and words be kept; some are used only by the shaman, or priest, and some only for dancing.

The songs are divided into sections, each having specific rhythmical characteristics. The tempo of the voice and the percussion accompaniment (drum or rattle) are often synchronized, which is not always true in Indian music. The use of rests is a distinct characteristic of the Yuma style. It is not just a rest for breathing, as the note before the rest ends the phrase in a quite definite manner. Another typical trait is the skipping of the melody to a higher register for a brief stretch, and back again to the main phrase. This rise may repeat or imitate the main motive or introduce new material. The Mohaves accompany their songs with rattles, basket drum, pounding of feet, or nasal grunting. They also have flutes, whistles, bull-roarers, and notched sticks.

The bird songs used for the big annual ceremony, which takes place about the Fourth of July, are well loved by the Mohaves. The songs are accompanied by a rattle and end with explosive, staccato nonsense syllables: "Hah-Hah-Hah." Many of these song series end with such special effects. The Mohave are said to have learned the bird songs originally from the Yumas though their songs are now different, simpler in melody and rhythm.

Pueblo (meaning village) was the name applied by the Spaniards to the Indians they found living in permanent villages built of masonry, and the term is still used. These people are divided into four different language families: Shoshonean (Hopis), Zunian (Zunis), Keresan (Santa Anas and others), and Tanoan (San Ildefonsos, Taos, and others). There are three main groups of villages—the Hopi pueblos, the Rio Grande pueblos, and the Zuni pueblos.

The Hopi villages are perched on three rocky mesas where these gentle people took refuge from their enemies. The entire population lives in ten villages, with three mesas of three villages each. The tenth, Moenkopi, is some distance away. Each village is independent in government and ceremonies.

The Hopi, like other Pueblo Indians, are divided into fraternities which control all the ceremonies. A great deal of the ceremonial life takes place in the *kiva*, or ceremonial lodge. The early or pre-pueblo people, when they first felt the need of a permanent home, dug into the ground and made a circular room which they roofed with mud and logs. It was entered from above by means of a ladder. As the people began to live in villages they probably maintained their relationships through preserving certain ceremonies conducted in these kivas. The modern kiva is the center of the clan and religious life of the Hopis. In Hopi villages the kivas are entirely underground; in most of the Rio Grande pueblos they are above ground.

In addition to the ladder entrance there is in the kiva a ventilator and smokescreen, a fire in the center, and most important of all, a hole in the floor, the *sipapu*, which typifies the entrance for the spirits from the underworld. The men conduct all clan and village business in the kiva and the preliminary services for every dance are performed there.

Like most primitive people, the Hopis ascribe human qualities to animals, plants, mountains, and clouds—practically everything. The *kachinas* are spirits from an outer world who come to live in the Hopi villages for half of the year, approximately from late January to July. During that period the Hopi represent these spirits by dancing in special masks and costumes and carrying out certain ceremonies. The kachina may be a masked dancer or a doll carved in cottonwood, dressed and ornamented exactly like the dancer. These dolls are given to the children as toys, or placed reverently on altars. A beautiful one was brought to me as a sign of friendship by my interpreter.

The dancing kachinas sometimes carry implements like those found in ancient ruins and often chant in languages so old that no one can translate the words. Their costumes are prescribed by ancient traditions—the face representing a bird, a beast, a monster, or a man. There are hundreds of kachinas, and some of them appear every year; most of them probably every few years. A continuous succession of masked dances takes place from January until the Home-Going Dance, called the Niman Kachina, in July when the gods return to their home near the San Francisco peaks. After that, the most ancient ceremonies, the Snake Dance, the Flute Dance, and other unmasked dances are performed. I witnessed a Long-Haired Kachina Dance in late August, but some of my Hopi friends sharply criticized the village for keeping the poor kachinas from their underworld home so late in the summer!

Clowns appear in many of the Hopi dances—for example, the Mudhead Kachina Dance which I recorded in Hotevilla, Arizona. The clowns are noted for their gluttony and obscenity, and there is no limit to their funmaking. Their bodies daubed with clay and their heads hidden in knobby sacks, also clay-daubed, gave rise to the name Mudhead. The Hopis believe that through an appeal to the dancing kachinas the prayers reach the kachina gods and the tribe will be blessed with rain and sun, good crops, and many children. Always they pray for blessings which will be not just for the individual but for the good of the whole community. In the Mudhead Song the prayer is, as usual with the Hopi, for rain:

> Come up, clouds, standing there,
> From the north, yellow clouds,
> From the west, blue clouds,
> From the south, red clouds,
> From the east, gray clouds.

The Mudheads, or clowns, appear in practically all of the dances throughout the year.

The kachina songs are, generally speaking, the most complex of all the Pueblo Indian songs. In this song, accompanied by drum and gourd rattle, many of the characteristics of Pueblo singing are evident; calls at beginning and end are frequent and the amazing Pueblo manner of voice production by continuous pressure on the vocal chords can be heard. The jaws and lips of the singer are barely apart, and the listener feels the muscular stress in the throat as well as the dynamic stress of the song.

The modern Zuni pueblo is the remnant of the legendary Seven Cities of Cibola sought by the Spaniards. Since it is somewhat remote from the other pueblos, it has kept its ancient customs with very little of the Roman Catholic intermixture which has become part of the Rio Grande pueblo life.

The Zunis are divided into six groups, each with a kiva, and each kiva group performs two dances a year at some ritual. The kivas are above ground and built into the block of houses, probably to make them inconspicuous to the outsider. Boys are initiated into the kiva at eight years of age and again at twelve. Girls are initiated only if they are visited by the spirits in dreams. Certain masks are the property of the kiva; those of the Zunis are among the most elaborate; through wearing a mask a dancer becomes a supernatural being for the time he wears it, and has influence with the gods.

Zuni religion is still very powerful, and ceremonial dances go on serenely throughout the year. In the winter there is scarcely a week without a ceremonial. When spring comes, all the farmers are busy planting, but with the summer the dances for rain begin. The great festival *Shalako* takes place about the first of December. All rituals are in the hands of the priests, who have great power, the Sun Priest being the headpriest.

One of the most impressive recordings I made with the Zunis in New Mexico was the Harvest Dance, a very old ritual given at the end of the summer. I saw it in early October; there was dancing every day for a week. The dancing began in the late afternoon and continued till sunset, when the singers and dancers retired to the kiva and practiced their songs far into the night. The next morning the singers were very late in rising, but when they gathered to sing for me they recorded a new Harvest Dance song which had been learned in the kiva the night before and was to be used in the dance that very day. Thus new songs are added to the repertoire.

It was in Pátzcuaro in Mexico when I was a delegate at the first Inter-American Congress on Indian Life that I first met Mabel Dodge Luhan (one of the Dodge car heiresses) and her Indian husband, Tony. Later in 1940 I was a guest in their beautiful home in Taos, New Mexico. For years Taos, to many people, meant mainly that famous group comprising D. H. Lawrence, his wife Frieda, Mabel Dodge Luhan, and Tony. The colorful life led by these outsiders in the midst of an Indian pueblo perhaps overshadowed the fact that Taos is actually one of the most beautiful and vital American Indian communities of the Southwest. Here the Indians own and farm their land, have their own herds, vehicles, and work animals. The Pueblo Indians who built Taos, and other villages like it, were apparently already established as town dwellers before the Navajos and Apaches had even entered the Southwest. Like all pueblos, Taos had its own governor who regulated and controlled tribal affairs; its whole Pueblo Indian population lived in two famous community houses, each with several stories, sprawling over acres of red earth.

These honeycomb-like buildings, terraced back from the sides, are splendid examples of the pyramidal type of house built for defense as well as for communal living. Facing each other near a beautiful little stream, these houses, rising to four or five stories, are no doubt the most photographed pueblo dwellings in New Mexico. All around Taos are cultivated fields. The ceremonial life centers around the kivas, which are completely underground as in the Hopi villages. The entrances are flush with the ground but boldly announced by the tall ladder poles so that we would not make the mistake of going too near.

The Taos Indians used to make expeditions to the Great Plains to hunt buffalo. These trips could be made safely only in large parties and with the greatest care against attacks from the Plains Indians. The communal hunting of antelope, deer, buffalo, and elk, which provided food and clothing in the early days, has been discontinued, but rabbit hunts still go on.

Many traits of the Plains Indians are evident in the Taos group; for example, the men wear their hair in braids wrapped with fur or flannel, in the same manner and style.

Both Taos and San Ildefonsos belong to the Tanoan language group. In the San Ildefonso pueblo the common prehistoric arrangement of dwellings around an enclosed court from which the upper stories recede is still to be found. During the wars with the Spanish in the late seventeenth century, the inhabitants of San Ildefonso, now peaceful people famous as potters of a special black pottery, showed themselves great warriors. In the end the Indians were subjugated; they accepted nominally the Christian faith, but have always continued their native religious practices.

Among Rio Grande Indians, Pueblo Indians, dances are allotted to certain seasons and the Corn Dance is an ancient and very beautiful summer dance. It is a prayer for growth and rain, given in most pueblos on the day of the saint for whom the Spaniards named the village. If the saint's day comes in the fall, as it does in the Jemez pueblo, this dance is given when the harvest is brought in.

For most dances nowadays, the dance of the public performance begins with a Catholic ceremony. There is apparently no connection between the Mass for the saint and the ancient ceremony which begins with the clowns rushing out of the kiva, their painted bodies and costumes of corn husks and rabbitskins reminding the onlooker that they are spirits of the dead. All day they perform bits of burlesque from time to time. The dancers, men and women, enter from the kivas in brilliant costumes, shells rattling, bells sounding, with the leader carrying a pole topped with yellow feathers, a symbol of the sun inviting the rain to fall. A large chorus of chanters, marking time with hands and feet, hour after hour, calls on the gods for clouds and rain with singing and drumming.

The Comanche song which I recorded with the San Ildefonso singers may represent a large group of songs borrowed from the Comanche tribe. Sung with great gusto by practically all Pueblo Indians, this illustrates the borrowing of songs from tribe to tribe. This particular song may have belonged to the Comanches or it may be a part of the San Ildefonso Comanche War Dance, formerly used to arouse the tribe to defy invaders.

The modern Pueblos have many legends connecting them with the inhabitants of the ancient cliff dwellings and the great communal villages like those on Mesa Verde, which is claimed by the Hopis as their source. The Santa Ana Pueblo Indians, who belong to the Keresian language family, believe that the Rio de los Frijoles was their ancestral home. The medicine men make pilgrimages to the ancient sites and the present ceremonial observances are linked with the past. Among the Keres the clowns use their jokes to correct evildoers by holding them up to the ridicule of their townsfellows, a very effective moral agent in the community, like the songs of satire among African natives. Here, instead of singing they often perform in pantomime, the beginnings of an indigenous theater movement.

The more nomadic tribes, such as the Utes, Apaches, and Navajos, retain fewer material possessions than the town-dwelling, house-dwelling Pueblo Indians, but their social organization, their complex economy, and their religion, a strange admixture of pagan and orthodox Christianity, provide equally fascinating study.

The language of the Apaches, like that of their Navajo brothers, belongs to the Athapascan linguistic family; they probably migrated from western Canada about the same time. They have always been hunters, living on the wild things which the country offered. Always fierce warriors, they were feared by the village and pueblo dwellers. (The name "Apache" is a Zuni word for enemy.) The strategy, endurance, and fierce spirit of the Apaches made them hard to conquer. But after forty years of war they yielded to the superior numbers and strength of the American army. By 1886 all tribal members were captured and put on reservations.

Now the Apaches live chiefly on four reservations, the Jicarillas and Mescaleros in New Mexico, and the White Mountain and San Carlos Apaches in eastern Arizona. In all there are about seventy-five hundred of them.

The Apaches got horses very early, not through gifts from the missionaries, like their more peaceful neighbors, but by raiding the mission stations and by waylaying small parties of whites or Indians. With horses they could then retreat and live at a safe distance from their enemies. Those in the east near the Plains Indians lived in the tepees; those away from the Plains lived in wickiups of arched boughs covered with grass.

The wandering life of the Apaches made any strong tribal unity impossible. There were no societies, no kivas no kachinas. These restless, nomadic people, who divided into small groups, have farmed to a very limited extent but they are quite successful at herding sheep, goats, and cattle. The Jicarillas are the most successful shepherds, with an average of around sixty sheep per person. The nomadic life of the Apaches has prevented fixed dates for ceremonies, and there is no trace of the elaborate ceremonial life that is found among the sedentary Pueblo people. Nor are there great communal rituals, as among the Pueblo Indians, held for the good of the whole community.

At the present time the Apaches have combined all their ceremonial observances into one big annual festival around the Fourth of July. The government encouraged this plan to prevent them from being called away to various ceremonies during the growing season and thus neglecting their farms. This four-day ceremony is primarily for the blessing of the young girls who have reached maturity during the year. Even though the whole community participates, this ceremony is not communal. A medicine man is hired for each girl by the family. He is very well paid and does not work for the community, but for the girl. A man and wife are found to act as sponsors for each girl during the ceremony and, thereafter, throughout her life. The woman chosen must be industrious and virtuous. For four days the girl is considered sacred; she wears the ceremonial costume of buckskin, and dances from time to time; the medicine man sings certain prescribed songs.

On the fourth night there is a great public ceremony—the Crown Dance, which I recorded in Mescalero, New Mexico. This seems to be a combination of several old Apache ceremonies. Spruce trees were set up at the four points of the compass to typify plenty, for in the old days they found plentiful game in the spruce forests.

On the western side, a skeleton wickiup was erected with four poles, piñon, walnut, cedar, and oak, which represented the trees from which the little girl would gather fruit when she was mature. At sunset the medicine men began to sing and the girls danced until midnight. At midnight, or somewhat before, the spirit dancers appeared, wearing towering crowns, their faces hidden by masks of black buckskin. Their bodies were blackened with spots, stripes, and zigzag streaks of red, yellow, and white. Long, fringed buckskin kilts and high boots completed the costume. The great spectacular superstructure or crown towering about two feet above the dancer indicated the personality of the spirit. These crowns were yellow and beautifully decorated with symbols of rain, clouds, thunder, and lightning. The dancers carried yucca swords decorated with the lightning symbol; there was a set of four crowned dancers and a clown, dressed in loincloth and white mask, for each girl. The dancers are called *gahe* (spirits) and did not talk at all but gave high cries like the weird call of the hoot owl, sacred to the Apaches. They danced with a queer straddling sort of step, with knees bent and swords held outward from flexed elbows like wooden figures. It was a very angular dance with a fierce wildness about it.

The musicians accompanied their song on a huge drum similar to that used by the Plains Indians and the eerie calls of the gahe could always be heard above the singers.

In many areas of this spectacular country, stretching west from Texas to the Colorado River, the earth has been sculptured by the elements, through countless ages, into incomparable contours. In Arizona's Canyon de Chelly (pronounced dà sháy), wind-worn walls of brilliant red-orange color tower higher in some places than the Empire State Building. The ruins of ancient cliff dwellings are almost hidden in deep niches, sometimes quite inaccessible, except for finger-and-toe holds cut in the sheer rockface by ancient Navajos whose stronghold it once was.

In January 1864, Kit Carson and his men rounded up eight thousand Navajos from the Canyon de Chelly and drove them to a reservation, but a few hundred still eke out a sparse living in the canyon.

While working in New Mexico, I was invited on a journey into a remote part of the Navajo country. Musically this was richly rewarding for me but it might well have ended in tragedy for all of us had we not had so experienced a guide.

Román Hubbell was a much-loved trader with a large popular Indian post founded many years earlier by his father, who had married into a fine old Spanish family and had built up the best-known trading post in the Southwest. Román spoke the dialects of all the important tribes but he was, I felt, closest in spirit to the Navajos.

Part of our route lay right through the glorious Canyon de Chelly. It was a dry river bed, no more than a twist of dusty earth wedged between towering cliffs, which served as a rough highway for the few automobiles whose owners felt inclined to expose them to such a tortuous route. We were still winding our way along the narrow pass, dwarfed by the wind-scarred rocks, when behind us we heard a faint roaring sound that quickly swelled into a crashing crescendo rumbling down the canyon.

Recognizing the sound of cascading water from its first faint whisper, Román accelerated, driving the car at top speed, jolting and rocking over the rough river bed in an effort to get us through the narrow pass. No sooner had we bounced out of the canyon and gained the safety of a promontory of stony earth on what might once have been the riverbank than a towering wall of water fifteen or twenty feet high came thundering through the gorge, piling up, swirling along, sweeping all before it—uprooted trees, sheep, goats, and dogs. Even a couple of whirling motorcars tumbled in the path of the flood while we stood helplessly by, weak and shocked by the narrowness of our own escape. The thought of water in that barren river bed was inconceivable. A cloudburst higher up in the mountains had sent the trapped flood-waters hurtling through the pass to find an outlet in the desert beyond.

A young student traveling by car through the Southwest had been close behind us. He had not been so fortunate and had just managed to scramble free of his vehicle before it was swept away. We helped him up to the higher ground beside us, and watched his car with all his belongings disappear under a mounting pile of red sand and rubble.

The flood quickly vanished into the thirsty earth and within a few hours we were able to drive on, but the road, such as it was, had now almost disappeared and the country was strewn with sad reminders of those less fortunate than we.

With Román as guide, I was able to collect some excellent recordings among the Navajos. Román was a great friend of these proud people, who in the early days wandered about continually fighting and harassing the more peaceful Pueblo Indians. Now peaceful, pastoral people, some 115,000 in number, they herd their sheep in the mountain pastures in the summer, and in low, sheltered regions in the winter, always on the move searching for better grazing. They also practice a limited amount of agriculture. During the winter they live in a warm hogan (house) built of logs and earth; in the summer, in a brush shelter. Since the Spanish introduced horses and sheep, they have become famous as horsemen and shepherds.

The Navajo family is matrilineal: The woman owns the sheep and the hogan, and the children belong to her clan. With her wool she weaves beautiful blankets which bring the family a good income from the traders; the men make the splendid silverwork which has brought fame to the tribe.

Whenever Navajos meet to work, worship, or play, they sing hour after hour, night after night—riding songs, running songs, love songs, songs learned from other tribes, and sacred chants, always in their proper season.

Navajo ceremonial life is very elaborate. Most ceremonies are curing sings, conducted by the medicine men. Perhaps all Indian music was originally in the field of the medicine men, or those who had acquired magical powers through a dream or a vision. Through singing, the medicine man puts forth his spirit power for the benefit of the tribe or an individual. Among the Navajos there are many thousands of ritualistic songs. They follow a few definite patterns, perhaps forty in all. The curing songs are extremely numerous, with very elaborate song texts, and the medicine man is the chief singer and sometimes the only one. The entire success of the curing ceremony depends on the accuracy of the medicine man, who is commonly called the singer or the chanter.

There are many special rituals: the Night Chant, the Mountain Chant, the Blessing Chant. In a nine-day ritual hundreds of different songs are sung, and they must follow one another in definite order. A single mistake in the order of songs or even in the order of the nonsense syllables will ruin the cure. Some of the medicine men know several ceremonies, some know only one, but that one may have four or five hundred songs in addition to all the sand paintings, prayers, dance steps, and other ritual details which must be remembered.

To become a good medicine man requires first of all a good singing voice, a remarkable memory, a certain spiritual quality, and long and strenuous training. The apprentice may have to study twenty years before he is trusted to lead a big nine-day sing. The sings play a remarkably important role in the social life of the community by bringing together great numbers of Navajos from their large and sparsely populated reservation. The astonishing unity throughout the whole tribe is largely due to the practice of the old medicine men who travel from sing to sing, holding the tribe together in the ancient faith and ancient traditions.

The songs which the medicine man sings alone, or with his assistant, are chanted and seem nearer speech than music. Yet they have definite musical form, beginning with an introduction, then a stanza giving the ritualistic text, and ending with a coda (like the introduction). The Navajo language has four distinct speech tones—high, low, rising, and falling—and in certain melodies the rise and fall of the melody is related to the rise and fall of the words of the song text. In these chants the musical melody does not depend on the speech melody, for the text has to fit into the chant pattern.

A well-known curing ceremony and social dance which takes place frequently in the summertime is the so-called Squaw Dance. This three-day ceremony was formerly a war dance, but now disease or illness is the enemy to be defeated. The Squaw Dance is the name given this dance by the white man because it is the only one in which mixed couples dance. The girl approaches the man, grasps him firmly by the arm or the belt, and pulls him into the circle of dancers. He must dance with her until he pays, and pays well. Payment used to be jewelry, horses, or even a white child brought back from the wars. Now it is usually money that the young lady prefers.

One of the healing ceremonies which I attended stands out in my mind above all others. It was held in the beautiful forest near the Lukachukai Mountains in the northern part of the reservation. Hundreds of Navajos had come from miles around to sing, dance, and gossip with their friends and relatives. Inside a great circle of covered wagons and tethered horses was a circle of many campfires where whole families, wrapped in colorful blankets, slept, ate, or sat quietly talking. In the center of this circle was a great bonfire where huge burning trees threw out heat and light for the circle of dancing men and girls. Giant trees towered into the sky, silhouetted against the moon. The dancing continued throughout the night, and from time to time we wandered back to our spruce shelter to revive ourselves by the family fires with chunks of boiled mutton and cups of steaming coffee.

The music was provided by a large group of male singers, accompanied by a small drum. Innumerable songs were sung, each one lasting perhaps only a minute or two. One by one, the singers led out with a new tune, and almost immediately everyone in the chorus had joined as one great voice. The lusty singing continued into the cold gray light of morning.

The group songs of the Squaw Dance not only illustrate a Navajo tribal style but indicate that within the tribe, even within a single ceremony, there are many different types of songs. For the Squaw Dance, aside from the medicine songs which are sung over the patient inside the hogan, there are group songs: serenade songs, sung outside the patient's house; sway songs, which are sung without dancing; and the *ahizhdi áhai sin*, which accompany the dancing. Even among these special groups of songs, the Navajos recognize two types, an old (which they feel is slower) and a new (faster) type. In my recording of the *nejnotahe* (the old type) the soloists, now here, now there, can be heard introducing their special melodies.

The Night Chant—called *Yebitchai* after the principal figure, the maternal grandfather of the gods—is perhaps the most sacred ceremony of all the Navajo chants, for in it the gods appear in masks made of sacred buckskin and assist in the ritual. The days of this sing are filled with the elaborate detail of preparing ceremonial properties, making sand paintings, and chanting prayers over the patient.

During the ceremony the initiation of the children takes place. They are lightly whipped by masked gods carrying yucca whips. Then the gods remove their masks, and the children recognize them as their neighbors and relatives. Later, initiation for the higher degrees (more whipping) may be held. No one is permitted to impersonate the gods until he has been through the initiation four times.

The last day is spent preparing for the public dance. The patient's family entertains the crowd but friends always help. The purification ritual and the sand paintings are now completed. When night comes, Yebitchai appears and dances with four masked gods. All night long a similar dance is performed by four sets of gods—the original number was four, but nowdays there may be more—each set with eight dancers, their bodies painted white, wearing kilts, masks, and coyote skins, and carrying spruce boughs. There is a clown with each set who imitates all their actions.

After the initial eerie calls of the god, "Hu-tu-tu-tu," the dancers shake their rattles with a sweeping motion from the ground to their heads, then whirl to the opposite direction and repeat the rattling. To the accompaniment of the rattles the gods begin to dance, stamping the ground vigorously with their right feet and singing a wild, rhythmic chant. The Yebitchai Chant is, to many people, the most haunting of all Indian music. The high falsetto of the god's singing is unforgettable.

"Ho-ho-ho-ho, he-he-he-he," syllables with no meaning, are sung hour after hour with insistent hypnotic power. Dance teams who have been practicing days for this occasion compete with each other until dawn. At sunrise the melodious Bluebird Song is sung by a group of unmasked singers, and this ends the dramatic ceremony.

My first experience with Indians of our Southwest had been in 1933 when, as a graduate student of the University of Chicago, with a grant from the American Council of Learned Societies, I was working with American Indians and, at the same time, experimenting with recording equipment in an effort to work out something adequate for use in the field.

I recorded flute sounds from the Winnebago Woodlands Indians, dance songs from the Sioux Plains Indians, San Ildefonso lullabies, ceremonial rites of the Apaches, and harvest songs of the Hopis, but especially I benefited from working with a Navajo medicine man.

Frank was the real thing among medicine men: sincerely devout, kind, and cooperative; a fine human being. I could wish for all young people in the field such a happy introduction into serious research. Frank was the son and grandson of medicine men and with such a background was highly skilled and respected in his work. As I have already stressed, the profession of medicine man among the Navajos is extremely exacting; and if too many mistakes are made, he may be out of his job.

Most Indians give the impression of being completely phlegmatic from the papoose riding on its mother's back through every age to death. Frank, not much taller than my five foot four, was squat and fat, very benign of countenance, and soft-spoken. Big brown eyes shone brilliantly from a round face with copper-colored skin and framed with long jet-black hair. He had a delightful, quiet sense of humor, and although the great body of songs he gave me were rare ritual songs, he sometimes sang amusing game songs, gambling songs, riding songs, and many others. The text of most of these songs, though scanty, were always highly entertaining.

In the process of working together, Frank and I became great friends; he is one of the people I would like to go back and find again after all these years.

During the project for the Indian Affairs Bureau (1940) I was to meet another medicine man, this time of the Hopi tribe, who lives vividly in my memory, not only for his beautiful songs but for the trust he placed in me.

While the three men from the Indian Service in Washington with whom I traveled went on their round of duties through the reservations, I settled down with specific tribes. It was at the Hopi reservation that the local government agent told me: "You won't get any songs here." So-and-so—he mentioned a musicologist by name—had just left and in three months he did not get a single song.

The Hopis have religiously guarded their ancient traditions and way of life and have always been very reluctant to part with their songs, which they hold very dear. Before I had been with them twenty-four hours, I was recording. By the time I left I had recorded songs from their most sacred rituals, the Snake Dance and the Flute Dance.

I got these rare and precious songs because I promised the medicine man to tell nobody, during his lifetime, that he had sung these for me. He made it quite clear that he would be killed if it became known that he had performed them for anyone outside the tribe.

As has happened so often in my life, the singer obviously sensed my deep seriousness in my work. He understood that my interest was not born out of curiosity but came from the heart.

We went a long way out into the desert, and under one of those weirdly shaped cacti (protected by law as a rare plant but providing absolutely no shade), I set up the recording gear and captured melodies which had never been recorded before.

The old man has now passed beyond reach of tribal retribution, and in the years between, many researchers have worked with the Hopis and perhaps have recorded some of this material. But I have kept faith and have never used these songs for demonstration or publication.

I learned very early from this fine man and from other great souls like him the value of a trusting friendship between the researcher and the informant. I have a great respect for the wisdom, the power, and the dignity of these two Indian medicine men who became my friends. It has been one of the real privileges of my work to know such wise and admirable personalities within such a trusting and binding relationship.

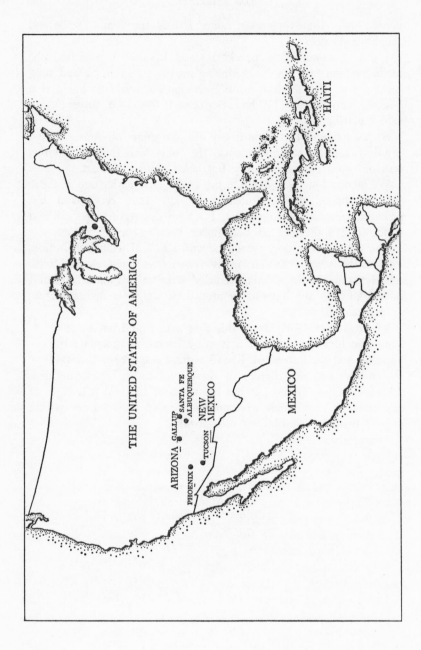

THE UNITED STATES OF AMERICA

ARIZONA
GALLUP
SANTA FE
ALBUQUERQUE
NEW
MEXICO
PHOENIX
TUCSON

MEXICO

HAITI

Chapter 27

THE FIRST MEXICANS

Mexico in 1940 was not the haven for tourists it has since become, and an expedition from the Sonora Mountains in the north down to the Isthmus of Tehuantepec in the extreme south was quite an undertaking. Traveling by train, car, and occasionally by donkey was extremely arduous. My usual heavy load of recording equipment and supplies was enlarged to include a folding bed board because of a back injury suffered shortly before this trip for New York's Museum of Modern Art was to begin.

Probably the hardest and certainly the loneliest thing I ever did in my life was the undertaking of this expedition, the first I had organized completely on my own. It was not a point in my life when I wanted to be alone, for simultaneously with my injury, my whole personal life had been disrupted. Two of my close friends, brilliant women, had become embittered and had gone to pieces when the continuity of their lives was suddenly broken. I was determined this would not happen to me. I know now that there is no tonic quite like concentrated work, and the acceptance of new responsibilities is the best cure for combating loneliness and for helping one to reassemble physical and mental resources. (To think that now I can dispose of that tragic period of my life in one paragraph! How time changes one's perspective.)

The decision to continue my work as if nothing had happened led to the acceptance of an invitation, from the head of an educational foundation, to attend the first Inter-American Congress on Indian Life, to be held in Pátzcuaro, Mexico.

At the same time a good friend, one of the trustees and founders of the Museum of Modern Art, offered to sponsor a museum project for me to work with the music of Mexico and to produce an album of Mexican Indian recordings, its publication to coincide with the museum exhibition of Mexican Indian art planned for the following year. This proved a turning point in my career. From this time on my expeditions were to be one-woman undertakings.

Mexican Indian music, like Mexican Indian art, has tremendously influenced modern composers and artists. All that we know of the pre-conquest period we have learned from the early illuminated manuscripts, from the records of the first Spanish missionaries, and from actual musical instruments, many of which have been found while excavating ruined temples and tombs.

Aztec music, poetry, and dances of remarkable beauty, no doubt built upon the musical heritage of preceding cultures (Archaic, Tarascan, Toltec, Mayan), have been described in detail by Spanish missionaries of the sixteenth century. There were apparently several types of music: the singing of poetry, military music, the songs for great dance ceremonials, and the narration in song of tales and of events resembling troubadour music. One illuminated manuscript shows a drummer, a flutist, and a juggler; another shows a group dancing around a pole, reminiscent of a dance still performed by the Mayas. Rattles are frequently represented, sometimes with the *huechuetl*, a large cylindrical drum made from a hollowed-out tree trunk with a membrane stretched over the top.

Some feeling of the earlier music has been preserved in the indigenous music of certain groups still practicing their traditional rites in remote localities of Mexico, for instance the Yaqui, the Seri, and the Huichol Indians.

The musical tradition of the Indian was indeed so strong and so deeply rooted that when the Spaniards came they were unable to destroy it, so they accepted it and compromised by adapting the pagan songs and ceremonies to the Christian rites. Some of the Yaqui music I recorded is an excellent illustration of this combination, expecially the ancient Deer Dance, which was adapted for use in the Easter week celebration of the Catholic Church.

In turn the Indian assimilated some of the vast amount of new music the Spaniards brought into Mexico. From the beginning of the conquest, the Church plain song was taught to the Indians and much of the secular Spanish music no doubt provided the basis of popular peasant dances of today such as the *jarabe* and the *huapango,* for the Indians lost no time in transforming many melodies from Spain into something typically their own.

The *corrido* or folk ballad in Mexico grew out of the Spanish romance; even courtly dance music, European chamber music, and, in the eighteenth century, Spanish, Italian, and French operas had their influence on Mexican music.

Carlos Chávez, Mexico's most eminent composer, is an ideal example of this welding of the old to the new. In 1921 he began writing compositions based on Mexico's ancestral Indian music. The legends, paintings, sculpture, and architecture of the ancient people and the aboriginal melodies, still to be heard in certain remote regions, were a great source of inspiration to him and his colleagues in their effort to create a musical art which would be truly Mexican.

During this renaissance many young musicians became fully aware for the first time of the vital importance of their native traditions and nourished themselves from these fertile sources. This raw material, a racial heritage with roots deep in the earth, gave sincerity and power to modern Mexican music; the elemental and universal qualities of Indian music have been called "the living voice of an ancient culture."

My headquarters in Mexico were at the San Angel Inn on the fringe of Mexico City where the other members of the museum were also staying. This inn with a charming Old World Spanish atmosphere was directly opposite the studio of the famous Mexican artist Diego Rivera. He was painting at the time a portrait of Paulette Goddard. (I was still in Mexico when, suspected of involvement in the Trotsky affair, he found his life in danger and made a quick escape over the border in Miss Goddard's plane.)

Rivera was very friendly and helpful and offered to let me study his wonderful collection of early Tarascan art, especially the musical instruments, which I did quietly while he was painting the portrait. It was a rare opportunity to watch his working habits, to listen to his entertaining conversation while painting, and at the same time to have moments of his attention during brief breaks from work while he discussed and demonstrated these unique musical instruments for me to record.

One such instrument was an early Tarascan ocarina from Colima which was made of terra cotta in the form of a bird, about three inches long with four finger holes. Another ocarina of terra cotta found in a tomb at Colima was made in the shape of a cobra. It was only one and a half inches long, one and a half inches wide, and had seven holes. Rivera thought it was probably used not only to call the snakes but also to calm them. Two precious sixth-century stone flutes, one single and one double flute, which he played and eventually gave me, are now in my collection at Columbia University.

In Mexico City I recorded many more ancient musical instruments of the Indians in the National Museum. One of the earliest instruments, probably used for hundreds of years before the Aztecs, is the conch shell. We have no way of knowing at present whether the conch shell was used as a war horn to call the warriors to battle, to proclaim triumphant victory after the battle was won, or, as with the West African Kru war horn, used from the beginning and throughout the fighting. The conch shell appears in use in the ceremonies of countries as far-flung as Polynesia and Tibet. We do know from the evidence found in illuminated scrolls that it was ever present during battle with the warriors.

The *teponaztli,* a slit drum made from a hollowed-out log, is another early instrument; its two wooden tongues, formed by cutting a letter *H* along one side of the wooden cylinder, produce different tones when struck. The teponaztli is sometimes carved to represent an animal like many of the slit drums I saw in West Africa. In the museum there are also rattles of various types, shapes, and sizes; rasps or notched sticks of wood, bone, and stone; ocarinas and whistles of different sizes and forms; flutes of clay capable of producing exquisite tones; and ancient bronze bells of different sizes, sometimes incorrectly described as rattles, for bell-shaped rattles of clay have been found in some of the ancient ruins.

An ancient Tarascan friction instrument of stone which I recorded was similar to the wooden rasps still played by the Yaqui in their Deer Dance; even the method of playing was identical—rubbing one stone against another. The one made in hard limestone from the Tarascan region was about sixteen inches long with nineteen notches and each end beautifully carved in the form of a bust, the face one inch, the body one and a half inches, with hands clearly showing the five fingers.

In the Museum in Mérida, Yucatán, I examined and recorded

ancient instruments of the Mayas, who two thousand years ago were architects, mathematicians, corn farmers, and musicians. As architects the ancient Mayas during the fourth to eighth centuries built great cities of stone, and their lofty pyramids supported magnificent temples which were the forerunners of our modern skyscrapers. They also built monasteries for their priests, palaces for their rulers, ball courts where a game resembling our modern basketball was played, and observatories for their astronomers.

The study of astronomy began among the Mayas probably several hundred years before Christ. Since they were primarily farmers, they were vitally concerned with the measurement of time, and the Mayan astronomer-priests—sometimes called the Greeks of the New World—far excelled the Egyptians and Babylonians in their knowledge of the movements of the sun, moon, and other heavenly bodies. Their greatest achievement was the invention of a calendar as accurate as our own.

The ancient priests were so efficient in their weather predictions that the Maya civilization was practically founded on the sucessful production of corn. This wealth allowed time for concern with loftier things than the means of keeping body and soul together, and such arts as architecture, sculpture, painting, feather working, and music were highly developed.

Uxmal (pronounced *oosh-mal*) and Chichen Itzá were great centers of early Mayan civilization. The Mexican government and the Carnegie Institute of Washington (I was a guest in Yucatán of the well-known American archaeologist Sylvanus Morley who was in charge of excavations) have reconstructed many remarkable ancient buildings which can be seen by the modern traveler. In Uxmal one of the most famous ruling families was the Xiu (pronounced *shoo*). Their genealogy has been traced back accurately to the year A.D. 1400. The descendants were still living near their former capital in the village of Ticul where I visited them in 1940. The old slit drums, or *tunkul*, formerly used for signaling, were brought out, the musicians called together, and I was given true Mexican hospitality while recording present-day rhythms on ancient Mayan instruments. No one knows what the ancient Mayan music was, but the many musical instruments shown in early Mayan sculpture reveal that music was by no means neglected among the arts.

Nowdays the fiddle and the guitar are popular in Yucatán villages; however, there are still many of the ancient slit drums that have preserved their beautiful resonant tones, on which present-day Maya musicians performed for me with all the dignity and solemnity of their remote ancestors. Two drums, one large, one small, with two tones each, were played simultaneously by the same man. The *tunkul,* similar to the teponaztli of the Aztecs, was made of *chicozapote* wood, the tree which also provides chicle for chewing gum, and is played with the butt of a palm leaf which was said to give it a better sound. The large and small tunkul were always played together and followed by another drum called the *saraktan.* Later in New York when a young American composer heard the recording I had made of these instruments, she was so delighted by their tones that she wrote a short symphonic piece utilizing many of them, together with a modern flute and clarinet.

I was helped greatly on this expedition by Oscar Straus, the grandson of my first sponsor, who was at that time at the American Embassy in Mexico City. He accompanied me into certain remote regions, providing transportation for me and my assistant, a specialist on Mexican Indians, and filming the ceremonies of many Indian tribes, including the thrilling *Los Voladores,* the Flying Pole Dance in Puebla, and the beautiful Plume Dance and the fireworks ceremonies in Oaxaca.

The traces of ancient races are especially numerous in Oaxaca, west of the Isthmus of Tehuantepec. Long before Columbus discovered America, there flourished here great civilizations which modern scientists are learning to interpret and relate to each other. It was here that Dr. Alfonso Caso discovered the renowned ruins of Monte Albán, and while I was working with local Indians nearby, he took me to see the beautiful frescoes and the famed jewels unearthed at Monte Albán. Not far away is Mitla, "the town of souls" or "the place of the dead," whose ruins demonstrate so marvelously the building genius of the early Toltecs. Mitla was the burial ground for early Zapotecan kings.

There are numerous cultures of great interest in the Oaxaca area, some of which have unusual traits and special ceremonies. These include complex ancient rituals for clearing land, for sowing crops, for harvesting the first ears of corn (like the first-fruits ceremonials in many parts of the world); various types of harvest festivals; rituals for hunting, marriage, and birth; rituals for sponsors of festivals and for becoming village officials; ceremonials to divine the cause of sickness, and the name of a thief or murderer; and healing rites reminiscent of the practices of African medicine men. Some rituals have kept their pagan form and show very little Christian influence, but with the Zapotecs the public rituals are usually connected with a saint's day of the Church, and often include some phase of Spanish history.

Of the seventeen groups which now inhabit this region, the Zapotecs are the largest and with the Mixtecs are thought to be the descendants of the great Toltec nation, which disintegrated in the twelfth century. Historians tell us that several groups of exiled Toltec warriors migrated southward to settle in Teotitlán, where they established their first capital in the thirteenth century. These settlers were called Zapotecs, "people from the land of the *zapote* trees."

In a picturesque Zapotecan village, on its saint's day, I recorded the Plume Dance of the Conquest, one of the most colorful dances of the Mexican fiestas. This represents the meeting of Montezuma, the Aztec king, and his courtiers, wearing tall headdresses of gorgeously colored plumes, and Cortez, escorted by his soldiers. In some districts this dance is performed for New Year's when the Zapotecs believe Montezuma joins in the dance bestowing health, good crops, and blessings on all who bring him offerings.

Fireworks were an essential part of these fiestas and the villagers were taxed to pay for the making of papier-mâché giants, dwarfs, little bulls with real bull horns, and a great castle, all of them covered with firecrackers, adding to the excitement by exploding in showers of colored sparks.

A drummer and a musician playing either the *chirimía*, a wide-mouthed flute about one foot long with detachable mouthpiece, or a brass trumpet or bugle supplied the music. Each of the papier-mâché creations had its own particular fireworks music.

The little bull or *torrito* was first to come out, charging about, scattering sparks among the crowd until, amid great excitement, he burned himself out. The weird tones of the chirimía accompanied by a solitary drum—a hollowed-out log about two feet long covered with a goatskin membrane and beaten with two thin sticks —provided thrilling "bull ring" music for this scene.

Then the giants appeared, male and female dancing opposite each other as the firecrackers went off. The dwarfs danced a wild fandango and the grand finale was the enormous castle, which went off in a crackling blaze of glory.

At most fiestas there was also a band of from twelve to twenty musicians who played modern instruments in preference to the traditional chirimía and log drum, but these two were still the favorite instruments for church feasts, playing throughout the days of preparation for the feast day and officially announcing the fiesta around four o'clock in the morning before settling down to play all day long in the churchyard. The modern chirimías are thought to have the same range as the ancient flutes, which they have now replaced.

Musicians of either the modern or the traditional order could play for such secular occasions as weddings or the visit of a distinguished guest, but the traditional instruments were regarded as absolutely indispensable for religious occasions, such as church rituals, funerals, and fiestas for the village patron saint. As a result, a Zapotecan musician enjoyed considerable prestige in the community. He was exempt from taxation and from all public service; his payment, at least when I was there in 1940, still consisted of food, drink, and tobacco. If entertained at supper before coming out to play for hours on end in the fireworks fiesta, the musicians considered themselves handsomely paid.

In the state of Puebla, the Otomis have a dance which goes back to a very early period in Mexican history. *Los Voladores* (The Fliers) embraces a symbolism many centuries old. The performers dance at the top of a pole as tall as a ship's mast, and then fly to earth on unwinding long ropes. Most of the Indians have forgotten the symbolism of their sky dance; only the very old men remember. The fliers are dressed as birds with tail-feather headdresses representing the sacred birds that guarded the points of the compass. The ceremony—for it is much more a ceremony than a dance—was closely connected with the old calendar representing the Indian century or cycle of fifty-two years, which was divided into four groups of thirteen years each. The dances and the songs of *Los Voladores* were in groups of four, and the four fliers made thirteen rounds each while flying to earth—four times thirteen, or fifty-two, the number of years in the cycle.

The dance began with the performers, four dancers and a musician, scrambling up the seventy-foot pole to a tiny platform only twenty-four inches in diameter. One by one, they danced at this dizzy height while the others bunched precariously together on the fragile framework surrounding the dancing platform. Each man performed for about two minutes with the exception of the *malinche* (the man-woman), who danced twice as often as the others. Finally, ropes which had been wound around the pole on a sort of spool below the platform, were tied about the dancers' waists, and like birds startled from a branch they suddenly dived from their seats on top of the pole and hurtled into the air. As the ropes unwound, the men descended in ever-widening circles until they reached the ground.

This ceremony calls for enormous courage, and the dancers usually prepare for it by consuming a considerable amount of tequila with the result that they sometimes lose their balance while dancing, fall, and are killed instantly. The framework on top of the pole has also been known to break, crashing them all to earth; the ropes may break or the pole itself snap under their weight. I was told that the ceremony was at that time prohibited by law, and that this village and two others were able to continue the practice only because of their remoteness. Watching from below I wondered why anyone would choose to perform such a ritual in the name of dancing. At the performance we recorded, the Otomi villagers grouped below watched breathlessly, roaring their approval when it was accomplished without mishap.

The accompaniment for this hair-raising spectacle was supplied by an older man on the platform who provided music for the dancers by playing a flute and a little drum simultaneously, until the final flight song when he, too, pitched head downward from his perch, catching the rope with his feet, still playing the flute and drum while flying earthward.

There were thirteen different melodies which I recorded, two for each of the four fliers, four for the "man-woman," and one for the flight.

The old man who played the flute and drum of the flight song in my recordings was very famous throughout the countryside because he had survived more than thirty years of flying in this precarious dance, and locally was accorded the same adoration as a popular bullfighter.

On the return trip from this village, the rough roads were too much for the car, and after hitting an unavoidable bump, oil started pouring out. My Scandinavian assistant knew the local scene well, as she had spent all her mature life in Mexico. She was a model of resourcefulness. We were all ordered to "get out and chew!"

The three of us had sore jaws for days afterward from chewing raw chicle, the sap of the indigenous trees which provide the essential ingredient for chewing gum and which, fortunately for us, grew beside the road, where we had had our accident.

After what felt like hours of continuous chewing, we had softened enough great chunks of this gum in the raw to stop up the gaping hole temporarily and crawl back into Mexico City. The car was irreparably damaged and had to be replaced, but we blessed the old one for getting us home and not leaving us stranded in that deserted spot. We would have had a long trek back on foot or at best, a tedious donkey ride of several days.

To the north of Mexico City in the mountains of Sonora is one of the most unspoiled cultures to be found in Mexico. There are several thousand Yaqui still living in Sonora, but when I was there practically the whole male population had been enrolled in the Mexican army and three exclusively Yaqui regiments had been deported to other states in southern Mexico and Yucatán. The history of these people has been one of persecution.

When the Spaniards came to Mexico, the Yaqui, courageous, resourceful, and powerful, were living on the Yaqui River in Sonora, northern Mexico, and fought desperately to retain their independence. From the arrival of the earliest invaders onward, they resisted all attempts of landholders to take their territory.

Yaqui history, dramatic and heroic, consists of a long series of wars, for they refused to submit to the political domination of the Mexican government and it is only since the presidency of Cárdenas (1935) that the policy of the government has been friendly to them.

Their tribal unity, however, survived all of these trials and they have managed to retain a great deal of their primitive culture. Being extremely conservative and distrustful, they cling to their ancient customs and ceremonies and pine to return to the homeland in Sonora, if not to live, then to be buried with their ancestors.

I found the Yaqui pagan dances closely connected with Catholic Church festivals, especially evident during Easter Week. The first week of Lent started the preparations for this fiesta, and during Holy Week the Chapayecas, or Pharisees, in impressive masks, rule the village absolutely from Ash Wednesday until the Saturday of Glory. When they roamed through the village they took anything they found and exchanged it for alms for the festival. Anyone trying to reclaim his property was severely whipped—another festival privilege of the Pharisees.

During the Saturday of Glory and Sunday of Resurrection there was a great festival, with the dancers called the *Pascolas* performing the Deer Dance in the *enramada*, a specially prepared arbor.

This Deer Dance, perhaps the most primitive and dramatic of all the Yaqui dances, is thought to date back to an ancient magical ceremony intended to charm the deer and ensure a successful hunt.

The deer or *el venado* was the principal dancer and wore on his head a stuffed deer's head, gaily festooned with ribbons and flowers. He was bare to the waist but a cloth (a woman's *rebozo*) hung down to his knees and was held by a belt from which dangled rattling deer hoofs. Anklets of dried butterfly cocoons filled with pebbles produced a pleasant clicking sound while he danced; to augment these, the dancer carried in each hand a large gourd rattle. The dance mimed the hunt and death of the deer, and village dogs running about the dancers, barking excitedly as the performers put all their talent into the chase, provided a very convincing background for my recording.

There was a clearly defined parallel between the character of the music and the mood of the dancer. When the deer was calmly grazing, the rhythm was tranquil; when he was nervous and anxious, the mood was clearly reflected in the syncopation of the music.

The drum began with a slow rhythm followed by a weird melody on the flute; the deer dancer wrapped his head with a white cloth, put on the deer's head, and took up his rattles. The dance began with *el venado* roaming around, stopping, scenting danger, rushing away, stopping again, then resuming his grazing or perhaps drinking at a stream. Then the coyotes (the *pascolas*) discovered him, pursued him, and, in a frenzied burst of music from the flute, drum, and rattles in which all the village dogs joyfully joined, finally killed him.

The pascolas were inseparable from the Deer Dance. The entire group or dance was sometimes called *El Venado* or *Las Pascolas* or *La Pascola*. The pascolas did a great deal of clowning but they were associated with all ceremonies, including those of the most solemn nature, and I have seen them dancing with profound dignity at a funeral ceremony. Their steps were very intricate, and an intensive training under a severe tutor was necessary for the boys who were to become pascolas.

The pascola dancer, bare to the waist, wore a serape or blanket around his hips and thighs, held in place with a belt from which musical bells were suspended, and bound around the knees tightly like riding trousers. Around his ankles he wore several coils of cocoon rattles, and the hair on top of his head was tied into a tuft called a *vela* or candle. Each dancer wore a mask to cover his face during certain steps, and for others he wore it on the back of his head.

Each pascola had a rattle, a rectangular wooden frame which had inside brass or bronze disks which hung on rods and gave a loud jingling sound when shaken. It has been suggested that perhaps certain disks of shell found by archaeologists may have served a similar purpose in ancient times. The accompaniment consisted of primitive harp and fiddle alternating with flute and drum. Beside the drummer a small fire was kept burning so that he could tune his drum by heating the membrane over the embers in the same way that African drummers tune.

The drummer was an excellent musician, playing both flute and drum simultaneously. The little finger of the left hand held the strap of the drum, which rested against his knees. He supported the flute with the fourth and fifth fingers of the left hand, playing with the others. With the right hand he beat the drumhead.

The pascolas sometimes danced in front of the harpist and fiddler, at other times in front of the drummer playing the flute. The harp and fiddle were of somewhat primitive manufacture but produced charming music which reminded me of Spanish quadrilles and other early Continental dance music.

In addition to the drummer who played flute and drum simultaneously, the clatter of el venado's deer-hoof belt, cocoon-rattle anklets, and gourd rattles, there were two ancient rasps and a water drum which bear further witness to the antiquity of the performance. It was interesting to find highly developed instruments in the same ceremony with the primitive water drum and the notched stick.

The water drum was a large container of water in which floated a gourd that was struck by the squatting musician using a stick wound with straw or corn husk and called a serpent. One author suggests that this water drum may have been connected with some form of rain ceremony in ancient times. The rasp was a notched stick which was rubbed vigorously with another stick; it had a gourd resting on the ground serving as its resonator. This was clearly the descendant of the *omichicahuaztli* used by the Aztecs in their death cult. (I have also recorded a relative of this rasp in the ceremonial music of the Hopis and Navajos of our Southwest.)

The musician held one end of the notched stick with his left hand, pressing the other end against the gourd, while with the right hand he moved the rubbing stick over the notches or grooves. While doing this he sang in the Yaqui language some of their most primitive songs. The text was often meager but always expressive. The singing technique, like that of certain of our Indian tribes, produced sounds forcefully ejected with the mouth almost closed.

The dance of the *matachinas* was another ritual dance performed by the Yaqui as a part of the Easter Week celebration and during parades. For this, the dancers formed two lines, using dance figures similar to the quadrille. On Easter Eve they danced inside the church, and later continued outside under an arbor until noon of Easter Sunday. As a rule, the musical accompaniment for the matachinas was provided by two violins. Each dancer with a headdress of bright paper flowers carried a gourd rattle in his right hand and a feathered stick in the left.

This dance was performed by a ritualistic society whose members join for life, often dedicating themselves to the ritual as thanks for survival of an illness or avoidance of some personal tragedy.

Yaqui music is surprisingly varied. The music of the Deer Dance preserves an aboriginal purity, while their religious music, chanted in Latin and Spanish, has been affected by European music. The latter is chanted by *maestros*, men well versed in the rites of the church, and a group of about twenty women—*cantadoras* or singers—answer the litanies and sing during the ceremonies while a group of little girls sing the "songs of the angels" on the Saturday of Glory and during wakes for children.

Among the Yaqui there are as well many songs and ballads (*canciones* and *corridos*), typical mestizo music performed with or without the accompaniment of the guitar. The violin-and-harp music used to accompany the pascolas has strong Spanish roots; also, the music played on flutes with percussion instruments provides interesting study, melodically as well as rhythmically.

The harps, violins, guitars, flutes, and drums of the Yaqui were all made by local individuals who made a lifelong study of their craft. On one occasion I went a very long distance to visit a Yaqui violinmaker whose skill had brought him widespread fame, and found him making not only splendid violins but charming musical instruments in miniature as toys for children and attractions for sale to visitors.

Later when recording in southern Arizona among the large community of Yaquis who had crossed the Mexican border and settled there, I played for them some of the music that I had recorded among their people in Mexico. They were profoundly moved. Some wept for their country. It was the deepest hope of all of them to return to their own land to be buried with their ancestors. Their songs, dances, and ceremonies are a common treasure, and by meeting and celebrating together the festivals of their ancestors, they have maintained their tribal traditions and preserved the unity of the Yaquis wherever they have gone.

Chapter 28

AFRICAN SURVIVALS IN THE NEW WORLD

African survivals have been unearthed in numerous localities of North and South America; in Brazil, for example, I recorded songs that seemed to have just arrived from Africa although it was more than two hundred years since they had been brought by the slaves to the New World. But it is in the Caribbean Islands that the African traits have been most persistent. In various areas there is a similarity of beliefs which are followed under different names; in Rio de Janeiro the Negro religion is known as *Macumba,* in Bahia *Candombles;* in Jamaica and Barbados *Obeah* beliefs are strong. In Haiti the religion of the peasantry, called *vodun* (the term I shall use) from the Dahomey word *vodu,* for god or spirits, is so much a part of life that any mention of Haiti brings to mind voodoo or vodun rituals and drums.

I first visited Haiti in 1938 after four expeditions in Africa. Unlike the casual visitor who hopes to see vodun ceremonies out of curiosity, I was seriously interested in studying and recording its music. Yet, whenever I talked to government officials or members of the elite in Port-au-Prince at that time, I was hastily assured "Oh, there's no more vodun in Haiti." But I had been told that just under the surface even highly educated Haitians, no matter how many years they had lived and studied in France, believed in their hearts in the power of vodun.

I was fortunate to have had an introduction to Stanley Reser, the one person who could help me at that time when vodun had to be practiced surreptitiously. "Doc" Reser, as he was affectionately called, had come as a pharmacist with the American Marines who occupied Haiti in July 1915. When they withdrew in the 1930s, Reser chose to remain on the Magic Isle. He was a firm believer and had become a great authority on vodun, one of the few foreigners who had been accepted as a devotee. He had established a oneness with the local people, spoke their language perfectly, and could instantly catch their moods and rhythms. He lived alone in a simple house, and apparently his chief possessions were some Haitian paintings, vodun drums, and a shelf of books on medicine, philosophy, and art. He was rarely seen at functions of the white colony of Port-au-Prince or with the elite of Haitian society.

"Doc" Reser was a sturdy man, brown from the tropical sun, with straight features and graying blond hair. He had an otherworldly manner that made him seem different from other men. His knowledge of the religious and folk traditions of Haiti was formidable. He was a man of deep religious experiences with a keen interest in the history of world religions and metaphysics. The Haitian rites were extremely familiar to him; in fact, he was himself an initiate and knew the signs, symbols and meanings in vodun. He said, "To know voodoo is to know the people; not the elite, who are usually ignorant on this subject, but the peasants, who as small children learn the vodun prayers as soon as they learn to talk. Reser believed that the Haitian peasant is simply closer to nature than we are and therefore can do many things that seem to us abnormal, for example, perform unbelievable medical cures, or when ceremonially prepared, handle live coals without being burned."

Vodun is not, as Reser explained, a barbaric cult; it is rather a religion of ecstatic, magical observances. It is a religion with hundreds of priests and priestesses, definite places of worship, rituals, beliefs, and great power, which functions from within and can never be really understood by those on the outside.

On several later recording expeditions to Haiti, I worked extensively with these people and their music. The first voyage, sponsored by the Field Museum of Chicago, was on board a large yacht, the *Buccaneer*, cruising throughout the Caribbean Islands. It was possible to go to small islands that were rarely if ever visited and still completely unspoiled—Gonave, Petit Gonave, La Tortue. *Langage* (the ritual language of vodun songs and ceremonies) was carried over from ancient African rites and, as recorded here, was unintelligible even to my best interpreters.

The ancestors of the Haitians (brought as slaves) came from West Africa, mainly from Dahomey, also Ivory Coast, Gold Coast, Senegal, and as far south as Angola. Some were brought in by slave raiders from central and eastern Africa. They were from innumerable tribes with different languages, dialects, and religious beliefs, even some Mohammedans as well as pagan Africans. Since they had no common language, songs, or rituals, a culture developed out of these varied backgrounds and two main religious cults emerged in Haiti, the Congo-Guinea and the Arada-Nago. Each cult has its own beliefs, dances, rituals, songs, and drum rhythms.

Ceremonies are numerous and one never sees exactly the same one twice. The practices vary from village to village and from time to time, and there is seldom agreement on the exact meaning of certain specific symbols. Possibly no two people would describe in the same way even the same ceremony.

In 1805 a law was put on the statute books prohibiting the practice of vodun, but except for a brief period, it has been practiced continuously. The Church tried to exterminate it and burned ceremonial objects and vodun drums and even cut down the sacred *mapou* trees, but vodun continued. Clandestine ceremonies were difficult because drumming is essential in all ritual, and the type of ceremony is indicated by the rhythms played on the drums. But even when vodun was illegal, the rites somehow continued.

Around the major religious holidays and saints' days, especially Christmas, there are numerous ceremonies, but ceremonies may be held at any time, whenever someone needs assistance or consolation and is willing to pay for the essential ingredients for the ritual. It is expensive by peasant standards to provide the cocks, goats, pigs, and bulls for religious sacrifice.

According to the Haitian belief, as in Africa, there is a Supreme Being, but no human has the right to approach him directly. The supplications must be made through the *loa* (deities), forces or energies which must be appeased through rituals involving animal sacrifice. They do not regard these rites, which have existed thousands of years, as cruel, since the animal that is sacrificed is blessed, having died for that sacred purpose.

All ceremonials begin with a salute to Legba, the guardian of the crossroads, the loa of communication with the world of divinities. The color for Legba, keeper of the gate, is white. The rituals conclude with a salutation to Ghede, god of life and death; the cosmic world of souls includes the dead. Ghede is represented by black and is supposedly wise beyond all the others. He is a divine healer, the protector of children, and the final appeal against death. The cross is his symbol and he represents the beginning and the end.

Each loa has a special *vever* or symbol; for example, the heart is for Erzulie, goddess of love; a boat represents Agwe, god of the sea; crossroads is the sign for Legba; and the serpent represents the god Damballah, symbolizing mobility and strength, brought directly from the serpent worship in Dahomey and one of the most important loas. The area covered by the vevers is consecrated earth and although this line drawing is so fragile that it could be blown away by a slight breeze, it is more powerful than any outsider could imagine.

After the salutation to the *mustères* or loa, the *houngon*, or priest, lights a candle and by skillfully dripping flour or ashes through his fingers draws a vever appropriate to the loa being summoned around the center post where food offerings are placed for the spirits. These are very beautiful and reminded me of Navajo Indian sand paintings of our Southwest. Once they have been intricately and skillfully created, they serve no further purpose and are soon obliterated by the dancers. The *hounsis*, the priest's female attendants and dancing chorus, enter dressed in white, chanting prayers, sometimes in Creole, sometimes in *Langage*. These prayers, which usually continue for hours, begin the ceremony "in the name of the Father, the Son, and the Holy Ghost." As all Haitians, since the arrival of the first slaves, have been baptized in the Roman Catholic Church, their worship is a mixture of the two religions. Catholic rites have been reinterpreted into old African forms and old meanings are given to new loa and rituals. The climax is the sacrifice, which varies considerably in different ceremonies.

I was able to visit and record ceremonies rarely, if ever, seen by foreigners, thanks to Horace Ashton who had gone to Haiti as the cultural officer in the American Embassy and loved the country and its people so much that he decided to remain there after retiring. He was absolutely trusted and much loved by the Haitians, and his knowledge, interest, and belief in vodun made him a welcome guest at all ceremonies even in the most remote villages. Through him I met the most interesting vodun priest I have ever known, Dr. Duclos Richard. He was called "doctor" because of his remarkable curing abilities; he was actually an herb doctor but he cured mostly by faith; his fame was widespread; he was called all over the country, even as far as Curaçao. He was a profound mystic, and while I was recording his ritual songs I learned something of the mysticism of vodun. He had never gone farther in his education than the primary school in Haiti and had never traveled, but had a profound knowledge of people and of mysticism, possibly passed on by his father who was a famous *houngon* in northern Haiti. He had a remarkable power over his congregation, which clearly had great respect for him. In his *hounfor* (where the vodun ceremonies are held) he had about forty trained acolytes (*hounsis*) who sang the ritual songs and were the chief ceremonial dancers. In the daytime he was a carpenter and ship-builder. He was so devoted to Horace Ashton that he made him sponsor of his hounfor and insisted that he be present at every important service, such as when he dedicated an additional room of his hounfor, baptisms, and burials of members of the congregation. He had been around his father's hounfor since childhood and learned all the rituals.

Duclos was about six feet tall and probably weighed about 190 pounds, much larger than the average Haitian. He was very healthy and strong; his face was full of character, and his searching eyes penetrated deep into one. His deep bass voice and impressive manner of speaking created confidence in everyone who met him and faith in his ability, which contributed to his remarkable success and popularity. He never mixed in politics but he was interested in the affairs and condition of his people and always hoped to do something to raise their standard of living, although there was nothing he could do except to give them spiritual advice and help them bear their burden with more patience and philosophy. Haitians accept the events of their daily lives, however difficult, as the gift of God, and he encouraged them to accept their blessings with gratitude and pass on the benefits to others in the spirit of brotherly love. His own great generosity, understanding, and sympathy reached out to his people in many ways. Most of his congregation had full-time work; his *hounsis* sold produce in the market, were washwomen, cooks, and so on, yet when the services took place, they seemed to have energy to burn and sang and danced until daylight. The ceremonies are supposed to be confined to the weekend when the participants do not have to go to work the next day. Everyone knows when a ceremony is about to take place through hearing the vodun drums.

The drums may sometimes emit wailing sounds resembling the tones of a friction drum by sliding the fingers over the drumhead (a glissando technique). The huge *assotor*, much taller than the drummer, has great power and is played by a highly skilled musician while in trance, in the state of "possession." A big drum called *djouba* is used for certain death rituals. The *rabordage* is a miniature drum, the only one the women are allowed to play.

The most sacred instrument is the *asson* or rattle whose rhythms have power to call the spirits to join the ceremony. It also directs the movements of the "possessed" initiates who dance and leap about with the accelerated rhythms or relax as the rhythms become calmer. The asson is a calabash (gourd) in a net woven with snake vertebrae and porcelain beads of ritual colors. When shaken by the priest, it produces a frail sound which is usually accompanied by a small metal bell. The mystical and musical function of the asson makes it a symbol of priesthood.

The *vaccines* are bamboo trumpets played in groups of three or four for secular songs and dances. Each trumpet gives one or possibly two tones and the players tap on the sides of the bamboo with small sticks to provide a percussion accompaniment. It is an art for each player to come in with his note at precisely the right moment. I recorded marvelous examples of this music from a carnival orchestra moving through the villages followed by a group of dancers.

Haitian dances are purely African in style, and many are connected with the vodun cult. The cult dances may have their origin with the Nago from Nigeria, the Arada of Dahomey, the Ibo tribe of southern Nigeria, or from the Congo or Guinea. The Petro dance, associated with Petro cult ritual and a part of the Congo-Guinea group of rites, is accompanied by two drums with goatskin heads. The chief loa (spirit) of this cult is Dan Petro. (*Dan* has the meaning of snake in some West African traditions, but the cult probably was built up around Dom Pedro, a Brazilian emperor; another suggestion is that it derived its name from a former slave and well-known vodun priest of Santo Domingo, Don Pedro.)

While in Haiti, I saw ceremonies that I could not describe here—strange, weird, mysterious, not to be believed. At times I saw ecstacy rarely witnessed anywhere else in the world. Devotees have assured me that the initiation by fire which I attended recently is probably the most beautiful of all the vodun ceremonies.

One ritual which I attended with Horace Ashton in a village far up in the mountains is particularly engraved in my memory. This was called *Mange Loa* (Feast of the Gods); it must be given by each *houngon* or *mambo* every five or seven years according to his or her financial ability. If a houngon has a large following, he may afford a *Mange Loa* every year, but that is most unusual. The mambo in charge of this ceremony was Madame Oliver, a handsome Amazon, well proportioned, weighing about two hundred pounds. Her manner was calm and dignified, her expression intelligent and kindly. She was an extremely clever and psychic woman and a very popular and powerful priestess. She owned a large plantation of sugar cane and had inherited more than one *hounfor*. She was devoted primarily to the Guinea rituals. Her large following was mostly women.

The ceremony I witnessed was in the hounfor which she had recently inherited from a famous old *mambo*, and she had promised to give a *Mange Loa* there to satisfy that congregation. This ritual requires many sacrifices. I have never seen such an extravagant sacrifice—white cocks, red cocks, black cocks, a white goat, a black goat, a white sheep, a black sheep, and finally a big black bull. (I was told that sometimes, depending on their economic status, hundreds of chickens, possibly twenty-five or thirty goats or sheep, four or five pigs, and one or more bulls might be killed for the sacrifice.) The blood was buried in a hole in the ground for the spirits. Haitians, as Africans, believe that certain loa require sacrifices to appease them, and every year a definite number of chickens of certain colors, and at least one bull, must be sacrificed for them.

The service lasted for a week. Each morning the mambo drew the vevers around the *poteau* (center post) for the several loa to whom they were going to make sacrifices. All day and far into the night the ritual with music and dance continued. On the final day of the celebration the music and dancing reached a climax of excitement.

There were many cases of "possession," some of the dancers had experienced possession ever since childhood. Their belief is that the disincarnated spirit of someone who has passed on before wants to express itself on the material plane. The god or loa enters or "mounts" the possessed one, who then behaves with the characteristics of that particular deity.

The phenomenon of possession is found in many parts of Africa. It is difficult to explain why no pain is felt by falling in a fire or how a fragile little woman while possessed by a male spirit may speak with the deep voice of the male spirit that has mounted her. Sometimes the possessed one speaks in languages of which he or she has no knowledge. Apparently after possession there is no memory of anything they have said or done.

I have been told that no two possessions are alike. Also there are no two ceremonies that are exactly alike. A ceremony may last a few hours, several days, or a week, depending on its importance. As the singing, dancing, and drumming continue, the rhythms gradually sink into the bodies and souls of the devotees; they become one with their universe. The authorities may differ on the descriptions but all agree that the study of vodun mysticism takes an important place in the study of comparative world religions.

Vodun, with its secret initiations, baptism rituals, white-robed *hunsis*, choirs singing prayers and chants, dancers performing age-old dances, still follows the ancient rites. Through the mingling of remembered African practices with New World forms, the Haitians worship their loa to gain the blessings of fine health, plentiful harvests, and all good things for themselves and for their community.

Section IV

EUROPE

Chapter 29

GYPSIES IN THE MOUNTAINS OF HUNGARY

Gypsies first appeared in the archives of the Western world in the early fifteenth century. It is generally believed that they came from India and are possibly descended from the Jats, a bold race of northern India. When they were broken and dispersed in the eleventh century, thousands wandered west into Persia and eventually into Europe. The route of their migration appears to have been through Persia, the Balkans, and Syria to Egypt, Greece, Yugoslavia, Romania, Hungary, and from western Europe to Britain and America, eventually even into Brazil and other countries of South America.

In central India there were nomads known as *doms;* in Syria the word for gypsy is *dum.* In the Punjab they are *tchangar;* in Persia, the *zingan;* while throughout Europe they are given at least twenty or thirty different names, among them Bohemians, *ciganski, cyganie,* gipsies, *gitanos,* gypsies, *tzygane,* Zigeuner, and *zingari.* In France they are the *tsigane,* and in Hungary, where they first appeared in the mid-fifteenth century, they are called *cigany.* A further historical word (*The Gypsies,* Charles G. Leland, Houghton Mifflin 1883) about the Jats gives us another connecting link between them and the modern gypsies: "They were without religion, 'of the horse, horsy' and notorious thieves."

The social customs of the European wanderers appear to have little in common with those of their Indian ancestors. Some present European gypsies, for instance, eat the flesh of animals that have died a natural death, which probably would not have

been the case in India; and along with their traditionally accepted occupations such as musicians, singers, dancers, peddlers, tinkers, smiths, and fortunetellers, they are reported by early historians to have had no qualms about accepting the task of "carrying corpses," considered by their ancestors in India the lowliest work of all.

We speak of their language as Romany. *Rom* means a gypsy and *romni* means a gypsy wife. Gypsydom itself is embraced in the one Romany title *Romnipen*. Romany is an Aryan tongue which appears to be related to that of the Jats. The adding of the letters *ni* to denote feminine gender is distinctly Hindi.

Wherever they go in the world gypsies are a closely knit group. In America they now travel more often in Cadillacs than in covered wagons, and pretty gypsy women, who have set up fortunetelling businesses in the main American cities, bear only slight resemblance to their nomadic ancestors. However, in times of stress or emergency, even in the heart of a great city, they form one strong united body resisting any force working against them, which may well explain their survival under the harsh conditions which, as a race, they have endured for centuries. When the daughter of the "King" of the gypsies in America was seriously ill not long ago, I was told that the entire group came and kept vigil in the reception room of the hospital day and night quietly waiting for the crisis to pass, withdrawing only when assured that the girl would recover.

In Hungary during the last hundred years, some of these wanderers settled long enough to build small huts at the edge of villages, for winter habitation only, and find work as smiths, basketmakers, and other craft workers. However, it is as musicians that they are chiefly known all over the world; but, as Béla Bartók so succinctly put it: "Those who believe that all Hungarian gypsies were born with a violin in their hands are wrong." According to statistics, Bartók said, only six percent of Hungarian gypsies have become musicians, and even these are not consistent in their method of playing or in the material they perform.

It was surprising to find how few of the village and nomad gypsies played any instrument at all. Although they sing their songs in Romany, the Hungarian gypsy musicians took many of their songs from old Hungarian folk melodies—as in Romania, where the gypsies played Romanian folk songs. They do, in fact, adopt the indigenous music of any country they inhabit, making it their own by playing it in a highly individual and ornamented style.

Gypsy orchestras, usually comprising first and second violins, contrabass, clarinet, and cimbalom, are the traditional entertainers in Hungarian cafés and restaurants everywhere, their performance always referred to as "exuberant" because of the excessive ornamentation of the melodies and the complete spontaneity of their performance. The ensemble is usually undisciplined, with frequent interspersion of free rhythm (except for the dance tunes, which keep strict rhythm), and the first violin, the leader, often playing quite independently of the others.

Eventually, according to Bartók, there came what he described as an infamous usurping of the throne of folk music; it was called "gypsy" music but was, in reality, the free performance of songs composed in a folk style. It is obvious that this type of music-making is not of true gypsy origin but simply an adaptation of the music with which they found themselves surrounded. In other words, gypsies are, in Bartók's opinion, an excellent example of musical acculturation. This applies to town musicians obviously for the music of the nomadic gypsies is quite different from that of their urban brothers.

Zoltán Kodály in his *Folk Music of Hungary* (Macmillan, 1960) wrote, "Abroad something called 'Hungarian Gypsy Music' is known, but this is not real gypsy music but popular Hungarian folk music played by gypsy bands. It is not a gypsy creation but music which their orchestras have made famous. There are other gypsies who live and travel as nomads throughout the country, and their music has no connection with the music in town, which is composed by town gypsies, or based on old Hungarian tunes played by the town bands. There is, in Hungary, real peasant music which has northern Turkish sources; this music was created in ancient times and has been passed on to the present and is the basis of the present Hungarian art music.

"This is not to say that real gypsy music does not exist; it consists of short songs in Romany which are known and sung today mainly by nomadic tent-colonies and to a lesser extent by settled village gypsies; the civilized town gypsies, and hence the musicians, do not know them at all.

"Still unexplored territories, these songs have essentially nothing in common with the Hungarian popular style or with true folk songs. A more thorough-going stylistic analysis may someday make it possible to trace the origins of certain features in gypsy composition but gypsy composers at best are never more than second-rate imitators of the regular Hungarian style."

When I was invited to the Hungarian Music Festival in Budapest in 1959, it was the music of the nomadic gypsy tent-dwellers that held me in Hungary after the festival and eventually took me into the mountains of northern and eastern Hungary to record their music. The gypsies whose winter settlements were on the fringes of Bogács and Gyöngyös were nomadic in the summer and their wagons and horses still played an essential part in their life. They seemed so much more children of nature than the gypsies I was to visit on my second trip in the summer of 1964. Possibly they were more primitive than those who had settled near Szentendre, now a small city of about thirty thousand not far from Budapest, but in the north in 1959, I found groups completely uninhibited and certainly more exuberant than the gypsies I recorded who had been forced to live in a collective farm in Communist Romania. Here their gaiety and exuberance, always so much a part of the gypsies' nature, had been greatly subdued due to their imposed work load.

The governments of the eastern European countries considered gypsies to be unproductive parasites on society, and many of the gypsy men and women now have to work on small farms, on big collective farms, or in factories in the towns.

My companions in 1959 on the journey to Bogács and Gyöngyös were Rudolf Vig and Balint Sarosi, young musicologists from the Hungarian Academy of Science. Rudi spoke Hungarian, fluent Russian, and some Romany, but no English; Balint spoke Hungarian, a little French, and no English; I spoke English, French, and no Hungarian, so as we traveled by car through the glorious countryside up into the mountains we had to work out a system of communication. Rudi had a Hungarian–English dictionary; Balint had a dictionary of Hungarian–French; and I had a French–English dictionary. And so we were able to converse, animatedly and often hilariously and, as it turned out, with great efficiency, for in spite of this linguistic impasse, I collected beautiful Romany songs, as well as vivid photographic studies of the gypsies.

Arriving at the mountain village of Bogács, we went directly to the farm of Rudi's aunt where she and her delightful family had made wonderful preparations for our visit. It was a very compact farm with fruit trees, birds, flowers, and farm animals all cozily installed in the family compound. As always, I carried my bag of rice and package of tea, a habit formed many years ago because of my difficulty in adjusting a sensitive digestion to the vicissitudes of strange diets all over the world. I had worked out a way of not hurting my hosts' feeling by refusing their food. Upon arrival as a guest I would take the earliest opportunity to confide to my hostess that I had recently suffered a stomach upset and that I could eat only boiled rice and drink only tea, supplies of which I had brought with me. This protective measure could quickly be dropped if, as in this case, I made a speedy recovery when meals of delicious new potatoes, chicken, and corn from the farm garden appeared on the table.

My room in the farmhouse was the one reserved exclusively for brides, and it was opened especially in my honor (there had not been a bride in the family for some years). The walls were covered with photographs of bridal couples, former occupants of what must have been the softest bed in the world. I, who for years have had to sleep on boards because of a back injury, found myself enveloped in feathers, but I was later grateful for their warmth when the autumn nights turned cold.

The main room—used for sitting, dining, and as my recording studio—was constantly crowded with family and friends coming and going, eating, chatting, singing. There was even a gay corn-husking party one evening. The farmers sang as they worked, and their songs are some of the most beautiful folk melodies in my collection.

On Sunday morning I was taken to church and, concealed in a balcony, recorded a most unusual type of village religious service, entirely vocal. The chief singers were old women who had preserved a special type of singing. The priest supplied the only male voice in the service. The men and boys amused themselves in the churchyard smoking their pipes and gossiping while their wives prayed for their souls and the old women sang. I found that it was typical throughout Hungary that usually only the women attended church services.

The gypsies in the north were immensely volatile. Their moods could change in a second. A man or woman might be caressing a child one moment, and at the next, for the smallest irritation or interruption, strike out with such force that the child would be knocked to the ground. Such blows had only a momentary sobering effect because the children, immediately on their feet again, merely kept out of range and carried on as though nothing had happened. This impetuous temperament was something I had never before seen, even among primitive societies of Asia and Africa. Gypsy behavior is so unpredictable and changeable that I could never be sure from one moment to the next how anyone would react.

As with gypsies everywhere, the females were the most adorned, flamboyant in soft blouses and full skirts in combinations of brilliant and fantastic color. Their gayest costumes and brightest beads were saved for village forays or for begging in nearby towns. When I arrived with my recording equipment, it suddenly became a great occasion, and the women disappeared, to emerge again from their tents in all their finery. Children came running from everywhere and crowded about, their great black eyes fixed upon me; the tiny ones were nude, and the larger ones were in ragged clothing. One small girl seemed more unkempt and even dirtier than the others, and for some reason I felt drawn to this neglected creature; perhaps she personified for me all the wild gypsy lore I had unconsciously absorbed since childhood.

Her hair, which I am sure had never in her six or seven years seen a comb, was so matted and tangled you could barely find her eyes. She peered through this shaggy fringe like a watchful dog, clinging all the time to the legs of a huge and most impressive man with a stunning mustache and a tremendous air of challenge and authority. He was described to me as "King" of the gypsies, and although he barked harsh commands to old and young, he was touchingly tender in his attitude to the child clinging to his knees.

Even though one knows many of them capable of being rogues and pilferers, it was refreshing, in this age of conformity, to come upon such completely uninhibited people; and I did not welcome the idea that there might come a time when there will be no roaming gypsies singing their haunting Romany songs and dancing their spirited dances. I was involved in more than one argument with the governmental powers during my last visit by stating the unpopular opinion that gypsies add much to the gaiety of nations and certainly have made a very interesting contribution to music.

The nomad gypsy, like all primitives, pours out his heart in music with the slightest encouragement. I remember an occasion when driving to a country wedding in Romania with my assistant and interpreter, we were nearly late because I saw a group of gypsies camped in a nearby field and insisted on stopping. We left the car on the roadside and within minutes of tramping across the field, my Nagra tape recorder was running and the whole colony was gaily singing and dancing for me, for which I gave them a handful of coins. I have never seen people anywhere in the world who could at the drop of a hat stop everything— cooking, hammering, mending harness, shoeing a horse, sewing, building fires, laughing, crying—and burst into a spontaneous riot of song and dance. It was like the sun coming out from under a black cloud or flicking a switch to flood a room with light. The whole group—men, women, and children—converged into one rousing cascade of song that set my blood tingling.

To be with gypsies in their open-air, natural environment was a great contrast to seeing them in the cities, where the women swept along the streets in their long skirts and the children begged from people passing by. Here in this green field under the open sky, the elders had a dignity and the young people had a vibrant charm that seemed to wither once they breathed the city air. The small children, too, were appealing in spite of their tatters and grubbiness. It was hard to believe that these were perhaps the same children we had seen the day before in town making nuisances of themselves.

They were so friendly to three strangers visiting their little domain that we were quite unprepared for what happened next, after they had escorted us in a body back to our car. Once out of the field we were no longer guests but prey, and they were the grasping mendicants that people know in towns and cities throughout the world. We were suddenly besieged on all sides for more money, and several tried to climb into the car to keep us from leaving.

When I returned to Hungary for the Conference of International Council of Folk Music in August, 1964, I had the opportunity to renew my acquaintance with Zoltán Kodály, who was president of the council. I had first met Kodály and his compatriot Bartók in the forties on two separate occasions when they had come to New York for performances of their music. These two fine composers, and László Lajtha, whom I also met in Hungary, are the three best-known composers of present-day Hungary, and have been intimately connected with the studies of Hungarian folk music, studies which have now made Budapest one of the important centers of the world in systematic ethnic-music studies.

Bartók and Kodály especially used Hungarian folk music to a great extent in their compositions, and Kodály became the chief spirit in the movement of systematically preserving, studying, and publishing the rich folklore of his country. In 1959 I was entertained in his home and heard much about the idea of making Hungary "a nation of musicians." When I returned in 1964, I found that Kodály, then an octogenarian, had been joined in this project by his young and beautiful wife, who had been one of his former students.

Kodály told me in a recorded interview: "I have always maintained that the music teacher in the small school of the tiniest village is more important than the director of the Opera; he affects the musical life of many more people." He felt that it was essential that everyone in the country know and appreciate serious music, and in his old age, he was satisfied that such music had reached into all corners of his country. He believed that music must start with the very young and be taught regularly each day in all schools. In 1964 there were a hundred music schools for children from six to fourteen years where there were two hours of singing lessons every day and twice weekly choir rehearsal. Students may, if they wish, learn to play any instrument; only the singing classes are compulsory. These children also have classes in sight reading and in complicated part-singing and are taken to concerts and taught to appreciate serious music. The seven-year-old son of my friend, Rudi Vig, sang rather complicated part-music with his father.

Kodály's face was animated as he told me, "This is just the right moment to elevate the public to appreciate Bach and other great composers but at the same time to remain Hungarian." It was more than forty years ago that he began working on this idea of creating a public in Hungary for serious music. When I asked him if he thought that music was the greatest export of Hungary today, mentioning the vast number of Hungarian composers, conductors, violinists, and pianists we have in America, he said, "This is possible," and added emphatically, "This is a happy moment now in Hungary that art music and folk music have met and 'married' together." He felt that it was extremely important that at the Academy in Budapest they are now publishing true Hungarian folk music. I learned from him that some fifty years ago this true folk Hungarian repertoire was sharply divided into the three main age groups: the young, the middle-aged, and the old. The middle-aged and the old people in the villages generally did not know the songs of the young people, and certainly the young people did not know the songs of their elders, who sang rarely if at all. Village etiquette recognized the right only of a married man or woman to sing at weddings, in church, and on some other exceptional occasions; even then singing was permissible only when indoors. Old men or women found singing out-of-doors would certainly have been accused of being intoxicated; to sing in the streets and the fields was a privilege reserved entirely for the young. Differences in occupations—industrial and agricultural workers, shepherds, and servants—also once caused markedly different categories of songs to arise; the well-to-do wished to be distinguishable even by their songs.

Even today the more important the landholder, the less interesting he becomes to the musicologist. Once he owns more than a certain amount of property, it is no longer considered correct for the farmer's daughter to sing, and even less correct for the farmer. The industrialist rarely offers material of any musical interest. In the more civilized areas, the repertoire of even the poorest peasant has now come under the influence of life in a town.

There is also a distinct classification according to sex, certain songs being sung only by Hungarian women, others only by men. Women generally have a richer repertoire, knowing the men's songs as well as their own. In fact, Bartók maintained that the feminine spirit tends to be the guardian of folk religion and superstition, as it is also the storehouse of music and poetry.

The strictness of this unwritten law as to who may and who may not sing, and where, varies according to districts, but in any part of Hungary it is often hard to get the older people to sing. Apart from traditional rules, the Hungarians are naturally shy and, being highly civilized, are perhaps self-conscious about their folk songs.

Kodály assured me that there were some young composers who had the same interest in this folk music that he and his contemporaries had, but said: "There is also another group that is trying to make a school of dodecaphony [twelve-tone compositions] but they are very imitative. They have not yet attempted electronic music because they do not at present have the proper equipment."

I questioned him about the state of the gypsy and his music in 1964, and he told me: "Gypsies are now being given better houses and are slowly becoming useful citizens, but the gypsy musicians, whose music is known abroad, have been civilized for more than a hundred years and are an entirely different group from the nomadic gypsies. Now there are gypsy doctors as good as any Hungarian doctors. One of the teachers in the Conservatory in Budapest, Professor Bonda, comes from a famous generation of gypsies. He is the great-grandson of a former gypsy band leader who, fifty years ago, had one of the best groups of instrumentalists in Hungary. Professor Bonda is himself a very good musician, probably the best professional cello player in Hungary."

With obvious pleasure Kodály added that recently with the tremendous emphasis on Hungarian folk music the gypsy orchestras have been forced by public demand to learn and play true Hungarian folk music, especially those accompanying singers on the radio. So now true folk music is taking the place of composed popular songs with the gypsy bands.

Kodály was one of the most impressive figures in the musical world. Small in stature, with blue eyes and long, thick, snowy-white hair brushed backward and down toward his shoulders, he had about him what might almost be termed a protective aura of quiet dignity and reserve which even the most extrovert admirer could not fail to respect. He was in every way a quiet man; even in the midst of a hustling crowd he managed to remain withdrawn, apart, and yet when questioned he gave most generously of his vast store of knowledge.

Although my last visit to Hungary was limited in time, I was once again, with the help of my friend Rudi Vig, invited to visit gypsy communities. One group had been living on the fringes of Szentendre since 1951, and although a few horses grazed nearby and there were two or three caravans in the settlement, the one-roomed huts had a very settled and lived-in air.

We were taken directly to the house of "the old one," clearly the matriarch of the group. I learned later she was only fifty-seven, but by their gypsy reckoning hers was a ripe old age. The color of her clothing, once brilliant and flamboyant, had, after much exposure to the sun and numerous washings, become beautifully muted. Her big brown eyes were soft and kind and over her black hair she wore a silk scarf sprinkled with pale pink flowers. An ecru satin apron covered the front of her full skirt, and her ecru silk blouse, with sleeves rolled to her brown elbows, was quite transparent, showing what must once have been beautifully formed small breasts.

The earthen floor of her tiny house was swept bare, clean curtains were hung at the windows, and the furniture comprised a bed, a table, one bare seat, and a small stove for use in the winter months. All the glass had gone from the two windows, as well as from the top portion of the door, and with the temperature in the eighties, I wondered if perhaps removal of the glass in summer was as close as these gypsies could get to their natural outdoor living. What wall space remained between door and windows was covered with colored prints of old paintings of Madonnas and an enormous print of the sorrowing Christ, crowned with thorns. In one corner a small rough shrine had been built with what appeared to be family photographs clustered about it. On the bed lay a sleeping baby, swathed, in spite of the intense heat, in a cocoon of woolen clothing; only a snub of nose and a wisp of black hair protruded to show the bundle contained any form of life at all.

While I set up the recorder, the woman seated herself on the side of the bed and took the baby and rocked it in her arms, singing a haunting Romany air with deep concentration and an indescribably faraway look in her eyes. Up to this point there had been only a small group of gypsy women and one or two men with us; now, as though the old one's voice had unleashed a flood, the little room swarmed with life. The baby woke up and, managing somehow to free a fist from the enormous sleeve of its enveloping blue woolen sweater, tugged at the microphone cord, trying to stuff it into his mouth. So many people crowded into the tiny hut that we thought the walls would crack. Children shouting and singing ran in and out. When the singer began a gay and lively song, her son supplied a boisterous accompaniment with the staccato snapping of fingers and a rhythmical booming sound made deep in his throat and issuing through his cupped hands. Little boys, in an assortment of cut-down clothing, so supple that they appeared to have no bones at all, hurled themselves into a spontaneous display of dancing with a stunning variety of steps.

As entertaining as all of this was, the extraneous noises were hardly conducive to a good recording so I decided that we should all move into the town, about a kilometer away, where we could control the crowd and achieve something approximating studio conditions. In Szentendre, Rudi arranged for us to record in the Cultural Center Library, and while waiting for the gypsy group to walk into the town I browsed among the shelves and was amazed to find in this small town massive volumes devoted to Byzantine paintings and the work of Picasso, Gauguin, and many others. On the wall was a calendar of magnificent color prints of treasures from the museum collections of Russia.

When the gypsies arrived, the singer occupied the solitary chair and the others squatted on their haunches around her. Of all the women who sang for me, "the old one" had the most perfect voice; she was, in fact, one of the finest singers I have recorded. Her tones were very true within the Eastern scale, though if judged by Western standards, her singing would have been considered far off-pitch.

All these village gypsy women were handsome and flamboyantly outgoing, but it was Biri who immediately won my heart. She had a beautifully formed face with very high cheekbones, her skin was dark and lustrous, and her thick black hair, under a white silk scarf, swung in two heavy braids over her breasts. Her salmon blouse was sprinkled with big yellow and pink flowers, a navy-blue apron covered the front of her long bright yellow skirt, and she wore clean white socks with brown sandals.

She was a very tall woman, but her big frame had not an ounce of superfluous fat; she was vibrantly gay and easily broke into song and dance. She was, in fact, the perfect gypsy type. Her smile, naturally dazzling, was made more arresting by the prized acquisition at some stage in her forty-five years of four silver-capped teeth, two on each side of her mouth. These gleamed and sparkled with every smile. Through the interpreter she asked with great interest if my teeth were real and was as delighted as a child when I demonstrated that they were. Biri had a deep, beautifully mellow voice, and when she came to the microphone to perform, she bowed to me, almost ceremoniously. She had about her a deeply ingrained elegance that was most impressive. As she snapped her fingers rhythmically while singing a lively song, I saw a gold wedding ring flash on her right hand. Later, while singing a lament, Biri suddenly burst into tears and ran weeping from the room. Rudi explained to me that the lamentation began: "My husband is dead, my children are dead, I think of them . . ." and I noticed that the librarian who had been standing by, completely engrossed in the singing, also had tears running unashamedly down her cheeks.

We went out to the gypsy woman and begged her to come back and sing something gay once more for us. At once she dried her eyes (on a very clean handkerchief, a point I deliberately make since all gypsies are universally regarded as being inherently dirty), returned, and sang the gayest song of them all, with the old one's son joining her with that strange, exclusively Romany accompaniment made deep in the throat, as deep as a drum and just as rhythmic. At once all the young women and the old one, too, were snapping their fingers, bouncing and swaying to the rhythm, and if there had been room within those dignified library walls, I am sure the whole group would have been whirling in a dance. As it was, Biri persuaded me to dance with her and, pleased with my effort, she patted me, leaning over to kiss my shoulder. A little later when a small girl of about five rushed over and put out her hand in the typical begging gesture, it was Biri who pulled her away reprimanding her with cross words and then, in her low musical voice, apologized in Romany.

In spite of the reputation of the gypsies, never in my visits among either the mountain nomads or the village settlers did I have anything stolen. Expensive cameras, recording equipment, and various small personal things were often left unattended while I was working but nothing was ever taken. At the same time, when Rudi was about to smoke a cigarette and lacked a match, Biri pulled up one skirt after another, and finally from deep within one of several pockets on her third or fourth petticoat produced matches. There can be little doubt that the full gypsy skirts with pockets within several flouncing petticoats had their practical uses.

Biri was the perfect example of the volatile gypsy temperament, immediately changing from her tearful outburst to singing and swaying, fingers snapping. Her eyes, so filled with tragedy the moment before, now sparkled with joy. She was the complete extrovert and warmly generous in her continual praise by gesture, by word, of the performances of the others. Of the old one she said: "She is very *sápe* [beautiful]!" When I replied that she, too, was very sápe, she flung back her magnificent head and laughed. "Oh no!" she exclaimed through the interpreter. "I am too black. I am a hooligan!"

Settled though these village gypsies appeared to be, in their music, as in their moods, they were totally unpredictable. So adept were they in the art of improvisation that I often suspected that the gypsy did not know when he was improvising. There is certainly no guarantee with a gypsy performer that you will ever hear a song repeated twice in the same form. True Hungarian music, by comparison, I have been told, is completely static. Record a Hungarian today singing a folk song of six verses, and six months or six years later he will probably sing you the same six verses in the same order and in the same manner. However, instead of the six verses the gypsy originally sang for you, he might, within half an hour, decide to sing ten entirely new ones, I am told, or switch the text from another song to the first melody, or he might sing the same six verses to an entirely different melody. All of this makes the task of the musicologist in this particular field not only an exciting challenge but a highly diverting, stimulating, frustrating, and fascinating one.

Chapter 30

BALKAN EXPERIENCES

I first visited Yugoslavia not long after World War II, before the country, recently torn by civil war, had been opened to tourism. It was a terribly difficult period of struggle, yet one could feel the upsurge of spirits. The Yugoslavs' dream to drive invaders from all their lands and reclaim their fields had come true after centuries of struggle. The West since 1918 was no longer ruled by the Austro-Hungarian Empire. The Macedonians, although divided between southern Yugoslavia and northern Greece, were free from Turkey; but in some remote villages in Macedonia, Moslem women had removed their veils only a few weeks before our arrival, we were told, although the law prohibiting veils had been passed in 1947.

The southern Slavs migrated to the Balkans from the Carpathian Mountains and for hundreds of years struggled against the Roman Empire on the west, the Byzantine Empire on the south, the Francs in the north. They eventually succeeded in setting up independent states which flourished for a time, but eventually these fell to powerful neighbors: Italy, Austria, Hungary, and in the fifteenth century, Turkey. The small state of Montenegro alone was able to resist conquest by the Turks because the bravery of its people was greatly aided by the mountainous character of their land.

Yugoslavia has been geographically at the crossroads of history; every inch of its frontiers has been disputed at some time. Albania, Austria, Bulgaria, Byzantium, Greece, Hungary, Italy, Rome, Romania, Turkey, and Venice have all owned parts of it at times, and each of them left behind something of its own culture and attitude of mind.

The frontiers are open to all invaders, but topographically the country is divided by vast mountain barriers which have prevented each area from communicating with its neighbors. Local patriotism, fierce clan pride, and medieval folklore preserved through centuries have added to the dissension among the people of Yugoslavia, heirs to a fantastic, even ferocious history. It is definitely a triumph to have united into one nation people so different as those of Serbia, Croatia, Slovenia, Bosnia-Herzegovina, Macedonia, and Montenegro.

Traveling throughout Yugoslavia's six republics is almost like visiting six different countries. I found people kind, gracious, and hospitable beyond belief. The Croats are persevering, idealistic, and quietly strong; the Serbs, vital, dynamic, and military. The Croats developed under the orderly rule of the Hapsburgs, while the Serbs grew up in constant warfare. The extreme differences in personality between the Serbian and Croatian cultures date back to the division of the Roman Empire; Croatia and Slovenia were placed with Europe and the Vatican, and Serbia with Orthodox Byzantium.

The Dalmatians on the Adriatic coast have been influenced by the civilized colonization of the Greeks and then of the Romans. Under the Roman Empire, Dalmatia was known as the province of Illyria and was under Venice's sovereignty until 1808 when Napoleon's troops occupied it. After the fall of Napoleon, Dalmatia became part of the Austro-Hungarian Empire.

The Slovenes had a kingdom briefly in the ninth century, but in the tenth century they were conquered and Christianized by Austria, and for nine hundred years they were divided into three Austrian provinces with German as their official tongue. Not persecuted, they did not develop as strong a national feeling as Serbs and Croats.

Montenegro—the name means "the land of the Black Mountains" —is the only area of Yugoslavia that has been almost continuously free. Under the four hundred years of Turkish dominion the tall, handsome, and brave Montenegrins pillaged, resisted, conquered, and hated the Turks, living on captured booty with subsidies from Austria and Russia. They remain today fiercely nationalistic.

Very little is known about Macedonia's history after the kingdom of Alexander the Great collapsed in the second century and was conquered by Rome. We do know, however, that in 1371 Macedonia became a province of the Ottoman Empire, a domination which was to persist until the end of World War I.

Bosnia-Herzegovina, a frontier between the cultural, political, and economic aspirations of Asia and Europe, has always been involved in world events. In Sarajevo, its capital, the assassination of Ferdinand, Austro-Hungarian heir to the throne, led to the outbreak of World War I; and in World War II this area was the site of many bloody battles. It is sometimes called the "Orient of Europe" with its noisy bazaars, fine mosques, excellent carpets, and music with strong oriental flavor. This beautiful country of snow-capped mountains and lovely lakes and rivers shows many traces of the long Turkish rule, especially in the architecture of the mosques, the Turkish baths, and the covered markets. Three religions have met here: Roman Catholic, Islam, and Serbian Orthodox. In 1463, when the country fell to the Turks, great numbers accepted Islam, but the majority are Serbian Orthodox. Numerous churches and mosques bear witness to the three religions, and the folk songs and costumes show remarkable differences with the various religions. The population is made up primarily of Croats and Serbs.

I went to Yugoslavia in the summer of 1951 as the musicologist of a UNESCO cultural mission headed by Chauncey Hamlin, president of the International Council of Museums (one of the several international organizations sponsored by UNESCO). A professor of art from the Fine Arts Institute of New York University was also in our party, and we were joined in each area by the local museum director. In Serbia I had an assistant from the Musicological Institute in Belgrade; in Macedonia and other regions assistants were assigned to me upon arrival. We traveled mostly by car. The road from Dubrovnik on the coast to Lake Ohrid in Macedonia had been built by Caesar, and I was sure that it had not been repaired since.

Ohrid today has grown into a great center, especially for Byzantologists, who are eager to visit the Saint Sophia, Saint Clement, and Saint John monasteries which have now been completely restored. But in 1951 when I went to Lake Ohrid, it was little known to the outside world. Though many houses in Ohrid are Islamic in style (built under the long Turkish domination), the city is nonetheless a remarkable example of Byzantine civilization. Practically every house now has a sign placed by the government proclaiming, "This is a Historical Monument," and the government provides money for the repair and decoration of these houses. But of even greater interest is the careful work spent in restoring the city's Byzantine churches (made mosques under the Turks). As recently as 1949, Saint Sophia was completely dilapidated and used by the local Communist Youth League as a boating club; now beautifully restored, it attracts Byzantologists from all over the world.

I first glimpsed the frescoes of Saint Sophia as they were emerging inch by inch from under the white plaster that had hidden them for centuries. The invading Moslems had covered these remarkable examples of Christian art in the fifteenth century as part of their effort to convert the populace to Mohammedanism. The frescoes, dating from about 1058, are intensely human, and rank among the greatest achievements of medieval European art. Depicted are stiff, priestly figures with sloping eyes, angels (flying and kneeling), evangelists and apostles in deep concentration, and, around the front of the apse, the twelve disciples, walking toward the meditating Christ. The fluent, firm composition and drawing and the beauty of the colors—brick red, slate blue, pearly gray—all contribute to the moving aesthetic quality of the frescoes.

The fourteenth-century frescoes in the Church of Saint Clement on the hilltop portray vividly scenes from Mary's life. One of the finest of these is the scene of the death of the Virgin, in which Christ stands by her outstretched body, carrying in his arms her soul in the form of a babe in swaddling clothes, surrounded by angels with gold halos. Though the painting is rich in detail, the technique cannot compare with the work found in Saint Sophia. It is thought that the drama and mystery of the Orthodox rites influenced the art of Byzantium. Like the Italians, the Byzantine artists did not paint for sheer joy, but to express profound piety. The eleventh-century frescoes of Ohrid far surpass later Byzantine art of the sixteenth and seventeenth centuries.

The frescoes of Saint Sophia and Saint Clement were so remarkable that we made a strong recommendation that UNESCO help in the undertaking to uncover them, for we knew that without skilled aid the project might go on indefinitely. When we were there, the only workers were a professor from Belgrade and some of his students who had voluntarily given their vacation time to picking off bits of the age-old plaster. However, with the help which later came from various foundations, UNESCO, and certain specialized groups, the frescoes were finally completely uncovered. When I went back in 1961 for the World Byzantine Congress, it was with great joy and gratification that I saw these frescoes perfectly restored.

Leaving Ohrid with the first light of dawn, we headed for Skoplje where musicians had been rounded up and were waiting to record for me. There were moments during that daylong car trip when, jolted and bumped by the appalling roads, I was sure that I would be buried in Macedonia. In Ohrid I had been very ill, and when we arrived in the early evening in Skoplje, I felt more dead than alive, but I set up my equipment and recorded through half the night. I have often been too ill to eat, but I have never been too ill to record.

The music of Yugoslavia provided so broad a canvas that I had to be content with only a glimpse of the amazing cultural heritage that these strong and vital people have passionately preserved and passed on from generation to generation.

For centuries the cultural development of southern Yugoslavia almost entirely ceased, but the Turks could not destroy or diminish the vital creative spirit of these people. They might stop them from painting and building, but they could not stop them from singing. The Yugoslavs sang of their past glories and of their heroes, fallen in battle, and these epics remain some of the finest folk literature in existence. The national poetry compares in literature with such beautiful works as the *Iliad* and the *Odyssey*. When Goethe read some of it in translation, he was so enchanted that he learned Serbo-Croatian in order to read it in the original. Some of these epics or historical songs are extremely long. One I recorded has ninety-six verses; another has thirteen thousand lines.

Choral societies, which were, in fact, secret political groups, flourished and exercised enormous influence throughout the long periods during which the people were under the heel of one conqueror or another. Their songs and their dances were filled with hidden meanings aimed at keeping alive their intense fight for freedom. Whether under the sufferings inflicted by Hitler or under the Turks five centuries earlier, they still sang, and under guise of entertainment they encouraged one another and preserved their hopes, traditions, and ambitions. Yugoslav religious art also reflects this continual struggle against aggression, and many tragic tales may be read between the lines. Even saints were depicted with drawn swords in their hands, and sometimes sorrowing people, who in the paintings were weeping over the crucifixion or the martyrdom of the prophets, were really lamenting their own sufferings and oppression.

The Yugoslavs possess an intellectual fervor that is very moving, even today when in so many other countries traditional art expressions have almost completely vanished. In the arts there is evidence everywhere of concentration on theater, opera, symphony orchestras, films, painting, and sculpture. But while their cities continue to grow, the peasant villages, the folk music, the dances, and the national costumes are not just for tourists, but are a source of great national pride.

If I were asked to choose one word of description for the music and dances of Yugoslavia, that word would be vitality. Despite the fact that Yugoslav women are expected always to dance sedately, there is nevertheless striking vitality in their movements. In the vigorous and colorful dancing of the men, the exuberance is beyond description. The flexibility, the feather-lightness of the tall, handsome Montenegrins, for instance, is particularly breathtaking. The dancing from all six Yugoslav republics is alive with vibrant movement and expressive beauty that moves the senses. The costumes too, reflect these people's vigorous imagination, in their infinite variety and glorious combinations of color and design.

Throughout the country I found many types of instruments: long and short flutes, some single and some double, bagpipes, trumpets, and stringed instruments of all shapes and sizes, from the *gusle* (one-string and bowed) to the modern and beautifully melodious *tamburitsa*, (similar to a mandolin). There seemed to be almost no limit to the forms and uses of these fascinating instruments within each republic.

Not only the town musicians but peasants from remote mountain villages and farms showed inherent musical talent. Some of the loveliest melodies I have recorded anywhere were played by shepherds in Macedonia on the *kaval*. This primitive, long flute is played almost exclusively by shepherds. They are often played in pairs and can vary in length from twelve to thirty-six inches with six holes. It was entrancing to hear shepherds amusing themselves while herding their sheep on the hillsides by playing soft, plaintive melodies on these instruments in the same manner as they have done throughout the centuries. One Macedonian love song I recorded was sung by three girls in unison to the accompaniment of two kavals. The song itself, like so many Yugoslav songs, was very practical and down to earth:

> Sevdaline, my little girl
> Are you still at home, my sweetheart?
> You have taken all my money from me,
> Five hundred piasters,
>
> Give me back a little money, my sweetheart,
> That I can buy some trousers,
> So that I don't have to go through the village exposed,
> So that the dogs don't bark at me,
> So the watchmen don't laugh at me.

Many of the Serbian and Croatian songs are called "women's songs" to distinguish them from the heroic, narrative men's songs of ten-syllable lines usually accompanied by the *gusle* or by the *tambura* (a form of tamburitsa). The women's songs are lyrics or narrative poems with lines of various lengths and sung, for the most part without accompaniment, by women—or very young men—simply for their own pleasure.

The grand finale of my 1951 trip to Yugoslavia was a festival in Opatija on the Dalmatian coast. Each of the six republics sent village singers, instrumentalists, and dance groups. More than seven hundred musicians and dancers came to share the beauty of their arts with each other and the world. I had previously recorded many of them in their villages, and seeing them again was like encountering old friends. They brought their songs and dances—appealing shepherd melodies, plaintive laments, and joyful chants, many handed down from rituals of a long-ago era when sacrifice was an essential part of ceremony. There were also the wedding songs of Montenegro, songs composed on the ancient nontempered scale and other scales, originally modal, which had evolved to include tones of the tempered scale—a change attributable to the influence of the modern, nonfolk instruments, like the accordion. It was an unforgettable ten days of song and dance, and I recorded day and night to preserve the wonder and color of the event.

My travels in Turkey began in 1953 at the invitation of the Turkish Information Service which provided most cordial hospitality and wonderful assistance and cooperation for my work. I landed in Istanbul on a Friday and my hosts said: "You cannot get any work done this weekend; why not sail down to Büyük Ada, a favorite resort island in the Bosporus?" As in Yugoslav Brioni, (Tito's summer island), where I had visited, there were no motorcars, only fine horses and gay surreys. There was nothing to do for a whole weekend but drive around the island, swim in the blue waters, or lie in the sun and dream—a complete departure from my usual routine. On arrival, I was met and taken to the Splendid Palas, owned and run by a man whose wife was the daughter of the last great Pasha. The hotel had numerous distinguished guests including the first woman educated in England, and founder of the first school for girls in Turkey. Another impressive figure was a very tall, distinguished Negro who, I was told, had been a eunuch in the Pasha's court, well-educated and with considerable influence.

A highlight of my Turkish visit was a fascinating journey as guest of the government on a small ship which was taking President Bayar all the way to the Russian border on the Black Sea. The voyage was chilly and at times very rainy, but the scenery was beautiful; and at every stop, crowds greeted the President with flowers, dancing, and singing, so I was able to get splendid recordings of the songs and dance music. At the ports nearest the border, I found interesting primitive music which showed a strong Russian influence.

Leaving the ship at Trabzon, I remained there for a while to work. Though this was 1953, eastern Turkey was still very primitive. Even in Trabzon, on the Black Sea coast, my hostess, whose American husband was there on government duty, had to go marketing with a Turkish woman. I was told that both had to wear heavy coats even in midsummer to avoid being pinched black-and-blue by the men in the marketplace. Women who were not at home in the harem or were not veiled were considered fair game for anyone. I heard many tragic stories of Western women who did not understand this ancient, lusty, and primitive approach to life.

My host was in charge of building a road to Erzurum, an ancient city in eastern Turkey. I went with him by truck over his new road, a hazardous trip because of unfinished construction and the wildness of the country and the natives. With the help of American army officers who were in Erzurum training Turkish soldiers, I was successful in rounding up people to sing for me. One of the most interesting of the many melodies I recorded there was an old folk song which later became a popular song in America introduced by Eartha Kitt, who had heard it sung in an Istanbul café and adopted it. The original from Erzurum in my published album of Turkish music has very different words from the modern version and a final improvised verse which tells how the mountain people came to Erzurum especially to sing for me. It is an ancient but typical Turkish mountain love song performed by a male soloist answered by a male chorus;

> SOLO: The water of the valley flows sideways,
> Do not open my wound.
> Blood will flow!
> Oh misty mountains! Hey!

> CHORUS: You are from the valley! Hey!
> You are very charming. Hey!
> You are my love. Hey!
> You are mine. Hey!

Turkish music seemed very familiar after working in Macedonia where, after five centuries of domination, Turkish influence was very evident. The variety of cultural groups, music, and musical instruments provided a fascinating field for a musicologist. In Turkey, too, the music had tremendous vitality which radiated from young and old.

On my first visit to Turkey, I marveled at the inspiring monuments to early Christianity. In Greece and Yugoslavia I had seen priceless treasures of Byzantine architecture—paintings, icons, and other rare objects. But of all the reminders of ancient Byzantium, none was more impressive than the supreme masterpiece of Byzantine architecture, Hagia Sophia or Santa Sophia (Holy Wisdom). Originally a Christian church in Constantinople, it was built in 523–37 by Emperor Justinian on the site of earlier Christian churches which had been destroyed. It is considered to be one of the greatest buildings in the world. In 1453 with the Turkish conquest of

Constantinople, it was transformed by the Moslems into a mosque; the magnificent mosaics of the interior were covered with plaster, and other Christian symbols were obliterated. Many of the surviving mosaics have now been cleaned and restored to view by American archaeologists, the first of whom was Thomas Wittemore, who began the work and established the Byzantine Institute. In recent years Dumbarton Oaks has carried on this work.

Chapter 31

A GLIMPSE INTO BYZANTINE AND ORTHODOX MUSIC

During five or six months of each year since 1960, I have been working with Neo-Byzantine and Orthodox music, from Greek monasteries—for example, St. John's Monastery on Patmos, where St. John wrote the Revelation—to the cathedrals of Constantinople and Ethiopia. This work has been done with a generous grant from Harvard University's Center for Byzantine Studies, Dumbarton Oaks. This beautiful estate in Washington, D.C. was formerly the home of Mr. and Mrs. Robert Woods Bliss, who, with remarkable wisdom and foresight, presented it to Harvard with an endowment to support research in all phases of Byzantine culture.

My work with Eastern Orthodox music, begun in Greece in 1953, has continued to be my most consuming interest. In 1961 I returned to Yugoslavia to work on Serbian Orthodox church music as a part of my project for Dumbarton Oaks. With the expert guidance and assistance of Dr. Dimitri Stefanović, authority on Serbian chant at the Musicological Institute in Belgrade, I recorded Serbian liturgy in the monasteries and convents of Serbia and Macedonia.

These monasteries have been kept open and active, both as medieval museums and as centers of worship. The Orthodox faith is strong and has been a power to preserve the national consciousness of the people of Yugoslavia during long periods of foreign occupation, and religious feeling is still strong in many places. It was inspiring to see the ecclesiastical architecural monuments—Nerezi, Studenica, Sopocani, and Decani—with their beautiful twelfth- to fourteenth-century frescoes, images of saints, and libraries of illuminated manuscripts, but none impressed me more than those of the early churches at Ohrid.

It was the music, as always, that was of paramount importance to me. While recording at the Church of St. Demetrius in Skoplje, I was interested to see that the priest sang according to the neumes (symbols of the early notation) from printed books (usual practice in Greece but rare in Yugoslavia). In Tetovo at Saint Cyril and Saint Methodius on their Feast Days I recorded the archbishops's liturgy with the first Metropolitan of Macedonia present. The vesper service which I recorded at the convent in Lesok was extremely moving. The abbess, Marina, was very ill and everyone, aware that this was probably one of her last services, sang fervently and very beautifully. At the seminary in Prizren the seminarists led by their music professor sang lustily and well, demonstrating the eight modes in use.

The finest singing was at the convent at Ravanica. The Metropolitan of Sarajevo, the Bishop of Zica and the Bishop of Branicevo were present for the bishop's liturgy. There was a choir of about twenty nuns, mostly peasant girls whose only training had been in the convent, who sang like angels. I have never heard a more moving "Cherubic Hymn" although I have recorded it innumerable times.

In the Serbian church the liturgy is sung in four parts, as in the Russian Orthodox Church, in contrast to the Greek Orthodox Church where the chanting is a melodic line sung in unison with a bass drone.

The cantors in the present-day Greek Church sing the chants with the nontempered intervals, with a nasal quality which on first hearing may seem monotonous and too oriental for the Western ear. Many of them claim that the liturgy is still sung exactly as it was sung during the early days of the Church; pure vocal melody rides above a bass drone.

In the Eastern Orthodox Church, the Greek liturgy, as in most Orthodox rites, the entire liturgy is sung, and no instruments are used. (Ethiopia is a notable exception; the priests accompany certain chants with drums, and sistrums [similar to the rattle used in the worship of Isis in Egypt]. Due to centuries of isolation from the rest of the world, in this remote land the traditional music patterns have been preserved longer than in other countries. But now, even there, as His Majesty, Haile Selassie, remarked to me, "Ethiopian music is of late developing rapidly with a great deal of improvisation and change.")

There are hymns for every day of the year, the oldest going back to the very beginning of the Christian Church. Among the most beautiful I recorded in Greece were those attributed to Romanus the Melodus, the great sixth-century composer, who lived during the golden age of Byzantine hymnology. It was believed that those early composers received sacred melodies from on high, from the "Choirs of Angels and Celestial Hosts."

As the music itself was divinely inspired, new hymns were created simply by giving new texts to old melodies. Many of these melodies have persisted and are still treasured as truly sacred music. But another school of thought refuses to acknowledge anything sung today as authentic Byzantine music; it is argued that the only original melodies are those preserved in the ancient manuscripts. The earliest musical notation is found in Byzantine manuscripts of the tenth century. A second phase of notation was used from the twelfth through the fourteenth century when a third notation evolved which is still in use today in a revised form.

Early music manuscripts have been uncovered, especially in the monasteries of Greece, and considerable work is now being carried out in this field. The study of Byzantine music is approximately in the state in which Gregorian chant found itself about a hundred years ago, according to the great Viennese musicologist Egon Wellesz, of Oxford University, one of the few experts who have deciphered the earliest manuscripts of Byzantine music. Very little had been written about Byzantine music until recent years, although much had been written about Byzantine art.

Scrambling up mountains to isolated monasteries on mule and donkey or sailing in treacherous little boats to remote islands, I could never forget for a moment that time was not on my side. I always had a feeling of "mission," realizing that even the religious music is changing, especially in the larger cities.

Already in the cathedrals of the big cities the choirs are beginning to depart from the old form of unison singing with a bass drone; more chords are creeping in. On the Greek island of Corfu, lying close to Italy and subjected constantly to Western musical influences, it was possible to hear from one church in the small square in the center of the city music performed as it was in ancient days, from another congregation four-part singing common to the Western Church, and from still another section of the square the liturgy sung partly in the old style and partly in modern Western form.

One of my earliest and most rewarding experiences in the project for Dumbarton Oaks was at the Patriarchate in the Phanar district of Old Stamboul (formerly Constantinople), the seat of His Holiness Athenagoras, the Ecumenical Patriarch of Constantinople, revered by the whole Orthodox world. During Easter, the most inspiring holidays of the Eastern Orthodox Church calendar, this towering, bearded cleric (seven feet with his high, priestly hat) was a most charming and helpful host. He speaks excellent English, as he served in New York City for about twenty years as the Greek Orthodox Archbishop of North and South America. He had in advance graciously granted permission for me to record the Easter services in St. George Cathedral in the Patriarchate in the Phanar (Fener). I recorded all the services, which continued through Easter Tuesday—the beautiful, fervent liturgy of Maundy Thursday, the Good Friday mournful music, the glorious liturgy on Saturday night which continued from nine in the evening until three o'clock Easter morning. Just after midnight came the victorious hymn "Christos Anestis" (Christ Is Risen). With the Patriarch leading, the high clergy, the choir, and the entire congregation marched out from the Sanctuary around the church three times; then the deeply felt joy of the entire congregation found expression with the joyous exclamation repeated three times: "Christ Is Risen."

After four hours of sleep I was back to record the Easter morning liturgy at the Cathedral. A multitude of bishops, priests, and laymen had assembled from many lands where the Orthodox Church adheres to the Byzantine rite. I recorded the scriptures read in Greek, Russian, Serbian, Bulgarian, Romanian, Lithuanian, Old Slavonic, Albanian, Ukrainian, Armenian, Egyptian Coptic, Syrian, Amharic (Ethiopian) and English.

It is difficult to describe the majesty, joy, and beauty of that Easter service. The archbishops and high clergy from various countries in splendid brocades looked like austere sculptured saints of old. The Patriarch with his long flowing white beard and piercing black eyes dominated the scene. The beautiful icons glowed in the light of hundreds of candles. The singers in two groups at the left and right of the altar facing each other were as unmoving as statues. The realization struck me that, after centuries of struggle under Turkish rule, the greatest triumph of the Patriarchate is that it survived at all. Here in what remains of the Greek Church in Constantinople, my thoughts turned briefly to descriptions I had read of the former grandeur and pomp of the church ceremonies of ancient Constantinople. Seated with my recorder under beautiful icons near the singers on the right with the chief cantor, I was poised to capture every note.

The choir began with a special tone which established the mode for the choir and the congregation. The two dominant tones were sung quietly, slowly, as a background for the traditional melodies which were strictly followed by the precentor. The choirmaster's hands continually indicated the rise and fall of notes to express the finest shades of tone. His voice soared and fell around the firm bass drone of the choir. While the precentor and the choir on the right followed the traditional melody, the choir facing kept the fundamental tone. Then the two choirs changed roles, thus alternating throughout the liturgy. They sang with devotion and fervor the melodies passed on and preserved from the early Church with no thought of adding anything original, individual, or spectacular.

Although scores of mountain monasteries from Thessaly to Crete, from Macedonia to the Peloponnesus are veritable museums of Byzantine architecture, mosaic art, iconography, frescoes, murals, history, and Eastern ecclesiastical music, some of the greatest treasures are found on Mount Athos, the Holy Mountain on the Chalcidice Peninsula in southern Macedonia. About the middle of the ninth century, Christian hermits began to settle on Mount Athos. When the rise of Islam destroyed thousands of Christian communities in the Near East, Mount Athos was a refuge. In the Middle Ages great scholars came together here, and it was an important intellectual center. The Mount Athos monasteries are storehouses of rare examples of Byzantine art and priceless manuscripts. Among them are early music manuscripts which in recent years are finally being transcribed by a few expert Byzantologists.

This active, religious community is now a semiautonomous republic of less than two thousand members. (In earlier days there were about five thousand.) The world's oldest democracy, it was well established when William the Conqueror landed in England in 1066. The old monks are dying off and young men today do not choose a life of solitude and austerity in this mystical, other-

worldly atmosphere. In the hope of attracting a new generation of
novices, they founded a school in 1953 at Karyes, the capital of
this small republic. Most of the monks are from peasant stock and
are gardeners, fishermen, carvers, or icon painters. There are still
hermits who live in caves or in huts clinging to the mountainsides
existing by dangling buckets to the fishermen below to fill. However, there are still some scholarly monks working on the manuscripts and caring for the treasures.

Life on the Holy Mountain has changed little for a thousand
years. For eight or ten hours daily the monks chant the divine
office. Some of the monks are regarded as living saints. Although
the numbers of monks have been greatly reduced, the monasteries
have an amazing power of survival.

Mount Athos cannot support a large population, but the monks
feel an urgency to preserve what has been built up through the
centuries—fertile fields which they have created out of the stony
mountainside, magnificent monasteries built with long years of
unbelievable labor, libraries of rare manuscripts, and icons of great
beauty.

In 1963 the millennium of monasticism was celebrated at Great
Lavra Monastery. Great Lavra, the oldest of the twenty monasteries
of Mount Athos, stands on a five-hundred-foot promontory. It dates
back to the tenth century and still houses eighty Greek Orthodox
monks. It is a storehouse of great treasures: bronze doors donated
in 1004, bejeweled relics, precious icons, rich murals, and priceless
manuscripts.

In my work in the Greek monasteries I had learned much about
Mount Athos, the Holy Mountain on the Athos Peninsula which
stretches into the Aegean Sea, where no woman may visit. Legend tells that a ship carrying the Virgin Mary to Cyprus was blown
to Athos by a storm. The pagan idols spoke ordering the inhabitants to pay homage to the Mother of Jesus who claimed the mountain as her private garden, forbidding the entrance of other females.

Eager to see Mount Athos, I went to stay in a small village
called Prosphori, named for a huge stone Byzantine building that
rose on rocks from the sea. "The Tower," as it is called, was formerly
an outpost of the monastery of Vatopedi on Mount Athos, and is the
last point on the peninsula to which women can go. In its present
form it was rebuilt about seven hundred years ago, but it is thought
to have had a much earlier foundation. I was the guest of Mrs.

Sydney Loch, whose husband had been given permission in 1928 for them to live here while he was writing his book *Mt. Athos The Holy Mountain.* They loved their life in this village and his wife remained in the Tower even after his death.

Beyond the wall the peninsula stretched for twenty-five miles and at the tip of the peninsula the Holy Mountain rose. Villagers went to work for months with the monks, and the monks came out to stay in the village occasionally, usually when ill or in need of a diet of milk and eggs denied them on Mount Athos, as no cows or hens were allowed. To the villagers, the Holy Mountain provided a constant source of conversation and curiosity.

My daily walk from the Tower took me along a path which meandered from the village between vineyards and pastures, and led across the mouth of a small stream. From there it turned inland toward pine slopes, past the ruins of a castle built in the thirteenth century, through an olive grove. The path ended in a stream bed and along the other side was a low crumbling wall stretching on into the distance. This was the boundary of the Virgin's garden, where I could go no further. I photographed the wall and garden, and a monks' house by the sea. Sometimes the girls picking olives or watching their herds scrambled over the wall to use the well, but they did this with great trepidation.

On my first visit to the Tower, I made the treacherous trip by boat completely around the peninsula. The winds often change suddenly, making navigation all but impossible, and more often than not the boats have to turn back to the Tower long before they reach the point of the peninsula. But we were blessed with good weather, and I was able to photograph all the monasteries from the sea and could at that time enter their ports, although recently new regulations forbid this privilege.

For the millennium celebration of the Great Lavra Monastery, as at all times, only men were allowed to step onto the sacred soil of the Holy Mountain. (Not even the Queen of Greece was permitted this privilege.) I returned to the ancient Tower of Prosphori for the occasion and there was great excitement with distinguished visitors coming and going constantly. On the day of days, I went with a local boatman to Great Lavra, and although it was not possible to visit the monastery itself, it was thrilling to be in the harbor surrounded by battleships, the Greek Royal Yacht, and ships from many different lands, listening to the bells of Great Lavra, joined by those of other monasteries on the Holy Mountain in a rhythmic accompaniment to the distant chanting of monks welcoming a gathering of Orthodox Christian leaders, probably the most impressive in the century: Athenagorus I, Ecumenical Patriarch of Constantinople and spiritual leader of the Orthodox Church; the Patriarchs of Jerusalem, Romania, Serbia, and Bulgaria; the Archbishop of Athens and all Greece; and more than a hundred prelates from Russia, Czechoslovakia, the United States, Cyprus, Poland, Finland, and the Near East. Guests including the head of the World Council of Churches, Catholic monks, delegations from the Coptic Church of Egypt, Nestorians of Iraq and Syria, and representatives of the Armenian Church and the Ethiopian Church, all were led by King Paul of Greece up the steep road to the monastery.

My assistant, being a man, had permission to attend and to record all the services connected with the celebration, so fortunately we have the entire liturgy beautifully recorded.

Following the Mount Athos celebration, the Patriarch visited several Greek cities and islands; I was invited to record the liturgies of all these celebrations throughout the country with the Patriarch officiating. It was touching to see the love for him and deep devotion expressed by the multitudes everywhere.

In September 1961, on the sunny Greek island of Rhodes, a Pan-Orthodox conference was held. Fifteen national churches, headed by Patriarchs and held together by a common tradition of liturgy, make up the Eastern Orthodox Communion. Twelve of the fifteen main churches were represented at this congress which had been called together by the Ecumenical Patriarch of Constantinople, who (since the schism of Christendom between Rome and Constantinople about 1050) has been the first among equals "in the Eastern Orthodox Church." His Holiness, Athenagoras, very much aware that the Orthodox Church must rid itself of ancient animosities if it is to have any influence in the modern world, had worked on the organization of this conference for a decade. That it really took place is one of the greatest achievements of many centuries.

Its purpose was to prepare for a synod of all the Patriarchs, the first in more than ten centuries, which would revise the liturgy, reform the calendar, and work out the various differences between the churches. The conference was presided over by the Venerable Chrysostom, eighty-one-year-old Metropolitan of Neapolis Thasos, and Philippi in Greece. It was run by Chrysostom, the Metropolitan of Myron (Athenagoras' representative), who was the executive secretary of the meeting. In the opening liturgy, he said in his sermon, "If I could characterize the Pan-Orthodox Conference in one word, I would not hesitate to say that it is a conference for the projection of orthodoxy on a scale which is Pan-Orthodox, Pan-Christian, and worldwide."

The three Eminences, Athenagoras, Pope John XXIII, and Moscow's Patriarch Alexei, were absent but were very much concerned with the deliberations. Pope John and Athenagoras were agreed in their efforts to bring unity in the Christian world. Athenagoras, as Archbishop of the Greek Orthodox Church in North and South America, had had much contact with Western orthodoxy; and Pope John, having lived in Istanbul for nine years as apostolic delegate, understood well Eastern orthodoxy and was sympathetic to it. They were close friends and were working together to bring peace not only in orthodoxy but throughout the world. Moscow's Patriarch Alexei was represented by Archbishop Nicodemus, thirty-two years old, the youngest Bishop of the Russian Church, which has about 95,000,000 of the more than 130,000,000 people that make up Pan-Orthodox worshipers.

Each morning for about two weeks I recorded the matins in a different language as the services were conducted in turn by clergy from all over the Orthodox world. Special services took place from time to time with splendid musicians who had come from other choirs. In the cathedral, the liturgy was beautifully sung.

Orthodoxy is modernizing itself slowly and planning certain liturgical reforms and greater unity. Athenagoras has said, "Christians must realize that they have one church, one cross, and one gospel, and every church must put its treasures into a safe-deposit box and issue a common money of love which we need so much."

Section V

AFRICA

Chapter 32

AFRICA REVISITED—ETHIOPIA

When I first glimpsed the fringes of Ethiopia many years ago, I knew that this was a place to which I must return. But most of the experiences in this book were to take place before the opportunity to return presented itself in 1962.

Since, I have been back four times and still this beautiful country remains for me shrouded in mystery. Much of the country's music until recently had been entombed with its ancient culture. So little work has been done by musicologists that everything one does here is a new and exciting adventure.

Ethiopia has been an enigma to the world throughout recorded history. Founded centuries before the Christian era by Semites from southern Arabia, Ethiopia has little in common with black Africa. These immigrants established a monarchy, became the ruling class over the indigenous brown-skinned Hamitic people, and imposed on them the Semitic culture and language, Geez. Long ago this language ceased to be spoken but it has remained as the language of scriptures and liturgy known only by the priests and *debtera* (deacons who may become priests). The official Ethiopian language is now Amharic.

This country, as large as France and Spain (or Texas and California), has been marvellously isolated by its majestic forbidding mountains (ancient geographers called it simply "Land of God"). It is a land with vast smoldering deserts bordering the Red Sea, serene inland lakes including Lake Tana, source of the Blue Nile, waterfalls seething through deep gorges, and gentle open plains for grazing—all this embracing a delightful, healthy climate. The fourteen provinces include an infinite variety of people, from primitive Negroid tribes to highly educated groups.

Ethiopia's civil and social customs, her language, and indeed her outlook upon the rest of the world had been little changed for centuries prior to Menelik II (1889). The country's initial integrity has been preserved against all outside pressures (even in a world that has moved in the past fifty years at a bewildering speed), for Ethiopia is the only country in Africa that has never been dominated (except for brief interludes) by an alien power. His Majesty, Haile Selassie I, recognized by the world as "the architect of modern Ethiopia," has had to move slowly in establishing the requisite institutions for a modern state. Government officials are now being trained to carry out the functions of democracy. It is a miracle that the Emperor, through evolution rather than revolution, has been able to unite all these widely differing peoples into one country and to preserve the extraordinary stability of this constitutional monarchy for more than fifty years as regent and emperor.

Whether at home in Addis Ababa, the capital, or visiting his provinces, he is in his office at nine in the morning; then at noon, as highest judge of the land, he receives anyone who has a legal problem or complaint; after a brief lunch and rest, he returns to the office until five, when he walks some three to four and one-half miles. He enjoys the evenings with his family whenever he can free himself from official functions. The Emperor has brought stature to his country and its people. Ethiopia was among the fifty nations that drafted the UN Charter, and His Majesty is staunchly supporting peace and progress for his country and the world. Through the OAU (Organization of African Unity, with headquarters in Addis Ababa), he hopes to help lead the turbulent African states to peace and progress. His personality is tremendously impressive. During the visit of General de Gaulle to Ethiopia in 1966, I was a guest at the state banquet, and despite the General's giant stature, the presence of the Emperor seemed to overshadow him.

The very name Haile Selassie has become synonymous with Ethiopia. His Imperial Majesty, crowned Emperor of Ethiopia, King of Kings, Elect of God, and Conquering Lion of Judah, is two hundred twenty-fifth in the Solomonic line, the oldest and longest continuously reigning royal line in recorded history, claiming to have its origins in Menelik I, son of the mysterious Queen Makeda (Queen of Sheba) and King Solomon. Tradition tells us that Menelik I visited Jerusalem and brought back the *tabot*, the sacred Ark of the Covenant, approximately 1000 B.C.; Ethiopia followed the teachings of the Old Testament until Christianity was introduced soon after the crucifixion when an Ethiopian convert of the apostle Matthew, it is believed (according to other authorities, Philip), spread the gospel throughout the land. Ethiopia was the first country to make Christianity the official state religion (about A.D. 327), with the emperor as head of the Ethiopian Orthodox Church. The Church is powerful but there is tolerance for all faiths. The second most important religion is Islam; Roman Catholics and various Protestant denominations worship freely; and pagan rituals are still followed by certain tribes.

The Ethiopian Church was separated for 1500 years from Western and Orthodox Christianity, partly due to its isolation by almost impenetrable mountains, and because it was branded as heretical owing to its adoption of the Monophysitic teaching that Jesus had one nature in which human and divine were mingled. (This doctrine was condemned by the Council of Chalcedon in A.D. 451.) The archaic liturgy has been preserved; no reformations have reached it; no modern language has replaced the ancient liturgical language, Geez; no modern instruments have changed the music. The Ethiopian church gives us a glimpse of the earliest Church practices.

It is due entirely to the zeal of the early Ethiopian Christians that we have anything remaining of their early scriptures and musical manuscripts, for during the invasion of Islam most of the churches and monasteries were destroyed. The dedicated ancients dug themselves in, hiding church treasures and manuscripts in remote caves in impenetrable mountains and on islands in the lakes; for example, Lake Tana has thirty-eight small islands which shelter ancient monasteries with a wealth of ecclesiastical treasures, most of which may be seen only by men. (Although these may be visited today in a powerboat, it is more romantic to travel in the traditional papyrus *tankwa*, which dates back thousands of years to the sixth Egyptian dynasty. It reminded me of the American Indian papyrus boats which I saw on Lake Titicaca in the Peruvian Andes.)

When I went to Axum, the Holy City, being a woman I was

not allowed to enter the Church of St. Mary of Zion, the holiest sanctuary of all Ethiopia, where, according to tradition, the tablets of the Ark of the Covenant rest. However, the chief monk of this Holy City, who guards the thrones on which past emperors have been crowned, brought out many treasures for me to see. Included among the crowns of the emperors was the splendid bejeweled crown used in the coronation of Haile Selassie I. The present church is on the site of the old one dating from the fourth century, of which only the platform and wide steps remain.

It was difficult for me to imagine that this small town of Axum was once the dazzling first capital of a kingdom described by the Arab historian Mani as one of the four greatest empires along with Babylon, Rome, and Egypt. It was here in 980 B.C. (conjectured date) that the Queen of Sheba lived in her huge palace; it was here that she first heard of the great wisdom of Solomon and went forth on the expedition which, according to legend, resulted in her abandoning the worship of sun, moon and stars, accepting King Solomon's religion, and giving him a son. Archaeologists are gradually uncovering more and more relics of this kingdom.

I was extremely impressed by one of the great stelae (mistakenly called obelisks), the only one still standing in a garden near the church. About seventy feet tall, it dates from the third century A.D. The recently deciphered inscriptions, mostly in Hebrew and Greek, reveal pre-Christian history, giving further evidence that the ancient Abyssinians accepted the precepts of the Old Testament. The peculiar method of architecture, a wood-and-masonry technique brought to this ancient capital by the Semites, was imitated in the decoration of the pre-Christian stelae and later adopted in building the early Christian churches. In Axum I was fortunate in acquiring two small ancient parchment scrolls of scriptures for my collection at Columbia which compensated in some small measure for not being allowed inside this holiest church to record the liturgy, although I did record some very interesting nonchurch music here.

Just to the south of Axum are the amazing rock-hewn churches of Lalibela, the capital of the ancient Zagwe dynasty in the remote mountains of Lasta. These magnificent structures hewn out of solid rock are among the wonders of the world. They were inspired by King Lalibela, who reigned for some thirty years toward the end of the twelfth century, a builder-king now worshiped as a saint in the Ethiopian Orthodox Church. While the Romanesque and Gothic art flourished in the West resulting in the famous European basilicas, King Lalibela and his Coptic stonemasons were hewing out these unique architectural structures that will stand for all time. The names given the eleven churches indicate that the King intended Lalibela to be a holy city, a new Jerusalem in the heart of Ethiopia.

European archaeologists are discovering, embedded in inaccessible mountains, some of the world's finest and most unusual medieval churches, with their treasures never before seen by any but Ethiopian eyes. Although many conventional churches were destroyed by invaders, at least a thousand incredibly beautiful rock buildings, many of them churches, have been found unmolested (mostly in the north country of high plateaus slashed by terrifying chasms), saved from destruction by their inaccessibility and strength. There are three kinds of rock church architecture: churches built inside caves; those hewn out of the mountainside; and the monolithic churches carved from blocks of rock cut free from the surrounding mountain or from the plateau and formed into churches. (The solid blocks of rock were cut out of the plateau by hewing great trenches around them. These giant blocks were sculpted into buildings with impressive carved or pillared façades, and then hollowed out inside.) It is impossible to measure the labor, love, and dedication that must have gone into these rock churches. I tried to picture the ancient carvers, having hewn a vast block from the earth, faced with a great wall of rock, setting out to cut and hack and chisel it with hand instruments into a church with aisles and altars, arches and steps. The largest of these wonders, called the Redeemer of the World, is more than one hundred feet long and seventy-five feet wide and is surrounded by an external colonnade; the interior is divided by twenty-eight columns into five aisles of eight bays. Other rock churches have remarkable carved ornamentation including reliefs of the saints and the king. Many of them are "living churches," still used for worship by the local villagers today.

These architectural treasures have been slowly but steadily disintegrating since they were sculptured into the mountain about 800 years ago. They belong to the cultural heritage of the world and must be preserved for posterity. A committee has been formed for the preservation of the Lalibela churches with Princess Ruth Desta, the granddaughter of the Emperor (who studied at Columbia University a few years ago), as the dedicated Committee Chairman. James A. Gray, chairman of the International Fund, is working with the Ethiopian committee and specialists on monument restoration with finances from U. S. Counterpart Funds and contributions from sympathetic individuals. The important work of the technicians began in December, 1966 and the project is progressing well under splendid management.

In Ethiopia with its half-million square miles, where the Ethiopian Orthodox Church plays such an important role in cultural and social life, there are more than 100,000 priests, I was told. Everyone is expected to go to the priest with all his problems. The rural priests are generally not well educated but in the towns they are now university-trained and are being sent to Greece, Germany, and even to America, to study. The *debteras* are an intermediate class between clergy and believers. Only the priests and the debteras know the liturgical language, Geez. Few are trained in musical theory, as they usually learn the songs and chants through many long years of training, and they perform entirely from memory as in the earliest days of Christianity. Many times I have sat on the steps of churches listening to the training of young boys who hope one day to become debteras or priests. I marveled at the patience and devoutness of priest and pupil alike as they repeated the Scriptures phrase upon phrase a thousand, thousand times still employing the simple timeless method of rote. It was to me a vivid reminder of all the priceless treasures that have been handed down the centuries through the miracle of memory.

During my visit in 1963, I recorded only church music. In 1966, sponsored by the Ethiopian government, my work was systematically planned throughout the whole country. With the expert guidance of a government official assigned to assist me and act as interpreter (he is now working in my department at Columbia), I was able to collect many recordings of indigenous secular music throughout most of the fourteen provinces. Also I recorded a wealth of Ethiopian Church music that was complicated and unique, differing considerably even from that of the Egyptian Coptic Church. While other Eastern Orthodox Church choirs sing a cappella, certain pagan elements, adopted in the early religious music, have remained here; the Ethiopian Church has followed literally the Old Testament, making "a joyful noise unto the Lord" with songs, drums, and sistrums. All of this provides invaluable little-known material for the collections at Dumbarton Oaks and Columbia University.

Ethiopian Church music is basically antiphonal unison chanting by choirs of priests and debteras, singers trained for years in the liturgical music and poetry (in Geez), with responses of the congregation from time to time throughout the liturgy. Two debteras or priests may answer each other and for a special occasion an original composition may be sung by a debtera. Other Eastern Orthodox churches have no instruments, but in Ethiopia several instruments are connected with religious music. In the night prayers and the dawn service (which begins at 1 A.M. Sunday and continues until the liturgy begins at 7:30) the debteras and priests accompany their chanting with the slow, persistent declamation of the drums and rattles. On weekdays the services are performed without drums. For special feast days, which are numerous, the stately Dance of David is performed by priests and debteras. The instruments used in the Church, in addition to rhythmic hand-clapping, are drums (*kebero* and *nagarit*), rattle or sistrum (*tsanatsel*), bell (*kac'il*), metal gong or large bell (*dawal*), staff (*makwonia*), and "harp of David" (*bagana*).

The kebero or church drum may be called the bridge between traditional church and secular musical instruments. It is the most widespread of all instruments and has different names in different areas. It is barrel-shaped, made of wood with skins stretched over both ends laced together with thongs. The ones I recorded were from two to three feet in length, but the size may vary from huge to small (played by women or children). It is struck with the palm of the hand. When used for sacred ceremonies, only the priests may play them. The ancient nagarit was considered a royal drum in the old days as it was used not only for rhythmic accompaniment for church dances but was also used to summon the people to war or to announce proclamations from the chiefs or king. The root word *nagar* means in Amharic "to tell." These huge drums range from three to five feet in length and are made of silver, brass, copper, or wood, with hide stretched over both ends.

The tsanatsel (sistrum) is used only for liturgical music and is one of the oldest instruments in use today. It resembles an ancient

Egyptian instrument. The brass frame, from eight to ten inches in length, has three wires (representing the Trinity) stretched from the sides of the frame with three metal disks sliding on them. It is used by the priests and debtera for a rhythmic accompaniment to the chanting. It is played outside the church only on rare occasions such as the Feast of the Epiphany. Kac'il, a bell of silver or brass about six to nine inches in height and from three to five inches in diameter, is used at times as a rhythmic instrument in the same way as the sistrum. The dawal, a large bell or metal gong, is used to call the congregation to services and to announce holidays. The makwonia has many uses. It is a staff from four to four and a half feet in length topped by a T-shaped ornament usually of metal or carved ivory. During the long, fatiguing periods of chanting (especially during the long night prayers) the priests and debteras use this staff as a support. It becomes a musical instrument when used to beat time by striking on the stone floor of the church. It is also used as a baton to direct the priests' dancing. The priest who carefully keeps his staff for his lifetime may refer to it as the "company of my years."

The *bagana* belongs to the lyre family and is one of the oldest and perhaps the most respected of all Ethiopian instruments. It is called "the harp of David," and is believed to be the harp on which King David accompanied his psalms. It resembles a Roman harp or Greek lyre and may be from four to four and a half feet in height. The wooden resonator, about fourteen by fifteen inches, is covered with tightly stretched goatskin. Ten (sometimes eight) long strings of gut passing over a bridge are fastened to the wide crossbar with wooden pegs; they are plucked from the front with a horn or leather plectrum, while fingered from the back. The deep, humming, buzzing tones are conducive to meditation. This instrument is played by priests to accompany their much-loved Psalms of David and other religious songs sung in Geez, not in Church but at any gathering. These songs of Geez deal with Old or New Testament subjects; they may be Bible stories, songs of praise to the Virgin Mary, the saints, and prophets, or prayers for the Emperor. One of the most interesting that I recorded is about Saint Yared, the saint of music, to whom it is believed the religious music and musical notation were given directly from on high. When the singer has neither harp nor drum, he keeps the rhythm by finger-snapping or handclapping.

The musical culture of Ethiopia, enriched by age-old traditions, is as ancient as the country itself with tones and techniques that have come down from remote times, yet the music is always vibrant and at times seems modern, even sophisticated. The sounds are exciting and extremely varied. Ethiopian music today differs tremendously in various provinces and tribes.

The vocal music of Ethiopia reflects all the influences that have been superimposed on the ancient Semitic-Hamitic culture. In the west, for example, Arabic characteristics coming in from the Sudan have affected the singing technique especially; in the north in recent centuries Portuguese and Italian influences may occasionally be found. In the southwest, which borders Kenya, Negroid and Bantu musical traits are common. For example, the rhythms are extremely complicated and vigorous as compared with the simple and serene tempos and rhythms of the central plateau.

It is impossible to overemphasize the role of music in life in Ethiopia, as in the whole of Africa. Practically every activity involves music in some form. The repertoire, therefore, is extensive, including songs of love and songs of war, hunting songs and work songs—for planting and harvesting or building a house; that is, for anything that requires the combined effort of a group. There are joking songs (sometimes at the expense of an important person in the village), and songs in which a man recounts his whole life history. If he is an old man, it will be a very long song and may include the migrations of his tribe and even the origin of his clan. In some areas a musician with a *masinquo* (one-stringed fiddle) may travel from village to village singing the news.

The folk dances are numerous and are related to many activities; war, hunting, weddings, and other ceremonies. The dancers may enact man's struggle with the elements to survive; they may express pure exuberance or religious feelings as in the Dance of David.

The vocal music of Ethiopia reflects the many influences that have affected Ethiopian culture, especially in the singing techniques; for example, Arabic characteristics are often found in the songs.

Antiphonal singing with a soloist-leader and a chorus repeating the refrain can be heard all over Ethiopia, as in Africa everywhere. Responsorial singing may involve two soloists answering each other, a soloist and a group, or two groups.

In general, Ethiopians sing in unison, but interesting polyphony can be found especially in the southwest where certain tribes sing not merely unison and octaves but amazing part music. The vocal polyphony with the Dorzai tribe of the southwest, in particular, is an unbelievable design of melodic patterns harmoniously commingling in four or even as many as seven parts.

Tribes which I recorded in the high mountains and Rift Valley lakes of southwestern Ethiopia (for example, the Wallamo) have a startling singing technique which must require unusual lungs and vocal cords. They grunt and hiss and puff and yell with rhythmic sounds that would make our avant-garde composers and electronics experts seem old-fashioned and timid in their vocal experiments with "noise-words."

The instrumental music usually has melody and rhythm only. However, among the southwest tribes, there are ensembles of fifteen or more bamboo flutes, each playing one tone, which produce strange and quite sophisticated harmonies. It reminded me of the Hottentot bark flutes of one tone played as flute ensembles which I recorded in South West Africa.

The *washint*, a small four-holed bamboo flute, plays delicate and lyrical long-flowing melodies. It may be used either as a solo instrument or with other instruments.

The *embilitas*, open cylindrical pipes, are played in groups of three; each player has a set of tones which are tossed about to share in a melody.

The *malakat*, a long conical brass monotone horn, is played by a musician who sits in great seriousness poised to blow from time to time in impeccable timing its one unique tone. (His serious face reminded me of the ancient carvings of Axum.) The malakat, the embilitas, and the *kebero* are used for royalty, but especially the kettle drums are essential for royalty; I was told that there were eighty-eight for the Emperor, but there might be as few as twenty-two for a nobleman of lesser importance.

The *masonquo* is one of the oldest instruments of Africa. It resembles the Egyptian *rebab* which is found in many Islamic countries. The single string of horsehair is played with a bow, also of horsehair, and a fine masonquo player can produce amazing melodies (including microtones and embellishments) which often range over three and a half octaves. The masonquo may be a solo instrument or be used in a small orchestra.

Perhaps the most popular instrument in Ethiopia is the ancient

six-stringed Ethiopian *krar*. It resembles the Greek lyre and the
Roman harp. A good musician can perform with the skill of a
lutanist as he accompanies ballads, epics, and songs of love, pleasure,
and joy.

All of these instruments were used in a song called "Tezita,"
an extremely popular and interesting song which is loved all over
the country. My interpreter said, "It is the song from which all
songs are made." A male soloist sang about each instrument, one
by one, as they played in turn and finally all together. This was
one of the melodies I recorded with the remarkable ensemble
called Orchestra Ethiopia, at the Creative Arts Center of the
new Haile Selassie I University in Addis Ababa. About thirty
musicians were recently assembled from remote mountains and
villages: wandering minstrels, instrumentalists, narrators, and
dancers. There was no written music for the ancient songs and
musical instruments; everyone performed from memory. They had
never before shared their different musical traditions. A social
problem presented itself when the priest, playing the bagana, was
asked to perform with lay musicians playing the krar and masonquo. They have brought together their indigenous traditional sounds
and a new musical creation is evolving. They are learning new
rhythms and melodies (recorded on tapes) from various parts of the
country, and producing a new polyphony. Fragments of melodies
are tossed back and forth by the embilitas (horns), long melodic
lines are played by the washints, new rhythmic texture is produced
by the combination of the kebero, bagana, and malakat. The
bagana when used to accompany religious songs has ten strings but
for this orchestra it has eight strings and is used as a bass rhythmic
instrument.

These "minstrel-musicians" have been brought directly into the
present twentieth century musical world and are being encouraged
to preserve their music in spite of transistor radios and Western
films before the last remnants of Ethiopian and African culture
have been submerged or completely washed away.

EPILOGUE

After crowded, fruitful years pursuing music as a way of understanding people and their cultures, I am now in the School of
International Affairs at Columbia University as Director of the
Research Project on World Music. This new and imaginative
approach to international affairs through music, the international
language, provides a unique and stimulating project, and its
potentials are boundless. The prospect of reaching people on the
cultural level (noncontroversial) is more hopeful than that of
continuing to be torn apart by widely separated ambitions and
interests. In these days thoughtful people all over the world, interested in understanding other peoples of the world, are making
efforts to find peace. Music affords us an avenue toward such
understanding.

In this new environment, research and publications are concerned with studies in world music, including work with more
than 30,000 musical recordings in the Laura Boulton Collection
of Traditional and Liturgical Music, possibly the most compre-
hensive collection of ethnic and religious music in the world.
The liturgical material which I have brought from the twelve great
religions of the world is unique. Scholars from foreign and
American institutions working in collaboration with our center are
using the music and musical instruments in the collection for
comparative studies with material in the field. Our program of
publications aims to increase international understanding through
the knowledge of world music.

Since childhood I have been filled with the certainty that just around the next corner was a challenging adventure, and my life has proved it. The marvel is that I knew very early what I wanted to do and have been able to do it with single-mindedness. To find myself now in the School of International Affairs where the collection is surrounded by institutes representing every area of the world is ideal.

Also, to be working in Byzantine and Orthodox music is the culmination of all my work in the field of religious music. I shall always think of the Byzantine project for Dumbarton Oaks as perhaps the most momentous and gratifying of my life. To work with religious musical material so little studied is a constant challenge; to work with the sensitive, scholarly, and appreciative people with whom I have been associated there is a great honor and privilege.

Not long ago, following a lecture I gave in Boston, a listener said, "What a wonderful life you have had!" A friend amended the statement, saying, "What a wonderful life you have made!"

Much of my life's color, excitement, and achievement I owe to the faith, encouragement, and practical help given me through the years by many generous sponsors and assistants, by great figures of the music world, and by loving friends and tireless helpers around the world, many of whom have watched the Laura Boulton Collection grow steadily from the day I brought the first recorded primitive music out of an African rain forest on an Edison wax cylinder to the present collection containing some of the most elaborate melodies to be found anywhere.

However, the end is not yet! That absorbing direction which has carried through the terrible and triumphant is still with me, giving meaning to present and future. Geographically speaking, I have come full circle, for I have written the last chapter of this book in Africa where it all began.

APPENDIX

Record Albums by Dr. Laura Boulton

Published by Folkways/Scholastic Records
50 West 44th Street
New York, New York 10036

#8852—*African Music*
#8850—*Indian Music of the Southwest*
#8851—*Indian Music of Mexico*
#8801—*Songs and Dances of Turkey*
#4434—*Folk Music of Yugoslavia*
#4444—*Eskimo Music of Alaska and the Hudson Bay*
#4482—*Songs of French Canada*
#6805—*Songs and Dances of Yugoslavia*
#6807—*Songs and Dances of Switzerland*
#6828—*Ukrainian Christmas Songs*
#6836—*Christmas Songs of Spain*
#6845—*Christmas Songs of Portugal*

Record Albums to be published shortly

The Music Hunter (appearing with this book)
Byzantine and Orthodox Chants
Music of Angola
Music of the Northwest Indians
Polish Folk Songs
Voodoo Music in Haiti
Rhythm Around the World

INDEX